NUCLEAR COUNTRY

NUCLEAR COUNTRY

THE ORIGINS OF
THE RURAL NEW RIGHT

Catherine McNicol Stock

PENN

UNIVERSITY OF PENNSYLVANIA PRESS

PHILADELPHIA

A volume in the Haney Foundation Series, established in 1961
with the generous support of Dr. John Louis Haney.

Published by
University of Pennsylvania Press
Philadelphia, Pennsylvania 19104-4112
www.upenn.edu/pennpress

Printed in the United States of America
on acid-free paper

1 3 5 7 9 10 8 6 4 2

A Cataloging-in-Publication record is available from the Library of Congress
ISBN 978-0-8122-5245-3

For PJ

CONTENTS

PREFACE

THREE CHILDREN TOSSED AND turned on a hot summer night on the Northern Plains, trying to catch a whiff of cool breeze to help them fall asleep. They could have been any children, from any era. Then they heard a sound that only the children of the Cold War recognized: the roar of B-52 bombers leaving the air force bases near their homes. Each child wondered: was this just another training flight? Or were the B-52s leaving the bases to escape Soviet nuclear missiles headed their way? They knew that the American military had buried hundreds of intercontinental ballistic missiles (ICBMs) in concrete "silos" on the Northern Plains and that each silo was the target of a potential Soviet attack. If the Soviets had launched their missiles, the children had thirty minutes to live. A nuclear strike would destroy the silos, the bases, and all the homes, farms, and small-town businesses for hundreds of miles. It could even mark the beginning of the end of the world.

It is easy to imagine the terror that the children felt as they wondered whether they were going to die in an immense firestorm. Their futures were entirely in the hands of forces they could not control. And yet two of these children did not feel terrified. Tom Brusegaard, a farm boy from Gilby, North Dakota, and Tim Pavek, the son of a man in the hardware business from the Rapid City, South Dakota area, were afraid, of course. But they were also awed by the power of the B-52s and proud of the strength of the American military in its battle against communism. Like many other descendants of Euro-American homesteaders, they believed the presence of the air force bases made them safer overall and that their benefits—like new fast food restaurants and big box stores—outweighed their risks. The missiles too made them part of something important, something of national and even global consequence. Years later when they chose careers,

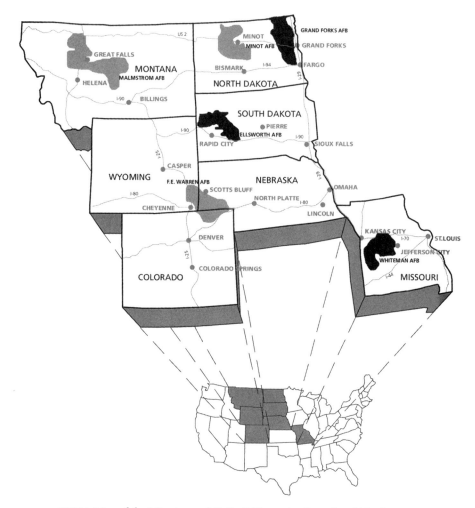

FIGURE 1. Map of the Minuteman Missile fields on the Central and Northern Plains from the late 1960s through mid-1990s. The areas that would have been destroyed by a Soviet strike, including by nuclear fallout, extended far beyond these immediate areas where the weapons were stored. Courtesy National Park Service, original by Historic American Engineering Record, Library of Congress.

Tom and Tim acted on these early impressions of the importance of American military strength: Tom tried his hand at farming but soon became involved in Republican politics. Tim joined the air force, learning how to keep the missiles mission-ready himself. Given the stakes, it "really wasn't a tough decision," he recalled.[1]

Young Delphine Red Shirt also heard the roar of the B-52s. But she did not share Tom's and Tim's sense of awe. Lying awake on the Pine Ridge Reservation, where generations of her family had lived, she worried about a Soviet strike. But she also wondered why the departing planes were flying so close to her house, close enough to rattle dishes on the shelves. She wondered if the air force was trying to threaten or intimidate the Lakota people, who throughout their history had protested racism and injustice. And while she wanted to join the military someday, neither the bases nor the missiles made Delphine feel safe.[2] Tom and Tim likely believed that American weapons were built solely to deter the nation's enemies in foreign countries. But Delphine knew that they also existed to assert power over local Native people by reminding them daily of the possibility that their land and lives could be taken again, this time by the mere turn of a key. Thus Delphine went on to do a different kind of political work: she became a writer, telling her people's stories and teaching their language, so that, barring complete annihilation, they would endure into future generations.[3]

Given their opposing social positions, it is not surprising that these children had contrasting views of militarization and nuclearization. Far more surprising is that both Natives and whites in the Dakotas had histories of resistance to American militarization, occupation, colonization, and war. The Lakota fought to survive in the face of genocidal attacks by the Army of the West; in the modern era they fought to maintain cultural and political sovereignty in the face of ongoing settler colonialism and state-sponsored violence. For their parts—and with no sense of irony—white settlers also resisted militarism, conscription, imperialism, and expansionism from the late nineteenth century through the early 1940s and again, more briefly, during the Vietnam War. But by the 1970s, most whites on the Northern Plains had adapted to a new reality: the presence of the military itself in their communities. During the Cold War, the air force built bases on the land and buried ICBMs beneath it, creating a kinship with residents that erased the conventional distinction between civilian and soldier and made all of their lives dependent on a well-funded national defense. Like Okinawans who lived near US Air Force bases, the Lakota experienced this potentially fatal reality as a "double colonization."[4] White people, on the other hand, could no longer see the American empire at work abroad or at home, instead becoming, in Manu Karuka's words, "white shareholders" in its project.[5] Doing their part to support the military, even if it meant losing their lives, was what they called patriotism.

South Dakota rancher and anti-militarist Marvin Kammerer recognized that whites and Native people shared a common position in the face of the military and the national security state. Between the bases, the ICBMs, and federal support for corporate agriculture, he said, the government "was making farmers and ranchers into the next Indians."[6] However ominous it sounded, Kammerer suggested that this potential racial leveling was in fact a promising turn of events. Perhaps the common experience of occupation and subjugation could finally bring the state's diverse people together to fight for peace and justice. Most days—and nights—it was a lonely position to hold.

INTRODUCTION

MIKE JACOBS, EDITOR OF the *Grand Forks Herald* during the historic 1997 Red River flood, won a Pulitzer Prize for Public Service when he made sure the paper never missed an issue, even when "hell and high water" destroyed its entire facility.[1] However indispensable to the community in crisis, Jacobs did not think that accomplishment was as daring, at least politically, as an essay he had written thirty years earlier. In September of 1967, Jacobs was both the new editor of the *Dakota Student* and a sandals-and-ponytail-wearing anti-war activist. In his first month on the job, he learned that one of the university's wealthiest alumni, Jack Stewart, wanted to sponsor an essay contest and give the winner a scholarship. Stewart suggested the topic too: "Our American Heritage—How Can It Be Eternally Yours?" Outraged by the idea that the university would essentially bribe students into expressing conservative views, Jacobs responded with an essay of his own: "The Prostitution of Patriotism." Young people in 1967, he argued, knew that "old ladies in furs and men in uniforms or business suits waving flags" had been trying to "spoon-feed patriotism" to them their entire lives. It was too late for that now. "Our generation is beyond it."[2]

Soon after "The Prostitution of Patriotism" hit the newsstands, angry letters began to pour into the university president's office. Some parents and alumni demanded that Jacobs be dismissed from his position or even expelled. Letter-writers berated, insulted, scolded, threatened, and mocked the young editor. One man suggested Jacobs should have encouraged students to participate in the contest: "But no, an editorial to this effect wouldn't have been any fun, not in keeping with the fashion. 'Protest' is the magic word. Raise hell with everything that is or has been . . . ridicule, tear down, protest. To be constructive is 'square.'"[3] Citing freedom of the press, President George Starcher let Jacobs stay on as editor. Many years later, Jacobs admitted the essay had created an enormous "kerfuffle" and caused Starcher a lot of "trouble." Even so he did not regret writing it.[4] Instead he regretted the gradual fading away of the liberal ideals that his generation had been so sure were in ascendance.[5] In their place conservatives like Stewart and many others had found increased political power and cultural authority. By the dawn of the twenty-first century, the angry letter-writers and the flag-waving men in uniforms and business suits would have the last word on regional politics—even if they could never get rid of the outspoken young editor himself.

It is hard to imagine that a student from North Dakota ever published an article in which the words prostitution and patriotism appeared in the same sentence. Both North and South Dakota have long been among the most reliably Republican states in the nation. Since the presidential election of 1920 voters have chosen only two Democrats—Franklin Roosevelt in 1932 and 1936, and Lyndon Johnson in 1964. In 2016 South Dakotans preferred Donald Trump by more than thirty points, inspiring a local journalist to say his state was "as red as a lazy August sunset."[6] Moreover, between 1968 and 1992, the majority of voters in both states came to embrace all tenets of the brand of conservatism associated with the New Right.[7] Overwhelmingly white and Christian, with large numbers of Catholics, conservative Lutherans, and rapidly increasing numbers of evangelical Protestants, Dakotans began to bring their home-grown cultural conservatism to the ballot box, promoting prayer in school and resisting abortion rights and marriage equality.[8] They also took a "law and order" stand on crime, gun rights, and incarceration, with a particularly chilling effect for Natives who had experienced interconnected and historic systems of de facto and de jure segregation, disproportionate rates of incarceration, and unprosecuted cases of sexual assault and murder.[9] Albeit more reluctantly, in the 1980s and 1990s, white voters in both states embraced the Reagan-era ideals of small-government-style fiscal conservatism and strived to become the most "business friendly" in the nation. In South Dakota special deals made with the finance industry kept unemployment rates low and corporate campaign donations high; in North Dakota deals with multinational energy corporations did the same and more.

But it is the region's support for national defense—the foundational pillar of New Right conservatism—that makes any reiteration of the

"Prostitution of Patriotism" unimaginable. During the Cold War, the air force built three large bases on the Northern Plains, one each in Rapid City, Grand Forks, and Minot. Beginning in the 1960s, the national security state installed 450 intercontinental ballistic missiles (ICBMs) in concrete silos beneath farm fields and grasslands surrounding the bases. As Dakotas became the "center of the bulls-eye" for comparable Soviet ICBMs in Siberia, "distant strategists" designated the region as a potential "national sacrifice area," should nuclear war begin.[10] This new reality, this *Nuclear Country*, essentially obliterated the distinction between soldiers and civilians. Since then, the people of North and South Dakota, like many other rural Americans, have created what J. D. Vance has called a "kinship" with the military and have enthusiastically embraced American culture's broad associations of patriotism with "supporting the troops" and their wars.[11] As they did, flag-waving became a nearly universal gesture, with flags flying outside homes, on windows, silos, and the sides of barns; festooned across shirts, jackets, pants, bandanas, and bikinis.[12] Of far greater consequence has been the overrepresentation of young men and women from the Dakotas in the regular military and National Guard.[13] In 2011 they ranked near the top of the list of casualties per capita in the Iraq War.[14] Yet the appeal of war endured. Adam Schumann of Minot, North Dakota, one of the "good soldiers" from the Iraq War, said that during his second deployment, every time he "[got] shot at in a firefight," it was "the sexiest feeling there is."[15]

But if we look back in time rather than ahead to the twenty-first century, Mike Jacobs' unapologetic 1967 editorial becomes far less surprising. In the decades before World War II, the people of the Northern Plains were not universally politically conservative; indeed, far from it. They certainly were not conservative in the ways that came to define the New Right. Instead they created a broadly mixed heritage of left and right that defies today's polarized bifurcations.[16] Many people in the Dakotas, including Republicans, supported experiments in agrarian democracy that incorporated ideas from Populism and Progressivism to socialism and communism. Likewise for more than a century, most rural Dakotans had belonged to left-leaning agricultural organizations including the Nonpartisan League, the Farmers Holiday Association, the Farmers Union, United Family Farmers, the National Farmers Organization, the American Agricultural Movement, and Dakota Rural Action. In each of these movements, they fought against "bigness" in all its forms: "bonanza" farms, out-of-state railroads, corporations, banks, corrupt political parties, and distant federal bureau-cracies. At the same time they demonstrated their faith that activist govern-ments, particularly at the state level, could protect ordinary citizens from the worst manifestations of concentrated power. They believed, as Sarah Vogel, the former North Dakota commissioner of agriculture put it, that government should always embody the principle of "people first."[17]

Creating democratic reform was not easy, however: Agrarian radicals consistently encountered opposition from wealthy businesspeople and large landowners. Furthermore, the reforms they sought were sometimes infused with ideas that we would see today as less than fully democratic. With important exceptions, Populists and their political descendants broadly shared exclusionary views on race, religion, and gender with their oppo-nents as well as with most other white Americans.[18] Nevertheless they left a legacy of institutions: a state bank, mill, and grain elevator in North Dakota; and political practices: initiatives and referenda and bans on corporate farming in both states—meant to exemplify the principle that government could and should work for the public good.

The story of the "agrarian revolt" on the Northern Plains is remem-bered proudly even today.[19] But the fact that Populist opposition to "big-ness" and concentrated power included opposition to the military has nearly been erased from memory. White Dakotans benefited immeasurably from the army's genocidal removal of indigenous people and appreciated the "small but reassuring numbers" of soldiers and forts that guarded the territory.[20] But with no sense of irony or complicity, they were wary of the culture of militarism, the establishment of a permanent standing army, and the expansion of American military power abroad.[21] Some had emigrated from countries with overseas empires and universal conscription. Many others were influenced by the socialist idea that wars only benefited the rich or the suffrage-era feminist belief that women's political activism could stop mass violence.[22] Members of Anabaptist sects believed that war vio-lated their religious beliefs. For those reasons and more, most Dakotans opposed American entry into every war in the first half of the twentieth century, beginning with the US expansion of the war in Cuba to the Philip-pines and extending to intervention in Hitler's Europe.

Every Populist anti-militarist—from South Dakota senator Richard Pet-tigrew, North Dakota governor "Wild Bill" Langer, and North Dakota sena-tor Gerald Nye to 1972 presidential candidate George McGovern, the region's final anti-war champion—faced harsh criticism for their views;

many people still believe their resistance, particularly to entry into the Second World War, was unforgivable.[23] After the attack on Pearl Harbor, Dakotans may well have agreed; South Dakota senator Karl Mundt, for example, threw away his files of correspondence with the anti-militarist and antisemitic America First Committee.[24] Until that date, however, most men and women on the Northern Plains returned again and again to their commitment to peace. Those who had served with courage and honor in one war counted themselves among the resistors to the next, testifying as did a North Dakota farm boy caught behind German lines in 1915: that militarism had the power to "hypnotize the people" and that war was "humanity gone mad."[25] Even after World War II, a few "old Progressives" from the region warned that a permanent state of military readiness and aggressive intervention overseas put the United States in danger. In 1952 as war in Korea raged, North Dakota representative and longtime member of the Nonpartisan League, Usher Burdick, wrote: "we cannot bring peace by furnishing guns."[26]

These two major shifts—from the complex political heritage of Populist-style agrarian radicalism to the tenets of new conservatism and from anti-militarism to support for a well-funded, "muscular" national defense—require an explanation. This book provides one by suggesting that we see these seemingly distinct developments as inexorably dependent upon and related to each other. Furthermore it demands that we see the experiences of rural men and women in one of the "reddest" regions of the country as illuminating of our own in ways we might only see by looking there. Whether there are nuclear weapons buried on our land or not, we all live in a country where war has gone, in Marilyn Young's words, from being a mere "shadow" to the "substance of American history."[27] And yet on the Northern Plains, there were nuclear weapons buried in land whose citizens had long decried the very idea of a permanent standing army. The Northern Plains in the late twentieth century, far from being a "flyover story," shine a bright light onto the all-encompassing nature of "the militarization of everything" in the current-day United States. Americans share this militarization so completely as to make its deep-seated consequences difficult for us to articulate or even to perceive.[28] That makes it all the more important that we try.

This book examines two of the most important historical developments in the Dakotas as well as the modern United States as a whole. Both have been written about at length—some have said too much length—but rarely together.[29] The book roots the first—the rise of the New Right in American politics—in the experience of men and women in a region perhaps less well understood than any other in the United States.[30] In the explosion of studies of new conservatism, the Sunbelt states of the South and West and the Rust Belt states of the deindustrializing North have figured prominently and the Northern Plains, indeed every rural state in the North, appear as an afterthought, if at all.[31] One reason is evident: in the mid-1960s Republican strategist Kevin Phillips and others believed the trick to creating an "emerging [New Right] Republican majority" lay in recruiting resentful southern whites and northern blue-collar "ethnics" who had voted as Democrats before. However much this might have been, in Richard Nixon's words, an "American" rather than a "southern strategy," early operatives like Phillips nevertheless largely ignored the states of the Northern Plains.[32] Aware of but unconcerned by the radical agrarian and anti-militarist countertraditions within the states' Republican voting patterns, Phillips assumed that rural voters in the North would simply stay in the conservative fold even as the party's ideas about what conservatism meant changed. But their presumption was as ignorant and arrogant then as it is now. The political traditions of the Northern Plains included strains of thought that simply did not fit into an emerging new conservative view of the world. Furthermore, Dakota voters had only voted fully in concert with white southerners twice between 1890 and 1980. So it would take significant changes to the political and economic culture of the Dakotas and a repurposing of its own cultural conservatism, led at times by national organizations and media, to transform the region into a bastion of the New Right.[33] In short, the emergence of the New Right on the Northern Plains—what I call the Rural New Right—was anything but assured. The story of its complex and contentious ascendance suggests that, given the perils of our own time, Republican strategists still err when they take the political landscape of the Northern Plains for granted.[34]

Essential to the emergence of a Rural New Right on the Northern Plains was the coming of the military and national security states to the countryside. Thus the second development addressed in the book, the militarization of society and culture in the Cold War years, recontextualizes the history of the Dakotans within the story of American imperialism.[35] In experiencing rapid militarization and nuclearization, Dakotans were far from alone. While its footprint "abroad" began in westward expansion and other imperial efforts in this hemisphere, during World War II and the

Cold War the United States Department of Defense built an "empire of bases" around the globe; the national security state established an "empire of nukes" near overseas bases, on remote proving grounds, in submarines, and on aircraft that flew twenty-four hours a day on alert.[36] By 1960, a million soldiers, civilian employees and their families were stationed at 815 bases in 41 countries. By 2010 the number had risen to 70 countries and a variety of new facilities—sometimes called "forward operating sites," "zones of protection," or secret "lily pads"—were planned throughout the Middle East and Central Asia. The cost of maintaining what Daniel Immerwahr calls "Baselandia" is at least two hundred billion dollars per year.[37]

The expansion of the American military empire had social, cultural, and political consequences. Wherever they went in the world, American military men and, in time, women brought with them American norms, frames, and practices of race, class, gender, and sexuality. During the Cold War, for example, servicepeople carried the arrogance that accompanies victory as well as long-held ideas of racial and cultural superiority. The ritual practices of "military masculinity," with its all-but-required performance of aggressive heterosexuality, led to the establishment of "hybrid" spaces just outside American bases, like "Hooker Hill" in Itaewon, South Korea, where "drinks, drugs, and women" are available, racial segregation tolerated, and instances of sexual violence common.[38] Overseas bases are also among the most dangerous places for enlisted American women. As one serviceman put it, "You can't expect to treat women as one of your own when, in the same breath, you as a young soldier are being encouraged to exploit women on the outside of that base." Several American servicewomen died of dehydration in their tents in 120 degree heat in Iraq rather than risk drinking water and having to use the outdoor privies where several sexual assaults had taken place.[39]

A major figure in the modern history of indigenous resistance, the Ojibwa Dennis Banks, knew exactly what was expected of him both as a Native person and as a young male when he arrived at a base outside Osaka in 1954; his experiences would later sharpen his ability to see American empire in operation at home. Like many other Native men and women who have served in the military, Banks had been proud to join the service and "kill a Commie for Christ"; in fact he had felt "so patriotic it was ridiculous."[40] He tried to ignore the fact that whites still called the enemy "Injuns" and their missions "Injun fighting."[41] After a long trip by sea, Banks and his shipmates arrived at the Sunagawa Air Force Base; soon they were looking for something to do. Even though the air force rules stated clearly, "No fraternization" with the Japanese, Banks knew that, far from forbidden, sex with local women was practically required.[42] "We were surrounded by bars that were right off base. We called them the Thousand-Yard Strip—saloons, pawnshops, clip joints, and whorehouses. It was said that if you didn't hock your watch, drink a gallon of beer, and get laid, you were not a man." Thinking back on it later, he realized that "They tell you you're going to see the world, have a woman in every port. Then when you are actually there, you're supposed to be macho and use women as sex objects."[43]

Banks did not learn his lesson, falling deeply in love with a Japanese woman, Machiko Inouye; in her company he felt liberated for the first time from the ever-present glare of white racism. He felt this liberation so fervently that when asked to shoot to kill Japanese anti-base protesters, he became unsure if he was on the "right side" of his gun. After all, his indigenous ancestors had also been vanquished in battle, their land stolen or degraded, their culture demeaned or destroyed, their women sexually assaulted, exploited, or murdered. What was he doing "guarding the ramparts of Empire?"[44] To officials in the air force his marriage and his refusal to follow orders did not just show bad judgment. They were criminal. He was arrested and put on a plane back to the United States, never to see his wife again. But Banks continued to believe that America was misusing its military power, particularly against people of color. In 1968 he helped to found the American Indian Movement and in 1973, with other Native veterans, fought the "vanguards of empire" closer to home, at Wounded Knee, South Dakota.

While the American government was building bases around the world—and inadvertently inspiring critiques of American power among local people and servicepeople of color alike—they were also building them in the United States. Some, like the army's Fort Bragg in North Carolina, were first established in World War I.[45] Others, like the air force bases scattered across the Dakotas, Montana, Nebraska, eastern Wyoming, and Kansas, were established during or after World War II and expanded with the introduction of nuclear weapons.[46] As in Europe and Asia, not all Americans welcomed the bases: protests against the establishment of Pease Air Force Base in New Hampshire, for example, succeeded in delaying construction. But most communities welcomed, even competed to acquire, bases. By 1980 the strategic dispersion of military bases across the United

States meant that there was at least one base in every state and nearly a thousand in all; in states like California, Florida, and Texas there were a dozen or more.[47] Hundreds of thousands—even millions—of military personnel cycled in and out of local communities in the Cold War era, making themselves very much "at home."[48]

The presence of the military as a constitutive part of American society, not a separate or anomalous entity, amplified social and cultural tensions already present in local communities, in the Dakotas, as much as overseas. Wherever it is, a military base is made up of large numbers of young men, new to the area, looking for "drinks, drugs, and women"—or just any kind of diversion. Some return from deployment having refined their conception of military masculinity and racial and cultural superiority. Thus hybrid spaces—like Box Elder, South Dakota, near Ellsworth Air Force Base; or Emerado, North Dakota, near Grand Forks Air Force Base—boasted bars, liquor stores, pawn shops, and sex workers, as comparable spaces do abroad.[49] Conflicts over race and religion and the meaning of full citizenship also arose at domestic bases. In the early parts of the century, whites in some southern communities rioted when African Americans were trained at bases nearby. In the 1960s servicepeople of color experienced discrimination in their base communities—Rapid City, South Dakota, among them—and filed complaints to civil rights commissions. They had come to see that racism and colonialism were baked into the military's structure and history.[50] In the early 1970s African American servicepeople, including a group at the Minot Air Force Base, protested how seldom blacks were promoted and how often they were disciplined.[51] Meanwhile, in the wake of the loss in Vietnam to a military force of nonwhites, some veterans founded paramilitary units and other white power organizations to fight for "their race" in Rhodesia, South Africa, and inside the United States.[52] At Fort Bragg in the 1980s and 1990s, the presence of white supremacist groups was well-known; membership was not even a violation of base regulations.[53]

The military also arrived in the American countryside in the form of defense-related civilian industry; these too influenced culture and politics. As Dwight Eisenhower warned, the "military-industrial complex" connected military needs to diverse sectors of the economy—from manufacturing to finance and university research.[54] In World War II and the early Cold War, the Pacific coast and other parts of the American West received such enormous federal investments in wartime industries that one historian deemed it the "largest peacetime militarized zone on earth."[55] At first, major manufacturers were slow to relocate to the remote interior West but the officials in the nuclear weapons industry, which required both secrecy and low population density in case of an accident, thought it was perfect. By the mid-1950s, boomtowns like Rocky Flats, Colorado; Amarillo, Texas; and Hanford, Washington—as well as the sites eventually chosen for the installation of missiles—owed their low unemployment rates to the manufacturers of nuclear weapons. At first, workers were told neither that they were handling toxic materials nor what they were making.[56] When they found out, they saw their work as part of the larger national project. By the 1970s and 1980s, these workers' experiences and ideological commitments also began to influence their political views. Kristen Iverson, who worked at the Rocky Flats plant, came to resent antinuclear protesters whom she dismissed as "Boulder [Colorado] crazies," "kooks," and liberals "who cared more about wildlife more than people."[57] Soon some of her coworkers translated their prodefense and anti-liberal views into local political organizations and votes for conservative candidates of the New Right. In Jefferson County, Colorado, where Rocky Flats was located until 2006, Republican presidential candidates won a majority of the vote in every election between 1980 and 2004. By and large voters made a singular calculation: even if the military put their lives at risk, why risk the military's commitment to the local economy? In places large and small, the growth of corporate capitalism, funded by and affiliated with the military, overcame anti-militarism among workers on the "front lines" of nuclearization.

However consequential the impact of bases and nuclear weapons industries has been for local communities, militarization as a whole has had even more wide-reaching ramifications.[58] Militarization is an all-encompassing experience, one with deep implications for the economy, politics, race, gender, sexuality, immigration, the environment, and much more. In her study of Fayetteville, North Carolina, Catherine Lutz concluded that "we all live in an Army camp" where "we have raised war taxes at work, and future soldiers at home, lived with the cultural atmosphere of racism and belligerence that war mobilization often uses or creates, and nourished the public opinion that helps send soldiers off to war or prevents their going."[59] Even so it can be difficult to see, and certainly to write about, this "Army camp." Gretchen Heefner adds that the "very normalness [of militarization] renders it illegible."[60] But if we try, it is there: where children play video games of war and new recruits are trained on similar systems; where khaki is a fashion statement; where police attack protesters with leftover military-grade weapons; where a memorial is being planned for the Mall in Washington, DC, to honor the dead in a war that has not ended; where some refugees from our wars, including those who fought on the American side, are cast as, and cast out as, our enemies.[61] Last, the universal army camp is where most Americans—both Republicans and Democrats—consider questioning war to be at odds with "supporting the troops," even though veterans themselves increasingly demand that we do so.[62]

Just as we struggle to discern the consequences of militarization in our lives and yet know it is there, we struggle to fathom its costs—perhaps as much as a trillion dollars a year.[63] We have been paying for what Mary Dudziak calls our "war-but-not-war" for so long that we cannot imagine the country we might have built with even a tiny portion of that fortune.[64] In 2019, Jessica Mathews, longtime president of the Carnegie Endowment for Peace and a past member of the National Security Council, warned: "The political momentum that drives [increases to the military budget] . . . threatens to become—or may have already become—unstoppable. The consequences are huge. At home, defense spending crowds out funds for everything else a prosperous economy and a healthy society need. Abroad it has led us to become a country reflectively reliant on the military and one quite different from what we think ourselves to be or, as I believe, wish to be."[65] During the Farm Crisis, some activists from the Midwest did imagine a country that supported human needs more than military ones; in fact, they demanded it, calling for "Farms not Arms."[66] From our vantage point nearly forty years later, we can see that their worst fears are close to being realized. The Northern Plains may be becoming more devoted to arms—as well as the multinational corporations that profit from them—than farms. And if that region is, so is the country as a whole. As early as the 1950s, President Eisenhower urged Americans to understand these trade-offs: "Every gun that is made, every warship launched, every rocket fired signifies, in the final sense, a theft from those who hunger and are not fed, those who are cold and are not clothed."[67]

A decade later, on March 18, 1968, a very different politician, Robert F. Kennedy, made the same point in a speech he gave to hundreds of student supporters at the University of Kansas. The University of Kansas was the state's flagship public institution, as was the University of North Dakota where Mike Jacobs had published "the Prostitution of Patriotism" just months earlier. Kansas also shared with the Dakotas a history of agrarian activism that included anti-militarism, yet during the Cold War it came to house military bases and ICBMs.[68] Moreover, in the 1960s, Kansan young people, like many in the Dakotas, were not yet ready to abandon their radical heritage; yet their commitment to peace and justice fueled their conservative opponents' fire. By the end of the twentieth century, Kansas would be such a fortress of the New Right that it would be hard to imagine that Robert Kennedy had ever dared travel there.

But he did and he did not disappoint. Kennedy reminded students that America's finest ambition was to seek peace and justice. He used an extended metaphor about what lay behind a bland statistic: the nation's Gross National Product (GNP). Kennedy argued that the nation's enormous GDP, which President Lyndon Johnson cited frequently as evidence of his success in office, measured little of real value. Rather it measured things that reflected the American tendency toward violence, racism, and war. It measured "air pollution and cigarette advertising, and ambulances to clear our highways of carnage. It counts special locks for our doors and the jails for the people who break them. . . . It counts napalm and counts nuclear warheads and armored cars for the police to fight the riots in our cities. It counts . . . the television programs which glorify violence in order to sell toys to our children." In other words, it measured "everything . . . except that which makes life worthwhile. And it can tell us everything about America except why we are proud that we are Americans."[69]

Both the aspects of militarization that can be counted and measured, and those that cannot, help us understand how the people of the Dakotas came to abandon anti-militarism and believe that war might be "the sexiest feeling there is." Furthermore, they help us see how the coming of military bases and nuclear weapons to the region and the experience of militarization writ large made possible, perhaps even inevitable, the region's shift from Populist agrarian radicalism to new conservatism. When the military came to the country, so did new facilities, new jobs, new associated industries, new exits off the interstates, new fast food stores, new big box stores, new bars, new housing, and more. Most importantly it brought new people—largely young white male military people. Along with personal needs for distraction, these military men—who after 1973 came disproportionately from the South or rural communities in other regions—brought conservative religious traditions, political beliefs, racial practices, and ideas about gender and family, forged by their upbringing and reinforced through the institutionalized conservatism of the military. As time passed, hundreds of thousands of service personnel, military staff, and their families cycled through the region. Each one, even if he or she only served their time and accepted a transfer to a warmer station, influenced their communities. But others came to stay, settling in, finding a local partner, starting a business, or coming back to the region to retire. These active-duty and retired military people volunteered, coached, attended church, supported veteran organizations, and joined school boards. A few got involved in local electoral politics, generally as prodefense Republicans. One became the mayor of Grand Forks, the third largest city in North Dakota—and, after he was licensed to carry a concealed weapon, a top-tier member of the NRA.[70]

The coming of the military also affected regional political culture by reinforcing or recontextualizing long-standing local ideas and practices. Both Populists and their opponents had long been suspicious of concentrated power and bigness; it was at the root of both their prewar antimilitarism and their concerns about the New Deal. And while Dakota communities largely welcomed the bases, individual farmers and ranchers whose land was taken by the national security state for missile sites began to resent a distant, secretive, sometimes incompetent federal bureaucracy with new vigor. At the same time, the people of the plains shared values with the military too, particularly culturally conservative views about race, religion, gender, and sexuality. Thus while some Dakotans joined the antiwar, antinuke, and feminist protests of 1960s and early 1970s, more resented activists who flouted social conventions, especially support for the military. When in the 1970s Dennis Banks' American Indian Movement organized protests in the region that sometimes turned violent, Dakotans found common purpose with resentful white southerners and northern "ethnics," and created a multiregional coalition of whites who were determined to restore "law and order" and willing to engage militarized state violence to do so. At that moment, while Republican operatives were looking elsewhere, the success of the "Southern strategy" was complete.

While embracing the need for a strong national defense and rejecting liberal social ideas, Dakotans adopted the third plank of New Right ideology—fiscal conservatism. They did this more haltingly, however, as it brought full circle the changes in priorities that militarization required of them. Strains of Populist agrarianism in economics—and pride in their "people-first" political traditions—had persisted in both states. Again and again voters made sure they sent representatives to Congress who would push legislation to support farmers and farming. Dakotans had long distrusted big government and many did not like the agricultural programs members of Congress had designed. But they liked Ronald Reagan's threat to get government "out of the farming business" even less. At the same time, however, Dakotans voted against tax increases that their "New Populist" leaders needed to solve the states' fiscal problems. Without them, officials sought private solutions to the most public of problems. They encouraged large-scale corporate investment and ensured that the states would remain "business friendly"—even when the corporations they enticed damaged farmland, exploited local consumers, and either directly or indirectly profited from, even helped to prolong, war. In time, these efforts to diversify the states' economies would succeed beyond anyone's wildest dreams. They represented the final triumph of conservative politics in the region. Yet in Matthew Lassiter's words, what they really did was "social[ize] risk for major corporations and privat[ize] risk for ordinary households, an underlying feature of modern American politics."[71] They also created conditions for the rapid consolidation of farms and the collapse of many small towns where rates of suicide, addiction, and child death remained among the highest in the nation. Of course had the federal budget, or just a trillion dollars of the federal budget, been allocated to farms—or to schools, addiction treatment centers, suicide prevention hotlines, or hospitals—rather than to arms, those hard choices might never have had to be made.

Nuclear Country locates the gradual commitment to all aspects of New Right conservatism on the Northern Plains in the experience of militarization and nuclearization. It argues that, over the course of several decades, white men and women in North and South Dakota from both sides of the aisle figuratively shredded the evidence of their commitment to Populist anti-militarism as surely as South Dakota senator Karl Mundt literally destroyed his. On the other hand it does not claim—however tempting it might be—that militarization and nuclearization are the sole reasons for these shifts. At the very least the out-migration of small farmers in the postwar period, long the backbone of Populist organizations and the Democratic Party, indisputably changed the political landscape, particularly because they have been "replaced" by military families and energy workers. Instead it contends that militarization and nuclearization, the full scope of which remain hard to discern, were the historical developments most essential to the creation of the Rural New Right, that they can be best seen in

FIGURE 2. Airmen honoring the American and South Dakota flags at Mount Rushmore, South Dakota. iStock Images.

this often-overlooked region, and that they link men and women in the Dakotas to people in the rest of the country and even the world. More personally, this book makes clear my view that a great deal is lost when "material" values of militarization and global power take the place of more "spiritual" values of seeking community among our diverse humanity.[72] And it seeks to imagine—indeed demands that even the most skeptical reader imagine—a country in which, rather than having the occasional unpopular war, war itself has become unpopular, even un-American.[73] As did Martin Luther King Jr., I refuse "to accept the cynical notion that nation after nation must spiral down a militaristic stairway into the hell of nuclear annihilation." Furthermore I agree that a nation that promotes war cannot also promote justice.[74]

Again writing about Fayetteville, North Carolina, home to the army's Fort Bragg, Catherine Lutz suggests that the normalization of permanent war, nuclear catastrophe, injustice, and inequality does not have to remain a defining part of American culture and its role in the world.

Fayetteville's people have enjoyed a unique . . . history, but they have also suffered a history only partly of their own making. Like people across America, choices made in Washington about war and war preparation have deeply shaped their lives. . . . the sacrifice and suffering war exacts from the home front has often been denied by official narratives, even as the costs abroad have been. But however permanent the present may seem, other histories—both of the past and the future—can still be made from the insights of all the people who have lived under war's shadow and nursed its hidden injuries.[75]

This book is written in the hope that such new histories can still be made and that all Americans can write them together.

CHAPTER 1

"UNDER GOD, THE PEOPLE RULE"

IN 1883 HAMLIN GARLAND left Dakota Territory, putting its harsh climate and windswept towns behind him. He had seen too many men and women broken—killed, driven mad, or bankrupted—trying to carve a farm from the deep-rooted, arid soil. Yet the land and its people called Garland back. Soon he put pen to paper, blurring the line between literature and politics to communicate what life on the "middle border" was really like—and why. He hoped someday that his stories and novels, rather than just achieve artistic "beauty," could help "spread the reign of justice."[1]

In "Under the Lion's Paw," Garland recounted the struggles of Tim Haskins, who, with his ailing wife, newborn baby, and two young children, fled his Kansas farm after grasshoppers destroyed what little he owned. Homeless, the Haskins family wandered the roads until they stopped at a farm where an older couple, the Councils, took them in. Steve Council finally arranged for Haskins to negotiate a two-year tenancy with a local landowner who in turn agreed to sell Haskins the land for $3,000 when the lease expired. It seemed like a dream come true: hard work, thrift, and some luck with the weather assured Haskins of becoming a property-owning member of the middle class, a virtuous yeoman-citizen in the true Jeffersonian tradition. Yet it was not to be. Haskins worked "ferociously" on the land and saved every penny he could.[2] But after two years the land-lord, Jim Butler, claimed that the improvements Haskins made to the land had made it more valuable. He demanded $5,000 instead. Enraged, Haskins nearly attacked Butler with his pitchfork, but after seeing his baby daughter, hung his head and returned to work. He remained a landless—and powerless—tenant.[3]

Garland read "Under the Lion's Paw" at the 1892 Omaha convention of the People's Party, already generally known as the Populist Party. It brought the audience to tears. Like many small farmers and tenants, the Haskins family did not realize that the system was rigged against them by landowners, bankers, corporations, and politicians.[4] At one time Jim Butler had owned a store and "earned all he got." But he discovered that speculating on land and extending credit to poor farmers was an easier way to make money. He could take fishing trips and sit "around town on rainy days smoking and 'gassin' with the boys'" while tenants like Haskins worked themselves "nearly to death" in the hope of "pushing the wolf of want a little farther from [the] door."[5]

In the late nineteenth and early twentieth centuries, tens of thousands of farmers like Haskins, and their wives, decided they had had enough. They joined radical agrarian movements that swept across the rural United States like a "political prairie fire."[6] The best known was the Populist movement, which had coalesced in the region but gained widespread national prominence in Omaha in 1892. Its members stretched from the cotton fields of the Southeast, up and down the Great Plains, and into the Mountain West. In some of these states, historian Lawrence Goodwyn contends, Populism was more "moment" than movement.[7] But on the Northern Plains, commitment to the ideals of Populism—expanded access to economic opportunity and political decision-making—lasted far longer than the initial insurgency. With controversial political leaders and famously persuasive barnyard organizers, they carried forward the goals of Populism, enhanced at times by socialist and communist strategies, into many aspects of progressive Republicanism, the Nonpartisan League (NPL), and Depression-era organizations such as the Farmers Holiday Association.[8] Together these movements made up an inspiring chapter in the history of the American left, as they put ordinary people first and honored the productive work they performed.

But Garland revealed even more about the political culture of the Northern Plains. Radical agrarian organizations, however fondly recalled, never held a monopoly on political ideas or ambitions. To the contrary, plenty of landowners, bankers, politicians, and small businesspeople like Garland's antihero, Jim Butler, held power in the small towns of the region. They actively opposed the reforms proposed by radical farmers, year after year. These conservatives did not fear the concentration of economic and political power as much as they feared the diminution of their own. As they fought back against the "upstart" farmers through the business-friendly wing of the Republican Party, they prepared the political landscape for a future generation that would, during the Cold War era, try to extinguish the region's political prairie fires for good.

The roots of the Rural New Right on the Northern Plains lay not only in how agrarian radicals and small-town conservatives saw the world differently but also in how they saw it the same way. In the 1960s and 1970s, cultural issues would come to dominate political debate nationwide, creating deep, seemingly intractable, divisions between Republicans and Democrats. But in an earlier era, a "common logic" around religion, gender, and race could instead form the glue that bound members of diverse white ethnic groups together, even when they disagreed vehemently on party politics.[9] For example, the vast majority of Euro-American Dakotans, immigrants or native-born, Populist or conservative, tenants or landlords were Christian; like Garland's Good Samaritan, Steve Council, they believed that Christianity's moral principles made it the "only religion" there was.[10] Furthermore, many people on the Northern Plains belonged either to doctrinally conservative denominations like Roman Catholicism or to one of the more conservative sects of larger Protestant denominations like Lutheranism, Methodism, and Presbyterianism.[11] Consequently, even some Dakotans who supported women's suffrage believed in the patriarchal heterosexual family where men were the sole proprietors and authorities.[12]

Most fundamental to social order in the Dakotas, as in the rest of the United States, was a racialized hierarchy predicated on the idea that whites were superior to all nonwhites and, most immediately, that whites "deserved" to settle on Native land and extract profits from it.[13] For all their enmity, Haskins and Butler did not argue about *whether* the land should be plowed and its crop sold, just *to whom* the profits belonged, *which* of the two white men who claimed it. Furthermore, they surely agreed that homelessness and dependence on the charity of others was a fate even worse than tenancy. It threatened to equate poor white farmers with Native people, whom most Americans believed were incapable of citizenship and were going to "die out" within a few decades.[14] In an era where whiteness "conferred both citizenship and the right to own property," Populists fought not just for their right to earn a living, but for their right to be white.[15]

* * *

Few homesteaders new to the Northern Plains expected the task ahead to be easy. Whether they traveled from nearby states like Iowa or Minnesota or distant communities in Canada, Germany, Scandinavia, or Russia, they were far from home and often on their own.[16] Plowing the deeply rooted and arid sod of the plains and building homes where few trees grew tested their physical and emotional limits. Added to those challenges were cycles of wet and dry years, prairie fires, grasshopper plagues, tornadoes, blizzards, and an endlessly blowing wind. For all living creatures these conditions could prove fatal. In the winter of 1886 to 1887, snow came early and never quit. By its end hundreds of thousands of cattle had frozen to death. Just two years later, the temperature dropped sixty degrees in less than an hour and snow fell so fiercely it was hard to see your hand in front of your face. By its end, dozens of schoolchildren and their young teachers, 235 people in all, had died. Some were found frozen in haystacks and snowdrifts. A few died only feet from their homes.[17]

But it wasn't nature, or nature alone, that radicalized farmers. It was also that the prices they received for crops and livestock were increasingly dependent on a globalizing economy far outside their control. At the same time, the concentrated power of big corporations, big banks, and big political parties squeezed them for every last cent.[18] This rapid economic transformation shifted the center of power from rural to urban areas, deepening regional inequalities. South Dakota Populist Henry Loucks put it bluntly: in 1830, farmers had owned 75 percent of the nation's wealth; by 1880, less than 25 percent.[19] Historian R. Alton Lee writes, "In coming to the plains, [farmers] had hoped to find a utopia of relatively free, rich land, but they came at a time when modern America was emerging and attaching increasingly less importance to the agrarian way of life."[20]

Inequitable railroad fees radicalized Dakota farmers first. In many small towns on the Northern Plains, there was only one railroad to bring crops or livestock to market. And there were no regulations, not even "reasonable maximum" rates, to limit the monopoly these railroads enjoyed—even as they neglected to pay taxes they owed to the state.[21] Farmers were literally captive to the out-of-state corporations: they could pay railroad fees or let their crops rot. Incredibly, Jon K. Lauck writes, "From certain points in

Dakota, it was cheaper to ship wheat to Liverpool than to Chicago or Minneapolis."[22] The "middlemen" who represented large creameries, mills, or storage facilities also had unassailable power over farmers' livelihoods. An agent could lie, for example, when he graded a crop's quality and thus lower its price. And farmers' problems did not end trackside. If the only local bank provided the terms for a loan, how could a farmer negotiate better terms? If politicians from both parties were being wined and dined by the same corporate executives; and senators were appointed, not elected, how could a farmer create change?[23]

The challenge of making ends meet on a farm was not new in the late nineteenth century. The inequity between farmers and the institutions of economic and political power, however, certainly was. When a drought and recession in the 1880s further multiplied farmers' troubles, Charles Macune founded the Farmers' Alliance in Texas, a model for cooperation rather than competition in agriculture that quickly spread north. The Alliance encouraged farmers to band together, extending their traditional "habits of mutuality" like barn-raisings and quilting bees, to larger economic organizations like stores and storage facilities.[24] He also encouraged them to demand support from the state. Soon some Alliance members advocated third party political action. Among the economic reforms they demanded were: an increase in the money supply through the coinage of silver; the creation of a long-term "sub-treasury" system so farmers could store crops until the price had risen; crop insurance; and state ownership of banks and utilities. In politics they advocated for the direct election of senators, the more secret "Australian ballot," and implementation of the initiative and referendum system, which allowed voters to decide on new legislation directly. They believed that as a third party, the People's Party, their candidates could withstand the corrupting forces of the current political system. At first the idea seemed to work well. In the 1892 presidential election, the People's Party candidate James Weaver of Iowa received over a million votes and won five states in the West; the party also won six governorships.[25] Even so they did not win the White House.

In 1896, the Populist Party abandoned its third-party strategy at the national level and "fused" with the Democratic Party. To some this was the compromise that changed an authentic democratic insurgency, full of possibility for radical change, into a mere "moment."[26] Even so the Populists found their best-known champion: William Jennings Bryan of Nebraska. While he may have only been fully committed to the silver issue, throughout 1896 Bryan used his considerable oratorical gifts to advocate for the central place of farming in American life. "Burn down your cities and leave our farms, and your cities will spring up again as if by magic; but destroy our farms and the grass will grow in the streets of every city in the country."[27] Meanwhile, his opponent, William McKinley, sat on his front porch in Canton, Ohio, giving press conferences and listening to the advice of business leaders.

While Bryan failed to win the nation's highest office in three tries, the ideas and ideals that he endorsed so enthusiastically endured in many rural places. On the Northern Plains they even thrived. As Howard Lamar writes, Populist efforts "established a precedent for political flexibility that made it easier for . . . future third-party movements . . . to be heard."[28] Dakota farm leaders created innovative practices to fit their local circumstances. In South Dakota, where farmers had organized the first Farmers' Alliance in a northern state, the charismatic newspaper editor Henry Loucks publicized its successes in every issue of the *Dakota Ruralist*. His colleague, Alonzo Wardell, experimented with a form of cooperative crop insurance that the national movement soon called "the Dakota system."[29] South Dakota Populists also enacted the initiative and referendum which has remained an essential part of the state's political culture for over a century.

But the Populist Party's success in South Dakota may have also been its curse; it had never fully dominated state politics and when rumors of corruption and opponents and money from outside the state targeted its leaders, the magic began to fade. In 1892, for example, South Dakotans elected their first governor, the Populist Andrew Lee, by only 319 votes. Though reelected in 1896, Lee lost a 1900 election for Congress in a landslide after his rural credit scheme failed. Likewise Senator Richard Pettigrew, a leading voice for Populism and anti-imperialism, lost his reelection bid in 1900. In a preview of the New Right's campaign to defeat George McGovern in 1980, the national Republican Party spent an astounding half million dollars to push Pettigrew out of the Senate. Marcus Hanna, President McKinley's top adviser and chair of the Republican Party, traveled across the state attacking Pettigrew. From the "viciousness" of his attacks, it was hard to tell which Hanna wanted more—for McKinley to win in November or for Pettigrew to lose.[30]

While the Populist Party was in decline, the adoption by progressive Republicans in South Dakota of several key items in its platform demonstrated how the movement created the "roots" of both Progressive-era and

New Deal reform.[31] Governor and three-term senator Peter Norbeck, for example, boasted that he was a true "champion of the needs of farmers."[32] He was the first governor of South Dakota to have been born there: in a dugout on his Norwegian parents' homestead. Like the Populists before him Norbeck believed that the state should be used to help farmers in their fight against the powerful interests of corporations, banks, utilities, and corrupt political parties; he believed that cooperation between and among farmers was one key strategy. He supported a state-owned cement factory (approved by voters in a 1919 constitutional amendment), the 1907 ban on corporate farming, a rural credit program, state hail insurance, and, in time, women's suffrage.[33] But Norbeck's reforms were just that—Populist ideas without their agrarian ideals. Hardly a farmer, he owned a well-digging business and invested in land, coming close to joining the "millionaires club."[34] More importantly, he loathed the "disloyal" programs proposed by a new agrarian organization, the Nonpartisan League (NPL), and temporarily barred its most effective organizer, the former socialist A. C. Townley, from the state.[35] In the early 1930s he strongly supported the New Deal's Agricultural Adjustment Act, even though many farmers were alarmed by its requirements. Finally Norbeck added a new reform: conservation. He introduced the first regulated hunting season and established several state parks, including Mount Rushmore. Farmers, he may have forgotten, traditionally had little interest in conservation, at least of land. They preferred to produce more not less.

Enhancing the role of women in the public sphere was a goal Populists and Progressives largely shared, albeit in different eras. Nationally, female leaders like Kansan Mary Lease were well-known orators and authors: among many legendary stories about her, Lease reportedly told farmers in Kansas to "raise less corn and more hell!"[36] Like Lease, female leaders in South Dakota did not speak solely to "women's issues." Sophia Harden of Huron and Elizabeth Wardell of Butte County organized for both the Farmers' Alliance and the suffrage movement.[37] They promoted rallies as social events for the whole family, diverging from the fraternal political culture of the time. Nevertheless, organizers found that many farm women—Scandinavian and German women, in particular—struggled to attend meetings given the long distances they sometimes had to travel, their extra responsibilities for household production and child care, and their husbands' opposition.[38] Two early South Dakota women who made their careers in radical agrarianism were unmarried. Alice Lorraine Daly, a socialist organizer, became involved when a fellow teacher in Madison was promptly fired after starting a union.[39] Gladys Pyle was the first woman in American history to be elected (rather than appointed) to the United States Senate when she succeeded Peter Norbeck in 1937. Like Norbeck, Pyle was a progressive Republican dependent on the farm vote. In the late 1930s she found a way to champion the farmer and criticize Roosevelt at the same time. Far from doing too much, she said, the New Deal had "not done enough for the state."[40]

*   *   *

Populist ideas endured even more robustly in North Dakota, despite constant opposition from conservatives. Early farm organizers there faced one obstacle that their counterparts in South Dakota did not: an established political machine. By 1900 Alexander McKenzie controlled the Republican Party in the state through his powerful connections with corporations and investors in the Twin Cities. Famous for holding all of his most important meetings in a smoky backroom at the luxurious Merchants Hotel in St. Paul, McKenzie derided immigrant farmers, their ethnicity, poor English, and political beliefs. He was known to have boasted, "Give me a bunch of Swedes, and I'll drive them like sheep."[41]

Facing McKenzie's power base, Alliance members and Populists (like members of the NPL later) took a different approach to organizing farmers: They treated them and their concerns—both local and national—seriously. They did not travel by luxury train car but by wagon (or Model T) to farms in remote sections of the state, encouraging farmers to organize cooperatively in their own communities and take up the issues that mattered most to them. They saw the possibility that the Alliance meetings could double as social outings in areas where isolation was one of the biggest problems farmers faced.

The records of the Alliance organization in Romness, North Dakota, show how neighborly cooperation and socialization melded easily with politics.[42] At each meeting the first order of business was the needs of members and their families. In November 1892, for example, the Romness Alliance voted to donate twenty dollars to Nels Thompson who needed his leg amputated and a family whose crop had been lost to hail. Second, the group discussed their efforts to establish a cooperative store. They concluded each meeting with a discussion of "political interest." They thought the moral purpose of their work was so closely aligned with Christianity that they appointed a chaplain. On January 24, 1891, he told them: "The wealth of the nation is accumulating . . . in the hands of a few—mostly now on corporations of which the leaders are [becoming] millionaires in a short time. [Mean]while the farmers and laborers have to work hard for the necessaries of life. But, Brothers, let us unite and stand united and work by every lawful means in our power to better our conditions. Not as the nihilist and anarchist with explosives, life and property destroying elements. But as good moral law obeying and peace preserving citizens."[43] Fourteen years later, in "the revolution of 1906," it was not an Alliance member or a Populist but a progressive Republican candidate for governor, John Burke, who finally overthrew the McKenzie machine. Working with state representative Lars Ueland, Burke established systems for direct democracy, including initiative and referendum.[44] But like South Dakota's Norbeck, Burke was no farmer and definitely no radical. By 1915, many North Dakotans determined that progressive reform would not solve the economic problems they continued to face.[45]

At this moment, the two most talented farm organizers in history, A. C. Townley, a former socialist activist, and attorney William Langer, forever remembered by friends and foes alike as "Wild Bill," arrived in the state to launch a truly radical political organization, the NPL. Both men's approach was less reform, more takeover; their goal was to establish "people-first" alternatives to laissez-faire corporate capitalism. They demanded that the state acquire many kinds of businesses that profited from the farmer's labor: creameries, packing plants, terminal elevators, flour mills, grain inspection stations, and banks. They promoted state hail insurance and the exemption of farm improvements from taxation. They also made sure that farmers knew that their concerns really mattered. Townley insisted, "If [the farmer] likes religion, talk Jesus Christ . . . if he is afraid of whiskey, talk Prohibition, if he wants to talk hogs, talk hogs—talk anything he'll listen to, but talk, talk, talk, until you get his Goddamned John Hancock to a check for six dollars [the price of a membership]."[46] The son of another early organizer, Frank Vogel, remembered that "Wild Bill" Langer also "had a genuine interest in the ordinary people. . . . If Bill Langer was speaking in a German speaking community, he would throw in a few words of German, a joke or a pun or some remark about a political enemy who did not speak German. He always loved to refer to local people in his speeches . . .

and he got lots of laughs, keeping the crowd in stitches a good share of the time."[47] North Dakota NPL organizers also worked to include and elevate women. However much it may have seemed like a violation of the nineteenth-century doctrine of "separate spheres," women served as NPL orators, organizers, and secretaries. Many did not see the contradiction. Ruby Craft, an NPL leader in Turtle Lake explained: "A family is the 'Heart of Politics.'" She and other NPL women circulated their own newspapers and fought for improved educational opportunities both for their daughters and themselves. An NPL woman in Montana explained the seriousness of her work: "We are not going to talk about recipes for rhubarb . . . we want to know about the great battles for human rights so that we can vote straight when the time comes." After the passage of the Nineteenth Amendment, NPL women took up the cause of voter registration to "make the women's vote as strong as the men's."[48]

After a year of organizing in fields, barns, kitchen gardens, porches, and sitting rooms, the NPL boasted forty thousand members in North Dakota and entered its golden era of political power. Soon its newspaper, the *Nonpartisan Leader*, had twice as many subscribers as the next biggest paper in the state. In 1916 North Dakota voters elected NPL candidates Lynn Frazier, a farmer who had never served in public office, for governor, and William Langer for attorney general; the NPL also seized the house and put large numbers of candidates in the state senate.[49] In a flurry of legislation, lawmakers established three institutions that still stand today—a state-owned bank, elevator, and mill, as well as a state-level Industrial Commission, chaired by the governor, to oversee them. But NPL leaders had more "take-over" in mind; they aimed to acquire and manage even more sectors of the economy. Over a century, the NPL (since 1956 the D-NPL) created a living legacy for the American left as a whole. Michael Lansing writes, "At the very moment most American intellectuals gave up on a central role for the people in politics . . . the League showed the ongoing potency of carefully organized and platform-focused citizen politics." Even though their initial control of the government was fleeting—Governor Lynn Frazier and other officials were recalled by voters in 1921—the NPL "transcended cynicism to create enduring—if regularly ignored—legacies that hold the potential to reshape politics today."[50]

*   *   *

Dakota farmers faced their hardest times in the twin economic and environmental crises of the Great Depression and Dust Bowl when low crop prices combined with drought, heat, hordes of grasshoppers, and "black blizzards of dust" to render it impossible for farmers to make a living. Farmers struggled to pay back their loans or buy seed and feed, creditors foreclosed on their property, and local businesses shuttered. And the crisis on the Northern Plains started well before it did in other regions. In 1929, 16-year-old North Dakotan Ann Marie Low wrote, "there seems to be a furor in the country over a big stock market crash that wiped a lot of people out. We are ahead of them."[51] When journalist Lorena Hickok visited the region in 1932, she wrote "a more hopeless place I have never seen. This is the Siberia of the United States."[52] By 1933, 90 percent of residents in some counties qualified for federal emergency relief.

Throughout the United States, men and women responded to the Great Depression with a wide variety of alternative political and economic programs. On the Northern Plains farmers held a distinct advantage: two generations of experienced politicians and radical agrarian organizations. One new group, the Farmers Holiday Association (FHA), began in Iowa and quickly headed northwest to South Dakota. Like other radicals before them, members of the FHA believed they needed to work cooperatively to stop creditors from obliterating family farming. They argued that since bankers took a "holiday" to keep panicked depositors from emptying out their vaults, farmers should do the same. In the spirit of Bryan, one FHA leader averred: "we'll eat our wheat and ham and eggs and let them eat their gold."[53] Across the upper Midwest, farmers blocked roads to market, attacked those who tried to get through, and threatened bankers and lawyers who tried to foreclose on local farms. They even surrounded farm houses set to be auctioned, so that no one could get to the sale.[54] Angry farmers and others looking for change elected Tom Berry, the second Democratic governor in South Dakota history.

The NPL's unique legacy in North Dakota prepared farmers for even more sustained and institutionalized action. In 1932 voters elected NPL leader William Langer governor and almost immediately he earned his nickname "Wild Bill." Langer ordered an embargo on wheat exports until prices rose. He banned foreclosures on farm properties as well as corporate ownership. He was rumored to have said, "Treat the banker like a chicken thief. Shoot him on sight."[55] Langer's colleague and longtime NPL leader, William Lemke, was elected to the US House in 1932. He quickly gained a

FIGURE 3. Members of the Nonpartisan League (NPL) blocking access to a farm auction in the Great Depression. Courtesy State Historical Society of North Dakota.

reputation for standing up for farmers. In 1934 he cosponsored, with then senator Lynn Frazier, a bill that forced banks to give bankrupt farmers five years to repay their loans. When Frazier-Lemke was ruled unconstitutional, he submitted a revised version, the Farm Mortgage Moratorium Act of 1935, which was renewed until its 1949 expiration.

But the crisis of the Dust Bowl did not simply provide renewed opportunity for flexible political responses in the tradition of radical agrarianism. It also transformed the nature of the agricultural economy itself, bringing white farmers into a new and enduring relationship with and dependence on the federal government.[56] Their "consent" to this transformation was born of extreme necessity, etched by deep ambivalence, and punctuated by both traditional political and "everyday" habits of resistance.[57] New Deal interventions—reductions in production, increases in conservation, and resettlement—could not have departed further from what farm leaders had long proposed. Farmers saw domestic allotment, in which the Agricultural Adjustment Act (AAA) paid farmers to leave fields fallow, as a stark rebuke to those who prided themselves on producing food. To make matters worse, Congress passed the AAA after the 1933 planting and birthing season had begun, meaning that, to receive benefits, farmers were required to kill their newborn pigs and plow under their crops. The chance to destroy the products of their labor was hardly what farmers had fought for over half a century. Likewise payments scaled to help large landowners more than small contradicted their foundational principles. Forced to choose between participating in programs they opposed or losing their land entirely, almost all farmers, in the new federal lexicon, "cooperated." It occurred to many, however, that the federal bureaucracy was now just another source of concentrated power rigged against them.

Farmers resisted domestic allotment on the political front first. Just after Roosevelt's inauguration, Emil Loriks, representing the FHA, and John Simpson, representing the Farmers Union, went to Congress to promote an alternative to domestic allotment: the "cost of production" plan. Cost-of-production would guarantee a minimum price on crops so farmers could produce as much or as little as they chose, without the interference of an "army of [government] workers."[58] In other words, they proposed a plan where a sympathetic interventionist state would provide aid to farmers while also respecting their ability to manage their own industry. Simpson advised: "Never try to regulate the farmer. Turn him loose. If he is fond of work, he will have a big excess that he does not get much for; but what the home folks use he will surely get paid for it."[59] Loriks put it more bluntly: changes in the farm industry were best left up to "you and me."[60]

When Congress rejected the cost-of-production plan and passed the AAA, large numbers of Dakota farmers—as many as 95 percent in some counties—signed up to "cooperate." Before long they began to receive benefits based on the value of the average yield over five years on the acreage they promised to leave fallow. And yet their "cooperation" did not signal an end to their resistance as much as its relocation from the political to the "everyday" sphere. Roosevelt insisted that AAA programs be administratively decentralized, overseen by county boards with local men and not "outsiders" as members. As a result, local men were empowered to make the single most important decision: how many acres each farmer had to keep fallow and how many he could put into production. Quite often, farmers succeeded in "overestimating" their five-year average yields so they could produce more going forward. It is possible they kept poor records. But it is far more likely that the commissioners—their friends, neighbors,

and fellow parishioners—looked the other way and allowed them to produce more than they were allowed.[61] County boards found plenty of "reasons" to explain their abnormally high acreage figures to the Department
of Agriculture: property lines had been "mixed up" or census figures had
been inaccurate, or "slow-minded German-Russian and Indian" farmers
had gotten confused. A federal agent who oversaw the local boards in Ren-
ville County, North Dakota, expressed it more candidly: some of the farmers were just "liars."[62]

Farmers, who had hoped for federal programs they could control,
learned instead to control what they could. They worked the system to their
benefit when possible, learning to live with and profit from, if still not
endorse, federal intervention. For decades they consistently voted for the
candidates who vowed to protect federal farm supports even though they
still disliked the logic behind them and the bureaucracy that operated
them.[63] Two decades later a new form of federal power with an even more
impenetrable bureaucracy arrived on the plains in the form of air bases and
nuclear weapons. When it did, when the warfare state joined the welfare
state on the Northern Plains, Dakotans worked from the playbook they
knew: they welcomed the economic benefits of militarization, created strategies to provide the best results for local people, and voted for politicians
who acquired increased funding. From time to time, however, even the
most "patriotic" Dakotans admitted that when the warfare state combined
red tape and incompetence—secrets and lies—the consequences could be
fatal.

*   *   *

However much radical agrarian organizations were like "political prairie
fires," they also faced opponents determined to extinguish them. Small-
town conservatives in the "probusiness" wings of the Republican Party
ardently opposed radical farmers and their proposals. While they were not
conservative in all the ways the New Right would be, they were both conservative and plentiful enough to enable the rise of the New Right in later
years despite the region's radical heritage—provided that the right mixture
of global, national, and local factors coalesced to support their cause.

First and foremost, conservatives in the Dakotas put their faith in American business and laissez-faire economics. They believed in competition not cooperation. Thus they also opposed any organization, politician, or program that advocated for the use of the government to regulate the economy—whether Populist, NPL, or New Deal. Rather than decry the growth of corporations and the globalization of commodities markets, they tried to emulate these trends.[64] Some of the leading business owners in the region had moved from eastern states with money and educations in hand, planning to accumulate large-scale farms and ranches or launch small businesses. Most of these hardware stores, general stores, banks, and small manufacturers stayed small; some failed completely, especially in the 1930s.[65] But a few were on the ground floor of what would become the country's most powerful agribusinesses. Cargill Corporation began in Iowa but quickly moved west and by 1885 had one hundred storage elevators in the Dakotas.[66]

Dakota conservatives also defined their role in society through the lens of their class position. Whether their establishments were large or small, Dakota businesspeople counted themselves among the "best families" in their towns, usually attending the largest "mainline" Protestant churches—Presbyterian, Lutheran, Methodist, or Episcopalian—and belonging to the most prestigious social clubs and organizations. Compared to farmers, they were more likely to be Protestant and more likely to be born in the US; if they were immigrants, they were more likely to come from Canada or Scandinavia, rather than Germany or Russia. They were heavily invested in "traditional Protestant concerns with upright behavior" and stood against the sale of alcohol, gambling, and even dancing.[67] Further as employers and creditors, they also had the power to reward or punish those in the community who violated their values. Conservatives looked askance at anyone who depended on local charity or aid. The editor of the *Woonsocket News* wrote, "Any able-bodied man is able to make his own living without begging. Make him work for what he gets."[68]

From the late 1890s onward, businesspeople and other conservatives implemented a variety of economic strategies, political maneuvers, and legal actions to foil agrarian reformers. On the regional level, this set the stage for the national movement of businesspeople against the New Deal and, subsequently, the rise of new conservatism.[69] South Dakota bankers and attorneys, for example, upended Progressive governor Peter Norbeck's plan to create a state-run rural credit bureau. In North Dakota, Alliance and Populist legislators faced fierce resistance from what remained of the McKenzie machine.[70] When legislators proposed regulations on the railroad, for example, conservatives allied themselves with powerful railroad commissioners and demanded to know why anyone would want to inhibit the railroad, when they "have done and are still doing a mighty work toward the prosperity and material advancement of our State."[71] Conservatives stymied Governor Eli C. D. Shortridge, too, as he endeavored to push through reforms. Though funding for a state-owned elevator was approved and a few other bills passed, it was a "well-known fact," according to Shortridge, "that every bill brought before the Legislatures of the past, that was not satisfactory to the corporations, and could not be otherwise defeated, was either stolen, mutilated, or destroyed."[72]

North Dakota conservatives met their match in the NPL and "Wild Bill" Langer until conservatives turned some of the radicals' trademark tools against them. Because Langer and other NPL candidates ran as a branch of the Republican Party, for example, anti-NPL voters organized their own. They created the Independent Voters Association (IVA), held their own rallies, and published their own newspaper. Still outnumbered by NPL Republicans, they used the legislative process to block the NPL's attempt to write a new constitution.[73] They sought every piece of evidence that state-owned institutions were poorly managed, including the claim that the state bank wasn't investing the money it had and that some NPL leaders were really supporting "Big Biz."[74] Finally in 1921 they weaponized one of the NPL's most important political reforms against it: they organized and won a recall vote for three party leaders, including Governor Frazier, and won, replacing them all with men of their own.

With Twin Cities railroad men, corporate interests, and powerful judges and attorneys on their side, IVA leaders worked to get "Wild Bill" Langer out of office by any means necessary. They saw their best chance in the 1930s when it was revealed that Langer, by then the governor, had required state employees to buy a subscription to the *Nonpartisan Leader*. For that offense they got a guilty verdict that sent Langer to prison.[75] But the verdict was overturned and, after two more trials, Langer returned to the governor's mansion. In 1940 he was elected to the US Senate, but immediately faced an ethics committee investigation when opponents back home forwarded to Washington "evidence" of Langer's allegedly corrupt practices as governor.[76] Langer was cleared of those charges as well and served as a senator until his death. Perhaps apocryphally, North Dakota farmers were said to have written his name on their ballots for years after his passing.

To conservatives dedicated to laissez-faire economics, the protection of their own wealth, and the authority of their moral views, New Deal reforms seemed like the end of the world. If farmers were disappointed with the reforms and resentful of bureaucrats, they at least received benefits they believed their particularly unpredictable industry merited. Conservatives, however, saw the New Deal as an attack on their position in society. First, they worried that new programs diminished their economic independence and cultural authority. In a letter to President Roosevelt, for example, a mainline Protestant minister in North Dakota complained that there were no controls on how men on relief spent their money: as a result, in his town, there were four thriving saloons and seventeen bootleggers, while the church's coffers were bare.[77] Other conservatives were concerned that they had neither the power to select the men who would oversee federal programs nor the authority to get rid of them if they were not doing their jobs. Most crucially Roosevelt's policies hurt conservatives in their wallets. This "class traitor"-turned-chief-executive increased taxes on upper-income families, gave workers the right to collective bargaining, and attempted to create a system of wage and price controls.

Dakota conservatives faced a more personal crisis when some discovered that their families qualified for federal aid, both emergency cash payments and works programs. Writes R. Alton Lee, this prospect filled many South Dakotans "with disbelief and dejection."[78] For some the only solution was to refuse to accept relief, a public sign that they were incapable of managing their affairs. Lois Phillips Hudson of Eldredge, North Dakota, whose father owned a local store, remembered how often her school lunch pail was empty while her friends' were full and sometimes held a bright red "relief" apple. Even though she was desperately hungry, she, like her father, was also "really proud" that she had nothing.[79] When she toured the states for her friend Eleanor Roosevelt, Lorena Hickok found a family with a single business suit left, which the father and son wore on alternate days when they looked for work. They preferred that desperate scheme to accepting relief.

However difficult their own circumstances, Dakota conservatives worked to find a new strategy to defeat New Dealism at home, where Democrats had surged in South Dakota and NPLers—while hardly fans of Roosevelt themselves—held the reins of power to the North. In both an echo of the World War I era and a preview of the Cold War, they found new and effective ammunition in accusations of socialism and communism.[80] In South Dakota, for example, conservatives took advantage of many farmers' resentment of the federal agricultural bureaucracy to defeat Democratic efforts to create state and local planning boards. Not fooled by the use of the faux-Populist language of "cooperation," German Russian farmers complained that these planning boards sounded just like "Soviet-style five year plans." To others they just sounded like another set of rules and regulations dreamed up by bureaucrats. Democratic governor Tom Berry traveled by train across the state, trying to get farmers to equate planning with familiar "habits of mutuality." In Huron he said, "We have got to try to cooperate with one another instead of trying to buck one another. That is why we have been trying to do what they call 'planning.'"[81] Even a visit by Roosevelt in 1936 did not bring most residents around to the idea of a centrally planned economy. The Beadle County Planning Board resigned en masse rather than continue to participate in a "useless commission." The Edmunds County Planning Board did the same, and called both its work and that of the county welfare board "shams, jokes, and money wasted."[82]

The 1938 election in South Dakota began both the slow decline of agrarian radicalism on the plains and the first signs of a reinvented "new" conservatism, articulated first through what historian John Miller calls "McCarthyism before McCarthy." [83] The Republican Party, whose progressive wing was already less influential, swept the state, delivering a shocking condemnation of the Berry administration. The November 9, 1938, edition of Sioux Falls *Argus Leader* provided one reason voters had changed course so drastically: "South Dakotans Repudiate New Deal." But that may not have been their only motivation. Accusations of communism also helped defeat at least one radical agrarian leader and elevate a rising conservative star. In his congressional campaign against Emil Loriks, a Farmers Union and FHA leader who had originally opposed the AAA, Karl Mundt linked Loriks to labor radicalism, support for the New Deal, urban-style political organizing tactics, and—most damningly—communism. He bragged to an audience in Sisseton, "The Communist Party of South Dakota is now openly holding political rallies to defeat me and I accept their opposition cheerfully . . . I have been fighting the un-Christian and un-American doctrines of Communism . . . for over ten years."[84] By the end of the campaign, Loriks, a World War I veteran who "loved his country more than anything," was forced to prove his loyalty to voters over and over.[85] They remained unconvinced. In victory, Mundt would go on to show to the nation what he thought true love of country required, working side by side with Senator

Joseph McCarthy to eliminate communists in the government and force other Americans to prove their loyalty too. When years later a young congressman named George McGovern challenged the veteran Mundt for his senate seat, he experienced these same red-baiting tactics. After the loss, he vowed never to run against Mundt again and instead to aim for South Dakota's "other" Senate seat. Even so McGovern found he could not escape conservative attacks that associated liberalism with un-Americanism. More than forty years after Mundtism ended Emil Loriks' political career, its ideological descendant—Reaganism—would end George McGovern's too.

*   *   *

As politically divisive and difficult as the 1930s were, Dakotans of Euro-American descent found ways to reinforce shared values through a celebration of their history. The Depression coincided with many communities' fiftieth anniversaries of settlement. To mark the occasion townspeople held pageants and parades, put on skits, and published local histories about the "old settlers'" days. Some members of the Roosevelt administration, particularly those in the Department of Agriculture, believed that the settlement of the arid plains had been a mistake. But the mistake, at least politically, was theirs. Uniformly and vehemently, white Dakotans rejected their conclusions and responded by performing their parents' and grandparents' historic courage, self-reliance, persistence, and success. Meanwhile they censored anything the government issued that suggested different.[86]

But as in Garland's story about the conflict between Tim Haskins and Jim Butler, the people of the plains had more in common than their "pioneer" history. The very fact of their common identification with the cultural symbol of the hard-working, independent, white pioneer at once depended upon and reinforced three beliefs so logical, so fully "embedded in the everyday," that only rarely did they need to be explained.[87] Long before they faced dust storms and far before they faced nuclear weapons, Dakotans of all political stripes shared a commitment to the protection of Christianity (sometimes exclusively Protestantism), patriarchal gender and family norms, and white supremacy. They did not express these convictions in the same ways, with some Dakotans promoting the use of violence and others eschewing it, for example. Most importantly some Dakotans then as now strongly opposed xenophobia, racism, and injustice.[88] But if Dakotans sometimes disagreed on how best to maintain their shared culture, or even on which ethnic groups counted as fully "white," they largely agreed on what their states had come to constitute: a "white [Christian] man's West."[89] By the end of the Great Depression, when some Eastern bureaucrats, artists, and intellectuals argued that farmers should never have ventured onto the Northern Plains in the first place, Dakotans created a shared past to codify—in the case of Mount Rushmore to literally set in stone—the story of why they did, including what they had achieved and why it mattered. In this way they carried out the process Jason Pierce describes as "myth and reality bec[oming] inseparable, each supporting the other."[90]

In the states' first fifty years, Dakotans of all political persuasions believed that being Christian was fundamental to good moral character and constitutive of citizenship. They were hardly outside the nation's norm. Nationwide, few Christians felt any compunction to hide their antisemitism. Henry Ford, for example, accepted the German lie that Jews were responsible for starting World War I. Every new car he sold came with a pamphlet explaining this view.[91] Thirty years earlier, some Populist leaders incorporated antisemitism in their political language.[92] Three well-known Populists in particular, Ignatius Donnelly, Mary Lease, and Tom Watson, distributed pamphlets that warned farmers about the conspiracies planned against farmers by "Jewish bankers." One particularly popular tract told of a Jewish banker who planned to "bury the knife deep into the heart of America."[93] Tom Watson put his antisemitic views into action when, in 1915, he unabashedly rallied fellow Georgians to lynch Leo Frank, a Jewish manager of a textile mill where a young girl had been raped and murdered. He warned "the next Jew who does what Frank did is going to get exactly the same thing that we give to Negro rapists."[94]

While no Jews were lynched in the Dakotas, many felt isolated and distinctly unwelcome in a region where there were "more United States senators than rabbis."[95] Few Dakotans objected, for example, when NPL leader William Lemke ran as presidential candidate in 1936 for the Union Party, and quickly became associated with the vicious antisemitism of its creator, Father Charles Coughlin of Michigan. Among other things, Coughlin called the New Deal the "Jew Deal"; like many other Americans he argued that Jews had "taken over" the government.[96] In the Dakotas as elsewhere in the Midwest, discrimination against Jews in housing was not required by law but broadly practiced, allowed in the deeds of homes, and rarely investigated. As late as 1961, Jack Stewart, the conservative alumnus of the University of North Dakota who proposed the essay contest on "Our American Heritage—How Can It Be Eternally Yours?" did not allow Jews to stay at his resort, the Camelback Inn in Scottsdale, Arizona. Even so, the university's president, George Starcher, regularly met there with the alumni association, drawing the ire of activist undergraduates.[97]

But, in an era when the very definition of whiteness was in formation and religion was among its battlegrounds, some Dakotans did not consider all Christians to be equal. Protestants targeted Catholics with sustained hatred and sporadic violence from territorial days through the first decades of the Cold War. Jon K. Lauck writes that marriages between Protestants and Catholics were scandalous; children were taught simply that "you can't mix wheat and potatoes in the same bin."[98] These religious schisms had consequences beyond marriage. Many Dakota Populists as well as nearly all conservatives sought to ban card playing, saloons, the sale of alcohol, and even dancing.[99] NPL governor Lynn Frazier, for example, claimed never to have had a sip of alcohol and canceled some parties that had customarily featured music and dancing. But other important members of radical farm organizations, especially German Russians, deeply resented such attempts at forcible assimilation through "moral reform." By the 1920s, the NPL in North Dakota stopped endorsing the national plank of Prohibition.

Dakotan anti-Catholicism became more organized and violent in the early twentieth century, an era that Nell Irvin Painter identifies as a peak in American history of racial differentiation among white ethnic groups.[100] Across the Midwest in the 1920s, Protestants organized "klaverns" of the Ku Klux Klan, which, in its second iteration, targeted immigrants, Catholics, and Jews. In the Dakotas its "respectable citizens" terrorized Catholics especially.[101] In Grand Forks the minister of the most prestigious mainline Protestant church in town, F. Hadley Ambrose, was found to be an imposter: an unordained man who moved to town to assume the role of "Grand Dragon."[102] He motivated church members to march against the growing number of Irish Catholics in the town, some of whom were on the local school board. Residents of South Dakota communities did the same. They marched in Rapid City, burning crosses in Lead and Sturgis and accused priests in Madison, Nunda, and Ramona of using dance and card and "booze parties" to convert members.[103]

Long after the KKK had fallen out of public favor in the Dakotas, anti-Catholicism remained. In the 1940s legislatures in both states banned nuns from wearing habits in their classrooms; as late as the 1960s athletic teams from Catholic schools could not compete for state championships.[104] Some Dakotans were as alarmed by the candidacy of Massachusetts Catholic John F. Kennedy in 1960 as they had been by the candidacy of New York Catholic Al Smith in 1924. When Robert and John Kennedy came to South Dakota to stump for George McGovern, Bobby worried that they had actually hurt him. He was probably right. Some South Dakotans thought that if McGovern, the son of a Methodist minister, was friendly with the Kennedys, then he must be a secret Catholic himself. One admitted that, with five children, he would "make a pretty good Catholic."[105]

Whether they perceived it in the early years or not, the shared experience of attending largely conservative denominations gave many Protestants and Catholics on the Northern Plains at least one worldview in common: a traditional view of women and family. While in the 1960s some large Protestant denominations became active in social justice work, including second wave feminism, in the prewar decades the churches most Dakotans attended were relatively theologically conservative. For example, German and German Russian immigrants might be either Lutheran or Catholic. Both, however, sought to protect their parishioners from the modernizing influences of American society, by retaining German language services, for example, at least until 1918 and in some places longer. Many of the Lutheran parishes they and other immigrants established would later become part of the Missouri Synod, the most conservative branch of the Lutheran church.[106] Even early twentieth-century Presbyterians in the Dakotas—a "mainline" and largely "Yankee" denomination which in the 1910s became associated with the "social gospel" theology—considered themselves "old school."[107]

The tepid, even "timid," response of many rural Dakotans to women's suffrage reflects these common views—as well as the degree to which social life in rural areas centered around the church.[108] Populists, Progressives, and Nonpartisan Leaguers in both states had involved women in their movements, welcoming them to speak, organize rallies, and publish newspapers. Moreover, the South Dakota constitution made public universities and colleges open to both sexes and formally closed no occupations or professions to women.[109] Even so, change did not come for women on the Northern Plains as quickly as many had hoped largely because for many voters the idea of women operating in the public sphere as equals to men was still unthinkable. Some Dakota women shared this concern, organizing as "antis" and arguing that the special nature of women's difference from men would be destroyed if they became involved in partisan politics.[110] As a result, even the most dedicated activists played down the revolutionary nature of suffrage. The NPL's suffragists reassured legislators that women who voted would not become radicals, only more effective mothers and wives. Others downplayed any change suffrage would bring to the traditional relationship between men and women.[111]

Compared with other western states, like Colorado and Wyoming, the campaign for women's suffrage in North and South Dakota was frustratingly slow. Local suffragists brought the issue to a vote in South Dakota in 1892 and 1896, losing both times. In 1898 the National American Woman Suffrage Association actually pulled their support in South Dakota. Its leader, Carrie Chapman Catt, believed the many non-English-speaking immigrant women and country families in the state were "not yet prepared" for it.[112] South Dakota organizers such as Matilda Vanderhule also understood that any hope they had of winning over county farmers was to explain that the vote was nothing "radical," just an extension of the kinds of community organizing—church bazaars, for example—that women already did.[113] On their own, with no support from the national organization, they lost again.

In North Dakota the leaders of the women's suffrage movement took a somewhat different tack: they linked the vote to the campaign for Prohibition, largely supported by Protestants, both native-born and Scandinavian. With the vote, they contended, women could counterbalance the corruptions of secular society, including saloons. This drew the ire of German farmers, anti-prohibition groups, the McKenzie machine, liquor interests, and railroads. They lost in 1914 and 1915. In fact neither North nor South Dakotans granted suffrage until World War I and, in the case of South Dakota, perhaps only because it was paired with an amendment that banned some immigrants from voting.[114] Catt had been more right than she could have known. Many decades later when a second wave of feminists advocated for reproductive rights, among many other issues, they would meet with much the same hesitation from local people with conservative faith practices, by then including the evangelical movement. In those years, too, the "antis" took the lead to make sure that radical change did not alter the traditional roles of wife and mother they valued so much.

The most hegemonic component of the culture of the Northern Plains—the aspect furthest beyond debate or discussion—was the belief in the superiority of white culture. While all Euro-Americans had, in Toni Morrison's words, lived in the "shadow of the African," whites in the rural West lived more immediately "in the shadow" of the region's indigenous people, whose stolen lands they cultivated.[115] Even so the stereotypes they held about Natives—they were lazy, uncivilized, unintelligent, sexually degenerate, and immoral—overlapped significantly with those they held about other nonwhites and thus served at once to disparage them, to define core elements of whiteness, and to justify discrimination and violence. Most importantly, whites on the Northern Plains did not consider Indians to be advanced enough, perhaps not even human enough, to deserve to keep their land. The *Billings Post* stated bluntly in 1884: "It will be a great boon to this section, when these miserable, idle dogs are moved away, this valuable section of land thrown open to the use of people who will utilize it."[116] Whites believed that if Native people had no understanding of property, they were also incapable of self-government. In 1908 South Dakota governor William Beadle was asked why his state's politics often grew so heated: his citizens had a "race instinct for local self-government," he explained.[117] In the late nineteenth century, as white farmers' claim to land, and thus citizenship, became increasingly perilous, their decision to use the political sphere to protect it was at once a performance of their whiteness and a desperate attempt to define and salvage it.

As in other settler societies around the world, the federal government had done much of the dirty work that enabled white Dakotans to create communities on the Northern Plains. The Army of the West, surveyors of the Army Corps of Engineers, public-private partnerships that built the transcontinental railroad, and legislators who "opened" the west to homesteading cumulatively deprived Native people of their homelands and created a "continental empire."[118] On the Northern Plains, wars and treaties—some of which were broken before the ink dried—"removed" Lakota, Sioux, Crow, Cheyenne, and other indigenous people from the land and relegated them to the legal segregation and separation of reservations. When forced to give up yet more land under the Dawes Act in 1886, some Lakota turned to the Ghost Dance, a complex religious revival that began in Utah and spread quickly up the plains.[119] When a band of Oglala Lakota under Big Foot traveled to sacred sites in December of 1890 to perform the Ghost Dance, the Seventh Cavalry of the US Army opened fire on them near the hamlet of Wounded Knee, killing as many as three hundred men, women, and children. Many historians consider this "attack" the last chapter in the Indian Wars. Others see it as the first chapter in the modern history of pan-Indian cultural resistance. In either case it demonstrated that the federal government would meet with lethal force any attempt by Native people to determine their own future.[120]

After the state had "cleared the land," Euro-American settlers reinforced this new reality of white power. They did so with law, culture, and violence—all of which helped to bridge the gap of white ethnic difference. For example, while Native men and women were not forbidden from traveling off the reservation, border towns became de facto sites of violence and sexual assault. Ranchers organized vigilante groups to find Indians they suspected of stealing horses or food. In larger cities and towns, whites enforced structures of segregation in housing and employment, with "Indian towns" relegated to the outskirts of most communities and "no Indians" signs in the windows of businesses.[121] And settlers continued to press state and federal officials to take remaining reservation lands. "West River" settlers in South Dakota, for example, were well known to graze their stock on Indian lands illegally, and to take up arms against any Natives who left the reservation or tried to keep them off their lands. Looking for a solution to this volatile situation, the US commissioner of Indian Affairs under McKinley, William Jones, arranged a lease for rancher Ed Lemmon on nearly a million acres of land promised to the Standing Rock Sioux in north central South Dakota, which only whetted Dakotans' appetite for Indian land. Rather than appease Dakotans, such leases created even more calls for the end of Indian landholding altogether.[122]

Some early settler-colonists expressed sympathy for Natives and disagreed vehemently with those who, in the aftermath the Dakota War of 1862 believed that Indians should be wiped out.[123] Populist leader T. R. Bland, for example, spoke out against both the massacre at Wounded Knee and the policies of forced assimilation. He hoped that the government programs would help tribes hold onto their lands.[124] Some Dakota publishers supported the right to vote for Native men—even when they did not always support it for white women.[125] In later decades South Dakota senator Francis Case sponsored a bill to provide compensation to survivors of Wounded Knee.[126] "Wild Bill" Langer used his position in the Senate to investigate mistreatment of Indian youths in the federal prison at Fort Yates.[127] But these early examples of relative open-mindedness around race stemmed either from the belief that Native people would soon disappear, victims of the unstoppable forces of "progress," or from a general empathy with the

poor rather than a complex understanding of racial injustice or a commitment to full equality. Populist senator Richard Pettigrew, for example, was
very interested in Native people, but expressed it by collecting Indian artifacts—what historian Elliot West calls "a macabre competition . . . especially among private [collectors]."[128] Even Hamlin Garland advocated for
tribes to retain more of their land; at the same time, he was sure to buy
Indian land when it became available through forced dispossession in Oklahoma. Case strongly supported the forced assimilationist policies of the
1886 Dawes Act and fought the New Deal's attempts to restore Native culture.[129] In the postwar years, neither Case nor Langer stopped to consider
the impact on Natives of living in missile fields that threatened annihilation
every day.

In a final step to imprint their power on the plains, whites wrote a
history of the region that essentially erased Native people from memory. In
1923, progressive Republican Peter Norbeck hoped to draw tourists to the
Black Hills. He hired sculptor Gutzon Borglum, who had just finished scul-
pting a memorial to Confederates in Stone Mountain, Georgia, which also
served as a gathering place for the KKK—an organization to which Borglum belonged. Norbeck asked him to create an enormous sculpture on a
series of rock faces the Lakota called the "Six Grandfathers." But Norbeck
did not want Borglum to sculpt any Indian grandfathers. Instead Norbeck
asked Borglum to carve four American presidents—two of them slavehold-
ers and two of them advocates for the removal of Indians. In creating his
art, Borglum destroyed much of the rock face that had been promised in
perpetuity to the Lakota. Indeed he put more Dakota values on display than
he knew—particularly the erasure of Indian history by whites who had
commodified the land and put it to the plow.

As enduring as Mount Rushmore have been Laura Ingalls Wilder's *Little
House* books, written in the Depression years, and read by millions of
Americans since. In them, white "pioneer" families, independent and
deeply moral, works the land far from any government programs or
bureaucratic interference. They do so, as recent critics have recognized, on
a landscape where Indians have been erased and white families seem to take
ownership as if by magic. For example, Wilder began the original 1935
version of *Little House on the Prairie* by comparing Native people to wild
animals: "There [in the woods] the wild animals wandered and fed as
though they were in a pasture that stretched much farther than a man could
see, and there were no people. Only Indians lived there."[130] Today, this does

not go unnoticed by critics such as Ojibwa author Louise Erdrich, who wrote, "The Natives were . . . a vanishing people who were going to go away. And that's all one could feel about them." [131] But Wilder was far from alone in her effort to erase Native people and reify the myth of the pioneer. In 1932 the "Daughters of the Pioneers" erected a statue of a "pioneer family" in front of the new North Dakota "skyscraper" capitol. A man at the center, a woman and infant, and a male teenager face the future together. If any Indians could threaten them, they remained far away, perhaps already gone. [132]

*   *   *

In the early years of statehood, Dakotans disagreed vehemently on many things, particularly the power of corporations and banks and the role of the federal government. While at odds on economic and political issues like these, few voters in South Dakota disagreed about the fundamental world view represented in their state's motto: "Under God, the People Rule." [133] For South Dakotans the motto perfectly expressed their shared values and, in linking "myth and reality," brought diverse political factions and white ethnic groups together. Thus the everyday "cultural logic" behind this motto endured longer than the reformist political economy some citizens imagined. The "God" of both the Populists and their opponents was a Christian God, for some, an exclusively Protestant God; the people "under" him were white men, with women as partners but not equals. At the time the motto was written, it would still be twenty years before women could vote and thirty before Native people could "apply" for citizenship. As we have seen, by the 1930s, the ability of the people of the Dakotas to rule their own affairs had diminished considerably. In the decades to come it would diminish even more. By 1970 the famous faces on Mount Rushmore could be in the sights of a Soviet nuclear missile's navigational system. Yet Dakotans' conceptualization of who the people were and who their God should be would stand fast and, for some, even deepen as the risk of instant annihilation intensified each year.

CHAPTER 2

"HUMANITY GONE MAD"

IN THE WEEKS BEFORE the Japanese attack on Pearl Harbor on December 7, 1941, many Americans stopped by their local movie theaters to see the most popular film of the year, *Sergeant York*. The film depicted a pacifist, Alvin York, on the eve of America's entry into World War I. York had grown up on a hardscrabble Kentucky farm; after his father's death, he met a beautiful girl and became evangelized, making a personal commitment never to kill. When York was drafted he recalled he "was worried clean through. I didn't want to go and kill, I believed in my Bible."[1] He applied, unsuccessfully, for conscientious objector status. At basic training camp, two officers who recognized York's talent with a rifle and were also, apparently, persuasive interpreters of scripture convinced him that killing was sanctioned in the Bible if the cause was just. On October 9, 1918, York killed twenty-eight Germans and single-handedly took 132 prisoners in the infamous Battle of the Meuse Argonne.[2]

Sergeant York was promoted as a film about war, but a strikingly large percentage depicted York's life on his Kentucky farm, perfect for the intended audience of the time: rural Americans, particularly those from the upper Midwest and Great Plains states, who had resisted both the expansion of the Spanish-American War and American entry into World War I. Throughout the 1930s these Populist anti-militarists—called "isolationists" by their critics—had fought passionately against American participation in a second conflict with Germany.[3] True to fifty years of Populist-inspired politics, they believed that war only served to profit the rich and expand the power of the federal government. Some had seen for themselves the carnage of war and the distinctly undemocratic nature of military life. In the 1930s their congressional representatives sponsored laws, including three Neutrality Acts, to ensure the United States did not intervene in any new international conflicts. But by 1940, as Hitler marched through Europe and bombarded London, President Roosevelt became desperate to persuade Americans to change their minds. He turned to his "men in Hollywood." By producing *Sergeant York*, and "a few [other] good movies about America," Jack and Harry Warner and other studio owners set out to do just that.[4]

But how could a film depicting a rural man reluctant to go to war convince other rural men to go to war? First, filmmakers were careful not to lampoon rural life. Rather than a dirt poor and ignorant "hillbilly," like the ones satirized in the popular cartoon, *Li'l Abner*, they portrayed York as a thoughtful man with essential moral goodness.[5] The director also rejected pinup girl Jane Russell for the part of York's sweetheart, casting instead a 16-year-old newcomer, Joan Leslie, who neither smoked nor drank. The film elevated rather than diminished rural experience. It suggested, for example, that York's skill as a backwoods hunter helped make him an effective soldier—using a turkey gobble to entice Germans out of hiding, for example. Most importantly, the film showed that leaving the countryside and going to war did not change Alvin York. He returned to his sweetheart and his pacifism after the war. In 1940, when he saw the film for the first time, the real-life York apparently liked everything about it—except the killing.[6]

In the end, *Sergeant York* succeeded beyond the filmmakers', or the president's, wildest dreams. It earned more money than any other film that year, won two Academy Awards, and was nominated for nine others. Best of all, *Sergeant York* convinced many a reluctant warrior to fight—some going directly from the cinema to the recruiting station. According to historian Lynne Olson, "in the process of making the film" York himself "became a convert to interventionism"—again.[7]

However inspiring, *Sergeant York* still left many anti-militarists in the Dakota countryside unsettled. A small handful, like North Dakota senator Gerald Nye, remained unconvinced that war against Germany was necessary even after Pearl Harbor.[8] They called the film "an instrument of propaganda" and studios like Warner Brothers "the most gigantic engines of war propaganda in existence."[9] Senator Nye complained that the film was unrealistic. It did not show men "crouching in the mud . . . English, Greek, and

German boys disemboweled, blown to bits."[10] Populist anti-militarists saw in the film the growing power of the federal government to control information, media, speech, and even political beliefs when a crisis "required" it. They saw what they had feared for more than two generations, through World War I and the Great Depression: that the United States was becoming more like the militarized states of Europe with powerful, sometimes despotic centralized governments, and permanent standing armies where "it was impossible . . . to be both militarized and free."[11]

Nye and many others from the Northern Plains knew a different story about what could happen to conscientious objectors during World War I. They also knew Warner Brothers would never make it into a film. Josef and Michael Hofer were young Hutterite men from the Rockport colony in southeastern South Dakota. Like York, the Hofers applied for conscientious objector status based on their religious beliefs and were denied. Unlike York, no officers could ever persuade them to give up their pacifist beliefs. They were what military officials called "absolutists."[12] In 1918 a military court sentenced the Hofers to twenty years' hard labor at the notorious federal prison on Alcatraz Island. When they arrived and still refused to wear a military uniform, the Hofers were imprisoned in small basement rooms with wet floors and given little water and no food for the first five days. They were also "high cuffed": forced to stand for nine-hour stretches chained with their hands above their heads and only their toes touching the floor. Both men died within days of being transferred to Fort Leavenworth. Only then did the US military succeed in putting uniforms on them—in their coffins.[13]

Dakotans themselves shared some of the blame for the Hofer boys' fate. Before the war they had largely lived in peace with their religiously absolutist neighbors, finding common ground in the view that working the land was good and war was bad. When the war arrived, however, some Dakotans became as suspicious of Germanic Hutterite practices as the military authorities.[14] A few local people stole Hutterite cattle, set fire to their barns, and attacked their leaders. They ultimately succeeded in cleansing the countryside of these radicals, newly seen as "un-American." In 1918 residents of Rockport abandoned the colony, relocating to Canada. But the memory of these attacks only reinforced anti-militarist fears, even in those who perpetrated them. Having witnessed the militarization of their society in the late 1910s, Dakotans resisted war even more ardently in the 1930s. They asked, as Chicagoan Jane Addams had in 1917, "Was not war in the interest of democracy . . . a contradiction in terms, whoever said it or however often it was repeated?"[15]

* * *

The "political prairie fire" of Populism and its political descendants has long captured the attention of historians, even as they have debated whether its legacy belongs to the American left or right. But these same historians have largely overlooked the movement's extension of its critique of concentrated power to the military. Over the course of three wars between 1890 and 1941, agrarian radicals—at times with the consent and cooperation of their conservative opponents—made undeniably clear their dedication to anti-militarism and their opposition to a permanent standing army.[16] It was a defining element of their political tradition, which once alienated from economic agrarianism, left the region vulnerable to being militarized itself.

A cursory glance at the Omaha platform of 1892 might suggest that any discussion of the People's Party's foreign policy could be quick reading. Only a single "sentiment" mentions the military: "Resolved, that we pledge our support to fair and liberal pensions to ex-Union soldiers and sailors." But the silence of Omaha platform and subsequent Democratic platform in 1896 about traditional matters of foreign policy also spoke volumes. Populists, like Alliance members before them and Midwesterners as a whole, were not unsophisticated rubes. They had a global perspective on markets and supported free trade. They certainly knew that global markets affected the price for crops and other agricultural commodities. A group of Kansas Populists even began its own colony on the west coast of Mexico.[17] Likewise Populists in the late 1880s and 1890s knew full well of the Republican proposal to strengthen the navy and increase the United States military presence around the world, whether in Hawaii, Japan, China, or South America. Even so, they believed strongly that industrial-era economic transformations had to be ameliorated at home before any action could be taken abroad.[18]

As it did for many Americans, the Spanish-American War, which began with the media-enhanced "destruction" of the battleship *Maine* in Havana harbor, forced Populists to define their views on the American role in the world. David Lee Amstutz contends that Populists were "strongly opposed to empirical rule, or imperialism." At the same time, they "accepted the idea of self-determination of nations, and they also thought fostering democracy would safeguard American security."[19] As a result, most Populist leaders supported the war in Cuba, expecting that a victorious US would grant Cubans full independence and would not pursue further imperialist adventures elsewhere. When conservatives in Congress advocated the annexation of Hawaii and the broadening of the war to the Philippines, Populists instantly lost enthusiasm for the war.[20] Leaders from the Northern Plains, including William Jennings Bryan, Richard Pettigrew, and Andrew Lee, led the first Populist anti-imperialist movement in Washington and local capitals. As time passed and one war became another and then another, they learned both how difficult it was to fight against war—and to fight in one.

A national figure and a "godly hero" to many rural Americans even though he had come to Populism only through its decision to fuse with the Democrats in 1896, William Jennings Bryan's views on war illustrate how rank-and-file Populists thought about war and imperialism. Throughout his life, Bryan believed that war-making was a violation of Christian principles. Moreover, his views on war overlaid his concerns about economic injustice, since, in his view, the upper classes profited from war while clerks and factory workers paid with their lives.[21] Nevertheless reports of Spanish atrocities in Cuba and the loss of American life aboard the *Maine* convinced Bryan that the United States needed to intervene. He accepted the offer of a commission in the Nebraska National Guard and picked two thousand troops from the scores of local Nebraska residents, young and old, who had volunteered to fight with him. In the end, Bryan and his troops never saw battle in Cuba, stationed (he thought imprisoned) in Camp Cuba Libre in northern Florida for the duration. Bryan's inactivity did not come from lack of commitment to the cause. Instead it reeked of political gamesmanship. Why would McKinley have given his rival an opportunity for glory during midterm elections if he did not have to?[22] When Bryan finally resigned his commission and left to campaign again, he joked, "I had five months of peace in the Army and resigned to take part in a fight."[23]

Fighting a limited war to "free" Cuba was one thing, but expanding it to the Philippines confirmed Bryan and his followers' worst fears about McKinley's original intent. They saw the war and subsequent treaty with the Philippines as nothing more than a naked imperialist land grab. Speaking to the Democratic National Convention in Kansas City, Missouri, in July 1900, Bryan argued that in light of the American tradition of self-government, colonization of the Philippines made hypocrites of all who called themselves lovers of freedom. He paraphrased Lincoln's belief that our freedom does not depend on militarization: "the safety of this nation was not in its fleets, its armies, its forts, but in the spirit which prizes liberty as the heritage of all men, in all lands, everywhere"; and he warned his fellow citizens that they could not "destroy this spirit without planting the seeds of despotism at their own doors."[24]

Echoing George Washington's concerns about "entangling alliances," Bryan was most concerned about how the creation of a standing army would affect the politics and culture of the United States. Not only would a vastly expanded professional military require immense amounts of money, it would also change the culture of the peaceful land and its people: "The army is the personification of force, and militarism will inevitably change the ideals of the people and turn the thoughts of our young men from the arts of peace to the science of war."[25] For Bryan and his many followers, imperialism begat militarism, and it was militarism they feared most, however much they had benefited from their own military's violent removal of Natives from the Plains.

Imperialists like Teddy Roosevelt and William McKinley were unlikely to take these criticisms lightly, especially when they came from such an esteemed figure. Rather than one-offs, however, their sharp responses foreshadowed attacks on anti-militarists throughout the twentieth century, including those who protested the war in Vietnam. They focused on anti-militarists' patriotism. South Dakota senator James Kyle claimed in an interview to be "deeply grieved" by his colleague Richard Pettigrew's "unpatriotic stand" on the war.[26] But opponents also assailed Populist anti-militarists' gender identities. As Kristen Hoganson has explained, they worked to make Populists and others who sought peace seem more and more out of the mainstream—not only of culture but also of gender.[27] Populists, for example, were increasingly accused of being "old women." Even the act of joining a third party (seen as an act of unmanly disloyalty) gave Populists the moniker of "she-men," "eunuch," and "man milliners."[28] In the presidential campaign of 1900, McKinley's heroic Civil War record was held high, while questions raged about why Bryan had not stepped foot in Cuba. Later the Democrat Woodrow Wilson praised "the young men who prefer dying in the ditches of the Philippines to spending their lives behind the counters of a dry-goods store in our eastern cities. I think I should prefer that myself."[29] Of course, Populists feared the moral and economic consequences of militarism far more than they feared any kind of less "strenuous" future, and the campaign in the Philippines did nothing to dissuade them of this view.

*   *   *

Bryan was well-known in his day and is historically well remembered. Even so, it was not Bryan but the almost entirely forgotten (and Indian-artifact-collecting) Populist senator from South Dakota, Richard Pettigrew, who led the anti-imperialist forces in the Senate. In fact, even after Bryan had given up, Pettigrew fought against increasing the size of the military and expanding the military beyond North America. He resisted the annexation of Hawaii, the war in Cuba, and the annexation of the Philippines. In each of these cases, his views demonstrated how the economic and political concerns at the heart of the Populist movement—regulation of trusts and the power of corporations; protection of American farmers and workers; maintenance of white supremacy—informed, even determined, its anti-militarism. As Kenneth Hendrickson argues, Pettigrew and other Populist anti-imperialists were "convinced that the plutocrats of Wall Street sought overseas frontiers for exploitation, and that the vehicle through which they worked was the Republican Party."[30] They were countered with the full ire of that party; in 1900 it coughed up a half million dollars to defeat him. Infuriated, he wrote an ally: "These fawning sycophants without brains who act as McKinley's advisers are disgusting in the extreme. They want to carry out the idea that their President is a sort of emperor and that loyalty to him is the only way of expressing loyalty to flag and country."[31]

Pettigrew took on the annexation of Hawaii first. This was nothing more, he claimed, than a deceptive play by the "sugar trust" to decrease competition and increase profits. As a Populist, he was against all trusts, of course. But this one hit home, as small farmers on the Northern Plains were trying to harvest sugar beets. He also perceived the hand of the American capitalist elite at work in the Hawaiian revolution, which had quickened calls for annexation. The first constitution for the government allowed for wealthy property owners alone to serve as elected officials or to vote. To Pettigrew this indicated just one thing: "They established an oligarchy."[32]

Pettigrew also wondered why the military needed to expand naval bases into the Pacific, which Hawaiian annexation would allow. To him and many other Populists, an expanded military merely allowed large corporations to increase their monopolies and profits. After all, who would profit from a major expansion of American sea power? The steel trust. Hendrickson explains, "Pettigrew viewed domestic exploitation and expansion as one and the same conspiracy, thinking that imperialism was merely a sham to increase the need for military spending . . . and increasing government purchases of armor plate from the steel trust."[33] Pettigrew supported the effort of the US military to "free" the people of Cuba from Spanish dominion.[34] But he also saw the naval vessels sunk in that conflict and needing replacement as yet another way in which expansionists could press for a larger military presence around the world. Last, he accused the military of dishonesty, of firing the first shot and then denying it.

Pettigrew's partner in Populist anti-militarism and anti-imperialism at home in South Dakota was Governor Andrew Lee. Once the war was declared, Lee had to muster troops and pay for them. As it happened, he was already struggling to cover state expenditures, since two years before, corrupt administrators had raided the state treasury. Lax taxation of railroads and the 1890s recession had also left South Dakota coffers nearly bare.[35] Even so the federal government asked for the same number of troops—one thousand—from new states in the West as it did from long-established states in the East. Lee complied and mustered the First South Dakota Volunteer Infantry in May 1898. Its members arrived in Hawaii just in time to shake the hand of the new American governor, Sanford Dole, before heading to the Philippines. While the war with Spain was officially over when they arrived, the First South Dakota was nevertheless put to work fighting insurgents in the Filipino jungle.[36]

Governor Lee's troubles had just begun. Lee was shocked that the government would use the First South Dakota in an action that had not been authorized by Congress, or by him.[37] True to his Populist perspective, writes R. Alton Lee, he also claimed that "any further use of the troops would only benefit capitalists."[38] McKinley thought little of Populists, of course, and less of their concerns about imperialism. The South Dakota soldiers fought on for 126 days, facing illness, injury, and death in a land unimaginably different from their homes on the Northern Plains. When his troops finally landed in San Francisco, Lee discovered the federal government had no intention of paying for the rest of their journey home, which cost the state $27,000.00. The bill was eventually repaid, sort of. After suing the federal government, South Dakota received $15,573, less a 20 percent attorney's fee.[39] Far from the Populists' ideal of an empathic, "people first" state, the American government seemed as eager to steal their money as banks and corporations.

Local politics further complicated Lee's and Pettigrew's reactions to war. Melvin Grigsby lost the Populist nomination for governor and served a contentious term as attorney general, including what Lee called "scandalous conduct on board of a sleeping car on a trip from Pierre to Huron."[40] With the outset of war, however, Grigsby wondered how service in war might improve his political position nationally. Grigsby, well-known for having escaped from two southern prison camps during the Civil War, mustered a volunteer force of horseback riders from several Northern Plains states, calling them "Grigsby's Cowboys." But unlike Theodore Roosevelt's famous Rough Riders, Grigsby's cowboys never made it out of camp in Chickamauga, Georgia. Far worse than the frustration men felt at seeing no combat was the poor sanitation, water, and food. Several men died of disease, when they were ordered to stay in camp even after the war in Cuba had ended. Hundreds of members of the soldiers' families wrote to Lee and Pettigrew demanding that the soldiers be mustered out. They couldn't understand why Grigsby would make his men stay. Lee and Pettigrew suspected that Grigsby was considering switching to the Republican Party so that McKinley could promote him to brigadier general or endorse him for Pettigrew's Senate seat.[41] When the South Dakota "cowboys" finally headed home, Lee wrote, "doubtless [Grigsby would] have allowed the boys to remain there until they were all dead in order to draw his salary."[42]

Even though their political leaders were skeptical, ordinary young Dakota men were excited to join the war effort. Echoing advocates of the "strenuous life," conservative newspaper editors stressed the opportunity of war to make South Dakotans more "virile." The *Rapid City Journal*, for just one example, reminded readers that "many a man was made in the war of the rebellion."[43] As happy as they were to take on the manly pursuit of soldiering, South Dakotans nevertheless discovered that democracy and self-governance ended at the muster tent's door. Upon arrival in Sioux Falls to join the First South Dakota, many discovered that "Uncle Sam's" rations were not exactly home cooking and, worse, as Herman Krueger of Lake

Country put it, were "carefully doled out, no help yourself."[44] The men resented the absolute authority of elite officers—who often enough were dangerously incompetent. Krueger wrote again and again to his brother about such concerns. He began by telling of the officers who chose a spot well-known to flood to make camp. It flooded. He also told about the time when the officers built a privy so unstable that several men fell in. The final straw was when the officers transported an injured man by dray rather than ambulance and the jostling caused him to bleed to death.[45]

Krueger and Thomas Briggs of Mitchell, South Dakota, also observed that militarization literally demoralized some of their companions. Briggs was surprised to learn, for example, when he was on board a ship to Hawaii, they had no "Sunday services" and that some men played cards to pass the time instead. In Manila, Briggs commented that many men were openly attracted to "the Spanish ladies, some of them extremely handsome, bareheaded [and] dressed in the light gauzy fabric proper to the climate."[46] Krueger was angrier about the hardening of character he saw as a requirement of military service. This desensitization became much worse after months fighting insurgents in the jungle. Krueger was shocked by the attacks some infantrymen made on native Filipinos, including prisoners.[47] He concluded in one of his last letters home, "Grant said 'war is hell.' It is. May God save our home country from war."[48]

∗   ∗   ∗

As the "lamps" went out "all over Europe" in August of 1914 and the "Age of Catastrophe" began, voices of resistance to militarism in the United States gathered strength across the country.[49] By 1914, as historian Michael Kazin describes, a complex and "ever-widening circle" of socialists, pacifists, feminists, anti-imperialists, immigrants, Southern Populists, and Midwestern Progressives had come together from every region in the country to create the "largest, most diverse, and most sophisticated peace alliance to that point in US history."[50] Moreover, the strength of the coalition and the unwillingness of some of its members to end their resistance to the war once it had been waged provoked the strongest state repression of dissent in our history thus far, presaging the "surveillance state" so familiar in the post-9/11 world. The well-known struggle against radicalism that followed the First World War—and would also follow the Second World War—began with a crackdown on Americans who stood against war itself.

Among the most influential of the anti-war groups were those whom Kazin calls "Midwestern progressives"—Republicans Robert Lafollette and George Norris, and the Democrat William Jennings Bryan. By 1915 Bryan had failed twice more to become president, but became secretary of state under Woodrow Wilson. His principled anti-militarism, informed by his Christian worldview, hardly diminished as the war intensified. Bryan's reluctance to give aid to the Allies even after the sinking of the Lusitania isolated him in Wilson's cabinet and ultimately cost him his post. But it barely diminished his support in the upper Midwest: after tendering his resignation, Bryan received hundreds of letters of support from farmers, workers, and small-town people, equally fearful of the advent of a world war. One traveling salesman in Minnesota wrote, "For 20 years when asked what I thot of anything you have done, my reply has always been, 'The King can do no wrong, you are my King.'"[51]

In 1914 and 1915 Dakotans were not just conflicted about the war; they were conflicted about which side they preferred. Germans and ethnic Germans from Russia and Hungary together represented more than a third of the foreign-born population in the Dakotas; largely rural communities still boasted German-language churches, newspapers, and school curriculum. Not surprisingly some of these immigrants sided with Germany early on or hoped for America to stay neutral, still a legitimate geopolitical strategy at the time.[52] Others, however, had fled their countries because of their militaristic and imperialistic political cultures and supported the Allies, believing that the horrors of the war were inevitable in a society built on its glorification. Even the editors of the staunchly conservative and probusiness *Fargo Forum* expressed ambivalence about choosing a side in the first few months of 1914.[53] As late as February of 1917, after Germans had renewed unrestricted submarine warfare, the editors maintained a somewhat open mind toward local pacifists, contending that the term "un-American did not apply to them."[54]

But once the US had entered the war in April of 1917, Dakotans found attempts at "common sense and moderation" a difficult line to walk. Both states' small but influential socialist organizations echoed the anti-war rhetoric of their European counterparts who saw the war as pitting one group of capitalists and imperialists against another in pursuit of wealth, with the poor and working classes sacrificing their lives. In Bowman, North Dakota,

Kate Richards O'Hare said that men who volunteered for the military were seeking to become "fertilizer" and their mothers "were no better than brood sows."[55] Local pacifists also doubled down on meetings and public lectures—although they increasingly found that both private and public facilities were closed to them.[56]

The Nonpartisan League (NPL), the fastest growing radical agrarian organization on the Northern Plains in the 1910s, made what historian Michael Lansing has called a "nuanced" argument about the war—though, unsurprisingly, few of their conservative opponents thought it so.[57] Like Populists Pettigrew and Lee a generation earlier, the leaders of the NPL believed that war was the tool of corporations, banks, and the elite to increase their wealth and power. Governor Lynn Frazier said simply that "North Dakota is not in favor of war"—indicating that war itself, as opposed to this particular war, troubled his constituents.[58] NPL founder A. C. Townley told a crowd that in wartime the US was "working, not to beat the enemy, but to make more multi-millionaires." He added that "in the heat and haste and confusion of war, they multiply their millions many times at your expense." The LaMoure, North Dakota, editor described American soldiers as being "farmed by the capitalist class."[59] In Iowa a speaker borrowed from a speech given by Georgia Populist Tom Watson, "On the pretext of sending armies to Europe, to crush militarism there, we first enthrone it here."[60]

But the radicals of the North Plains tried time and again to demonstrate that, even if they had been against the war—all war—they would not be disloyal to the American cause. Townley described this approach in 1917: "This nation of farmers are so patriotic that even though the government today may be in the hands and the absolute control of the steel trust, and the sugar trust, and the machine trust . . . we are going to do our best by producing all we can."[61] In fact Dakota farmers bought more than their share of war bonds and sent more than their share of soldiers to the front. Unlike some white men in the American South, the vast majority of Dakotans did not evade or refuse the draft.[62]

But few of the League's opponents desired to understand the subtleties of the NPL's position on the war. Instead big-business opponents of the League strategically attacked it for disloyalty to impede their economic reforms. Even George Creel, the leader of Wilson's Committee on Public Information, and no fan of the NPL, noted that opponents seemed to be doing his work for him, by attacking leaders for disloyalty.[63] Radical leaders were singled out throughout the region. Former South Dakota Populist senator and anti-imperialist Pettigrew was arrested after telling a reporter "there is no excuse for this war. We should back right out of it. We never should have gone into a war [while] the Schwabs make forty million dollars per year."[64] A. C. Townley and his manager were arrested for suggesting that wealth as well as men should be conscripted. Throughout the region NPL meetings were shut down by mobs, their leaders run out of town, in some cases tarred and feathered by mobs that knew they would face no retribution. In Bonesteel, South Dakota, two NPL organizers were captured and given to the sheriff, who in turn handed them over to a mob. In a rural area southwest of Mitchell, South Dakota, NPL organizer Emil Sudan was stripped naked, tarred and feathered, and dragged behind a wagon for miles.[65]

More complex were the attacks on Germans and German Americans on the Northern Plains, many of whom had recently joined the NPL due to its anti-war position. Beginning in 1917, and with the implicit permission of the federal government's Committee on Public Information (CPI), "patriotic" Americans across the United States sought out Germans and other immigrants from nations of the Central Powers and violently enforced their loyalty. States with large populations of Germans, like North and South Dakota, passed laws against teaching or speaking German, or possessing German-language books. As we have seen, small colonies of religious sects, such as the Hutterites in South Dakota, faced particularly intense discrimination.[66]

But the cruelty of mobs knew no religious test. German Lutherans, German Catholics, and even some Scandinavians dubbed "German-Swedish" faced attack. In Wentworth, South Dakota, local officials outlawed an NPL meeting because so many Germans were planning to attend. The local newspaper reported that the participants used "the German tongue exclusively in their homes, in their religious services, and insist[ed] on being educated in German and speak[ing] a broken English."[67] The council of defense in South Dakota, although significantly less active and violent than their counterparts in neighboring Nebraska and Minnesota, nonetheless simultaneously subpoenaed thirty-five people to investigate their loyalty. A German farmer and his wife fainted when the sheriff arrested them.[68]

Through the efforts of "Wild Bill" Langer, North Dakota prevented some of the worst of these kinds of attacks. As historian Charles Barber has shown, Langer, then attorney general, could speak German himself and regularly sent and received letters in German. He also took steps whenever possible to protect Germans from discrimination. When the county super-intendent closed a few schools in Cass County because they taught summer catechism in German, Langer immediately intervened, explaining that "the Constitution of the United States provides that religious liberty cannot be interfered with and that children who cannot speak English have a right to know God even though they are taught in German."[69] When he learned that Reverend Denninghoff, a registered "alien enemy of the government," was teaching and administering a school under the auspices of the German Evangelical Church, he wrote him that "it would be advisable for you to discontinue this school immediately." But he added, "This is not an order or anything of that sort, but is just a suggestion and I will be glad to have you come down to Bismarck at any time and talk this over with you."[70]

Recent historians have contended that the wartime attacks on the NPL, its members, and the German community only served to help it recruit more members.[71] In the short run, that may well have been true. And yet, when state and local governments violently attacked League organizers and threw them out of town if not into jail, they adopted a strategy that would become all too familiar and all too effective in the postwar period. Ameri-cans concluded that radicalism of any kind, and particularly the kind that looked to reform capitalism while at the same time bringing an end to war, was the antithesis of patriotic Americanism.

*   *   *

As they had in the Spanish-American War, Dakota men and women who served in the First World War saw firsthand both the undemocratic nature of military life and the inevitable horrors of war. At first glance, North Dakota farm boy David Nelson seemed an unlikely anti-militarist. From a relatively affluent family whose members almost certainly did not belong to the NPL, Nelson went to Luther College in Decorah, Iowa, and then to Oxford University as a Rhodes Scholar. He arrived in the fateful fall of 1914 and almost immediately chose to work for Herbert Hoover's Commission for the Relief of Belgium. For months, he wrote his mother, a German American, that reports of German aggression and atrocities were simply propaganda. But after a visit to occupied regions of northern France, his views changed radically and he began to see the true danger of a militaristic culture. He wrote, "militarism was in command . . . and militarism had hypnotized the people." To Nelson, no less than the Hofer boys who had refused even to put on a military uniform, war imperiled the very nature of humankind. "[War is] humanity gone mad. . . . How then believe in human kind? How reconcile [war] with any living creed or faith? These little crosses, this line 'mort pour la patrie' . . . this weeping mother, wife, or child—no do not tell me . . . that all this sacrifice signifies nothing, that I could stand indifferent by."[72]

The artist Harvey Dunn saw what Nelson saw but he used a different medium to describe it. Long before he painted sentimental, yet inspiring, images of "pioneers" on the Northern Plains—evocative of Laura Ingalls Wilder's books—Dunn served as a combat artist; in that context his images were not heroic or romantic in the slightest. In fact, they could not "have been further from the kind of art" his employer—the War Department— had hoped he would create.[73] Dunn had grown up on a South Dakota farm in the same county made famous by Laura Ingalls Wilder, but he sought every opportunity to follow his passion for art, eventually paying his own way through the Art Institute of Chicago and then volunteering for the American Expeditionary Force. His orders were to act much like a journalist, drawing what he saw, showing "war as it really is" but getting nowhere near actual combat.[74] Somehow Dunn moved up to the front lines anyway and, while initially thrilled by the courage of the soldiers and the righteousness of the Allied cause, he soon became overwhelmed by the carnage and needless suffering on both sides. His charcoal sketches reveal a universal anti-militarism, an opposition to war itself—but also a refusal, in Nelson's words, "to stand indifferent by."

Many of Dunn's anti-war paintings and drawings show the cost of war on individual men, what he called "the shock and loss and bitterness and blood" of it.[75] *The Sentry* (1918), for example, shows a gaunt, haunted young man who surrounds himself with weapons, as if for luck. But Dunn's most important and expressive anti-militarist painting shows the cost of war to a large group of men, to the community of humanity, without regard for nation or uniform. *Prisoners and Wounded* (1918) shows both injured Allied soldiers and captured German men. But the two opposing "sides" are rendered indistinguishable in the one-dimensional rain-soaked background and the monochromatic foreground of khaki uniforms, wet blankets, and

FIGURE 4. Harvey Dunn, *Prisoners and Wounded*, October 1918. Watercolor, charcoal, and pastel on paper. Dunn was a sketch artist for the army but often got closer to combat than he was commanded, so that he could show the reality of the war. Courtesy National Archives.

blurred faces with corpse-like gaping mouths. The men are also fully anonymous, random arms and torsos blending into one another until the line of men is more like a blob. In this way the painting takes on an even darker tone than the better-known John Singer Sargent masterpiece *Gassed* (1919), in which each living man in the line remains a distinct human being. As David Lubin suggests, Dunn's work resembles more closely John Stuart Curry's 1938 painting *Parade to War, An Allegory* in which the legs, arms, feet of soldiers headed to war blur all together but their faces—actually, skulls—are distinct. Like Dunn, Curry was from a small town on the Great Plains—the heart of Populist resistance to war.[76] As it happened, he was Dunn's student too.

*   *   *

When the war ended most Dakotans, like many others all over the world, hoped it would be "the war to end all wars." Only such an epochal outcome would justify the unspeakable suffering and loss. With that aim in mind, they created monuments in dozens of small towns, most of which did not glorify the war as much as encapsulate its horrors. The *War Mothers Memorial* (1924) in Bismarck-Mandan, North Dakota, like the celebrated Kathe Kollwitz sculpture *The Grieving Parents* (1932), primarily associates the war with loss; the cause is secondary; the idea of glory in war missing entirely. The town chose granite because boulders that had "withstood the storms and stress of the ages . . . best typif[ied] a mother's love."[77] Its inscription reads, "In Memory of Our Sons and Daughters who lost their lives in the world war so that liberty might live." A similar monument in the tiny town of Steele, North Dakota, reads simply "Our Boys."[78]

But Dakotans also created a living appeal to peace, one which for a time became known around the world: the International Peace Garden. Eastern activists in the peace movement initially imagined planting a garden on the American-Canadian border to demonstrate how a world with peaceful boundaries—or no boundaries—might flourish. North Dakotans quickly suggested a location near the Turtle Mountains, thirty miles from the geographic center of North America. At that spot, they had already formed an "international peace picnic organization" and families from both countries were accustomed to meeting, eating, and playing sports together. As members of the memorial committee wrote, the four thousand miles of border between the US and Canada stretches "free from soldier, fort, and cannon" unlike almost any other in the world.[79] More concretely, once the garden was in place, with fifteen hundred acres on each side, the border itself would be "wiped out." The garden would become a place without a country "inculcating" peace around the world. Fifty thousand people gathered for the opening ceremony to which both President Herbert Hoover and Canadian prime minister William Lyon sent congratulations.

In the first decade of the garden's formal existence, people around the world embraced the idea of a borderless world, even as threats to their own borders grew. In 1938 Glasgow, Scotland, hosted the Empire Exposition where an estimated eight million people viewed a replica of the International Peace Gardens. At a second opening ceremony in 1935 a member of the Canadian parliament commented, "If they had a string of peace gardens in Europe, do you think we should have a Mussolini moving into Ethiopia?"[80] However overly optimistic, even naïve, such statements were, they reinforced the commitment to peace and, more enduringly, to anti-militarism among people on the Northern Plains—in both the US and Canada. None could see at that moment that far from being triumphant, the movement against war was in its last stages of power and influence. North Dakota would remain "the Peace Garden State," even after nuclear weapons poisoned the soil beneath it.

*   *   *

There is no way to know how many Dakotans saw the anti-pacifist film *Sergeant York* in the weeks before Pearl Harbor, nor how many of the young men in the audience went directly from the cinema to the recruiting station, as filmmakers claimed. But we can know without a shred of doubt that the people of the Dakotas, along with other rural people in the Midwest, were its intended audience. Unlike the anti-war and anti-imperialist organizations in the 1890s and 1910s that brought together Americans from many different regions, the Populist anti-militarist movements of the 1930s centered in the broad middle of the country, perhaps even the Dakotas. Historians in our time blame the length of the war and its terrible cost in lives—including Jewish and Soviet lives—on America's delayed entry, even calling anti-interventionists "Hitler's American friends," and taking little time to understand their views more completely.[81] Populist anti-militarists did not come to their views quickly; nor were they attributable to their alleged ignorance of foreign affairs or the antisemitic beliefs they shared with many other Americans. While misguided in the context of Hitler's imperial and genocidal ambitions, they carried forward a tradition steeped in fifty years of resistance to militarization, fear of concentrated power, and experience in combat.[82] These were amplified by their simultaneous struggle against the increased power of the central government in the Great Depression.[83] John Simpson of the Farmers Union had worried that agricultural programs might usher in an "army of workers" from the government to oversee their businesses. He surely knew that was but a glimpse of the kind of army workers might be forced to join if the US went to war once again.

In the 1930s leaders of the isolationist movement made familiar attacks on the idea of going to war—and many of the leaders were familiar too:

Populist, Progressive, and NPL figures from the rural Midwest. In North Dakota Governor Langer was joined by the entire North Dakota delegation to Congress—William Lemke, Lynn Frazier, Usher Burdick, and Gerald Nye—to argue that war was nothing but murder, a means to line the pockets of eastern bankers and capitalist elites while young men went to their graves. They believed that the nation's experience in World War I proved their point. With broad support in the region, in 1934 Senator Nye led a "special committee to investigate the munitions industry." For two years the "Nye Commission" collected evidence that munitions manufacturers, Wall Street investors, and other "profiteers" had manipulated Wilson into declaring war in 1917. While they never found the conspiracy they sought, their well-publicized efforts were persuasive nonetheless. According to a 1937 Gallup Poll, 70 percent of Americans had revised their initial feelings of pride at their victory and believed instead that the US's entry into World War I had been a dreadful error.[84] The well-known Kansas publisher William Allen White warned "the next war will see the same hurrah and the same bowwow of the big dogs to get the little dogs to go out and follow the blood scent and get their entrails tangled in the barbed wire."[85] Reflecting these broadly held views, and revealing the degree to which many believed that simply not taking a side remained a viable option, Congress passed—and revised—neutrality laws in 1935, 1936, and 1937. As Elwyn Robinson wrote, by 1939 "what the country editors of North Dakota had written in their weeklies from 1914 to 1917 was the law of the land."[86]

North Dakotans may have led the way, but South Dakota's entire congressional delegation also adamantly resisted the idea of going to war or creating international alliances. Furthermore, they made sure the president and other interventionists understood that they were expressing their constituents' views. Senator Francis Case, for example, read into the official record of the Senate a resolution by the American Legion of South Dakota—a newly minted veterans organization—at its annual meeting in Pierre: "Resolved, that it is the sense of this assembled conference of the American Legion, Department of South Dakota, that as to the European situation, the foreign policy of these United States be: To mind its own business, become involved in no entangling alliances, and let Europe settle its own problems without our interference or intervention."[87] Case's counterpart, Senator William Bulow, used frontier imagery to argue against the Lend-Lease Act. He suggested that many South Dakotans would like to hang Hitler like a horse thief from a "sour apple tree." But "before [we] would get our hands on Hitler to hang him, we would sacrifice several million of our own good American boys, who are worth more to us than all of Europe."[88] In the week after Roosevelt's "Four Freedoms" address in early 1941, South Dakota congressman Chad Gurney read anti-war editorials from the *Yankton Press* into the official record of the House. The editor of the *Press* found Roosevelt's words stirring, but he also wondered why Roosevelt thought it was the duty of the United States to bring democratic ideals to the world—"something we failed miserably to do some twenty years ago."[89]

Populist anti-militarists from the region also fell back on antisemitism to make their points against the war. In sadly familiar terms, Nye and others warned against the international banking conspiracy, the influence of Jews on world affairs, and the impact of Jewish producers in Hollywood.[90] He joined many others in Congress to vote against allowing Jewish refugees from Europe to settle in the US. Together with William Lemke and Karl Mundt of South Dakota, Nye joined Minnesota's aviator-hero Charles Lindbergh's America First Committee and spoke on its behalf, including to packed houses at Madison Square Garden, Chicago's Soldiers Field, and the Rose Bowl. Lindbergh, of course, denied that he was antisemitic, while openly discussing the threat to peace that Jews represented and warning white Christians throughout the world to band together.[91] Privately he was even less oblique, writing several passages openly hostile toward Jews, including, "We feel that . . . it is essential to avoid anything approaching a pogrom; and that . . . it is just as essential to combat the pressure the Jews are bringing on this country to enter the war. This Jewish influence is subtle, dangerous, and very difficult to expose. . . . they invariably cause trouble."[92] After a particularly virulent speech in Des Moines that drew national outrage, Nye doubled down on his commitment to the cause. Coming to "Lucky Lindy's" defense, Nye blamed the interventionists for inserting a discussion of religion into the debate about war; he repeated that he himself was not antisemitic.[93] He was far from alone: 90 percent of the thousands of letters to Lindbergh after the Des Moines speech supported and even extended his antisemitic views. The Petersons from Minneapolis explained, for example, "[Jews] did wrong in Germany and Germany got rid of them because of it."[94]

Finally, Populist anti-militarists on the Northern Plains connected their experiences in the First World War with their struggles in the Great Depression, fearing that a new war could be yet another mechanism for the expansion of federal power. Populists were not anti-statists—far from it.

Throughout the first fifty years of statehood, radical farmers had contended that the state could be put to beneficial, democratic, and anti-plutocratic use. But it had to be done under structures of local leadership and control. The New Deal was only acceptable, if at all, because many programs, the Agricultural Adjustment Administration (AAA) in particular, were administered through county boards. But farm supporters and their conservative opponents alike resented the way New Deal programs empowered a distant federal bureaucracy. As the 1930s wore on, even some farmers who benefited from Roosevelt's programs withdrew their support for the New Deal. They worried too about the increased power of a president who ran and won an unprecedented third term, asking if Roosevelt had not brought European-style totalitarianism to America's shores.[95]

As the crisis in Europe grew, Dakotans suspected that Roosevelt and his planners were increasingly blurring the lines between domestic planning and military preparedness. They were not wrong. Historian Ronald Schaffer has shown that many New Deal programs flowed seamlessly from the governmental structures that had been designed for the "wartime emergency" of 1917. The requirements of the National Recovery Administration, for example, borrowed heavily from the price supports and regulatory structures of the War Industries Board; FDR even staffed it with WIB veterans. The Civilian Conservation Corps, what FDR called "Our Forest Army," was set up so much like an actual army—with its tents, rations, platoons, and uniforms—that many Americans complained that they actually were wartime preparedness facilities. In some cases they actually were.[96] Even the Agricultural Adjustment Act was merely the inverse in its purpose—to decrease production—to the wartime commodities programs' purpose—to increase production.[97] Montana senator Burton Wheeler saw a direct connection between the coercive statism of the First World War, the New Deal, and a new military imperative. In a direct reference to the AAA's requirement in spring of 1933 that farmers "plow under" their crops, he declared that Roosevelt's "triple-A foreign policy" would "plow under every fourth American boy."[98]

Populist anti-militarists on the Northern Plains were also concerned that overlaps between peacetime and wartime bureaucratic structures would create a permanent increase in executive power. When FDR ordered Atlantic patrols to enter war zones and to "shoot on sight," Charles Lindbergh accused him of conducting "government by subterfuge."[99] Nye saw the power of the wartime state at work in places where men and women would never expect: the movie theater. In short, Populist anti-militarists perceived a possible synergy between the increased authority of the federal government and growth of the military state to influence all parts of American life. For many reasons, Populist anti-militarists on the Northern Plains were wrong about delaying intervention in the war. Some of their reasons for doing so likewise were unjustifiable and the consequences are an inexorable part of our world today. But about their fear that such a war would usher in a permanent national security state and empower an imperial presidency, they were correct.

What they couldn't have imagined was that, by the time it did, few Americans would see anything wrong with it.

*　*　*

Pearl Harbor came as a shock to all Americans, none more than the leaders of Populist anti-militarism who, like Lemke, had believed that "there is no nation or combination of nations that are a threat to the United States."[100] Nye and Lindbergh continued to believe that Roosevelt had known about Pearl Harbor in advance or perhaps had even played a role in planning it. They had little company. The vast majority of ordinary Dakotans quickly silenced their remaining doubts, accepted the legitimacy of the war and the wartime government, and rallied to the American and Allied cause. They followed the example of Senator Karl Mundt and shredded—either literally or figuratively—any evidence that they had been involved in anti-militarist activities. Then, also like Mundt, they would do everything they could to support the Allied war effort. In the end families on the Northern Plains would sacrifice men and money in larger amounts proportionately than Americans in most other regions.

The entry of American forces into the war silenced most—though not all—talk of the United States as a "fortress" nation that should stay separate from the world. In 1963, Robert Wilkins wrote that the occasional "isolationist" argument from Langer, Case, or Burdick—regarding the Marshall Plan, the United Nations, or the war in Korea—had sounded like echoes from "a living fossil." In some corners these old Populist anti-militarists "drew snickers rather than applause."[101] Likewise, in Michael Kazin's words, the term "isolationism" itself "became a synonym for anyone blind to the dangers of well-armed evils from abroad."[102] To Brooke Blower, it became "a cautionary tale for the post–Pearl Harbor future, not an accurate depiction of the past."[103] A new generation of leaders in the Dakotas, men like Republicans Mundt of South Dakota and Milton Young of North Dakota, learned quickly that "loyal" Americans embraced the mission of an interventionist military and, in the context of the Cold War battle against communism, rejected radicalism of all kinds. Rather than fearing a permanent standing army, Dakotans soon dedicated themselves to creating a place for it in their communities. When they did, they broke the bond between Populist agrarianism and Populist anti-militarism. Except for a highly controversial restoration during the Vietnam War and a far more muted one during the Farm Crisis, the proud Populist tradition would go forward unhinged from what had been its most distinctive element.

CHAPTER 3

"100% AGAINST COMMUNISTS"

IN 1948 WHEN THE federal government dispatched a "Freedom Train" full of historic memorabilia on a nationwide tour to "sell America to Americans," they badly misunderstood the people of the Northern Plains. So many people stood in line in North and South Dakota to see the Declaration of Independence and the Gettysburg Address that attendance records were broken again and again. Even San Francisco couldn't match the number of people who waited in terrible heat and terrifying thunderstorms in Rapid City, Pierre, Jamestown, Bismarck, Minot, Fargo, Grand Forks, and Sioux Falls. Informal estimates at the time suggested that a higher percentage of residents of North Dakota had seen the train than had residents of any other state.[1]

Even if Dakotans did not have to be sold *on* America, they may have felt the need to sell themselves *to* America. Through the 1930s, they had been nearly unanimous in their resistance to a second war in Europe; some had waited until December 7, 1941, to change their minds. And their resistance to American involvement in World War II was not the first but the third chapter in a multigenerational effort to stop military expansionism, imperialism, and war itself. To make matters worse in the age of the second "Red Scare," they counted among themselves socialists, communists, and other agrarian radicals from the prewar era. Perhaps this very history and the suspicion of the region it had created explained why the train made so many stops there. Along with their stamina, Dakotans visiting the Freedom Train displayed their respect for the military and their fear of a new enemy, the Soviet Union. In Rapid City, residents allowed veterans from the nearby hospital to go to the head of the line even though at least five people had already fainted from the heat. In Sioux Falls, the week of the train's visit was officially declared "Rededication Week." The climax was Medal of Honor air force pilot, Joe Foss, leading a squadron of B-29 bombers to "defend" the city from a "Soviet attack."[2]

Throughout the late 1940s and 1950s Dakotans found many ways to "rededicate" their communities and redefine themselves. Although a handful held their ground, the vast majority of Dakotans turned against Populist anti-militarism and began to support most aspects of an interventionist foreign policy. Meanwhile they passed restrictions on union activities, reorganized political groups to marginalize agrarian radicals, used anti-communist smears to beat political opponents, instituted loyalty oaths, and purged political radicals from at least one university and two farm organizations. One of the region's senators, Karl Mundt, even became Joseph McCarthy's right-hand man. Blending their historic suspicion of a distant federal bureaucracy with fears of totalitarianism, leaders on both the right and the left made it clear that they were, in newly elected Senator "Wild Bill" Langer's words, "100% against Communists in every way, shape, form, and manner."[3] Historian David Mills argues that Dakotans did not go to "absurd" lengths to ferret out communists. Perhaps not, but they did respond to the imperatives of the era with a marked turn toward political conservatism and antiradicalism, finding opportunities in both the voting booth and everyday life to express their commitment to postwar American ideals.

Of course not all Dakotans changed their Populist-inspired views on the economy or the military all at once; a few never changed them at all. In North Dakota in particular, the socialist-inspired heritage of the Nonpartisan League (NPL) and its enduring state-owned institutions could not be erased so easily. Likewise, every leader did not suddenly become an uncompromising hawk. Politicians from both states and both sides of the aisle expressed concerns about the war in Korea and the long-term impact of certain forms of universal conscription, concerns that would reappear more forcefully during Vietnam.[4] But gradually, the culture of the Cold War would lay deep roots on the Northern Plains as it empowered local conservative political groups and contributed to the deradicalization of others, eventually revising even how the radical heritage of the region was remembered.[5] Moreover the culture of the Cold War began to blur the distinctions between and among supporting the military, fighting communism, and embracing conservative cultural and religious ideals, including new forms of evangelical Protestantism. As war, or what Mary Dudziak calls "war but not war," became a permanent part of American life, this elision of conservative politics and conservative cultural views with patriotism started to become permanent too.[6] It was a first step in the creation of a nuclear country.

*   *   *

When the US declared war against Japan and Germany in 1941, South Dakota congressman Karl Mundt knew exactly what he had to do: quickly disassociate himself from what critics called "isolationism" and groups such as America First. So he "emptied his office of every newspaper clipping, speech, or memorandum that recorded his opposition to the conflict."[7] Even though he was over forty years old and a member of Congress, he volunteered to serve in the military. While he was counseled to remain stateside, no member of Congress would support the war more ardently. Likewise, when the war ended and the nation's foe turned from Nazis and Japanese to Soviets, and voters elevated Mundt to the upper chamber, he earned a national reputation as a relentless anti-communist, unearthing its evils both at home and abroad.

Mundt was hardly alone in his rapid conversion. Fellow South Dakota congressman Francis Case had voted consistently against measures that brought the United States closer to war and even sponsored a bill that would have required a national referendum before any declaration of war.[8] But after Pearl Harbor, he too offered to enlist. Across the Northern Plains, men and women who had resisted the entry of the United States into a second world war quickly came to believe that the defense of their nation and its ideals was not only necessary but honorable—even heroic. During the war, South Dakotans bought $328 million worth of war bonds and donated more than $2 million to the Red Cross; in 1944, North Dakotans put a higher percentage of their income into Series E savings bonds than the people of any other state. Their sacrifice was personal as well as financial. Families said farewell to 110,000 recruits of whom nearly 4,000 never returned.[9] They died in battles their families had hoped the world would never witness again.

By 1944 nearly all Dakotans came to see that their commitment to Populist anti-militarism in the late 1930s had been a mistake. But other Americans had long memories. Whenever it served their interests, politicians reminded rural people—Dakotans and others—that they had been part of "America's greatest mistake."[10] National leaders sometimes used the memory of Dakotans' support for organizations like the America First Committee as a bludgeon to gain support for other projects. As late as 1950, President Harry Truman visited the region to check on flood damage and reminded local men and women that a "rebirth of isolationism could bring on war." He added with a touch of sarcasm that the "economic isolationists" of 1950 were no different from the "yes-but-boys" of 1936.[11] So endless were the accusations that "isolationism" nearly cost the world its freedom, according to Brooke Blower, that hawkish Cold Warriors could easily grasp the chance to "lead the country [unimpeded] . . . into . . . world leadership."[12]

As if to answer these critics, voters in North Dakota made their rejection of prewar Populist anti-militarism crystal clear when Senator Gerald Nye— the outspoken and unapologetic anti-interventionist with a national profile—came up for reelection in 1944. The state Republican Party still housed a probusiness and a Nonpartisan League faction, so the conservative wing contemptuously nominated Nye, whom they judged to have been "unAmerican and a joy to Hitler." They thought Nye would easily beat the NPL-endorsed candidate, Usher Burdick, in the Republican primary. But they also forced Nye to accept a platform that included support for a postwar international organization. It did not work out entirely as planned. While he won his primary, on Election Day Nye lost to Democrat governor John Moses by a landslide.[13] Moses beat Nye even though no other Democrat won statewide office that year and even though he had been hospitalized during much of the campaign. Moses died less than six weeks after taking the oath of office.[14] Even then, Nye did not retain his seat and serve a third term. The new Republican governor, Fred Aandahl, appointed Milton Young to take Moses' spot instead. Young was, David Danbom writes, "a thoroughly conventional and conservative Midwestern Republican."[15] Hardly an anti-militarist, he would go on to champion the acquisition of two air force bases and three hundred ICBMs for the state.

Like Young, Dakotans did not simply aim to show the world that they had rejected "isolationism," they worked to place themselves at the center of a militarized, international future. At the behest of a local businessman, in early March 1945, South Dakota congressman Francis Case wrote President Roosevelt with a suggestion: wouldn't the Black Hills be a wonderful site for the newly created United Nations?[16] "'In the Black Hills there are no military objectives, and the gentlemen who are striving for the peace of the world can live at peace while the atomic bombs are falling.'"[17] Within twenty years, the plains themselves would contain "atomic bombs," but for now the congress members promoting the proposal used the state's remote geography to their advantage. The editors at *Time*—and a number of members of the selection committee—found the idea preposterous, and assumed their national audience would, too, saying: "the bleak Black Hills of South Dakota, where men are men and steaks are three inches thick."[18] A bit of elite sarcasm did not dissuade the people of the Northern Plains, however. In 1947, Master Sergeant James Lessman, an army recruiter in South Dakota, sent an invitation to President Truman to vacation in the Black Hills. He thought Mount Rushmore would be a particularly wonderful place for Truman to administer the oath of enlistment to new recruits, a "ceremony heard around the world."[19]

In those first years after the war, many Dakotans—influenced by their newfound, perhaps frantic embrace of the US's role in the world—sounded more like hawks than doves when they discussed issues of foreign aid, rearmament, and anti-communism. One 1948 poll, for example, revealed that a large majority of North Dakotans supported the Marshall Plan for the rehabilitation of Europe.[20] Likewise, when the Soviets announced the successful detonation of an atom bomb in 1949, the editors at both the *Bismarck Tribune* and the *Fargo Forum* reminded their readers that "missile work deserves priority."[21] Moreover, they reiterated the "lessons of Munich" to support a massive rearmament campaign, arguing that "appeasement will not stop a tyrant" and that "the men in the Kremlin" had learned their lessons "from Hitler."[22] Local editors and businesspeople boasted that the Midwest might play a big part in the job of rearming, a task that would presumably bring jobs.[23]

Support for an interventionist approach to foreign affairs was new for men and women in the Dakotas, but anti-communism and antiradicalism were not, at least not for some. Since 1890 Alliance members, Populists, progressive Republicans, "Leaguers," socialists, and communists had faced fierce opposition from conservatives and business interests. By the late 1930s Dakotans of many political persuasions, unhappy with the agricultural policies, the distant bureaucracy, and the emerging cultural authority of the New Deal, began to merge the rhetoric of anti-statism and anti–New Dealism with antiradicalism, a trend amplified in the new Cold War context. In 1938, for example, when Dakotans contributed to an essay contest sponsored by the *Dakota Farmer* on what Americanism meant to them, five of the six winners specifically contrasted American "freedom" and "liberty" with an authoritarian state. One submission by J. H. Boese, for example, defined Americanism as "something that grants every individual and every family the right to put himself on his own feet, independent and self-directing."[24] Mrs. L. A. Philbrook agreed: "Americanism is every honest man striving to solve his own problems . . . keeping us from Communism, Nazism and fascism and all other isms. Except Americanism."[25] Edgar Syverud wrote, "Americanism admits of no superior, overlord, king, or dictator."[26] The "real Revolution" in the world, the *Bismarck Tribune* agreed, occurred when governments allowed for individual freedom from the government itself.[27]

Political leaders who fought to maintain Populist-style organizations and "people first" policies during the Cold War—sometimes called the "old Progressives" although the monikers "old Populists" or "old Leaguers" suit them better in the Dakotas—developed what Charles Barber has called an agrarian ideology of "anti-communism on the left."[28] Like many of their constituents, they linked communism not to its attempts to reduce the power of an economic elite—something they continued to endorse in their own work—but to the dangers of a state with too much concentrated power. After the Second World War, Senator "Wild Bill" Langer maintained that "the doctrine of Socialism had within itself the seeds of dictatorship as much as did the doctrine of Capitalism."[29] Speaking at the Mandan Elks Club in 1950, Langer made the connection explicit. Communists, he said, were "highly educated. They obtained their education in the United States and wormed their way into the highest councils of government. Then trusted by the president and holding the most important government positions, they have been found working toward the destruction of our nation." Langer proposed the franchise and the people as the antidote to the communism of an educated elite.[30] Mrs. Anna Corbin from Livonia, North Dakota, seemed to agree with Langer when she wrote the *Bismarck Tribune*: "It seems to me that our government is only by a Few, in place of by and for the people."[31]

Some "old Progressives" were also old anti-militarists and, as such, they did not forget that the central government's power to send men to war was one of its most anti-democratic. Both Langer and Representative Usher Burdick, for example, were skeptical about the war in Korea. So were more conservative South Dakota senators Francis Case, Karl Mundt, and Representative Harold Louvre, who demanded the immediate withdrawal of American troops. They saw the military as an expression of an overheated, overempowered government. Ordinary Dakotans, many of whom were veterans, worried that the military was inefficient and top-heavy while the individual soldier was underpaid.[32] They also did not forget that corporations benefited the most from war, and working-class people paid the price. In 1951, the North Dakota state senate passed a resolution to support the conscription of wealth as well as manpower "when this nation's security is imperiled." There was little debate about whether the rich should pay more for war; instead, state senators debated whether it was appropriate actually to call the military a "dictatorship." Those who endorsed the term reminded naysayers that "the army . . . can tell you when you can get up, what you can eat, and when, what you can and can't do . . . and that a man hauled before a court martial is guilty until he is proved innocent."[33]

These long-simmering fears, expressed by Dakotans on both sides of the aisle, concerning communism and any expression of an overly powerful, anti-democratic state led to outbreaks of what John Miller has called "McCarthyism before McCarthy" in the region.[34] In the prewar years farm organizations like the NPL, the Farmers Holiday Association (FHA), and the United Farmers League (UFL) were inspired by socialist principles of cooperative marketing and state ownership of agricultural facilities and drew their best-known organizers from socialist or communist groups.[35] During World War I and again amid the Dust Bowl, law enforcement officials and vigilante-style gangs of local people sometimes took violent action to oust known or suspected communists from their communities. In northeastern South Dakota, for example, in early 1934, seventeen activists were arrested for "rioting" at a foreclosure sale. In July 1934 a mob beat five UFL members in Britton. According to historian William Pratt, the "incident was followed by a Legionnaire attack on the [UFL] 'Farm School on Wheels' in the same county. Several individuals were beaten . . . the facility was driven from its site."[36]

In South Dakota, the election of 1938 introduced the state to red-baiting, a strategy employed by conservatives to beat left-leaning opponents. To beat FHA leader Emil Loriks, for example, Karl Mundt adopted a clever, if cynical, approach. He endorsed the Loriks' own brainchild, "the cost of production" alternative to domestic allotment. At the same time, he—or his spokespeople—accused Loriks of being a communist because he had promised to work with the CIO and had been praised for doing so in the Communist Party's newspaper, the *Daily Worker*. The Sioux Falls *Argus Leader* told voters that "we are not saying that Loriks and Fosheim [the Democratic candidate for governor and president of the Farmers Union] in fact are Communists. . . . Candidates who endorse politics that are communistic in nature should not be surprised when they, in turn, receive the blessings of the Communists."[37] But Mundt supporter Arthur Bennett of Milbank, South Dakota, felt no compulsion to be nuanced in his conclusion about the pair of candidates. He distributed a pamphlet that averred, "South Dakotans Wake Up—Tomorrow may be too late! Communism is knocking at our very doors . . . disguised as 'progress.' . . . [It will] deprive us of everything we hold dear."[38] Similar strategies were employed to defeat Democrat Fred Hildebrand.[39] This election returned power in Pierre to South Dakota conservative Republicans where it would stay—with one brief but crucial exception—through the first decades of the twenty-first century.

As part of this rightward turn, South Dakotans also passed the nation's first "Right to Work" law in 1946, effectively ending the ability of unions in the state to require membership for all workers in a place of employment and severely restricting the ability of union workers to picket or boycott a place of employment. In the 1930s and 1940s, many South Dakotans distrusted large organized labor operations. The closed shop, they believed, was antithetical to capitalism and the doctrine of American individualism and opportunity upon which it depended. Historian Matthew Pehl writes: "In postwar South Dakota, economic freedom became synonymous with opposition to labor power."[40] Furthermore, because the New Deal's Wagner Act had empowered unions nationwide, they engendered the hostility of anti–New Deal Dakotans of all political persuasions, even some left-leaning farmers who had supported workers in the 1920s. One South Dakotan, Rex Batie of Webster, characterized "labor racketeers" as aspiring to become "a little Stalin of USA."[41] According to one reporter in the Black Hills, home to the powerful Homestake Mining Company, "if any union organizer should appear in Deadwood or Lead . . . he would simply be thrown in jail."[42]

Businesspeople felt particularly vulnerable to work actions taken by the Teamsters, who had developed a reasonably strong presence in eight cities on the Northern Plains and led a major coal strike in Sioux Falls in 1938.[43]

In 1945, the Custer Chamber of Commerce wrote President Truman demanding that "government intervention" (presumably troops) be sent to end a shipping strike before their crops were ruined. Anti-labor activist William Wilson echoed these sentiments, "It is high time that the people of this country take a firm hand in the handling of these strikes."[44] In 1948, Senator Francis Case introduced a law that would, in his words, if successful "break every union in the country."[45]

In North Dakota the years before what historians identify as the "McCarthy era" also saw a strong conservative backlash against perceived "creeping socialism," unionism, government corruption, and "Langerism." For most of the state's history, the Republican Party had been split between business-friendly voters from the Red River Valley and the Nonpartisan League–affiliated farmers and ranchers in more western counties. Democrats, while gaining strength in the Roosevelt years, were still more often than not "viewed as curiosities."[46] Essentially, this meant that the state had a single party system split into irreconcilable factions. But in 1943, a group of business-friendly Republicans schemed to oust the NPL from their organization once and for all. New leaders like Fred Aandahl and Milton Young believed that conservative Republicans, anti-Langer members of the NPL, and unaffiliated young people might unite behind a conservative banner. In 1944 this strategy produced the Republican Organizing Committee's (ROC's) first platform, which accepted the ongoing presence of the NPL-established state-owned businesses and state-funded crop insurance. But every other plank revealed the growing consensus among conservatives around the country that Americanism was defined by economic freedom, support for business, and a small and efficient federal government—a repudiation, in other words, of the public-private partnership that characterized the New Deal.[47] Even more important—top of the list for the ROC—was support for "the Armed Forces of our nation."[48] In 1944, Aandahl won the governorship. The *Fargo Forum* proclaimed upon Aandahl's death in 1966: "[Aandahl] is the man who started the conservative branch of the Republican Party in North Dakota on its longest period of control in the State's history."[49] In less than a decade, the NPL would leave the Republican Party entirely, merging with the Democratic Party and creating what has been known as the D-NPL ever since.

* * *

These shared cultural histories and political strategies prepared Dakotans to rededicate themselves to anti-communism during the 1950s, both in Washington and at home. On the national stage, South Dakota senator Karl Mundt joined Joseph McCarthy to assist in his investigations into communist subversion inside the United States. Born in Humboldt, South Dakota, Mundt carried the banner of anti-communism throughout his career, first as a congressman elected in 1938 and then, beginning in 1948, for three terms in the Senate. In 1947, he was the first congressman to call for the registration of communists and members of front organizations.[50] In the upper chamber, he contributed directly to the Internal Security Act of 1950, which had originally been named the Mundt-Nixon Act.[51] A champion debater, Mundt was well-known for his fiery and colorful rhetoric. In one attack, he said that "for eighteen years [the country] had been run by New Dealers, Fair Dealers, Misdealers and Hiss dealers who have shuttled back and forth between Freedom and Red Fascism, like a pendulum on a cuckoo clock."[52]

Mundt's most public association with McCarthy came when he chaired the "Army-McCarthy" hearings, called to examine subversive activities in the United States Army. One case involved an army dentist who had not signed the required loyalty oath, but had been recommended for a promotion nonetheless. When McCarthy insisted that he be dishonorably discharged, the army refused. The subsequent hearing was part investigation and part "ordeal, combat, theater, duel, confession, catharsis, the testing of will—all accomplished through a flood of talk."[53] Mundt was barely able to maintain order as McCarthy misused a common parliamentary device called a "point of order" to interrupt witnesses, threaten and harass them, and bring up new topics for discussion. Televised live with no commercial interruption on the fledgling ABC network, the hearings ran for thirty-six days and were seen by more than eighty million viewers.

In the early stages, voters on the Northern Plains largely supported Mundt, McCarthy, and all the associated efforts to ferret out communist subversives. In regard to the Mundt-Nixon Bill, later named the McCarran Act, L. A. Forkner of Elm Springs wrote Senator Case, "No country can hope to live unless they retain the right to curb any subversive activity."[54] When Senator Langer spoke out against the bill, and even helped to filibuster it, he received plenty of pushback from voters. He explained that, should the bill pass, any member of the NPL would have to submit to federal investigation, whether they had ever been communists or not. Such a bald attack on dissent and political experimentation reminded Langer of the Sedition Act of 1917 which had led to violent attacks against Leaguers, Germans, and other anti-war protesters. However much he hated communists, Langer felt the act evoked the cultural politics of that terrible anti-democratic era.[55]

When it came to the televised debacle that was the Army-McCarthy hearings, however, Langer found he had a great deal more company in his opposition to McCarthy and Mundt. Dakotans, like other Americans, began to wonder how the desire to keep America safe from communists had veered so badly off course. Furthermore, Mundt's inability to keep the hearings on track or on schedule was not lost even on his closest allies back home. On June 11, publisher Fred Christopherson wrote in the *Argus Leader* that Mundt was trying to please too many people—by implication McCarthy—and that he simply had to take control. "Mundt should let all know who's boss," he wrote. "The time has come to swing an iron fist!"[56]

The question of whether McCarthy should be censured by the Senate put Mundt, his regional colleagues, and their constituents in an especially tight spot. Francis Case, known for his equanimity, was chosen to serve on the Senate subcommittee tasked with making a recommendation on censure to the full Senate. Like both McCarthy and Mundt, Case made use of the political capital of anti-communism to target opponents at home. As a result, Case struggled with the Senate's movement to censure McCarthy. At first he stood steadfast in McCarthy's defense. But when the six members of the Watkins Committee initially agreed to censure him, Case backpedaled. First he suggested that McCarthy apologize and be exonerated; then he decided not to vote on one of the censure charges. Finally he voted for a different charge, in effect splitting the difference and pleasing no one. By way of explanation, *Time* magazine noted that the senator from South Dakota "is up for re-election in 1956 in a state where McCarthy has powerful political friends."[57] The charge was not unfounded. Throughout the hearings, mail from South Dakota and around the country poured into Case's offices in support of McCarthy.[58]

Ironically, by the time Case ran again in 1956, it would not be his support for Joe McCarthy that he would be compelled to explain. For several years the farm economy on the Northern Plains had been in crisis; thousands of Dakotans had left their farms and rural communities; many even left the region. Meanwhile President Eisenhower's secretary of agriculture,

Ezra Benson, a member of the John Birch society and an avid anti-communist, sought to cut all remaining New Deal farm programs. He saw them as forms of socialism and wrote approvingly of a *Harper's Bazaar* satire that depicted farmers who accepted them "pampered tyrants . . . with a minimum of two cars."[59] When Benson had traveled to South Dakota for an appearance at the National Corn-Husking Contest in Sioux Falls, South Dakota, farmers pelted him with eggs.[60] Even worse for South Dakota's Republican Party, as the decade came to an end, a newcomer to state politics, George McGovern, was going farmyard to farmyard, determined to rebuild the South Dakota Democratic Party from scratch. A decorated war veteran and preacher's son who knew how to speak the traditional language of Populism and religious faith, McGovern supported farm programs and even the agencies that administered them. Moreover he believed they might even play a role in maintaining global peace, which remained among his primary goals. Farmers—and others in South Dakota—started to listen. [61]

* * *

When Dakotans sought out communists in their own communities, schools, and organizations, they maintained their unique regional view of what made communism so bad—not that it sought to equalize economic opportunity but that it diminished local control and concentrated power in a centralized state. Although they did not go to the extremes seen in some other states, political changes in the 1950s would reverberate long into the region's future.

Anti-communist agitation began at the University of South Dakota (USD). The FBI could only identify thirty-seven card-carrying members of the Communist Party in South Dakota. Even so veterans' organizations, including the VFW and American Legion, demanded that public employees, including faculty at the University of South Dakota, sign a loyalty oath. It read in part: "I do not advocate, nor am I a member, nor have I been within a period of a year a member . . . of any political party or organization that advocates the overthrow of the government of the United States or of this state by force or violence."[62] When historian R. Alton Lee joined the USD faculty, his department chair advised him simply to sign it like everyone else.[63] Even so, Lee felt the task inherently "degrading." Moreover, he knew that McCarthyism engendered the "immeasurable" harm of making teachers self-conscious and "cautious" about political statements and content.[64] Hardly confined to a single era, the loyalty oath was required of all public employees in the state until 1974.

Even with the oath in place, administrators watched carefully for any known communists or other radicals who spoke or worked at USD, coordinating with the FBI when necessary. President I. D. Weeks, for example, considered cancelling a convocation appearance by Henry Pratt Fairchild, a sociologist who advocated nationalization of land. He need not have worried, however, since the student newspaper, the *Volante*, quickly identified his "pink complexion."[65] Two other professors also came under scrutiny: Bert James Loewenberg, the only Jewish professor on campus, had written a scathing critique of the 1927 prosecution of Sacco and Vanzetti and enthusiastically supported the New Deal and other federal programs, having himself served as the assistant director of the Massachusetts Federal Writers Project. Soon he became known as "that communist history professor."[66] Loewenberg later left USD for a job in New York City. Thus the only professor fired for his views worked at the Medical School. When he learned from the FBI of the professor's affiliation, Mundt called USD president I. D. Weeks immediately, who in turn told Dean Walter Hard to fire the faculty member. Weeks reportedly said that he "did not want a guy like that around." A covert investigation followed, "to keep an eye on him and his activities" and, when the professor continued to attend communist "cell" meetings in Sioux Falls, his contract was terminated.[67]

Anti-communists also targeted leftist farm organizations across the region, actions that would have far-reaching consequences for the region's politics over time.[68] After Karl Mundt and his allies attacked Loriks for, at minimum, coordinating with communists in 1938, Emil Loriks and other FHA leaders began to expel political radicals from their ranks, thinking that it was better to dismember their own organization than to have others do it for them. This compromise effectively brought the storied days of the FHA as an outside and independent political organization, rather than a lobbying group, to an end.[69] At the end of his life, Emil Loriks could not remember—or would not admit—that at one time he had stood fast against Roosevelt's New Deal, and particularly against top-down agricultural programs such as the Agricultural Adjustment Administration (AAA).[70] He erased his own radicalism from his mind, just as many Dakotans would soon erase it from their memories.

Conservatives attacked the National Farmers Union (NFU) even more pointedly. Since its founding in 1902, the NFU had included a "no political party test" in its constitution. For that reason and its persistent advocacy for small farmers and tenants, the organization claimed a Populist image and left-of-center political philosophy. Members held communist and other leftist affiliations; some state organizations endorsed Henry Wallace for president in 1948, who advocated disarmament and cooperation with the Soviets. National leaders loudly protested intervention in Korea, putting them directly at odds not just with anti-communist conservatives but also with anti-communists on the left. Then, in the fall of 1950, the American Legion announced that it had included the NFU on its list of subversive organizations.[71] Senator Styles Bridges of New Hampshire charged, "the time has come to rid the Farmers Union, composed for the most part of fine and loyal Americans, of the evil and subversive forces within the organization."[72] In response, William Langer, Karl Mundt, and Minnesota's Hubert Humphrey defended the NFU.[73] Senator Milton Young reported that he was a member in good standing.

Among the NFU leaders Bridges assailed was North Dakota's Glenn Talbott, who historian William Pratt believes "was the real power in the national organization."[74] Even as the American Federation of Labor and other leftist organizations purged themselves of radicals, Talbott passionately defended the Farmers Union as the "direct descendant of the Populists."[75] In the early years after the war, he supported maintaining third party efforts rather than working as an interest group within the Democratic Party. He spoke out against the Truman administration's loyalty oath and increased defense spending. If that weren't enough to attract the wrath of the right, he told NFU members in 1947 that "corporatism was a form of fascism . . . while communism was not enough of an issue to be worth fighting about."[76] Pressure on the NFU mounted even more until Talbott helped find for the union common ground with the Truman Administration policies, including those on the war in Korea. At home he endorsed an anti-communist program called the Crusade for Freedom and began the process of becoming "more conventional"—at least politically.[77] Most importantly, Talbott endorsed the NPL's merger with the Democratic Party in advance of the election of 1960, establishing a conventional two-party system in the state for the first time. In South Dakota meanwhile, comparable attacks on the Farmers Union extended beyond the 1950s, creating a phenomenon that Pratt names "McCarthyism after McCarthy."[78] In both states, these charges and the consequent concessions reduced the Farmers Union from a radical third party "movement" to a "business-oriented" lobbying group—part of the coalition of labor and business interests that defined mid-twentieth-century liberalism.[79]

*　*　*

Most men and women on the Northern Plains did not have the time to devote to hunting down communists in their midst. Even so, they found a variety of other ways—like standing in line for hours to see the Freedom Train—to show their respect for the military, their devotion to "100% Americanism," and their suspicion of political radicalism. These actions spoke volumes to the politicians they elected. Dakotans had come to live with a new reality, new kind of war, and a new enemy—one with representatives close to home. While they were not living in nuclear missile fields—at least not yet—they were coming to understand what it meant to live "under the shadow of war." During the Cuban Missile Crisis in 1962, they saw how close the threat of nuclear war, of World War III, actually was.

To support the American way of life some Dakotans pursued activities directly connected to the military. Veterans' organizations, like the American Legion and Veterans of Foreign Wars (VFW), soared in membership and community involvement in the late 1940s and 1950s.[80] When President Eisenhower changed the November 11 national holiday from Armistice Day to Veterans Day, veterans groups organized parades, fairs, and suppers. They also remained active in bringing soldiers' bodies and remains home from battlefields abroad. But the groups' strong anti-communism also gave them a distinct, if often implicit, political agenda. Before each high school American Legion baseball game or other activity, for example, youth involved recited the Pledge of Allegiance, said a prayer, and sometimes repeated the Legion's Code of Sportsmanship. To most people at the time, these rituals were not ideological but simply a part of everyday life in a time and place where "everyone in town shared a sense of patriotism."[81] When Jim Fuglie was growing up in Hettinger, North Dakota, his father served as the commander of the local American Legion post—but that was just one of many local leadership positions he held. It was only when Jim came home from two tours in Vietnam, went to a local Legion meeting, and spoke out in favor of amnesty for draft dodgers—and was met with a chorus of boos—did he realize he had "chosen the wrong audience" for his left-leaning political views.[82]

Dakotans could demonstrate their support for the military directly by volunteering for the Ground Observers Corps (GOC), an organization that trained local people to stand watch for enemy planes that entered American airspace. Since the Dakotas were the farthest northern points of the central United States, volunteer observers were trained to look for Soviet planes that had flown over the Arctic. Often this work was isolated and somewhat dangerous, as observers stood on tall forest service towers or their own locally constructed observation posts late at night.[83] Even so officials had no dearth of volunteers in the Dakotas; women were particularly well represented. Organizations such as the Daughters of the American Revolution in Dickinson and Flaxton, North Dakota, supported the local GOC through fundraising; other women organized and participated in GOC beauty pageants, ice cream socials, and fairs; in fact women made up 65 percent of actual observers.[84] Dakotans defied expectations in their enthusiastic support, even in the tiniest of towns, like New Hradec, North Dakota. Its thirty-five residents "accomplished what seemed impossible by establishing an observation post that required a staff of 100 members. Residents recruited volunteers from outlying areas and swelled the ranks of observers to 125."[85]

Dakotans also supported militarized anti-communism in their everyday lives through religion. As we have seen, religious practice, much of which leaned toward the conservative end of the Christian spectrum, was a part of the prewar culture of the Northern Plains that could unify people across the political spectrum. The famously liberal Senator George McGovern—who eventually found the liberal teachings of the "social gospel" when he was in college—grew up in a pietistic Methodist family and remembered a prewar childhood of endless religious revivals and camp meetings.[86] But after the war Dakotans—Catholics in particular—began to see their faith practices in a context beyond family and community; they saw them instead as part of the fight against "godless communism" and the threat of atomic war.[87] Historian Stephen Whitfield observes that Americans believed "not so much in the *value* of religion" as they believed that "religion was virtually synonymous with American nationalism."[88] In the early Cold War years, Dakotans recontextualized long-held religious practices and beliefs into national defense, anti-communism, and geopolitics, a change which would reverberate in regional politics for generations.

For some Dakotans, this recontextualization of faith drew them to investigate new trends in evangelical belief and practice. Historian Darren Dochuk has shown how the "plain folk" of the southern plains, after migrating to defense-industry-rich towns of southern California, combined Populist anti-elitism and anti-statism with anti-communism and white supremacy to launch the postwar evangelical movement.[89] Since the "plain folk" of the Northern Plains shared much of this worldview, they too were drawn to the lessons of sinfulness, redemption, and preparation for the coming apocalypse. Furthermore, they saw in evangelism a bold expression of anti-communism in an ever more dangerous world. While it would grow more slowly on the Northern Plains in the early Cold War than it did in California, evangelical Protestants in the 1950s set the stage for a surge in congregation-building in the 1970s and 1980s, when "mainline" Protestant denominations seemed to grow ever more closely allied with liberal culture.[90]

The connection between "plain folk" evangelists of the Sun Belt and the people of the Northern Plains was evident as early as 1950 when the evangelist Jack Shuler visited Sioux Falls. Nearly 40,000 people attended his services, so many that the city had to change the venue to the Civic Center Coliseum.[91] He told the congregants "to prepare their souls for the afterlife, lest atomic war catch them unprepared."[92] Likewise, in 1958 nearly 80,000 people gathered in an outdoor amphitheater in Spearfish for a series of performances of the "Black Hills Passion Play," which told the story of Jesus' life.[93] From Spearfish the Passion Play traveled to over 650 other locations.[94] Oral Roberts likewise filled Bismarck's Memorial Auditorium twice a day for four days; 1500 people filled out a card asking Roberts for healing before his first appearance alone.[95]

By the time the world's most famous Christian evangelist, Billy Graham, visited the Northern Plains, he had preached to Americans in every region and to international audiences on every continent. Moreover he had spread his faith in the inerrant words of the Bible, the possibility of personal salvation, and the imminent chaos of Armageddon through a broad network of conservative radio stations, bookstores, and television programs.[96] Unlike some evangelists, Graham made his Cold War politics clear: as Kevin Kruse says, placing himself soundly in the "McCarthy wing" of the Republican Party. He told an audience in 1949, "Communism is not only an economic interpretation of life—communism is a religion that is inspired, directed, and motivated by the Devil himself and has declared war against the Almighty God."[97] He shared more than anti-communism with conservatives, though, speaking in favor of deregulation and against unions and the New Deal. In the 1960s and 1970s, Graham would combine this economic conservatism with homophobia, antifeminism, and what Melanie McAllister calls "soft" support for civil rights, all the while acting as counselor to some of the best known Republican politicians of his time.[98]

Graham's visit to Fargo was an event few people forgot. Over the course of three days in June 1987, 22,000 people heard Johnny Cash perform, a 2500-member choir sing, and Graham preach. According to one volunteer, Wayne Hoglund, "there was electricity in the air, and it was a holy moment. A lot of people . . . went forward [for the altar call] and all those lives changed in some way."[99] Even more remarkable was the way his visit shed light on the conservative consensus that had emerged in the region in the Cold War. A Democratic governor, "Bud" Sinner—the last Democrat to serve in that position—introduced Graham. Leaders from every Christian church in Fargo, including the Catholic parishes, worked together to make the event a success. Cultural conservatism, it seemed, with deep roots on the Northern Plains, had flourished in the Cold War era and by the 1980s had found new and even more dynamic forms of expressions. The appeal and power of evangelism in the region made sense. Like Graham, Dakotans knew the apocalypse might bring them to the face of God at any time.

*   *   *

The United Nations was never located in South Dakota and President Truman never vacationed in the Black Hills or gave the oath of citizenship there. Even so on July 23, 1962, when twelve million people in seven countries around the world tuned in to see live images broadcast by satellite for the first time in history, they saw the Northern Plains.[100] Operation Telestar, like Radio Free Europe, used mass media to show those living in communist-controlled countries what life in a free country was like. What images could be better than the carved rock faces of four great American presidents paired with a conveniently timed—and dynamite-triggered—buffalo stampede, "a baseball game and the US-Canada border (with no guns or barbed wire)," and a performance by the 350-member Mormon Tabernacle Choir? The magnitude of the moment and the location was not lost on those who saw it live, either. A Latter-Day Saints (LDS) newsletter reported that members of the choir had been nearly overcome by the concurrent sense of national honor and the threat of its destruction: "The choir seemed to call up strange echoes among the cliffs—rich songs of progress, of vast migrations to better lands, of explorers, overtones from the marching pioneers. . . . But there were overtones of evil too."[101] To ward off these frightening premonitions, the choir sang hymns of battle: the well-known Protestant hymn, "A Mighty Fortress Is Our God" and the Civil War anthem "The Battle Hymn of the Republic."

It is hard to imagine another event that could have dramatized more clearly the transformation underway on the Northern Plains in the early Cold War decades. Just as those who had carved Mount Rushmore had erased the history of Native people and the "six Grandfathers," so the broadcast ignored the radical agrarian heritage of the plains and erased its anti-militarist tradition. Instead, the broadcast associated South Dakota with American exceptionalism and individualism: pioneers and progress, not deprivation and demand. Moreover, it connected South Dakotans to evangelical religious practices that within fifteen years would bring together diverse congregations, including evangelical Protestants, Catholics, and Mormons, into an interdenominational conservative political movement. Finally, through the choice of hymns, the program underscored the region's support for militarism itself. After the cameras were off and the Telestar satellite moved elsewhere on its orbit, all that remained for the people of the Dakotas was to build those fortresses and arm themselves for battle on the plains themselves.

CHAPTER 4

"AN ENTIRE WORLD IN KHAKI BROWN AND OLIVE GREEN"

TOM BROKAW'S CHILDHOOD IN South Dakota barely resembled his father's. Born in 1912 "Red" Brokaw grew up in his family's small Bristol hotel and, like many in his generation, rose before dawn to do hard physical labor. He quit school when he was ten to work for a local jack-of-all-trades. One day the older man lowered Red, upside down and hanging from a rope, into a farmer's forty-foot well to rescue a trapped piglet. As Tom put it, Red grew up when men and boys alike were defined by their work and their "work . . . produced tangible, useful things."[1] Tom, by contrast, felt he had never done anything "useful" at all. Red made sure Tom did his chores and always held a job, of course. But Tom was also in the Boy Scouts and played baseball, basketball, and football for town and school teams. He hiked the nearby hills, collected rock specimens, and attended club meetings. In high school he spent his free time at a nearby college drinking with sorority girls.[2]

Put in broad historical perspective, Red's and Tom's different attitudes toward the military were even more significant than their different life experiences.[3] Tom acknowledged that most people in the Dakotas resisted entrance into World War II and implied that his father may have been among them. When the war came, however, Red and his fellow South Dakotans were prepared to serve. Even so Red did not volunteer but waited to be drafted and was not disappointed when he was assigned to a construction job in South Dakota rather than a combat deployment. For Tom and his friends, on the other hand, "military service was mandatory" even during peacetime and they fully embraced the obligation.[4] Tom entered the University of South Dakota through the ROTC program and won its prize for best freshman cadet. After graduation he hoped he would be commissioned in the navy. He was devastated when the navy—and then the army—refused to accept him as an officer candidate because he had flat feet.[5]

What had happened to create such divergent attitudes and experiences over the course of a single generation? Tom pointed to December 7, 1941, as the day that "changed all that," the "historic hinge" on the Northern Plains.[6] But important changes in American society, Dakotan communities, and Tom's own family had begun before the attack on Pearl Harbor and encompassed even more than the region's rejection of Populist antimilitarism.[7] The expanded reach of the federal government during the Great Depression, for example, had helped pull Red and many others out of poverty. By the time Tom was a toddler, Red worked for the military, a vastly more powerful and expansive federal organization than the New Deal state, and earned $6.88 per day, doing construction at an ordnance depot in Igloo. Next Red and hundreds of other workers built a series of four huge earthen dams along the Missouri River under the auspices of the Army Corps of Engineers. There the Brokaw family knew the security of "a steady year-round paycheck, good benefits, [and] low-cost but comfortable housing."[8] In the years between Red's and Tom's childhoods, the military state had come to the country and it too had "changed all that." As Tom recalled, "My entire world, from the surrounding arid hills to the uniforms and vehicles, was khaki brown and olive green."[9]

In one respect the arrival of the military state on the Northern Plains was plain to see: it physically transformed the landscape. Along with the Fort Randall Dam, the Army Corps of Engineers built an entire town for dam workers.[10] Tom remarked on the "military precision" with which "Pickstown" operated, influencing even the ways men and women kept their yards, managed their households, and washed their cars.[11] He also noticed that a large number of workers were veterans; another subset had moved from southern states. Mississippians, North Carolinians, and Georgians introduced new foods, new words, new forms of religious expression, even a new kind of music—"country western."[12]

But the arrival of the military state also had an impact on society in ways Tom could not fully discern. When Tom entered high school, the family moved east of the Missouri River to Yankton, a long-established community that was far larger than Igloo or Pickstown. What Tom couldn't see was that Yankton had become a "tank town" too. American men of all backgrounds had served in the military in World War II; the businesspeople of Main Street shared a common worldview with the blue-collar dam workers from Pickstown. Everyone accepted the American military as a basic moral good and the repressive Soviet state as a direct threat to American ideals. Likewise they all admired military men, like Medal of Honor winner Governor Joe Foss whom Tom called a "man's man of the highest order."[13] And everyone supported the work of veterans' organizations and joined the teams and contests they sponsored. In his autobiographical descriptions, Tom confirms that during the 1950s militarization on the Northern Plains was so pervasive that it had become utterly ordinary.[14]

Across the Dakotas, other parts of rural America, and many distant and isolated corners of the world, the Cold War created "tank towns" where before there had been none. With them civilians became integrated into both the burgeoning wartime economy and the ongoing confrontation between East and West. In the United States, government spending on defense rose from 1 to 2 percent of GDP in the 1920s to 10 percent of GDP in the 1950s and 1960s, a 1,000 percent increase.[15] In 1950, the US spent 70 billion dollars on defense; by 1960 that number had moved to 170 billion; by 1990, 343 billion.[16] At the same time, new organizations like the CIA created the foundational structures of a secretive national security state, where tens of billions of dollars appeared only in "black box budgets." This explosion of investment over half a century created a "permanent war economy" that spread the dollars, personnel, and physical presence of the military to every state in the union and to every continent on earth. Between 1946 and 1989 Americans spent over sixteen trillion dollars to defeat communism.[17]

Men and women on the Northern Plains hoped to get "their share" of this mammoth increase in federal defense spending. As they had for generations, Euro-Americans still feared "bigness" and concentrated power and sometimes derided the incompetence and arrogance of the federal bureaucracy. But since 1941 white Dakotans had largely come to admire the military, fear communism, and accept the legitimacy of most forms of international engagement. They wanted to demonstrate their utter and complete rejection of prewar anti-militarism. At the same time the ongoing contraction of agriculture and resulting rural depopulation made any potential injection of funding and employment irresistible.[18] In Washington, DC, South Dakota senator Francis Case and North Dakota senator Milton Young, who chaired the Senate's Military Appropriations Committee, used their considerable influence to bring federal defense monies to their states.[19]

In the 1950s, Dakotans began to get their share. It came first in a form they had coveted: three air force bases, one each in Rapid City, Grand Forks, and Minot. In the 1960s and 1970s, it came in a form they could never have imagined: 450 intercontinental ballistic missiles (ICBMs) arrayed in "missile fields" around the bases. Before the Department of Defense decided where to locate the bases, boosters and elected officials in many Dakota towns battled each other for the honor—not to mention the jobs. Despite their previous anti-militarism, Dakotans did not worry that the bases would threaten local control of their communities. Instead they expected, perhaps due to their recent, albeit difficult, interactions with the New Deal, that the military would solicit community participation in the decision-making process. Before long they learned that, as James Sparrow has written, agencies of the warfare state "were far less beholden to state and local political interests than had been the case in the 1930s."[20] Unlike the New Deal administrators who cared that people saw programs as their "own," Department of Defense bureaucrats provided no processes for negotiation, no county commissions, and absolutely no convenient loopholes. Furthermore, their secrecy was legendary. In the end, Dakotans could not dictate where the bases would be, how many servicepeople would be deployed there, what their missions would entail, or how long the bases would remain. Far more than mere economic engines, the bases would become all-encompassing outposts of the military state whose presence over time transformed communities in ways few Dakotans could have anticipated.

*   *   *

The Cold War never spawned an apocalyptic showdown between the United States and the USSR. But the physical and political preparations for such a confrontation combined with smaller proxy wars left no spot on the globe untouched.[21] Many of these "local consequences of the global Cold

War," as Jeffrey and Catherine Carte Engel call them, will never be known due to covert actions and the secretive nature of intelligence systems. But what we do know took place—from the creation of huge weapons productions sites in Siberia, to the construction of nuclear submarine facilities in Scotland, the CIA's recruitment of indigenous people like the Hmong in Laos, and even the moon landing—shows that the Cold War knew no "real geographical bounds. . . . peoples the world over felt its impact."[22] By the year 2000, the United States had at least thirty-six hundred separate military facilities around the globe.[23] To equip them, the United States instituted the first-ever peacetime draft and left it in place for a generation; the number of Americans serving in the military in 1960, five years before the official start of the war in Vietnam, was one thousand times as high as in 1920. Finally the expansion of the military also linked the federal government, corporate industry, university research facilities, and the military into an enormous "military-industrial complex." At the dawn of the twentieth century, the US military was a small—inadequately small—operation. At the dawn of the twenty-first century, it was the largest employer and landlord in the world.[24]

Few places on earth were more thoroughly transformed by the Second World War and Cold War than the American West. First seen as what one scholar termed an "outdoor laboratory"—an appropriate location for secret experimental activities—the West soon became, to another, "a vast complex" of military facilities of all kinds.[25] Between 1945 and 1965, the federal government spent 62 percent of its budget ($776 billion) on defense. At least one-third of that ($250 billion) went to western states, where only 16 percent of the nation's population resided.[26] The construction of research complexes, mining and manufacturing facilities, military bases, experiment stations, and weapons sites created what historian Gerald Nash called "a federal landscape" in every western state. In Utah in 1965, one-third of personal income depended on defense spending.[27] While only one section of what Ann Markusen calls the nation's "gunbelt," the American West may well have been the most highly militarized region on earth in a time of "peace."[28] The region's representatives in Congress knew that their jobs depended on keeping federal money flowing and defining it not as "pork" but as a contribution to the nation's "greater good."[29]

During the early years of the Cold War, defense planners largely overlooked the Dakotas due to the region's lack of an industrial base or significant research facilities. In fact, by the mid-1950s, the Northern Plains was fast becoming a "fly-over zone" as far as the "permanent war economy" was concerned.[30] But the "fly-over" zone offered something few other regions could—air force pilots could literally fly over it. The Northern Plains contained vast miles of empty airspace, with no "encroaching urban areas." It had room not just for bombers like the B-2 and B-37 to fly but also for pilots to conduct target practice. In fact it was the perfect region for the Cold War air force to take up residence, as defense officials expected any Soviet planes to come over the Arctic Circle. In that scenario the Northern Plains were the nation's first line of defense. By the mid-1950s the race for the bases was on.

Rapid City, South Dakota, got a head start in that contest; in the end its leaders and those in Grand Forks also learned the most distinct lessons from their participation.[31] In late 1940, Senator Francis Case told city leaders that the air force was planning to build twenty-five new air bases across the country; if Rapid City was interested in being selected for one, its officials needed to make their best pitch. City leaders repeatedly wrote to and visited military representatives, promising full cooperation and emphasizing the vast amounts of open land and housing in the area. They repeatedly waited for some kind of response. Finally, the *Rapid City Daily Journal* announced that the base would indeed become a reality, due almost entirely to "Hard Work by Many Persons."[32] That was not entirely true. Rapid City was chosen for two reasons local leaders could not have controlled: first, a top air force general was a friend of Gutzon Borglum, the sculptor who had created Mount Rushmore.[33] Second, the area around Rapid City was so lightly populated—despite a small city and major reservation—that officials deemed it safe for a gunnery range, where pilots could practice dropping ordnance without putting civilians at risk, provided they hit their targets.[34]

As it turned out, the Department of Defense was just starting to invest in Ellsworth Air Force Base. In 1953 the Eisenhower administration sought to reduce the size of the standing military by prioritizing air power and expanded Ellsworth again; a few years later it did so a third time. Each round of expansion required acquisition of land from ranchers and homeowners, with little or no opportunity for negotiation. Even so expansion seemed to promise far more than it took away: new residents, construction contracts, road improvements, enlarged school enrollments, and more. Indeed, very few South Dakotans—even those who sacrificed land or homes—protested the gradual militarization of their land and communities during this initial period. Many years later Marvin Kammerer, a rancher near Ellsworth, would become a vocal opponent of the air force and the Pentagon. But in the 1950s, he remembered, "We didn't feel the same way about it. . . . We thought the Russians might be a real threat."[35]

The greater Rapid City community also rallied behind the base, recognizing not only its role in national security but also its potential to enhance regional economic development for years. The Rapid City Chamber of Commerce, for example, became one of Ellsworth's most important boosters, keeping close watch over the types of deployments, personnel, and support the air force might need. Early on the chamber recognized an important fact that set their priorities for the duration of the twentieth century: if the air force could open a base, the air force could close one too. In fact, the air force base in Glasgow, Montana, was shuttered only four years after it opened, stunning the local community and evoking comparisons to the wastefulness of the 1933 "plow-under" requirements of the Agricultural Adjustment Administration (AAA).[36] Over time Rapid City residents and state politicians would increasingly try to *anticipate* Ellsworth's needs and address them in advance, even if it cost the state or community money. What was good for the air force, they figured, was good for Rapid City. By making this calculation, city officials revealed just how fully Rapid City had become a militarized space, beholden to and defined by the Cold War's ongoing "wartime." Looking back, few could pinpoint exactly how or when it had happened.

*   *   *

The competition in North Dakota to acquire a large air base like Ellsworth felt like a bloody free-for-all, made all the more feverish by the secrecy of the military's decision-making process. At first most North Dakotans, including Senator Young, thought that Fargo and Bismarck would get the bases and their B-52 bomber wings. Both had been mentioned by name in the Military Construction Bill of 1953. Both had municipal airports that could be expanded and sufficient populations (38,000 and 18,000 respectively) to provide support services for incoming personnel. Both local chambers of commerce had reassured the air force that their respective citizenries were ready to "cooperate" in any way necessary.[37] But in the end, neither got a base. To everyone's surprise, a second site survey conducted in the spring of 1954 determined that neither airport could be adequately converted to military use, after all. It would work better, engineers reported, to find a "virgin site" in the larger Fargo and Bismarck "areas."[38]

The rivalry among communities near Fargo and Bismarck became fierce and ultimately bewildering. The prize was enormous: air force officials had informed leaders in Fargo that initially 850 men would initially be stationed at each of the two new bases in North Dakota, with a payroll in excess of $2.7 million per year. To prepare, the air force planned to make significant infrastructure improvements.[39] And yet, federal largesse would not be free or unlimited. As air force legislative liaison, General Joe Kelly, wrote to North Dakota senator Milton Young, "The Air Force has an obligation to the taxpayers of the nation to develop its base structure with a minimum expenditure of federal funds."[40] Thus one criterion for selection became "community support" and "economy of development." In other words, municipalities willing to put up funds for the base or to defray real estate costs got special consideration. Soon Bismarck voters agreed to raise $150,000 for land, Minot approved $50,000, and Valley City, $62,500. Jamestown offered land for free.[41]

Mayor Oscar Lunseth of Grand Forks and his friend, chamber of commerce president Henry Hansen, were particularly aggressive in their campaign to attract the air force. The chamber sent a representative to the original survey site in Fargo when military officials first visited. The next day Hansen sent a letter complete with a careful map of "four or five sections of very level, quite useless alkali land" west of Grand Forks that could be used for the base, should the air force decide against Fargo. He also claimed that land appraisers had decided "this morning . . . that none of this land would be appraised for more than $25 an acre."[42] Better yet, the mayor and chamber promised to raise $65,000 for the purchase of a different plot of land, if necessary. In a letter of solicitation to the Lence and Englund Construction Firm, Lunseth began with a reminder: "By making these contributions we are doing our part in the defense of our country." Then he got to the "practical and materialistic side to this new project": that economic growth in the area will benefit all concerned. "I trust that you will be able to contribute to this fund and share with us not only the costs but much of the benefits which will certainly accrue in the months to come."[43] The only thing that Grand Forks leaders did not do—although leaders of Fargo, Bismarck, Jamestown, Minot, Devils Lake, and Valley City did—was send a delegation to Washington in June when the final decisions were being made.[44]

On June 17, the Department of Defense announced its final decision: Grand Forks and Minot had been awarded the bases. Fargo and Bismarck citizens were outraged and charged that the air force had not followed proper procedures. The air force told them only that deciding factors were "operational suitability, community support, and economical development of the site"—meaningless bureaucratic jargon if North Dakotans had ever heard it, which of course they had.[45] More than one leader demanded that Senator Milton Young get some direct answers. How, for example, could Minot and Grand Forks be considered in the "area" of Bismarck and Fargo when both were more than fifty miles away? The air force responded that it relied on two new criteria: Grand Forks and Minot were in a "defense circle" set by the positioning of the new computerized radar systems; being farther north, they also were better positioned for interception of Soviet bombers flying over the Arctic Circle.[46]

The lesson of the past—that Dakotans and other Americans might be able to work with the federal government as a transparent, if distant and sometimes arrogant and uninformed partner—no longer applied. In the Cold War military bureaucracy, nameless decision makers not only had the "final say" as to where bases would be located, they could change their minds afterward and arrive at a different "final say." They could make communities wait for months, even years, for a decision. They could change the criteria without notice. They could play favorites based on economic contributions. They could "acquire" land from owners who hadn't offered it. And while this did not happen on the Northern Plains, they could even force a community to house a base when its leaders and citizens had explicitly asked—begged—the military to take their town off the list.[47]

North Dakotans had not expected the air force to be so secretive or inscrutable. But once the decision was finalized, they at least thought that the frustrating experience was over. They were wrong again. On December 7, 1954, military officials rejected the original location for the base—the "nearly useless alkali flats." Officials preferred instead a section of farmland farther west of the city near the townships of Mekinock and Emerado. Unfortunately, that land was useful indeed. Hardly alkaline, the farms collectively produced $162,400 in 1953 and included two large turkey farms.[48] Mayor Lunseth never would have offered that land for the base. Even Senator Young objected to the repurposing of such productive farmland. No matter. After months of legal wrangling, all the farm families in the area lost their land and, according to their attorney Richard King, they received less than the appraised value for it.[49] Some remained bitter for years. But for some of those who lost the most, having an air force base was well worth its cost. According to an acquaintance of the late Marijo Shide, whose father provided the largest section of land for the base, she always felt proud of the role her family had played in securing America's safety.[50] She still felt at home when she visited the base—just as any patriotic American would.

*   *   *

For all the rivalry and anguish that went into their acquisition; for all the concrete, asphalt, and steel that went into their construction; and for all the productive farmland that lay permanently fallow beneath them, the bases did not matter that much. They were not what changed Cold War politics and culture in the Dakotas. Over the course of fifty years the bases were merely physical manifestations of something far more consequential: the hundreds of thousands of military personnel who served there, whether rotating in and out of the region quickly or staying there permanently. In the heat of the race to acquire the bases, city leaders emphasized the financial benefits of militarization. And they were right to do so, as local economies indisputably benefited from the influx of funds. But over time, militarization—military people—brought changes that city leaders did not anticipate and problems they could not solve. Even so their dedication to the bases and their personnel did not waver. If anything it strengthened. By the end of the Cold War, when "realignment" threatened to close all three bases, the transformation of the communities and the region as a whole into militarized spaces, dependent upon and defined by the presence of and their commitment to the military, had long been fully established. The possible loss of a base felt more like a death in the family than an economic crisis. Even the region's history, its public memory of the past, became a casualty of wartime.

Historians may never know the precise number of military personnel and family members who served at the bases on the Northern Plains during the Cold War. City leaders and residents initially imagined a relatively low number of military personnel at the bases, but the estimates of 850 in the early 1950s grew to numbers approximating 6,000 at Grand Forks, 8,000 at Ellsworth, and 12,000 at Minot in the 1970s and 1980s. But since these

higher figures are only static snapshots of base population, they still do not tell the whole demographic story. They do not reflect the fact, for example, that servicepeople rotated through the region, on two-, three-, or four-year assignments or that during the wars in Korea and Vietnam, airmen were deployed abroad, replaced at the base, and, if they survived, might return. They also do not reflect the number of military dependents moving in and out of the base communities. As a result, the number of air force–affiliated people cycling through the region far exceeded initial projections. A conservative estimate suggests that between 1955 and 1995 as many as three hundred thousand service personnel and dependents were stationed at various times at the bases on the Northern Plains.[51] To put that number in perspective, the combined populations of both states in the same years never exceeded 1.6 million and declined throughout the era. The more military-affiliated men and women who rotated through the region, the more contact the citizens of the region had with their ideas, beliefs, and cultural practices. The more military people lived on the Northern Plains, in other words, the more the military mattered.[52]

While most servicepeople came to the Northern Plains, fulfilled their obligation, and were reassigned, others made their lives there. These men and women came to love the region's local towns, prairie landscape, outdoor recreation, and people—including some particularly special people. Wade Bertrand, an airman from Louisiana, recalled a common saying among retirees in Grand Forks: "The Air Force brought me here; my wife kept me here."[53] Over time veterans, retirees, and their family members

FIGURE 5. Community members visit the Grand Forks Air Force Base on Friends and Neighbors Day, 1979. Courtesy Orin G. Libby Manuscript Collection, University of North Dakota.

augmented the active-duty servicepeople in the base communities, and by extension the region as a whole. Of course, everywhere a major military facility exists in the United States, a disproportionate number of active-duty military reside; and it makes sense that some return when they complete active duty.[54] But base communities on the Northern Plains also attracted civilian employees of the military and a disproportionate number of veterans of other service branches who were drawn to the area's resources and support. By 2017, veterans alone made up over 8 percent of the white non-Hispanic population of South Dakota, nearly twice the national average.[55] In the area around Rapid City in 2000, between 25 and 40 percent of the population over age eighteen were veterans.[56]

The impact of migratory and permanent members of the military on small communities went beyond raw numbers, leaving in Gerald Nash's words, "a deep imprint beyond economic influences. Everywhere it served as a major employer; everywhere it determined the physical shape of cities and land controlled by military authorities."[57] Everywhere it also contributed to alliances between military elite and local political leaders. Black Hills State University professor Ahrar Ahmad suggests much the same: "Most people [in South Dakota] know somebody in the military. Consequently, many people feel a sense of personal involvement in military operations . . . they wear their association with the services as a badge of honor and support for troops is frequently translated into support for war."[58] Conversely, members of the broader military community give back to their communities in diverse ways, including volunteering at schools and churches and working at fire departments, rural police departments, and county sheriffs' offices. Since 2000 Michael Brown, a retired missileer, has served as mayor of Grand Forks.[59] In 1997 active-duty and retired servicemen and women rescued stranded residents in the devastating Red River flood. They housed the survivors both at the base and in their homes.[60] Air force officials even made it possible for students at Grand Forks Central High School to hold their prom on the base.[61]

Who were these people who became so important to their communities? Every service person stationed on the Northern Plains was a member of the air force, of course, the branch of the service with the highest education levels, longest average years of service, and, in the case of pilots, highest prestige and sense of "grandeur."[62] But only a small percentage were pilots, as the air force also trained security, maintenance, educational, and administrative personnel. In the 1960s the bases' bomber wings would be joined by Strategic Air Command (SAC) units that operated, manned, secured, and maintained nuclear weapons in surrounding launch facilities. Whatever their assignment, the vast majority of the military personnel on the Northern Plains were white men; small numbers of African Americans arrived in the early 1960s followed by women of all ethnic backgrounds two decades later.[63] For many who arrived, their assignment to a base on the Northern Plains was rarely their first move. Throughout the Cold War, service members might have been assigned to facilities in California, Texas, Illinois, Ohio, or anywhere across the world. During the Vietnam era, pilots and navigators had also been deployed to bases in Asia, including Thailand, Japan, Okinawa, and the Philippines, that served as launching points for air force operations. In fact, many had moved enough times to consider the air force their true "home," and its values—honor, duty, and sacrifice along with what one blogger called the "I am the King of the ville" attitude regarding race, class, gender, and nationality—to be their own.[64]

Yet most of the servicepeople who came to the Northern Plains had not been born and raised in the air force. They also brought with them the practices and values of their home communities—many in the American South.[65] Even before the Civil War, the South was the most "martial" of the regions in the United States; for whites in particular dueling, manhood, honor, and violence were closely intertwined.[66] The Cold War military buildup amplified this tradition by investing hundreds of millions of dollars for the construction or expansion of bases like Fort Bragg in North Carolina and manufacturing facilities like the Oak Ridge nuclear facility in Tennessee. So much money poured into the South in the Cold War that South

FIGURE 6. B-52 Bomber at the Grand Forks Air Force Base. Courtesy Orin G. Libby Manuscript Collection, University of North Dakota.

Carolina senator Richard Russell wondered if Charleston might fall into the sea.[67] But historian James Gregory writes that military service or federal defense work was also a well-trodden "path" out of the South, helping to create a "southern diaspora" throughout the nation.[68]

As important as it was in the 1940s and 1950s, the military-driven migration out of the South accelerated after the Vietnam War. When the Department of Defense replaced the draft with the All-Volunteer Force in 1973, southerners became even more overrepresented in the military, with 44 percent of all service members hailing from southern states by the early twenty-first century.[69] This trend may be explained by the fact that, according to the Center for Naval Analysis, one of the most important predictors of whether young people volunteer for the military is the presence of military bases in their home communities.[70] Five of the largest bases are in the American South. But the influence of the southern diaspora on military enlistment rates and culture might go deeper still. Californians are also overrepresented in the military; California is a state with a large number of bases. Moreover, as Gregory shows, California is also home to well over a million southerners who migrated there from the 1930s to the 1970s.[71] As military service has a multigenerational predictive component, it is likely that many second- or third-generation white Californians "inherited" their "southern" parents' or grandparents' positive views of military service despite their upbringing elsewhere.[72]

The cultural impact of southerners and "southerners once removed" among the military personnel who arrived in small rural communities on the Northern Plains was significant, and in one respect, transformative.[73] Beginning in the late 1940s, servicepeople introduced several communities to religious practices associated with evangelical Protestantism. As we have seen, the Dakotas had long been home to relatively theologically conservative Christian denominations, ethnic-specific parishes, and separatist synods. By the 1950s the region's faithful were also becoming familiar with Protestant evangelism through the national broadcasts and local appearances of celebrity preachers such as Jack Schuyler, Oral Roberts, and Billy Graham. But until the arrival of the bases and their personnel, local evangelical congregations were few. Quickly, however, service members from the South, Southwest, and California sought out places to practice their faith. In March of 1949, for example, six Ellsworth airmen who had previously worshipped in Church of Christ congregations began meeting at the Ellsworth Hospital and one of the base schools. By 1956 they had purchased land in Rapid City and completed construction on a facility of their own, while also traveling to Sturgis, Hot Springs, and Custer to found Church of Christ congregations there.[74] Likewise the two churches located nearest to the Grand Forks Air Force Base in its early decades were evangelical: the Baseview Assembly of God and the Calvary (Southern) Baptist church.[75] Ads like the one from the New Testament Baptist Church in Larimore, a few miles away, which described itself as "a friendly church where the Bible is the final authority," were reprinted in official military newspapers.[76] In the 1970s, when many Dakotans rejected the increased liberalism of "main line" Protestantism, evangelical Protestantism on the plains outgrew its military origins and expanded to include Christian schools, book stores, radio stations, and political organizations. Thus just when many regions in the US saw declining numbers of churches and churchgoers, the Dakotas showed the opposite trend. In fact, despite the shuttering of many isolated "prairie churches," far more churches were founded on the Northern Plains between 1970 and 2010 than before 1945. Few, however, were the kind that early settlers, especially those "business-friendly" Republicans from the "best families" in town, would have recognized. [77]

While Walmart did not arrive on the Northern Plains until the 1990s, it too originated in the South, had a commitment to the values of evangelical Protestantism, and owed at least part of its success to its self-conscious association with the military. A blogger named "Army Wife" wrote in 2012, "One thing I have always said for years is no matter where the military sends you in the United States, if you don't recognize anything else you are almost guaranteed to see a Wal-Mart close by." [78] She had observed a corporate strategy rather than a coincidence. Founder Sam Walton planned very carefully how to "roll out the formula" beyond the original Bentonville, Arkansas, stores, staying close to home at first and then building new stores in similar small-to-medium-sized southern towns, while also buying out competitors.[79] By the 1970s, however, stores dotted the south and southwest, often moving into towns near military bases. Walton knew that the migratory military families needed low-priced commodities and that they would find comfort and familiarity in the company's folksy approach to retail and their embrace of evangelism. Moreover, Walmart was also quick to publicize its support for the military, including the millions of dollars it gave to veterans-related charities, even though, as "Army Wife" pointed out in 2012, it did not provide in-store discounts for military families.[80]

On the Northern Plains in the 1990s, Walmart stores replaced many local businesses, some of which had barely survived the Farm Crisis of the 1980s. Old-timers complained that Walmart and other "big box" retailers, locating near malls or in other suburban spaces, would deliver the final death blow to the old Main Street.[81] But most Dakotans welcomed the stores, its part-time jobs for farm women, low prices, convenient parking, and the company's "carefully cultivated traditionalism." [82] Bethany Moreton writes that Walmart also introduced "Christian Free Enterprise" with its commitment to evangelical Protestantism, anti-communism, the free market, and traditional gender roles.[83] Far from just a store, then, Walmart was an engine of a new kind of political conservatism that was quickly replacing the "business conservatism" of former local elites. The Dakotas were far from Arkansas; but by the 1990s, the militarization of the Northern Plains made Walmart feel right at home.[84]

*   *   *

The influence of the military diaspora may have been even more significant when its practices and worldviews reinforced or redefined those already present in a community or a region. In the case of political conservatism it may well have done both. Before World War II, the political heritage of the Northern Plains was multifaceted; generations of conservative "business-oriented" Republicans vied with radical agrarian activists and organizations from the Populist Party to the Nonpartisan League (NPL). After 1945, however, Dakotans on both sides of the aisle largely rejected their traditional Populist anti-militarism and ousted socialists and communists in local organizations and schools. These trends leaned the region's precarious hybrid political culture to the right. At the same time the political views of men and women in the military became less multifaceted, leaning the military itself more to the right. By the last decades of the twentieth century, more members of the military, for example, identified as Republicans.[85] They also believed that the military had a positive role to play in the nation, particularly in defeating communism, and approved of increased funding for the military and for its missions abroad by large margins. Likewise they have admired the institution of the military itself. A 2009 Gallup poll found that over three-quarters of officers agreed with the statement that "civilian society would be better off if it adopted more of the military's values and customs," while just 25 percent of nonmilitary, nationwide, agreed.[86] Finally, while for many years military personnel believed it was important for them to stay "out of politics," by the late twentieth century the reverse was true: military-affiliated Americans were more politically active on average than nonmilitary Americans were.[87]

The conservative views of members of the military in the late Cold War decades on cultural issues—race, gender, and sexuality in particular—may have helped to redefine conservatism on the plains, replacing the prewar business Republicanism with its emphasis on economic issues to the new conservatism of 1980s and 1990s, with its added and distinctive emphasis on the "culture war."[88] Among military elite (officers and retired officers) in 1999, for example, 45 percent supported barring gay men and women from teaching jobs; a few approved of taking books that "supported homosexuality" from library shelves; 73 percent supported permitting prayer in public school; only 10 percent backed ending the death penalty.[89] Journalist Thomas Ricks wrote in the *Atlantic* in 1997 that being a Republican—particularly a Republican on the "hard right" wing of the party—"is becoming the definition of being a military officer." He based his conclusions in part on data collected by army Major Dana Isaacoff regarding the political views of cadets at West Point. Isaacoff found that they "pushed [conservatism] to extremes. The Democratic-controlled Congress was Public Enemy Number One. Number Two was the liberal media. . . . They firmly believed in the existence of the Welfare Queen."[90]

As we will see, the increasing size of farms, the out-migration of activist farmers, and even the introduction of soybeans played a role in the region's rejection of its mixed political heritage and its embrace of the New Right.[91] But some commentators have suggested that militarization was the essential precondition that set legislative priorities of rural whites before, during, and after these shifts. South Dakota historian Ahrar Ahmad, for example, has suggested that attitudes held by members of the military have rubbed off on Dakotans as a whole: "A state that benefits substantially from military facilities and expenditures . . . feels an obligation to respond positively to military needs."[92] Likewise, J. D. Vance argues that the closeness of rural people's "lived" connection to the military has made their views "increasingly distinct from those of urban people whose relationship with the military is more distant," and has shaped their increasingly conservative politics.[93] Beginning in the early 1990s, when Republican candidates began to attack Democrats for being "soft of defense," any meaningful distinction between Republican and Democratic candidates on support for the military diminished each year.[94] The resulting dynamic was nowhere clearer than in D-NPL incumbent senator Heidi Heitkamp's 2018 campaign.[95] Running behind, Heitkamp filled her social media accounts with her visits to local bases and meetings with veterans groups, hoping to optimize her share of the votes of the broader military community. It was too little, too late—and perhaps not even the point. Heitkamp lost by 11 percentage points; many voters cited her opposition to conservative Brett Kavanaugh's nomination to the Supreme Court as their deciding factor.

Military personnel in Dakota base communities also reinforced and redefined views on race, gender, and sexuality. In the early 1960s African American personnel stationed at Ellsworth air force base reported, as at other bases, that landlords, barbers, and restaurant and nightclub owners in Rapid City frequently refused them service.[96] Upon conducting their own study—the first of several of its kind over the next two decades—members of the South Dakota Advisory Committee to the US Civil Rights Commission, including Lakota leader and Episcopal minister Vine DeLoria Sr., reported that more than 90 percent of the owners of Rapid City bars and

FIGURE 7. D-NPL senator Heidi Heitkamp visiting Minot Air Force Base during her 2018 reelection campaign. Demonstrating her commitment to the military was an essential but nevertheless insufficient part of her strategy. Heitkamp suffered a double digit loss. Courtesy Office of US senator Heidi Heitkamp.

nightclubs in the city would not serve African Americans.[97] The number was nearly as high at barbershops, and well over 50 percent at restaurants and motels. African American military personnel had the most difficulty finding safe off-base housing for themselves and their families. In one survey, Rapid City residents were asked if they would object to living in a neighborhood with "Negroes," provided they were "well behaved." More than a third answered yes.[98]

Southern racial practices might have traveled with the diasporic southern military personnel and defense workers, just as country western music, evangelical churches, and Walmart did.[99] In fact some Rapid City businesspeople told the investigators that they "had to discriminate" because the "white airmen" insisted on segregated facilities and that if their businesses served "Negroes" they would lose white customers.[100] Other South Dakotans also believed that their racial attitudes were different from southerners and that the region did not share in the "shame of the South."[101] But even if businesspeople on the Northern Plains adopted southern antiblack racial practices because they thought they "had to," they were building upon similar practices already in place. One trailer park owner told an African American airman that he "didn't rent to Indians or Negroes."[102] In other words, he did not need to learn how to discriminate on the basis of race. Racial segregation of Native people had been engrained in Rapid City and other communities on the Northern Plains well before the military arrived.[103]

Military and local practices around gender and sexuality were also mutually reinforcing. Many historians have demonstrated that creating a "warrior" in the American military has long depended on and been defined by practices of misogyny, sexual violence, and homophobia.[104] The ritual practices of "military masculinity," with its all but mandatory performance of aggressive heterosexuality, lead to "hybrid" spaces just beyond American bases at home and abroad, where "drinks, drugs, and women" have been readily available and instances of assault relatively common.[105] The Ojibwa leader Dennis Banks remembered clearly that, far from forbidden, sex with local women was practically required. Thinking back on it later, he realized that "the military served as a training ground. . . . You're supposed to be macho and use women as sex objects."[106] White service members too recalled the peer pressure to "try a prostitute" as a form of male bonding; "kind of a joke."[107] This was true even at bases on the Northern Plains. When the air force chief prosecutor Col. Don Christianson's father was stationed at Ellsworth in its early years, strippers entertained officers over dinner.[108] In 1991 when airmen at Ellsworth heard that over one hundred women in the navy and marine corps alleged that they had been sexually assaulted at the Tailhook conference, most thought they were just "complaining." At that time it was still legal at Ellsworth for an airman to rape his wife. [109]

Like servicemen, Dakotans did not think of women merely as sex objects, of course. Nevertheless they held essentialist views of gender and sexuality that were founded on, reinforced, and in time politicized by the region's conservative religious culture. From the time of statehood when women's suffrage took longer than in other western states, many Dakotans saw differences between men and women as "natural" and "God given."[110] One of those "natural" differences was men's and women's roles in sexual intercourse and procreation: it was natural for men to be sexually aggressive, for unmarried women to resist their advances, and for married women to comply with them. Moreover Dakotans during the Cold War years largely believed that imprudent women bore the responsibility for unwanted advances, rapes, and unplanned pregnancies. Even at the end of the twentieth century girls in the Dakotas were sent away to church-affiliated "homes" to have babies whose existence families did not acknowledge. When Debra Marquart was a teen and eagerly welcomed new sexual experiences, she concluded that "by choosing pleasure over fertilization, I fear I have committed an act of extravagance that separates me irrevocably from the long line of agricultural women in my family."[111] Finally, while very little research has been done on LGBTQ history on the Northern Plains, it is likely that for some gays and lesbians, life there was isolating, if not life-threatening.[112]

The arrival of bases and thousands of airmen threatened heteronormative ideals of marriage and family. Local officials worried that they would see marked increases in both sexual assaults and sex work and that local women would be at risk. When the Grand Forks Air Force Base was set to open in 1957, commander Leon Lewis approached Mayor Oscar Lunseth to propose that the city build a club downtown for his enlisted men who had no place to "hang out." He received a resounding no.[113] Lunseth knew that Rapid City already had a USO club; it attracted a shocking amount of traffic, hosting eight thousand servicemen each year; two hundred on an average night and three times that number for special events.[114] Servicemen would not be the only people "hanging out" at the proposed club: sex workers and even local women dating airmen inevitably would be there too. However much Mayor Lunseth and the community council welcomed the military and wanted to support it, this was a bridge too far and before long the matter was dropped.

In Minot the problem of widespread prostitution was not theoretical. It was a long-established reality that grew more pervasive when the air force base arrived.[115] In 1960, US district attorney and NPL leader Robert Vogel launched an investigation into and a crackdown on the small city's reputation as a "center of vice"—illegal sales of alcohol, drug use, gambling, and prostitution. Convinced that publicizing the problem would help solve it, Vogel also assisted the Governmental Affairs Committee of the Minot Junior Chamber of Commerce ("Jaycees") in conducting its own inquiry. He reached out to newspapers to insist that they cover the story even if it meant "bad publicity" for the town. He provided the court records of dozens of sex workers as well as photographs of the houses, bars, and cafés where sex workers lived and worked, and transcripts of interviews with sex workers themselves.

This treasure trove of information revealed—doubtless to Vogel's horror—that Minot was a great place to engage in sex work. "Prostitute A" and "Prostitute B" (later identified by name in local news reports) both reported that sex work paid better in Minot than anywhere else in the Upper Midwest outside Sioux Falls. Their customers were hardly desperate or dangerous men; they were not even strangers. They were "high quality" men who either came from Minot or traveled from nearby Bismarck and surrounding towns. According to Prostitute B her customers included "businessmen, restaurant men, all kinds, men with pensions, men what [*sic*] were at times officials, things like that."[116] And, of course, they included men from the air force base, although Prostitute A said it was hard to tell how many airmen were among her clients since they rarely wore their uniforms and Prostitute B said she never asked to see credentials.[117]

Vogel's investigation revealed that the men and women of Minot shared a surprising number of views on sex and gender with the military. First of all, they told Vogel that they "had to have" a sex trade if they had the air force base.[118] They believed in other words that most men required, indeed deserved, sex; perhaps military men most of all. He accused the town of widespread apathy about the problem.[119] Furthermore so long as local white women were not involved in prostitution, the people of Minot did not perceive sex work as a threat to their community, homes, or families. Many sex workers, including both Prostitute A and Prostitute B, were from out of town—perhaps Chicago—and thus personified long-held ideas about women's demoralization in large urban settings. Moreover at least half of the sex workers in the area were African American, again demonstrating that they were not "from around here" and thus were not indicative of the corruption of their own daughters.[120] Aritha Robinson, for example, had been arrested in a raid on a two-story house in rural Ward County, where she and an unnamed man were caught "in assignation." She explained to the court that she was waiting for her husband, a member of the military, to return from his overseas deployment and could no longer afford the rent at the home they shared. Her new landlord claimed not to have any idea how she earned money.[121] While Aritha was found guilty, neither her "land-lord" nor her customer faced prosecution. Whatever personal problems Aritha faced, no one in Minot—perhaps not even Robert Vogel—felt responsible for her or worried about her future.

*   *   *

Between the end of World War II and the beginning of the war on terror, military and civilian life on the Northern Plains became integrated—demographically, politically, and culturally. By 2001 Rapid City, Grand Forks, and Minot were no longer just communities with military facilities; they were military communities. Accompanying this transformation were all the economic advantages their former leaders had imagined, and more.[122]

And yet, by the early twenty-first century, full integration with the military meant that the military's challenges became the region's too. Both Dakotas have a higher than average rate of veterans who have seen combat, including many younger veterans who have returned from tours in Iraq and Afghanistan.[123] These cohorts, as in the US as a whole, have higher than average rates of depression, posttraumatic stress disorder, and suicide.[124] Likewise, as military pay has not kept up with cost of living, despite the attractive benefits of service, some military families struggle with poverty; they qualify for SNAP, Head Start, and local social services.[125] That military families struggle to make ends meet is reflected in the built environment near all three bases, where fast food restaurants, pawn shops, and trailer parks dot the landscape. Drug use and addiction rates among active-duty and retired military have also risen, even at bases where the main mission is the maintenance of nuclear weapons.[126]

Women have paid an especially high price for the militarization of their communities. Both women in the military and the wives of military men and veterans face higher than usual rates of discrimination, sexual assault, and domestic violence. According to a 1993 survey, 12 percent of cadets at the Air Force Academy experienced sexual assault.[127] Meanwhile, female military spouses and partners nationwide experience a rate of spousal abuse two to five times higher than average. Throughout the 1990s the military considered domestic violence to be a private matter, a "relationship issue." Even twenty years later, a history of violence against women was not automatically considered a disqualification for military recruitment.[128] Finally sociologists have recently shown that veterans, especially those who have seen combat, have lower rates of criminality in general, but higher rates of sexual assault.[129] In 2002 an army recruiter in Rapid City, knowing that a white man accused of sexual assault on Native land could not be tried in state courts, arrived unannounced at a Lakota woman's home to perform a "required" physical examination. He then drove her to a remote area of the reservation and assaulted her.[130]

*   *   *

Despite all the challenges that integration with the military has brought, men and women on the Northern Plains remained wedded to the idea that bases are good for them and they are good for the bases. In 2018, the *Minot Daily News* could not say enough about the seamless bond between the "interrelated" civilian and military communities. The relationship was, above all, a two-way street: "There is a palpable appreciation for one another, affection and pride." The base was so important, the writer suggested, that "one wonders what the state of Minot would be were it not for the massive contribution from the base." He asked all readers to "thank any service member when the opportunity presents itself." He thanked the air force base for being "more than a good neighbor but rather an essential component of the heart of Minot."[131]

When they thought the air force might close Ellsworth in 2005, leaders of the Rapid City community went even further in their declarations of full integration with the military. Packing ten thousand residents into the Civic Center, speakers begged the Air Force Base Realignment Commission (BRAC) to change its mind.[132] They forthrightly denied that their community had ever protested against American entry into a war or ever worried about the culture of militarism that would accompany a permanent standing army. In fact in his introduction to the video that began the city's presentation to the Base Realignment Commission, Mayor Shaw said the very opposite:

> [South Dakota] is a place where men carve mountains and the stars and stripes and the eagles still fly. Through world wars and a history of conflict, they heeded the call of a nation, born from the simple premise that all are created equal, and that each shares unalienable rights worth defending at home and abroad. From the beaches of Normandy and the jungles of Vietnam to today's war on terrorism in Afghanistan and Iraq, South Dakotans have long served their country and still do so today surrounded by neighbors who welcome them home from their service, and in times of tragedy who never forget.[133]

Governor Mike Rounds also proclaimed the historic "love" that the people of South Dakota had "always" felt for the military. Needless to say, neither

Mayor Shaw nor Governor Mike Rounds mentioned their region's near-universal support for Populist anti-militarism in the 1930s. Nor did they recount the neglect, torture, and deaths of the pacifist Hutterite brothers, Joseph and Michael Hofer, in their basement cell inside Alcatraz in 1918. To save Ellsworth they needed to demonstrate and celebrate the kinship that had developed between the townspeople and the military. And that is exactly what they delivered, because after all it was the truth.

CHAPTER 5

SECRETS AND LIES

DURING THE HEIGHT OF the Cold War, all human beings lived close enough to nuclear weapons to be destroyed by them. Few lived as close as Shirley Norgard, however. She could see the launch control support building for a group of Minuteman-II intercontinental ballistic missiles (ICBMs) out the kitchen window of her family's farm near Cooperstown, North Dakota. Because the facility's underground launch control center directed a set of ten ICBMs, the Soviet military had almost certainly programmed the coordinates for her home into the navigation systems of similar weapons. Should nuclear war begin, everyone and everything inside and out would be instantly obliterated. Shirley knew this. But she was too busy to "get too excited about it."[1] At the end of the Cold War when the missiles around the Grand Forks Air Force Base were deactivated and the launch control support facility converted to a historic site, however, she "could almost brag" about having done her part. She liked having a base nearby and since many of her relatives had served in the military, she supported national defense wholeheartedly. Even so she admitted that the experience of having lived at "Ground Zero" of a possible nuclear war had left her having two "feelings at the same time": certain that the evils of communism had merited her risk and sacrifice but more suspicious of and irritated by the federal government than ever.[2] Nameless bureaucrats from Washington had taken her farm's "good land," paid far too little for it, and never given it back. Meanwhile, the secretive missileers were terrible neighbors, treating her family "like the enemy" and—in a grave breach of small-town etiquette—never even stopping by for a cup of coffee.[3]

The arrival of air force bases to the Northern Plains and the arrival ten to fifteen years later of the ICBMs had much in common. But living near a base and living near a bomb were also distinct experiences with distinct, albeit complementary, consequences. For those in the many communities adjacent to the missile fields, the secrecy, indeed hostility, of the national security state was not just frustrating, it was insulting and potentially lethal. It accentuated the distance between the government and civilians, even as the "nuclear mode of war" reduced the distance between soldiers and civilians.[4] For many Dakotans, the experience of living for decades in a potential "national sacrifice zone" reinvigorated their New Deal–era suspicions of the federal government.[5]

And yet it did not lead most Dakotans back to anti-militarism. Instead they forged a careful political path that disparaged big government and its bloated bureaucracy, while honoring the military and supporting increased funding for defense. Likewise they would come to see liberal protesters— antinuclear and others—as crazy at best, un-American at worst. In sum, men and women in nuclear country began to express, through lived experience, three of the most fundamental components of the ideology of the emerging New Right—even before they had the chance to cast a ballot for any of its candidates.

*   *   *

When the Department of Defense first considered putting air force bases on the Northern Plains in the 1940s, the idea that missiles could travel from one continent to another was but a glimmer in a military planner's eye. But after the Soviets detonated their own atomic bomb in 1949, the United States determined that developing an ICBM and then closing the (imagined) missile gap with the USSR was a top national priority.[6] First-generation ICBMs—the Atlas and Titan models, introduced in 1959 and 1962 respectively and housed in locations throughout the country—were far from perfect. They were cumbersome and time-consuming to launch.[7] The Titan was stored above ground and vulnerable to enemy attack. Both required liquid fuel that could only be stored in missiles for short periods. By 1961, however, scientists had discovered how to use solid rocket fuel. Missiles could be prefueled and launched from concrete underground "silos" "on a minute's notice." The "Minuteman" series of ICBMs evolved throughout the 1960s until the Minuteman III was introduced in 1971: a weapon 59.9 feet long, 79,000 pounds, with a 6,000 mile range, two or three warheads, and a price tag of $7 million each.[8]

Technical, geographic, and political rationales dictated the placement of over one thousand Minutemen on the Central and Northern Plains, with a disproportionate count of 450 in North and South Dakota. The semiarid climate that bedeviled white settlers was well-suited to the dynamics of the new solid rocket fuel that, in more humid regions, absorbed water vapor from the air. *New Yorker* writer Ian Frazier explained, "The easiest way to wreck a nuclear missile would be to keep it in a damp basement."[9] As it had for the B-1 bombers, the Northern Plains region afforded the missiles the best access to a flight path over the Arctic Circle. The region also had the advantage of being remote and relatively sparsely populated, should the Soviets launch an attack. James Mesco, a technical sergeant and historian for the Space Warfare Center in Colorado, explained, "It was best to place the missile sites as deep in the country as you could." This allowed for time to "retaliate before the first sites" were hit.[10] This notion—that some areas of the country might have to be sacrificed to keep others safe—was reinforced both by Robert McNamara's "no-cities" policy for targets and by navigation systems that allowed both sides to target each other's weapons directly.

Finally, military planners looked to the Northern Plains because Dakotans had fully committed themselves to militarization when the bases arrived and had remained steadfastly committed ever since. They were quite unlike the people of New England, for example, who had followed up their unsuccessful bids to stop the construction of Plattsburgh (NY) and Pease (NH) air force bases with a successful campaign to stop the installation of advanced ICBMs in New Hampshire and northern Massachusetts.[11] Before long, engineers would place missiles in geographically huge "fields" around the bases, with each missile at least three miles from any other, so the Soviets could not target them all at once. But dispersing the risk to weapons also dispersed the risk to humans. Each of the three missile fields in the Dakotas contained 150 missiles and covered up to 15,000 square miles, with a certain killing zone extending even farther than that. Most importantly, the Soviet missiles that targeted this huge area did not, indeed could not, distinguish between weapons systems they wished to obliterate and women standing at kitchen windows nearby. In fact, in the "nuclear mode of war,"

FIGURE 8. Minuteman II missile in its concrete silo, near Wall, South Dakota. Courtesy National Park Service.

the only distinction between the combatants at nearby bases and "noncombatant" civilians was that the combatants, once alerted, might have the chance to fly away to safety.[12]

From the beginning, nearly all Dakotans distinguished themselves from their New England counterparts with their enthusiasm for the Minuteman missiles.[13] ICBMs came first to South Dakota, where Senator Francis Case acted the part of local booster once again. Between 1960 and 1963 three Titan and 150 Minuteman missiles were deployed in the western portion of the state. From Case's perspective, housing the missiles was yet another opportunity for South Dakotans to demonstrate their commitment to the military and national defense. Case proclaimed in his constituent newsletter, "South Dakota has become a key area for defense planning in this day of long-range planes and rockets."[14] Case reflected many of his constituents' views that the increased status that would come with the missiles more than compensated for its concomitant risks. Suddenly a region whose citizens had once shunned the military was now the center of deterrence, the last best hope for peace in the world.

Even when early details about deployment were still hazy, Rapid City leaders welcomed the news of Minuteman deployment with hopeful expectations: Rapid City Chamber of Commerce president Tom Walsh predicted that the economic benefits of the Minuteman would be long-term. The *Rapid City Journal* ran a three-part series on the impact of Minuteman deployment. A January 17 story proclaimed: "Minuteman Promises Economic Lift."[15] Based on interviews with expectant real estate agents, labor groups, and construction firms, the paper asserted that "there is little doubt" the missile program "will herald vast economic benefits for the entire West River region, as well as Rapid City."[16] While no firm data could be ascertained and very few local companies had actually been contacted by the government, everyone interviewed agreed that good things were to come. If previous air force projects were any indication, some of that $60 million would surely go to local laborers and companies.[17]

The construction phase was likely to provide the largest number of jobs and the largest spike in new monies for the state. Indeed, defense officials estimated that at least four thousand construction workers would be paid more than $2.5 million per month in each missile field. Boeing alone was expecting to make $250,000 in local purchases each month.[18] Begun just months after the terrifying Cuban missile crisis, construction continued at a feverish pace: six or seven days a week, three shifts a day, even in the winter.[19] And all kinds of associated, if temporary, construction-related services went up to support the project, including trailer parks for visiting engineers; new housing for missile personnel; new, upgraded electrical service; and new road construction in the area of the missile fields.[20] Ted Hustead, a teenager at the time, remembered that the children of construction workers or Boeing engineers created a miniboom in the local schools. His father and grandfather, who owned the Wall Drug Store, benefited too, as laborers picked up breakfast—including free coffee and donuts—before work.[21]

Given the small size of the missile crews—just two missileers for each flight of ten weapons, plus a support staff of maintenance workers, a cook, and a security detail—local leaders likely knew ICBMs would never make a huge contribution to their budgets. But even so, they knew that as long as the missiles were in the fields, the air bases—a much larger source of revenue—could never be closed. In fact the Minutemen sounded so advantageous that letters streamed into Senator Case's offices from people in communities without a designated site, asking if he could get one for them. The people of Crocker, Crandell, Buffalo, Martin, and Lemmon all wondered how they could acquire a missile.[22]

In North Dakota, Senator Young championed the cause of acquiring Minuteman missiles just as he had championed the cause of acquiring air bases. He acted as a spokesman for the air force on all matters concerning the missiles and announced any new developments to the press. With the support of Governor William Guy, he worked to house as many of the missile wings in North Dakota as possible and, as a member of the Senate Appropriations Committee, scrutinized every detail of the process. In December of 1961, for example, he announced that he had convinced the Army Corps of Engineers to change gravel specifications so that the gravel available in the Grand Forks area would be suitable for the project. This decision, he announced in the *Grand Forks Herald*, "has almost assured construction of a Minuteman missile complex around Grand Forks Air Force Base."[23] Today, Senator Young's hometown, tiny LaMoure, North Dakota, honors his important contributions and "political clout" with a bronze plaque placed in front of an actual Minuteman II missile—the tallest structure in town.[24]

As it turned out, though, neither Case nor Young—nor anyone else in North or South Dakota—played any serious role in the decision to place three missile wings in the region. In a 2003 interview with Nathan Johnson of North Dakota State University, former governor William Guy remembered that neither he nor Milton Young had had any influence on the missile site selection process. While he had "close relations" with President Kennedy, Guy recalled, the missile selection process was "above the President."[25] Young also admitted that the military had greater authority than he did. He replied to a constituent, Mrs. Peter Peterson, who asked Young to ensure no more silos were placed in North Dakota, that missile location "was entirely a Defense Department decision."[26] If the senators did have influence, it was only in getting the air force to choose the state as a whole for installation. Other decisions were "above the president," and most certainly above farmers and ranchers who owned the land.[27]

Long before they arrived to "negotiate" with farmers and ranchers, military personnel had decided which landowners they needed to contact, which parcels of land they needed to acquire, how much they could pay for it (below market price), and where on that parcel the silo or launch control support building would go. When they had established this process in Montana in the late 1950s, they also learned they could simply condemn land they needed or take it by right of "adverse possession" if a landowner was reluctant to sell.[28] Years later local people remembered how this process worked. South Dakotan Ted Hustead recalled that "ranchers probably had lots of issues with having a missile in the middle of their field . . . but they were probably not asked, they were told."[29] Even so, Dakotans were not the type to give in or give up. In the Grand Forks Air Force Base battle over land, farmers had sought legal redress; in western South Dakota ranchers organized an association so that the military would be forced to negotiate with them as a group. The vast majority of landowners insisted that they supported the missile project as a whole but wanted a fair price for their land and a say in which specific sections would be used. Why did they have to use what Shirley Norgard called "good land" rather than "waste land?"[30] South Dakota rancher Gene Williams' father "offered to donate the ground to the air force if they would put it in the corner or basically just put it anywhere but in the dead center of the field."[31] Mostly they resented the way the military planners simply treated them as obstacles, rather than citizens. Gene Williams recalled that his father was even accused of being "unpatriotic" when he asked questions or made demands.[32]

When they realized they were "being told" not asked, Dakota landowners learned what city officials in Rapid City, Minot, Grand Forks, and all the other towns that had hoped for a base had learned a decade earlier. The warfare state, and particularly the national security state, was not the welfare state. The warfare state was opaque, secretive, and its budgets were not debated openly in election years. To the national security state, protecting the nation against both internal and external enemies was paramount. The concerns of local communities and property owners were not even close.

Once the "negotiations" for their land and subsequent disruptions of construction were over, thousands of men and women on the Northern Plains went back to the familiar hard work of farming and ranching. But now they cared for children, planted kitchen gardens, harvested crops, brought calves into the world, and repaired fences and machinery within sight of nuclear weapons. All the while, they knew that comparable Soviet missiles were targeting them. Like other Americans who lived near nuclear facilities, most Dakotans claimed that they had just "gone on with their business."[33] In 1988 farmer Tony Ziden reflected, "After you've walked around a barrel of dynamite for twenty years, and it doesn't hurt you, you sort of don't think about it."[34] Others relied on equal parts faith and what John Laforge called "bleak fatalism," saying that their lives and deaths were "'in God's hand'" and in any case, if a strike hit them, "'at least we would be the first to go.'"[35] As with the bases, improved access to consumer goods and chain stores made the dangerous conditions easier to swallow— sometimes quite literally. Tom Brusegaard, who lived on a small farm out- side Gilbert, North Dakota, recalled fondly when a Domino's pizza opened in Emerado, just a mile from the Grand Forks Air Force Base. At sixteen, if he got into his father's truck and floored it, he could be there in thirty minutes. For Tom, feeling that he was no longer just an isolated country boy with no access to the consumer goods so omnipresent in urban America made living with the fear of a Soviet nuclear strike almost worth it. [36]

But decades of living with the bomb on the Northern Plains had long- term consequences. First and foremost, it reanimated Dakotans' support for national defense as a whole, by putting their homes at its very center. By the 1990s, when the SALT I treaty demanded that some missiles be removed and destroyed, many Dakotans would brag that their sacrifice and vigilance had helped to win the Cold War.[37]

Even in the "difficult years of Vietnam" which included anti-war pro- tests at colleges and universities on the plains, most Dakotans believed it was important for the United States to have the strongest possible military, both to act as a deterrent and also to use in war. In 1983, ABC produced *The Day After*, a made-for-TV film about a Soviet attack on a missile field at Whiteman Air Force Base outside Lawrence, Kansas, and the widespread destruction it caused. Most Dakotans in the communities around the mis- sile fields hardly blinked. Rather than being convinced by the film that nuclear deterrence was suicidal, many Dakotans used it to confirm what they already believed: that the US needed to continue to improve its nuclear arsenal to deter just such an attack. Gene Kipp of Black Hawk, South Dakota, for example, wrote to the *Rapid City Journal* that nuclear deter- rence scared him more than the possibility of war. "The fact is for most victims of Soviet brutality, there is no day after," he wrote. "They're dead, victims of communist murderers. Given the Russian Penchant to bully and brutalize the weak by force, I personally think we need to strengthen and modernize our strategic and tactical nuclear weapons . . . until the Russians are motivated to understand serious mutual disarmament steps."[38] After the Cold War ended, missileer Wendy McNiel reflected that working in a

FIGURE 9. Snow removal around a Missile Launch Support Facility, North Dakota. Courtesy Orin G. Libby Manuscript Collection, University of North Dakota.

launch facility was "an invisible, thankless job. . . . [We were] almost invisible warriors." But she added that since World War III never came, that meant "we did our job."[39]

But before they could feel pride for doing their part, the culture of secrecy in the national security state made it impossible for Dakotans to know fully what their part was. They knew that sometimes the government lied to them, did not fulfill its promises, did not keep them informed, and was simply incompetent. It is even possible, for example, that many Dakotans did not know how many ICBMs were in the state. In the 1980s Nukewatch activists traveled more than thirty thousand miles over the Northern Plains simply to create a map of missile locations in each state. Said organizer John Laforge, "Even people living in the missile fields themselves" did not always know of their existence, unless they were "long-term residents who watched . . . the systems installed."[40] Nor did Dakotans know what the Minuteman missiles looked like. When the Minuteman on his land was taken out of the silo for repairs, Donald Lee of Devils Lake, North Dakota, was shocked. He told a reporter, "It's a huge thing. I never dreamt how deep that hole is. I've often thought about what would happen if I was on my tractor near the silo and that missile took off."[41] Even after seeing it, Lee could not have known exactly how much destruction it could cause. According to the antinuclear information group Jonah House, "A nuclear bomb launched from a Minuteman silo produces uncontrollable radiation, massive heat and a blast capable of vaporizing and leveling everything within a 50-mile radius. Outside the 50 square miles—extending into hundreds of miles—the blast, widespread heat, firestorms and neutron and gamma rays are intended to kill, severely wound and poison every living thing and causing long-term damage to the environment."[42] In this scenario, no preparations for evacuation or civil defense would be effective.[43] As Shirley Norgard asked, "What would there be to come out to?"[44] Even missileers were never given complete instructions for what to do after a Soviet attack.[45]

In the early 1960s, when civil defense preparations—however ineffective—were a national priority, some Dakotans wrote their senators to get more information about the missiles and what to do in an emergency. Mrs. Robert Lefevre, for example, wanted to know if it would still be safe to eat fruit and vegetables from the garden after the spring rains. Teacher Dennis Carter wanted information about how people would know when it was safe to come out of their fallout shelters after a nuclear attack.[46] Some letter writers also conveyed their growing suspicion that North Dakotans were not being told the whole truth. Harley Steffen of Garrison wanted to know why the missiles were only replaced at midnight and whether the water that drained from the silos onto his property might contaminate his crops. The senators had no answers. No one did. But in a side comment to Senator Karl Mundt about Mr. Steffen's observations, Senator Young remarked dismissively that "you get all kinds of weird stories about these missiles, usually from a small minority of people."[47]

However unfathomable, the risk from a Soviet strike paled in comparison to the risks Dakotans faced from accidents involving nuclear weapons—called "broken arrows." Just as the Minuteman was being developed and deployed on the Northern Plains, "broken arrow" incidents were increasing nationwide. Throughout the Cold War, air force pilots flew planes with nuclear bombs on board twenty-four hours a day, every day of the year, for immediate deployment if needed. Every crash or malfunction threatened an unintended release of weaponry. Among the most terrifying accidents was the explosion, ignited by a fuel leak, of a B-52 carrying two hydrogen bombs over Goldsboro, North Carolina. One of the bombs "went through all of its arming steps to detonate, and when that weapon hit the ground, a firing signal was sent."[48] It was kept from detonating by the actions of a single safety switch. Less potentially disastrous but still alarming was an incident at Vandenberg Air Force Base, California, in the 1960s, when an engine fell out of an Atlas missile and landed on a trailer home.[49]

An accident in a Titan missile silo buried under a dairy farm near Damascus, Arkansas, showed that it hardly took a catastrophe to create catastrophic possibilities. On September 18, 1979, during routine maintenance, a young worker dropped a tool down the missile shaft, which punctured the fuel tank. As the tank lost pressure, it might have collapsed on the warhead and caused a detonation. The control room crew was evacuated but the public was told nothing. With two airmen agreeing to stay on and try to open a vent in the facility, the weapons exploded and the warhead was released. When it was found in a nearby ditch, it had not detonated, for reasons unknown then or now. One of the airmen died and another was seriously wounded.[50] Of thirty-two broken arrows verified by the Department of Defense, six included the loss of nuclear weapons that still have not been found or recovered.[51]

While not officially classified as a "broken arrow," a serious accident took place at South Dakota's Ellsworth Air Force Base in 1964 and was kept from public knowledge for more than a decade.[52] Inside the Minuteman I silo near Vale, South Dakota, an airman used the wrong tool to take out a fuse on a security panel, causing a short circuit.[53] The electrical charge resulted in a huge explosion that detached the warhead from the missile. The warhead bumped and bounced its way down the missile shaft to the bottom floor. An off-duty airman, Bob Dirksing, recalled: "It could've been a lot worse. If the short had gone to the missile instead of to the retrorockets . . . the boys who were down there would've been fried."[54] Once it was established that the warhead was safe, the group had to improvise a procedure for bringing the warhead up the shaft and sending it for repairs. In the end, a young airman, Bob Hicks of San Antonio, Texas, came up with a system of nets, cables, and mattresses to lift the warhead very, very slowly out of the silo into the back of a truck. Hicks also drove the truck back to Ellsworth the next day, since it seems no one else on site "knew how."[55]

The list of "almost accidents" seared into missileers' memories is far longer than the list of actual accidents. Most of them were likely never reported up the chain of command, much less released to the public. Louis Brothag, a maintenance worker in the Grand Forks missile wing, recalled that one day in 1967 or 1968, he received a "frantic call" from a launch officer on alert. "He said his missile was trying to launch." This was such a dangerous situation that more senior maintenance crews were called and Brothag listened in on his radio. "Holy mackerel!" he heard one man shout. "It was a mouse!" As it turned out, mice liked to make their nests under the large doors that protected the missiles. On this particular day, "A mouse had gotten into the missile and was chewing on the wires, and shorted the wires out, and started the launch sequence." After that Brothag's duties included killing as many mice as he could around the facility.[56] South Dakota missileer David Blackhurst recalled the day when command and control officers at North American Aerospace Defense Command (NORAD) headquarters in Colorado Springs put his team on alert and even commanded him to put his key in the ignition switch and be ready to launch his Minuteman missile. Fortunately air force officials soon determined that rather than a Soviet attack on the horizon, they were "probably just seeing the moon."[57]

While they may not have known everything about the risks they took living in a missile field, Dakotans knew full well how the air force's culture of secrecy affected their day-to-day lives. Dakotans recoiled from the pervasive culture of secrets and lies that they persistently encountered in nuclear country. And they did not just live next to underground bombs; they lived next to underground bombers. They knew that missileers acted like men on "foreign soil" who lived in a "world of their own."[58] What they could not have known was that the isolated and cramped quarters of the launch control centers, overseen by the notoriously exacting Strategic Air Command (SAC), was in fact a world, if perhaps not foreign, unlike any Dakotans had encountered before.

To some local people, perhaps especially farm women like Shirley Norgard and her friends who worked in their homes during the day while their husbands were in the fields, the missileers, guards, and maintenance workers did not make friendly neighbors. They used their property for strange drills and procedures without announcing or explaining them.[59] When they brought a sick or injured serviceperson to the local clinic, they acted as if they were "protecting government property." Helicopters flew so low they rattled the dishes on the shelves and disturbed children's naps.[60] And while they occasionally helped to repair a fence, they also occasionally left a gate open allowing cattle to go free.[61] And they certainly never bothered to stop in and introduce themselves as most country neighbors did.[62]

To be fair, Dakotans could not have fully understood how the nature of the missileers' work and the rigidity of their specific command (SAC) contributed to their odd and aloof behavior. A former Minot Air Force Base missile crew commander, Mark Sundlov, blamed any unfriendliness on the relentless workload, all of which had to be completed after long drives—sometimes as much as three hours—over rough gravel roads in all kinds of weather. Once on site, the crew spent twenty-four simultaneously boring and terrifying hours in a confined space fifty feet below the surface.[63] Furthermore, they operated under the supervision of a notoriously strict command. Each day's series of routine procedures, tests, spot inspections, and checklists, as well as ongoing psychological monitoring, pop quizzes on rules and regulations, and health assessments reflected the seriousness with which SAC performed its duties. There was no room for even the smallest deviation from perfect performance. Michael Brown recalled, SAC's golden rule was: "To forgive is human, but it is not SAC's policy."[64] Missileers did not chat with the neighbors unless it was on their checklist. And it was not.

All missile personnel were expected to maintain site security under all circumstances. They were, after all, guarding one of the most powerful weapons on earth. They were required to keep all unauthorized people out, no questions asked. Former missile instructor Michael Brown remembered that one day a US Marshal arrived without proper paperwork and tried to get access. "I told security if he came on site to shoot him," he said. "You didn't play games out there. Shoot first and ask questions later. . . . They would be right to shoot you if you were in the wrong place."[65] Tim Pavek remembered that if a maintenance worker or any other air force representative—even someone they knew well—failed to provide the proper authentication code, military security would "jack him up": "get [him] down on the ground spreadeagle," search him, and send him "probably [on] a trip back to the base."[66] Missileers were even told to consider members of their own unit as potential security risks. David Blackhurst explained that one reason a missileer was required to carry .38 pistols when they were on alert was so that if their partner "freaked out, I was supposed to use it on him. . . . In the air force we didn't attempt to wound somebody, it was shoot them to kill them."[67]

But missileers, in charge of guarding so many military secrets, had a few of their own. The first was fairly well-known: most missileers did not want to be there. Some missileers would eventually retire in the Dakotas and call it home. But when they were first stationed in the region, most couldn't wait to leave. In Wade Bertrand's security training class, for example, recruits could pick five of 150 locations for assignment. None chose Grand Forks or Minot "but there were 90 openings there so that's where we went."[68] Southerners were unaccustomed to temperatures that dipped to minus forty degrees; those from outside the plains were shocked by the flat, treeless landscape.[69] Personnel from larger cities struggled to adapt to small-town culture.[70] Cleveland native Chad Jones remembered one night he spent on alert outside Grand Forks Air Force Base so well that years later it still made him angry: the local television channel had cancelled an NBA game to show "the class B girls' [state] basketball championship." He kicked the console so hard he thought he had broken it.[71]

The second secret was that few had wanted to be missileers in the first place. When Captain Marion Dinka, who was fluent in several languages and had hoped to work in intelligence, learned she had been assigned to missileer work, she cried. "I didn't put it anywhere on my dream sheet, I'll be honest."[72] Air force recruits perceived that missileers fell far below pilots in status and prestige, making it more difficult to get promotions or other recognitions.[73] And they were right: pilots were truly the "cream of the crop" across the armed services.[74] At the missile sites around Ellsworth Air Force Base, two popular songs made the point. One, set to the tune of "The Man Who Never Returned," featured a missileer who went out to the site and "never returned." The lyrics to the second read: "The pilots get all the gravy; the missileers get all the grit."[75] But the work itself was also a problem. Nearly all missileers felt pride in the role they played keeping peace between the US and USSR during the Cold War and were prepared to follow their orders to launch a missile.[76] But it was hard to "feel good about a job where, by definition, success meant you never actually did the job you were trained to do."[77]

For many missileers, then, the best way to get through the stress, boredom, and disappointment of a twenty-four-hour work cycle and a four-year deployment was to add some levity. Allowed to paint murals on the doors and walls, they chose comic book characters or other icons of popular

FIGURE 10. Captain Mark Wilderman at the commander's console in the
Delta-01 Launch Control Center near Ellsworth Air Force Base, South Dakota.
Courtesy Mark Wilderman Collection, National Park Service, Minuteman
Missile Historic Site.

and military culture. When officials were not around, they also cloaked
their doubts, fears, and frustrations about their work in jokes. When rabbits
or tumbleweeds set off alarms, security guards would sometimes say, "Off
to find the Commies!"[78] Similarly, missileers sometimes kidded among
themselves asking, "if a [Soviet] bomb hit us, would it bounce off the walls
or just come through 'nothing but net'?"[79] In that vein, the worst situation
was pulling alert duty with a guy who took the job too seriously. Dennis
Almer and his wife remembered a neighbor who was in charge of spot
inspections and did "everything by the book." All spot inspectors had been
"handpicked by the wing commander. That went right to their head."[80] In
1997 some of the missiles were pulled from their silos and deactivated and
the silos destroyed. The last alert teams signed their names and left mes-
sages that reflected their ambivalent feelings. One said, "Mission Accomplished, Gone Home." Others said, "Good Riddance."[81]

    Other kinds of secrets were held more tightly, contributing to the mis-
sileers' distinctive subculture. Most members of the missile crews, other

than the missileers, were very young—some still eighteen—and as a former crew commander from Minot Air Force Base admitted, they were often "very nervous" about their serious responsibilities. They were also away from home for the first time and unaccustomed to living with several other men in close quarters. Michael Brown remembered having to settle a dispute between enlisted men and the cook about what to watch on the only television: cartoons or football. He told them just to turn it off.[82] A third problem that accompanied youth new to the military was an all-encompassing lack of status. Second Lieutenant Bob Hicks, the hero of the Vale, South Dakota, accident, had just turned twenty. When he approached a high-ranking officer with his idea to use nets and mattresses to move the missile, he was summarily dismissed. "Airman, when I want an opinion from you, I'll ask you."[83] Fortunately for all South Dakotans that day, the officer relented and let a young man make a suggestion.

An underground launch control center, like a submarine, was a tightly enclosed, cramped space with only two men on alert at any one time; the above-ground support building was not much more spacious for the greater number of staff.[84] As a result, missileer culture contained both formal and informal controls on sexual activity and expression. Gay men served in SAC's missile wings, of course; in fact, to begin his path-breaking 1993 work on gays in the military, Randy Shilts declared something that may have shocked the readers: "Gay air force personnel have staffed missile silos in North Dakota."[85] Furthermore, servicemen who might not have identified as gay nevertheless have long found opportunities for playful gender transgression, like dressing in drag for a skit or joke.[86] Given the imperatives of the Cold War, however, when surveillance of gays in the military and other areas of employment was at its height, all airmen were carefully watched for any signs that they were not "real men."[87] Missileers and other launch staff thus understood that the public performance of heterosexual masculinism was a requirement of their work. Sometimes these performances overlapped with the young servicemen's need to feel more at home in a strange place, to push the limits on protocol, or to bring levity to an alternately stressful and dull job.[88] But however enjoyable, humorous, or seemingly ordinary, these performances were serious business. They were so serious, in fact, that, even years later, missileers refused to tell all but the blandest stories about what happened "on alert," maintaining the crew's secrets and continuing the performance long after the official surveillance had ended.

The most obvious ways in which military men, like many civilians, performed their heterosexuality was through humor—the familiar use of sexual images, bathroom jokes, sexual banter, homophobic teasing, and misogynist references. Some of this started at the top, modeled by boot camp officers, trainers, and supervisors—not to mention coaches, teachers, scout leaders, and other men whom the missileers had encountered before they had enlisted. When he was an instructor, lecturing missileer candidates, for example, Michael Brown gave the missiles female names, like "Miss Isle" and "Farrah Fawcett," to hold his students' attention. Later he acknowledged, with a twinge of nostalgia, that in an "integrated [male and female] class, I could not have done so."[89] And, as military men had for many decades, missileers brought visual imagery of their girlfriends, wives, favorite pinups, and sex workers with them to their workplaces. Even years later, Dennis Almer's wife remembered the fact that the men at his launch facility had a "*Playboy* drawer" and that they talked about it "all the time."[90]

The missileers also performed heteronormative camaraderie in ways that provided opportunities to blur the lines between permissible and impermissible behavior. Again and again, missileers reminisced about how "famous" their crews had been for their "sense of humor," "pranks," and "practical jokes." They were especially effective when "new guys" arrived. Dennis Almer thought many new missileers took their jobs—and themselves—too seriously.[91] A frightening prank might help put them in their place. But sometimes they pulled pranks on officers too. David Blackhurst recalled when a flight security supervisor did not have his identification and the young security guys "made him lay down in a mud puddle."[92] "If they are going to play funny games with us, we are going to play them with them too."[93] And yet, despite a remarkable unanimity that "pranks" were part of the launch control culture, the examples missileers provided to their interviewers years later were remarkably tame. Mark Sundlov admitted to teasing guys in their pajamas for "fighting a war in bunny slippers," "leaving little surprises for the oncoming crew, including putting all the tiny pieces of paper that gathered in the bottom of a shredder into their blankets" and "killing the breaker on the elevator."[94] Other pranks undoubtedly were less tame than these junior-high-style hijinks. But those details we will never know. When asked years later to describe their best pranks, some missileers refused to answer, explaining that "some things you don't talk about."[95] When asked to tell stories about "hanging out with the guys," Dennis Almer laughed it off instead—"I'll just write you a memo on that"—and went on to the next question.[96]

Inside the tight quarters of the two-man launch control centers that the air force called "no lone zones," where each missileer carried a pistol in case the other "freaked out," missileers understood that no authentic demonstration of intimacy would be tolerated.[97] They remembered these "rules" even years later. Aaron Bass and Chad Smith had served together on an alert team for several years and were reunited at the opening of the Ronald Reagan Minuteman Historic Site in 2009. During their interview, they chose to sit so far apart on the interviewee's couch that they appeared on the very outside edges of the video frame. Even so, they frequently reached over and tapped each other's shoulders as if to emphasize a point. But when asked about their longtime friendship, Bass downplayed it: "Well, we lived in the same apartment complex and went out and got stupid together, if that's what you mean." As the interview ended and the men were parting ways, Bass taunted Smith. "Are you going to cry?" Smith replied, "That's a negative. Not going to cry."[98] Dennis Almer likewise struggled when he was asked to discuss his "relationship" with an instructor who had become a close friend: "Relationship? Relationship? That's a kind of a tough word. [long pause] You look out for each other; you spend so much time together. You sleep with each other. Not in the same bed of course!"[99]

In these isolated and highly masculinized spaces, officials tasked with the integration of women missileers in the 1980s and early 1990s, were completely flummoxed.[100] A series of studies and reports outlined the potential pitfalls: What would air force wives think as they sat at home while their husbands were on alert with a female missileer? What would happen if a female missileer was promoted before her male counterpart? Would it hurt his morale? What if a female missileer were menstruating, pregnant, had recently miscarried, or given birth? Could she be counted on to be "emotionally stable?"[101] And would the vibrations and constant loud noises in the missile cause a miscarriage? Would the propulsion fumes cause birth defects? [102] Clearly, these "problems" focused on the negative effects of gender integration on men and their families, or on unborn children, rather than on women themselves. Beneath them all was a fear that those spaces would by definition be domesticated if women worked there, and perhaps the men would be too.[103] For many former missileers, having women at the launch centers would change everything—especially what Dennis Almer said were the "best parts of the job."[104] Even years later, when

FIGURE 11. Three airmen relaxing at the Ellsworth AFB military gas station after pulling a twenty-four-hour shift at the Echo missile launch facility. Courtesy Mark Wilderman Collection, National Park Service, Minuteman Missile Historic Site.

Wade Bertrand visited the Ronald Reagan Historical Site where he had once worked, he couldn't imagine why there was a women's bathroom.[105]

One last secret might have been the most important of all. It might have sealed the sequestration of missile crews from their Dakotan neighbors. As Shirley Norgard had suspected when her young daughter rode her bike up to a station guard and he pointed his rifle at her, or Gene Williams' mother had understood when she offered a missileer a glass of lemonade on a hot day and was reprimanded for doing so because his commanding officer worried she might have drugged it, missileers did consider local people to be the enemy—or at least potential enemies.[106] Tim Pavek admitted that missileers were trained to consider anyone—their crewmate on alert, an unknown visitor, a girl on a bike—a potential threat to national security and, when in doubt, to kill them. Furthermore they believed the threat of spies or just "convenient idiots" in the community to be "very real." They were taught that if a Russian agent was in the area, he or she could put together small snippets of information—overheard at the bar, in a restaurant, in a beauty salon—and put them together to discern top secret information about missiles.[107] Consequently missile crews were told to say nothing about their work to anyone—even their wives. When interviewed many years later, missileers and other launch center staff were still uneasy talking about their work. More than one said "maybe I shouldn't have said that" or asked, "is that thing [the audio or video recorder] on?" Their unease betrayed the intensity of their training to maintain strict confidentiality and view all others with suspicion. If Dakotans felt "this feeling of invasion and abuse of individual property," they were not far off.

*   *   *

When the Reagan administration advocated for a renewed nuclear buildup, the risks Dakotans had lived with for years suddenly seemed more immediate. At that point Dakotans, from local colleges and universities, liberal political organizations, and social justice–focused church groups joined the growing international antinuclear movement. They worked with Nukewatch to create a complete map of the missile fields, gathered for annual Easter vigils and scores of other protests, and launched an innovative multidisciplinary Peace Studies program at the University of North Dakota.[108] By then, Marvin Kammerer, a rancher near Ellsworth, who had once thought the Soviets were a legitimate threat but now considered his own government to be a greater one, took bolder action.[109] He joined forces with the American Indian Movement (AIM) and environmentalist groups to protest proposed uranium mining and the deployment of the new MX missile in the Black Hills. He helped organize the 1980 Black Hills International Survival Gathering that brought together twelve thousand people of different racial and religious backgrounds to protest what they believed could be "the annihilation of the species." Later he advocated reducing defense spending to end the Farm Crisis and used the family farm movement's new motto: "Farms not Arms."[110]

But Kammerer and other peace activists acknowledged that most Dakotans did not participate in these protests, were not interested in creating a multiracial liberal coalition, and derided the activists as "fruit loops."[111] A large majority of men and women on the Northern Plains had voted for

Reagan. As we will see, by the presidential election of 1980, they had determined that, despite the concerted efforts of anti-war protesters and their local champion, Senator George McGovern, to revive the tradition of anti-militarism, the region's commitment to all forms of national defense had come to stay. By the end of the Cold War fifteen years later, North and South Dakota would have become one of the most politically and culturally conservative regions in the country, with a reanimated antipathy toward big government and liberal elites. Their life in nuclear country had more than a small amount to do with it. Many Dakotans felt that the New Right's critique of "big government" together with its aggressive support for the military, hostility to leftist protest movements, and embrace of cultural conservatism echoed almost perfectly their lived experiences since the arrival of the military. They had been asked to give up land and any easements to that land. They had been paid too little for both and had had no say in the placement of the missiles. They had been made targets of annihilation and objects of sacrifice, and all the while the federal government had met their inquiries and concerns with a "wall of silence."[112] They had been treated suspiciously and dismissively by the isolated and sometimes disgruntled missileers, who themselves had developed an all-encompassing hypermasculine subculture. The "forgotten soldiers of the Cold War," Dakotans believed that the "brass" in Washington, DC, "never gave us a second thought."[113]

Dakotans began to blame the federal government for the problems that developed in nuclear country almost as soon as construction of the missile sites began—two years before Ronald Reagan, in support of Barry Goldwater's 1964 presidential campaign, gave his first national speech assailing big government. The projects were mammoth in scale: Curtis Anderson, an engineer from the Twin Cities, remembered that 350 men were housed in temporary trailers, four men to a trailer, outside rural Adams, North Dakota. Over 1,000 men worked on the Minuteman construction sites with fatalities as high as one death per month.[114] Unsurprisingly the projects involved plenty of headaches for local residents. Contractors had to truck in large numbers of workers and enormous quantities of materials to build so many silos and launch support facilities so quickly. The *Grand Forks Herald* estimated that "a road eight feet wide and three inches thick could be laid from Grand Forks to Williston with the concrete used. . . . [There is] enough steel . . . to manufacture 40,000 automobiles."[115] To handle the heavy equipment and service the silos, road crews graveled and upgraded three hundred and forty miles of roads. Meanwhile landowners endured the constant noise and light pollution of twenty-four-hour work cycles and sometimes had trouble accessing their own property. They also noted the high number of out-of-state workers, even though the air force had promised to give priority to local firms and workers.[116]

In some cases these short-term disruptions became long-term problems. North Dakota senator Milton Young received several letters from constituents about road conditions long after construction ended. Although roads were meant to be upgraded for the use of heavy equipment, some North Dakotans saw local roads used and, consequently, damaged without repair. Mr. and Mrs. Nels Peterson of Petersburg lived within two miles of a missile site; gravel trucks used many roads in their township and the government had not replaced the gravel.[117] Several other families had problems with water drainage. In 1965, the air force dug a huge ditch on George Johannsen's farm in Parshall, North Dakota, across the road from a missile site. Trouble was, by 1967, the government still had not filled it in. The ensuing water on Johannsen's land made it impossible for him to cultivate fifteen acres of corn. Then, wild oats went to seed on the same acreage and it cost him $75 to spray.[118] Young assured several constituents that the air force would provide funds for extra road repair, but the problems remained unsolved. Melvin Jensrud wrote as late as 1970 that "I can get no satisfaction as to who will fix these roads. . . . These missile trucks use all of our roads not only the designated ones. Can you help us with monies and designating who is responsible so they can quit passing the buck?"[119]

Landowners also complained about the amount of money the government was spending on the Minuteman project, particularly considering how little they had received for their land. To Gene Williams, the whole thing sometimes seemed like a "boondoggle." He described the government's new radar system installed in the late 1980s that cost "I don't know how many millions of dollars." At first they did not install it properly; then they spent more money to extend fence lines to make it work. Three years later they deactivated it entirely. Gene continued, "Well, I guess things change and everything but good grief you could have saved ten, fifteen million dollars."[120] And everyone on the Northern Plains knew the story of the Safeguard Complex, a six-billion-dollar anti–ballistic missile system installed outside of Nekoma, North Dakota, that was abandoned in 1974 within twenty-four hours of its completion.[121] The General Accounting Office tried to explain why the cost had skyrocketed: along with inflation, the bill included $112 million in "excess materials," $481 million in "lost effort," and $697 million in "schedule changes."[122] Embarrassed by his support of a similar defunct project, the mayor of Conrad, Montana, wore a sign around his neck: "Don't even mention ABM [anti–ballistic missile system] in my presence again."[123]

Dakotans responded even more vociferously when the government acted both wastefully and incompetently. On August 14, 1968, congressional representatives, members of the press, military brass, and local men and women gathered near Michigan, North Dakota, for a test firing of a Minuteman II. The "missile fizzled" and the launch failed—just as it had twice before, on October 19, 1966, and October 29, 1966. The *Grand Forks Herald*—a longtime defender of the military bases—initially worried that this setback might delay production of the Minuteman III missiles headed for the state. But its editors still reminded the government of the promise implicit in nuclearization: Dakotans who had accepted "without complaint" their "roles as the nuclear stronghold of the free world's defense arsenal" needed reassurance that they had done so for a "good reason" and not as guinea pigs in some kind of fatally flawed experiment.[124]

The *Devils Lake Journal* (ND) asked more pointedly, "Is this Protection?"[125] In a letter to Young, Lawrence Woehl of Carrington was also direct. "Well, with three tries I'm convinced that [Defense Secretary] Mr. McNamara sold the nation an Edsal [*sic*] for defending the nation. . . . They may be able to sell [their] slop to somebody else but not to me and a lot of thinking people."[126] After years of living with bases, bombs, and bombers, "thinking" Dakotans had learned—or, more precisely, remembered—not to trust the government, its promises, and its many outside experts, and certainly not to think the government had the best interests of rural people in mind. By 1968, Dakotans smelled the rotted food and spoiled milk of slop, and weren't afraid to say so.

*   *   *

Gene Williams understood exactly why the experience of nuclearization had led him to hold what may seem, to those outside the region, contradictory political views: ardent support for the military and an equally strong rejection of the federal government. He explained that, while some of the missileers "acted like jerks," he believed that they were just "fresh-faced kids" sent to what they must have thought was "God's forsaken half-acre."[127] The air force itself was a great organization; he was proud to have found a way "to do what was right for the country" as his relatives who had fought in World War II had done. "We are extremely lucky in this country that we have the military, the people in the military that we do have," he said. "We have the finest military in the world."[128] Whatever went wrong in the missile fields was the government's fault, plain and simple. Bureaucrats, Williams said, always proclaimed: "Trust us; we're the government and everything's fine." But the closer to Washington, DC, that any official lived, "the less he actually knew about the region's problems." In fact, in his view, there were only three things Americans could count on from their government: paperwork, waste, and being treated like a "peasant."[129] Over the course of the Cold War, Williams believed, his government had "fallen into the same trap that it's supposedly defending us from," resembling Soviet-style totalitarianism more every year.[130]

To Gene Williams and thousands of others on the plains at the end of the Cold War, the United States government was no longer credible, accessible, or even recognizable. The damage the warfare state and the nuclear weapons industry had done to ordinary Americans' faith in government was greater than anything the Soviets could ever have accomplished, short of nuclear Armageddon. We live with its consequences still.

CHAPTER 6

GEORGE MCGOVERN'S "LOST WORLD"

TWO THINGS STOOD OUT in James Moon's memory of his time serving a weapons mechanic in the 604th Special Operations Squadron in Vietnam, far from his home in North Dakota. He could never forget the sudden terror he felt when the North Vietnamese fired rockets and mortars at his Bien Hoa base. With no time to get to a bunker, Moon and his buddies hid under their bunks. But Moon also recalled the anger he felt "a couple of times" when he arrived back in the states "in uniform." As he got off the plane at various West Coast airports—"you know: 'Frisco, L.A., Denver"—he was "hollered at" by protesters. He tried not to dwell on either experience. He was no longer at war, no longer hiding under a bunk, and no longer forced to interact face-to-face with liberals in coastal cities. Once he was back home on the Northern Plains, people honored him for his service. He explained, "When you got into North Dakota, South Dakota, Nebraska, you didn't have to put up with that kind of thing [antiwar protests and hostility toward veterans] because people aren't that way in this part of the country."[1]

Moon is far from the only Dakotan who believes that no one on the Northern Plains ever "hollered at" a Vietnam veteran or protested the war. The 2018 Prairie Public Broadcasting series, *Prairie Memories: The Vietnam Years*, included interviews with only a handful of protesters among the dozens they collected.[2] Likewise, a middle school history curriculum published by the State Historical Society of North Dakota states flatly that anti-war protests in the state were "quieter than in other places" because the citizens had a heritage of "deep-rooted faith and patriotism."[3] In South Dakota elected officials got into the revisionist act as well. In 2001 Republican governor William Janklow dedicated the South Dakota World War II memorial only a few days after 9/11, using the event to declare the complete failure of 1960s liberal ideas. "There are no flags burning today," Janklow said. "No one is ashamed to talk about prayer in schools."[4] In 2010 Governor Mike Rounds encouraged South Dakotans not just to revise but to forget the difficult history of the war.[5]

Even if he was wrong about protesters, James Moon was right about the conservatism that differentiated the people of the Northern Plains from Americans in more urban parts of the country. Dakotans had long held right-leaning and increasingly evangelical Christian beliefs as well as culturally conservative views on race, gender, and sexuality. Since the 1940s, they had embraced anti-communism, welcomed the militarization of their communities, and adjusted—albeit grudgingly—to the nuclearization of their land. These experiences combined to make Dakotans far more likely to support a military effort in Vietnam than other Americans. Nevertheless, in a late resurgence of the regional tradition of Populist anti-militarism, some Dakotans, including veterans, questioned the war, the corporations that profited from it, and the government bureaucracies that conducted it. Tens of thousands of Dakotans served; more than four hundred died. But some found ways to avoid the draft or find a safer deployment. Others protested the war on local college campuses or embraced a countercultural lifestyle. A handful made veterans feel unwelcome when they returned home by stigmatizing them or the war itself. The truth is that Dakotans were deeply and, at least in the war's early years, nearly evenly divided about Vietnam. Those divisions gave them far more in common with people in "'Frisco, L.A., and Denver" than they recognized at the time or choose to remember today.

And yet, however real, this world—what Josh Garrett-Davis calls the "world of George McGovern"—was also doomed.[6] It was doomed to be ignored, revised, or erased by conservative politicians, historians, historical societies, and documentary filmmakers in the twenty-first century. But it was also doomed in its own moment. As the war dragged on, protests around the region and the country grew in size and vehemence and left-leaning, often young, Dakotans broadened their concerns from the war to the American social order as a whole. In counterprotests, letters to editors, and votes at the ballot box, conservative Dakotans matched and then surpassed their liberal neighbors' outrage. They felt, as Jefferson Cowie has put it, that all the social changes that accompanied the war tore America "in too many directions at once."[7] And these disruptions continued even after American troops left Vietnam. In the end, the tragedy of Vietnam coupled with the rise of freedom movements, the shock of several major Supreme Court rulings, and the seeming collapse of American military and economic supremacy fueled a conservative backlash that swept prominent Democrats out of office across the country.

In South Dakota conservatives targeted the most nationally prominent liberal Democrat of all. They did not hold back, successfully associating him not just with anti-war groups but with the increasingly regionally unpopular civil rights and feminist movements, too. By 1981 the world of George McGovern and the near-century of Populist anti-militarism at its foundation was lost, once and possibly for all. Thanks in part to the emerging hegemony of the Rural New Right on the Northern Plains, it was also well on its way to being forgotten.

*　*　*

Most young men from the Dakotas who served in Vietnam did so because they believed in the war, defeating communism, and serving their country. They may have also welcomed the opportunity to leave home and "become a man." They likely knew, furthermore, that the draft was structured in a way that allowed for creative strategies for deferment, particularly for the affluent.[8] But for many young men in rural America, "working the system" to get out of going to Vietnam was not only impractical, it was unthinkable. In his small town in the Sand Hills of Nebraska, for example, Tom Hager remembered, dodging the draft through some "maneuver . . . would not have crossed anyone's mind."[9] Of course, that was not entirely true. Crossing the northern Minnesota border into Canada absolutely occurred to author Tim O'Brien. But he went to Vietnam anyway. As much as he feared the Viet Cong, he feared the condemnation of local people in his hometown of Worthington, Minnesota, even more. He could imagine them talking in the local café: "some old farmer in my town saying to another farmer, 'Did you hear what the O'Brien kid did? The sissy went to Canada.'"[10] Hundreds of miles from the Northern Plains, in the isolated mining town of Morenci,

Arizona, nine young men enlisted together on July 4, 1966. "We were small-town people," one recalled. "We still believed in mom and apple pie. It was part of my duty as a man, growing up, to join the service. They didn't have to draft us."[11] Only two returned.

Many young men from the Dakotas were also the kind the government "did not have to draft." South Dakota veteran John Sweet's youth mirrored Tom Brokaw's world of "khaki brown and olive green" almost exactly, from Boy Scout troops to American Legion–sponsored activities. He recalled that, "Growing up in rural South Dakota with a strong deference for authority and a patriotic spirit . . . the thought of going to Canada or even voicing objection to the war was not even considered."[12] Fellow South Dakotan Mark Young had little choice but to go to the war. "I couldn't imagine taking off for Canada—I'd had five uncles in the service in World War II."[13] Richard Decker called those values and traditions "Midwestern farm ethics," saying, "One of these ethics . . . was that everything worth having had to be earned . . . what we have to enjoy as a country and government was fought for and preserved by the citizens of each generation."[14]

Despite these cultural and familial pressures, some young Dakota men and their families had reservations. Anthony Rangel confessed, for example, "I really did not want to go [to Vietnam] but I went to serve my country, which my father had done in World War Two."[15] Mark Young also admitted that he had "no desire to continue a [family] tradition of military service."[16] Sometimes it was not until they said their last goodbyes that some young men realized serving in the war might have terrible consequences. "There weren't any smiling faces to send off the draftees" from Custer County Courthouse in 1968, Young recalled. "My parents, Bill and Lorene . . . along with some Knights of Columbus . . . looked seriously concerned."[17]

Some families in the Dakotas acted on their concerns by encouraging their sons to find the safest possible way to serve. Some reasoned, for example, that avoiding the infantry was the best approach. Timothy Werlinger wanted to follow in his father's footsteps and join the marines. But Tim's father told Tim that if he joined the marines, "he'd shoot [me] in the head to save the Viet Cong the trouble. . . . 'You have two choices, Navy or Air Force.'"[18] George Shurr's parents advised his older brother to sign up early, avoid the draft which often led to combat assignments, and try to use his skills as a professional photographer to stay out of harm's way. Tragically, their strategy failed.[19]

Dakotans who served sometimes did not begin to express reservations about the war—or, more precisely, the government that was conducting it—until they were actually in Vietnam. Their frustrations resembled the views held by Dakotans who lived in communities around missile fields during the Cold War era. Rather than fault the military for the fear and frustration associated with living near a nuclear weapon, these Dakotans accused the federal government of being secretive, dishonest, overly bureaucratic, and incompetent. Soldiers in Vietnam did much the same. Some of the problems they encountered with government bureaucracy were funny—in retrospect. Bill Anderson laughed recalling how the draft board had promised he would have "a long time" to get ready to go; he was on his way in four days.[20] Other errors were a matter of life and death. Andrew Maragos served as a medical service corps supply officer sent into Vietnamese villages to provide medical care. Although the government had designated these areas as safe, he quickly learned that "no place in Vietnam was safe."[21] Even military hospitals might not be safe: after sustaining a life-threatening injury, Bill Rose had been "green-tagged": triaged into the medical bureaucracy's "don't waste your time" category. Fortunately two "corpsmen with sixteen weeks of medical training" ignored regulations and performed surgery.[22]

The later they served during the war, the more soldiers from the Dakotas blamed its horrors and frustrations on the federal government. "Morale was . . . declining fast," John Sweet recalled. "Most of us didn't see much point in what we were trying to accomplish."[23] Quite a few veterans were angry, believing the government had betrayed them and put them in harm's way for no good reason. Berwyn Place concluded that while the army could have won the war, "the U.S. quit. . . . It was the wrong war at the wrong place."[24] Robert Riggio likewise called it a "hopeless conflict" in which "we were sacrificing these boys for politicians both in the U.S. and South Vietnam." [25]

Veterans from the Dakotas exposed to the toxic herbicide Agent Orange condemned the government especially vigorously. Like workers in nuclear facilities in the early Cold War, servicemen and women in Vietnam learned too late that the government had put them in harm's way. They knew something was being sprayed from airplanes overhead, but they had no idea what it was. Just as the children who played near Dow Chemicals' Rocky Flats, Colorado, nuclear processing plant guessed that their fathers made "'Scrubbing Bubbles' or something," soldiers exposed to Agent

Orange guessed it was bug repellent.[26] Darrell Dorgan remembered, "[We thought] if the government was spraying with all this stuff, it must be safe."[27] On the website for the South Dakota Vietnam memorial, some veterans refused to tell their own stories, as requested; listing the names of men they knew who had died from exposure to Agent Orange instead. Jon Hanna, a veterans' service officer in Lisbon, North Dakota, saw the consequences of Agent Orange exposure every day. "The war is over," he commented, "but it still hasn't left our GIs."[28]

Only a small percentage of Dakota servicemen, fortunately, were unknowingly poisoned by their own government. But all who survived the war shared the difficult experience of returning from combat and trying to reassimilate into civilian life. Thus, like James Moon, some saved their strongest condemnations for protesters who harassed them. Returning servicepeople were required to leave the airports in uniform but many brought an extra set of clothes so they could change as quickly as possible. Even so they reported being stared at, physically accosted, screamed at, spit on and otherwise demeaned. John Rootham saw signs in San Francisco that read, "Dogs and Servicemen stay off the grass." His taxi driver advised him to change his clothes before they reached his destination. "The gun in my glove compartment won't help you once you get out of my cab."[29] The memories of returning to campus protests and outspoken celebrity activists still sting. In 2017 Jerome Cleveland warned: "Don't ever let anyone, like Jane Fonda, influence your thinking with her distorted and wicked views and unpatriotic thinking. People like her are as responsible for lost lives as the enemy themselves."[30] For Victor Robertson, the pardoning of those who fled to Canada was the final straw. "My greatest gift for serving in Vietnam has been an almost unrelenting anger that is inside of me all the time."[31]

Some returning vets even faced harassment in their own communities. The night he returned to South Dakota, for example, Calvin Olsen's father, a veteran himself, took Calvin out for a congratulatory drink at the local bar. Calvin recalled, "[My father] said, 'G—damn I'm glad to see you home. Things are tough over there.' About that time, some drunk jerk at the bar asked me if I was a 'baby killer or a dope addict.' . . . The bartender, wanting to avoid any trouble, asked me how old I was. When I answered, 19 years old, he poured my drink out and told me to leave, that I wasn't old enough to drink liquor in South Dakota."[32] They finished celebrating back home, alone in the garage.

Other slights were harder to shrug off. Dennis Lau was refused a job in Aberdeen at the local AT&T because, the manager said bluntly, "We are not hiring Vietnam vets."[33] Leo Powell was turned away from membership in his local servicemen's organization because its leaders thought that "Vietnam really wasn't a war."[34] That veterans of earlier wars did not always welcome the Vietnam-era soldiers is reflected in the updated mission statement of the North Dakota Vietnam Veterans Association: "Never again will one generation of veterans abandon another. We do not nor will not let any generation of veterans be treated the way we were when we returned home from our war."[35]

As it turned out, contrary to public memory, a few people actually were "that way" on the Northern Plains.

*   *   *

Historian Ahrar Ahmad has argued that the simple fact that South Dakotans elected two such completely different senators at the same time—the anti-communist Karl Mundt and the "peacenik" George McGovern—demonstrated voters' long-standing "ambiguities in terms of war and peace."[36] The numbers support his insight. In 1967 the Sioux Falls *Argus Leader* poll showed South Dakotans reasonably split between preferring to escalate the war and either staying the course or de-escalating it.[37] In 1968 Mundt—a close ally of President Nixon—discovered that only 10 percent of his correspondents fully supported the president's approach to the war. Nineteen percent—nearly twice as many—supported Senator McGovern's demand for immediate withdrawal of troops. Most found themselves in the middle of these two extremes. Seventy percent supported Nixon's moderate proposal of phased withdrawal from the war.[38]

In North Dakota, annual surveys that Senator Milton Young sent his constituents revealed a similar trend. In 1962, when Young first asked about Vietnam, 2,452 North Dakotans favored "sending US troops to help" if South Vietnam lost its civil war, but 3,660—nearly 30 percent more—did not.[39] By 1967 Young's questions about the war became more specific. Constituents' views were still decidedly mixed, but a growing minority of respondents now criticized how the American government was conducting the war, suggesting, like some soldiers on the ground, that they supported the war but not the president. In fact only just over 10 percent of nearly 11,000 respondents approved of President Johnson's "conduct of the war." Some who disapproved thought he was not being "strong enough." A large majority, for example, supported more widespread bombing and believed likewise that "stopping all bombing for a period of 60 days or more" would not "result in meaningful peace negotiations." At the same time 2,500 respondents favored "complete withdrawal from the war" rather than escalation.[40] As late as 1972 the same small proportion of respondents supported Nixon's handling of the war as had supported Johnson's. But the impact of a long and divisive war also influenced their answers, with 72 percent favoring Nixon's "proposal to abolish the draft and replace it with an all-volunteer force."[41]

Voter comments in the margins of their surveys—some with signatures attached—fleshed out the raw data. For example, some respondents who opposed Johnson's policies explained why. While he gave President Johnson a "fair" rating on his conduct of the war, Mr. P. Genwaldson commented that "we should not have been there in the first place."[42] To "get this war over," Mr. Cornell Swanson suggested, "stopping supply routes of the Viet Cong" and in its place "us[ing] the strategy that McArthur proposed to use in Korea (Radiation belt, etc. across supply lines)."[43] Most intriguing were the comments that echoed arguments made by Populist anti-militarists between 1890 and 1941. A creamery operator suggested, for example, that the Johnson administration had been suppressing the people's access to information.[44] W. F. Johnson refused to answer any questions and instead wrote in large letters diagonally across the survey: "Put everyone and all corporations on a wartime basis, freeze profits and prices. Make everyone realize we are in a war not for profit but for democracy."[45]

A few respondents commented—unprompted—on social and cultural issues, including the size of government, taxation, the federal budget, and social welfare programs. When they began to appear in 1966, these comments were unanimously conservative. While few in total, they suggest that once the war was over, cultural issues would dominate Dakotans' political priorities and draw them to the emerging New Right. First, like other Americans, some North Dakotans felt the war was becoming too expensive and the federal budget deficits too dangerous. Only a handful, however, supported cutting Social Security or programs for agriculture to pay for it.[46] What they did suggest cutting, however, were Great Society programs, the "welfare programs" which many Americans associated with urban people of color.[47] "We should follow the Bible," one farmer wrote. "Poor countries [and poor people] . . . should learn to help themselves."[48] They also had increasingly negative comments about the government's role in education and its regulation of business. "I say get the government out of business," wrote one man in 1967.[49] That same year a farmer added a PS: "Hope you will support the Dirkson [*sic*] amendment for prayer in schools."[50] Another named a politician from California whose views he admired: "Ronald Reagan seems to know where he is going."[51]

*   *   *

After compiling his survey data for 1972, Senator Young noted that one group of North Dakota voters answered his questions quite differently— and more frequently—than the others: those between the ages of eighteen and twenty-five. While most of his constituents seemed to be trending more Republican every year, young people were increasingly associating themselves with Democrats—strongly preferring a potential candidacy of Edward Kennedy, for example, over the incumbent Richard Nixon. They were also nearly unanimous—93 percent—in support of ending the draft.[52] But Senator Young did not need a survey to tell him that young people in the state were left-leaning and politically engaged. He could have simply called the presidents of the state's colleges and asked them. Campus protests on the Northern Plains may not have been as well attended and they certainly were not as violent as elsewhere, but they did take place—and with increasing frequency as the war went on. By the 1970s students on nearly every campus in both states had conducted at least one demonstration. President Nixon felt welcome enough in South Dakota to speak at the dedication of the Karl E. Mundt Library at General Beadle State College—now Dakota State University—in 1969. But even there, hundreds of miles from headline-grabbing universities in Berkeley, Madison, and Ann Arbor, a handful of protesters made sure that no place was safe for him either.[53]

As it did across the country, the long war was punctuated by events that mobilized student activism in the Dakotas: the Tet Offensive, the escalation of bombing campaigns, and the shooting of protesters at Kent State. But local issues and events also motivated protests, including compulsory

ROTC in South Dakota and appearances in 1967 and 1969 by Vice Presidents Hubert Humphrey and Spiro Agnew, respectively, at North Dakota State University. Whatever its impetus, local student activism took familiar forms: teach-ins, sit-ins, marches, strikes from classes, silent vigils, and occupations of academic and ROTC buildings, increasing in urgency as the war escalated. Until 1967, lone activists like Lester Galt at North Dakota State agitated against the war.[54] The first group of students to begin a chapter of Students for a Democratic Society (SDS) at the University of South Dakota (USD) needed only one table in the Student Union to hand out literature and answer—often hostile—questions.[55] But by 1970, five hundred students from five different colleges protested at the governor's inspection of ROTC cadets at South Dakota State in Brookings. They draped a flag over a mock casket and carried signs reading "All US troops out of Indochina now" and "End US Imperialism." Some of the cadets flashed a peace sign to protesters; twelve even "broke ranks, left their formation, and joined the demonstrators."[56] Just across the river from Fargo, at Moorhead State University—now Minnesota State University at Moorhead—the campus chapter of SDS opened a "draft information center" so that local men could learn ways to evade or avoid the draft. The FBI took note, despite the seemingly remote location. They compiled an extensive file on the SDS chapter's president, Larry Peterson, and more than likely placed an infiltrator inside the organization.[57]

The shootings at Kent State brought many protesters to a crisis point: wondering what good their dedication to nonviolence was if armed authorities would simply kill them. In the spring of 1970 students who had never marched before joined the protests, even those at smaller schools like Northern State in Aberdeen and religiously affiliated colleges like Augustana in Sioux Falls. At the USD, hundreds of students marched on the armory, where the president of the university met with them and allowed a one-night occupation. Many spoke of using violence. Father James Doyle pleaded with students: "We just have to search for every other possible alternative to violence, saying 'no' to war; saying 'no' to violence; saying 'no' to militarism; 'yes' to love, especially of our enemies."[58] The *Minneapolis Tribune* was quick to point out that the same Dakota State students from "small towns and farms" who had welcomed President Nixon and heard him speak out against "campus revolt" were marching against him a mere year later.[59]

Crucially in the late 1960s, student concerns began to extend beyond the war to larger issues affecting American society.[60] Connecting larger calls for "equality, freedom, and justice both at home and abroad," anti-war activists joined other students to engage with the civil rights, environmentalist, feminist, and, somewhat later, the gay rights and antinuclear movements. Soon, some just called it "the Movement . . . [and] everyone knew what it meant."[61] An anti-war rally at North Dakota State University in late spring 1971 was organized as a "rap session" so students could bring up any issues of concern. American withdrawal from the war was still the gatherings' most common discussion topic but students also went beyond it. They discussed the destruction of the jungle through the use of defoliants and the representation of Lieutenant Calley as a "scapegoat" in the wake of the My Lai massacre. They turned their gaze inward as well, asking why administrators were allowed to attend student government meetings and why so much money went to athletics.[62] Senior Mary Pat Graner asked the group to discuss several issues related to Women's Liberation.[63]

These new critiques spawned their own organizations, protests, and teach-ins separate from those sponsored by SDS or other anti-war groups, in time dividing "the Movement" as much as uniting it. Whatever their broader consequence, however, it is hard to imagine these groups so active in a region whose political culture, according to recent historians, was rooted in "essential conservatism."[64] Students at North Dakota State University, for example, demanded to know why so few African American students attended regional institutions and asked how more financial aid could be added to the budget.[65] Across the river at Concordia College in Moorhead, Minnesota, black students pointed to the extra burden they carried to "educate white peers and faculty about black exploitation."[66] At the University of North Dakota, Native students demanded that the university stop using the Fighting Sioux mascot and its corresponding cartoon character—"Sammie Sioux"—that even appeared on dinner plates in the student union. By 1972 President Thomas Clifford had officially banned any "demeaning" mascots that performed at games. Or, at least he thought he had.[67]

Urged on by students like Mary Pat Graner, college-aged women brought second-wave feminism to their institutions, challenging the culturally conservative social mores of the region. Between 1970 and 1975, women at Augustana College, Mankato State, and USD fought against sexist policies in dormitories, including requiring female, but not male, students to live on campus and allowing "visiting hours" in men's but not women's dorms. But this was not all: USD women also pushed their institution to open clinics and make birth control more accessible for both men

FIGURE 12. "Sammie Sioux," the caricatured mascot of the University of North Dakota used in the 1960s and 1970s. This figure was banned but fans continued to wear "Fighting Sioux" apparel even after the mascot was officially changed to the "Fighting Hawks." Original decal in author's possession.

and women. They spoke of the importance of recognizing and promoting women's "enjoyment" of sexual activity.[68] In 1971, five young feminist activists held a panel discussion entitled: "Women's Lib: Will It Never Happen Here?"[69] With honesty, courage, and foresight, they admitted that they feared it would not.

Small communities of adults in the Dakotas as elsewhere shared students' views on the war, civil rights, feminism, nuclear arms, gay rights, and the environment—and sometimes the countercultural lifestyles that went with them. When George Shurr's brother died, his mother—alone among all the women in her small farming community—became "obsessed" with attending protests, writing letters, and sharing her story.[70] In larger cities like Sioux Falls and Fargo, women organized local chapters of the National Organization for Women (NOW), opened women's centers, rape crisis and domestic violence hotlines, and joined feminist consciousness-raising groups, connecting the "political" with the "personal," or lived experiences of women. In South Dakota, women traveled the state on behalf of the South Dakota Commission on the Status of Women, established by Governor Nils Boe in 1963.[71] In North Dakota, women organized petition drives at local malls to support the Equal Rights Amendment, helping to win it passage in 1975, as South Dakotans had in 1973. Even so, as activists Mary Lynn Myers and Lona Crandall recalled, second-wave feminists in the region were careful, as suffragists had been before them, to endorse "no part of any radical organization of any kind," particularly any that threatened the patriarchal family. Instead they focused on "equal justice" issues such as the gender pay gap and access to the professions.[72] These issues, they believed, would seem like a "common sense way of thinking" to South Dakotans and to other rural voters across the region.

For some on the Northern Plains a commitment to the politics of freedom, peace, and social justice required the same commitments in their personal lives. Jay Davis and Kathleen Garrett moved to South Dakota in 1974 to work for the Association of Community Organizations for Reform Now (ACORN), the voter registration organization. They liked the state so much that they opened a record store, Prairie Dog Records, in Aberdeen, selling folk and feminist music, along with bongs, pipes, and rolling papers. As their son Josh recalled, kids would "come from 200 miles away" to "load up on glassware."[73] They raised Josh to care deeply about gender equality, racial justice, and the land. To stop his mom's tickling, Josh did not say "Uncle" like most children; he said "Ms."[74] The family shopped at the local food co-op for organic produce, put solar panels on their home, and participated in the Black Hills International Survival Gathering. For years, this was the only South Dakota that Josh knew, the South Dakota where guests once laughed when he, just a toddler, asked if they wanted "to smoke a bowl."[75]

But by the early 1990s, and particularly when his mother came out as a lesbian and left for Oregon with her lover, Josh realized that few of his friends' families shared his family's politics or values.[76] By then, the "world of George McGovern" had long since been "lost." Soon Josh concluded that "I too was queer for my surroundings, that I didn't live where I belonged."[77]

To the north and west of Aberdeen, outside tiny Napoleon, North Dakota, the farm girl Debra Marquart reached the same conclusion. After a decade of wearing bell bottoms with platform shoes, making out with farm boys in the back of a car, playing guitar, and listening to protest music, she acted the part of her television hero, Mary Tyler Moore, tossed her hat in the air, and put "North Dakota in the rearview mirror."[78] Neither teenager could know how much their decision—when combined with those of tens of thousands of other college-educated young people who either sought economic opportunity elsewhere or a place where they "belonged" —would affect the region's politics. The concurrent out-migration of left-leaning youth and displaced small farmers put political power in the hands of older and wealthier people, military families, Republicans, and, eventually, corporate representatives of the military-industrial complex. With them, young Dakotans carried away a piece of the most unique political heritage the countryside has ever known.

∗   ∗   ∗

It is hard to determine the precise moment when exasperated conservatives began to organize nationally to "reclaim" American institutions from the student anti-war protesters, mascot-bashing civil rights activists, conscious-ness-raising feminists, and pot-smoking record-store owners who inhabited so many corners of the country. Historian Rick Perlstein considers "Year Zero" to have been 1955, when William F. Buckley established the *National Review*, but he also acknowledges the importance of 1960s grassroots con-servative movements in the growing Sunbelt states.[79] Conservative men and women in every region took note of a series of Supreme Court decisions that outlawed prayer in school, provided access to both contraception and abortion, and, in 1983, stripped Christian colleges that refused to admit African Americans of their nonprofit status.[80] They also came to know new conservative political organizations, radio shows, and "celebrities," includ-ing some produced locally, while evangelical congregations continued to feed the national political influence of their spokespeople: Billy Graham, Pat Robertson, Jerry Falwell, and others.[81] As if to mark this "sea-change," conservative women organized to stop the Equal Rights Amendment (ERA), just as it was nearing final ratification, dead in its tracks.[82] But histo-rian Kimberly Phillips-Fein reminds us that, whenever and however it began, the seemingly diverse concerns of new conservatism were bound together by a constitutive ideology. They all "accepted a conservative poli-tics of God and capitalism, military might, and hierarchy in the workplace as well as in the home."[83]

The seeds of this change were visible in Dakotans' reactions to the cam-pus protests against the war in Vietnam. Protestors might have closely resembled Populist anti-militarists of the past, but an increasing number of

Dakotans saw them instead as dangerous radicals, not real Dakotans. No less a prewar anti-militarist than Karl Mundt championed conservative attacks against student protest.[84] He contended that protests only strengthened the enemy's hand. He participated in Senate investigations of the antiwar movement and even advocated reinstatement of the Internal Security Act of 1950. He also disparaged militancy of all kinds, including civil rights protests like the Poor People's March, as an attack on basic American norms of "law and order," a term soon to become synonymous with the New Right's strategy for appealing to white voters.[85] Finally Mundt implied that protesters were nonnormative Americans—perhaps not even Americans. Among other terms, he called some student groups "menacing" and "repugnan[t]."[86] Perhaps most revealingly, Mundt, like many others, also used the term "beatniks" to describe protesters, a reference to San Francisco area "beat" writers such as Allen Ginsberg and Jack Kerouac, well-known for being anti-militaristic, anti-materialistic—and openly gay.[87]

College presidents and other administrators also came down particularly hard on protesters and faculty members who supported them, thus limiting the influence of these forms of dissent in the region. As in the limited "purge" at USD in the McCarthy era, several faculty members were fired after helping students organize protests, or for speaking critically of the United States in their classes. Northern State College professor Frank Kosik lost his job for purportedly telling students "there is nothing good in America." President Hilton Briggs of South Dakota State fired Donald St. Clair for criticizing the United States in an off-campus presentation to a group of students.[88] Then Briggs fired Donald Crangle, after Crangle had helped students organize a protest. But he would not get rid of Crangle so easily. After they disrupted the ROTC commissioning ceremony, eighty protesters—including Crangle—marched into President Briggs' office. While most protesters sat on the floor, Crangle decided to sit in President Briggs' chair. Briggs then shoved the chair—and Crangle—to the floor. A fistfight ensued, after which Crangle was arrested and charged with assault and battery.[89] For the Board of Regents president, Richard Battey, enough was enough. "There is no place in our institution for radicals," he announced.[90]

In speeches and letters to their campus newspaper editors, conservative students—heard more loudly in the Midwest than in other regions of the country—blamed protesters for undermining the American military.[91] One student from South Dakota State said the protests "only prolonged the war" by boosting "the morale of the enemy."[92] At USD, one student echoed Senator Mundt and labeled protesters "so-called Americans."[93] Conservative students also suggested that most protestors were too afraid to fight, calling them "cowards who didn't have the courage to save our country from the threat of Communism."[94] The editor of the *Sioux Falls Argus Leader* described the moratorium march of October 1969 not as a demonstration but as a "mob scene" and its participants as "pathetically stupid."[95] The city planned a seminar to train police and other officials on how to quell a riot. Conservative students happily attended.

Like Senator Mundt, conservative students extended their rhetorical attacks to the personal qualities of the protesters. In USD's student newspaper, *The Volante*, for example, hawkish student opinion writers called the anti-war protesters "kooks," "appeasers," "hoodlums," and "punks," at a time when hoodlums and punks were increasingly associated with urban Latino or African American gangs.[96] Students subtly and not so subtly questioned the protesters' sexuality as well. In 1969 USD Student Association president Jim Dunn described protesters this way: "People you more or less could smell coming. You could see their attire, their costumes, their long hair. . . . [They are] usually . . . the left, the art department students."[97] Men from the "art department," like the Beatnik poets, were hardly imagined as "real men," but likely homosexuals. In one particularly colorful episode, more than three thousand leftist college students made a 1969 spring break trip to Zap, North Dakota—calling it "Zip to Zap." The town of 250 ran out of alcohol, food, bathroom facilities, and patience. It did not take long for Governor William Guy to call out the National Guard.[98]

The conservatives who organized counterprotests against anti-war groups took their liberal opponents seriously; they saw them as a real threat to American values, manhood, and the success of the war effort. The same cannot be said of their responses to campus feminists—usually disparaged as "women's libbers"—whose ideas were fodder for comedy. Even parents who wrote to administrators in response to the ideas of coeducated dorms used humor to make their points: "When you run cattle together, there will be an increase in the feedlot!" wrote one.[99] Male students chose sarcasm as their tool. When feminist students at USD held their panel, "Women's Lib: Will It Never Happen Here?," five men responded with a panel: "Why Women's Liberation Is a Lost Cause." One male student parodied the women activists by saying that what they really wanted was to be men themselves. "I am in favor of the two-sex system," he joked.[100]

While conservative men scoffed, conservative women organized against second-wave feminism just as they had organized against suffrage sixty years earlier—with deadly seriousness. Beginning in 1976 with the support of newly elected Governor Bill Janklow—informally called "Wild Bill" like North Dakota's NPL firebrand Bill Langer—Republican women, Catholics, and evangelicals worked feverishly to roll back the gains won by NOW, the Commission on the Status of Women, and other local groups. In 1977 Phyllis Schlafly traveled to Huron College to debate the ERA—again—with Mary Lynn Myers, a member of the board of NOW.[101] Just two years later, South Dakota voters chose to rescind their ratification of the ERA, one of only five states to do so.[102] As Matthew Pehl explains, by the end of the 1970s, the "individuality and autonomy" sought by second-wave feminists seemed far too drastic a departure from "traditional gender identities" for many rural Americans.[103]

With their largely conservative faith backgrounds, no issue energized anti-feminist women across the Northern Plains as much as abortion. As early as 1973, 41 percent of South Dakotans believed "abortion is like murder and ought to be severely punished."[104] In Fargo where there was an "efflorescent" feminist community, even local feminists did not all support *Roe v. Wade*. Like their South Dakota counterparts, they had no desire to seem "radical" or to upset the social order, saying, "We are feminists but we are not rabble-rousing bra-burners."[105] Nevertheless a subset of activist women in the area considered reproductive freedom to be the most important women's cause of all—one worth fighting for, no matter the cost or response. By the late 1970s they worked to open a clinic in the city. As they did, national antiabortion groups, like Lambs of God, formed alliances with local groups, including the growing number of evangelical congregations.[106] When the clinic opened in 1983, after struggling to find a landlord who would rent to them, protests began immediately and continued for decades. The antiabortion groups' relentless opposition and multifaceted strategies have ranged from putting junked cars in the driveway to firebombing the clinic itself to passing restrictive state laws that challenge *Roe*.[107] Even so, with the support of unique liberal politicians like Fargo's mayor, Jon Lingren, the clinic remained open, if under constant siege.[108]

*   *   *

In this rapidly changing political environment—what Daniel Rodgers has called the "Age of Fracture"—George McGovern planned his strategy for three Senate campaigns: 1968, 1974, and 1980.[109] But McGovern was not the only openly anti-war senator from the region; he was not even the only one targeted by the increasingly powerful national conservative political action groups. In fact both McGovern and North Dakota senator Quentin Burdick had been against the war in Vietnam from its start. Even more significantly neither opposed the war because this particular war was bad—expensive, unwinnable, or poorly executed—but because war itself was bad and the increasing militarization of American culture and society threatened to make war permanent. In this way they carried forward, indeed reinvented for a new generation, the region's prewar Populist anti-militarist heritage.

Quentin Burdick, his father Usher Burdick, and Bill Langer were what historian Robert Griffith called "old Progressives"—those who held onto the Populist views of their radical region even after World War II.[110] Quentin Burdick peeled back a layer of Cold War political orthodoxy with every vote he cast. First he rejected anti-communism, remembering the many poor farmers in the 1930s who "would embrace any ism that they thought would relieve them of this need, want, and suffering."[111] He was also no "kin" to the military, comparing his political strategy to one opponent's this way: "I walked the streets meeting everyone I could, while he hung around with his buddies at the American Legion Hall. You won't get new voters that way."[112] As for Vietnam, he had no fear of making a rare break with the Johnson administration. Raised in a Nonpartisan League (NPL) family, Burdick saw war as a mechanism for corporate profits, while farm boys paid the ultimate price.

The core of McGovern's views against the Vietnam War likewise harkened back to the traditions of Populist anti-militarism. While Burdick had sat out World War II due to a serious football injury, McGovern was a decorated B-24 pilot, having flown thirty-five missions over Germany—one with only one engine intact. He never lost a crewman.[113] But this experience did not incline McGovern toward pro-militarism or toward hanging around the Legion Hall. It had the opposite effect. As for veterans of World War I, McGovern's experience of being in combat and seeing its carnage—even causing it—deepened his resolve that war itself was wrong, that *all* war was wrong. The bombing at Hiroshima likewise led to his position against nuclear proliferation. He was convinced that "unless the nuclear monster can be contained, civilization would be destroyed."[114] In a 2003 interview he reflected, "I was never that gung-ho for the Cold War. . . . It seemed to me that both sides just went crazy, piling up 12,000 nuclear warheads on each side."[115] When he was already on record as being against the war in Vietnam, a visit to an army hospital reinforced his fear that war cheapened human life in the name of some other goal—honor, manhood, nationalism—of purportedly higher value. War made life as cheap and meaningless as the Purple Heart that one young soldier, whose body had been ripped apart by a landmine, had won. Rather than proud, the young man was "disillusioned and [in] disbelief."[116]

McGovern's anti-militarism reflected both the evangelical Methodism of his childhood and the mainline Protestant Social Gospel theology he adopted as a university student. Historian Mark Lempke argues that it is easy to forget McGovern's faith background, particularly since recently the term "Christian" has come to imply conservative not liberal views.[117] But for McGovern, there was nothing more important to his identity than being a Christian. Likewise nothing more fully informed his political views than his understanding of the meaning of Christianity as an outer-directed faith. Lempke concludes, "McGovern called for a politics based on compassion, inclusion and uplift for the most vulnerable. . . . In McGovern's progressive Christianity, people were called to transcend self-interest and live as though their salvation depended on others' well-being."[118] A leader who held such a view of Christianity could advocate for nothing short of ending poverty, hunger, and war—around the world.[119] Thus one of the most confounding attacks on McGovern in the 1980 Senate campaign against Congressman Jim Abdnor was a pamphlet that read: "Why as a Christian I Cannot Vote for McGovern."[120]

In his "war against war," McGovern echoed the speeches that Populist anti-militarists gave in the years before World War I, the paintings Harvey Dunn created during it, and the memorials citizens erected after it. He believed stridently, for example, that dissent in a time of war constituted an act of patriotism.[121] But McGovern knew that one of his predecessors' worst fears had come true: American society had become so militarized that war profited corporations as it damaged democracy. There was even a permanent standing army on the Northern Plains themselves. He also agreed with outgoing president Dwight Eisenhower that the power of the "military-industrial complex" was one of the greatest threats to the nation's future, declaring in 1963 that for all our military might we "have proved powerless to cope with a ragged band of illiterate guerrillas fighting with homemade weapons."[122] And yet year after year, the Pentagon requested more money for more weapons and more military bases in more countries.[123]

North Dakota's Burdick and South Dakota's McGovern shared many views about the war as well as the experience of nearly single-handedly rejuvenating their state's Democratic parties during a time of economic disruption in agriculture. But in the end, their different styles influenced their political longevity far more than their similarities. Burdick was known as the "silent senator." He rarely spoke on the floor of the Senate. Furthermore he did not like Washington and, incredibly, was known to come home to North Dakota almost every weekend where he could be found doing odd jobs in the barn "dressed in his grubbies."[124] No record or image exists of him attending any anti-war rally. Part of his secret was his well-informed realism about North Dakota voters. Fully admitting he was "too liberal for many of the conservatives out here," he prevailed, historian Dan Rylance wryly suggests, because "he did not brag back home about his liberal record."[125] Last, he had no interest in national prominence or higher office. He hoped to be remembered for nothing more than "working for the poor people of North Dakota."[126] Thus Burdick would survive two attempts by nationally funded conservative groups to oust him from the Senate, serving longer than almost any other elected official in US history.

George McGovern was not a silent senator. He did not take care to hide his liberal views. He did not travel home frequently. And he certainly aspired to higher office. Trouble from the right found McGovern early and often. In 1960 Karl Mundt successfully painted McGovern as a possible communist sympathizer. In 1968, when McGovern advocated for an immediate withdrawal from Vietnam, some influential newspaper owners in the state turned against him and a "handful" of right wing activists—who McGovern thought might be members of the John Birch Society—targeted his views on race.[127] One flyer showed McGovern's face in the center of a bullseye. Even moderate local voters blamed him for causing some of the chaos of the 1968 Democratic convention in Chicago and remembered their shock when he spoke at the National Moratorium March in the fall of 1969. Few had wanted him to run for president. Furthermore, his opponents did not just become more numerous, they became more hostile and more vocal. Author John Mollison's earliest childhood memory, for example, was his mother yelling at the television while McGovern spoke.[128] In the presidential election of 1972 more than eight in ten voters in some West River counties chose Nixon over the homegrown candidate. In 1973, 59 percent of South Dakotans thought McGovern's views had "encouraged the North Vietnamese to prolong the war and thus he hurt our POWs."[129]

There were many signs that McGovern was vulnerable in his own region. In 1974 McGovern beat the former prisoner-of-war Leo Thorsness, only when the farm economy, rather than the war, unexpectedly took center stage. Thorsness had explained that the idea of running against McGovern and winning his spot in the Senate had kept him alive as a POW in North Vietnam. McGovern and his team knew that beating Thorsness—who admitted to voters that he knew nothing about governance—by a mere 6 percentage points was hardly impressive. Another warning sign was Republican Larry Pressler's 1974 election to the House of Representatives and his subsequent election to the Senate in 1978. South Dakotans had long elected Republicans. But the Vietnam War and the economic troubles in the agricultural sector had brought a number of liberal Democrats to power in the state in the early 1970s.[130] Pressler's success suggested the "Democratic surge" might be short-lived. In 1974 Pressler prevailed even as a historically large freshman class of left-leaning "Watergate babies" headed to Congress and in 1978, he replaced Senator James Abourezk, considered by some to be more liberal than McGovern.[131] Pressler ran as a fiscal conservative with a probusiness, anti-regulatory, small government platform. Even more ominously for McGovern, he was a Vietnam veteran, the first ever elected to serve in the upper chamber.

In light of these trends, McGovern's team got an early start preparing for the 1980 campaign. Understandably, they worked foremost on combating the impression that McGovern was "soft on defense" and did not support the military. In 1976 the team had learned that even though most Americans were tired of talking about defense and foreign affairs, South Dakotans were not.[132] With local economies and communities fully integrated with the military, they believed that what was good for the armed forces was good for them. West River voters, in particular, who lived in and around Ellsworth Air Force Base, strongly favored expansion of the military and opposed the SALT II treaty.[133] In response McGovern's team prepared numerous mailings, memos, and press releases to explain his views. Avoiding even a mention of Vietnam, they reminded voters that McGovern himself was a decorated veteran of World War II. They argued that if voters used their common sense, they would see that McGovern's other dovish positions were reasonable: he had voted against the B-1 bomber, one memo suggested, because it "would not be a cost effective penetrator of Soviet air space into the next century."[134] He had traveled to Cuba only to confirm that the island nation "was not a democracy," and not out of sympathy.[135] He supported SALT II because "the world already had too many nuclear weapons."

South Dakotans, particularly West River voters, were not buying it. Over the transformational years of the 1970s, they had become increasingly critical of McGovern's positions on defense and increasingly alarmed that the United States, with the strongest military in the world, had lost a war to a small Asian country.[136] They were also shocked at the Carter administration's inability to solve the Iranian hostage crisis and warmed, by contrast, to Ronald Reagan's vigorous defense of American military might. Thus McGovern's opponent, Congressman Jim Abdnor, a "plain-spoken" farmer who liked to say he had "gotten off his tractor and gone to Washington," positioned himself on the opposite side of nearly every foreign policy and defense issue from nuclear weapons to the Panama Canal treaty.[137] And he knew that defense issues for many South Dakotans were in fact matters of life and death for themselves and their communities. In one letter to voters on Abdnor's behalf, retired Lt. Gen. Gordon A. Sumner claimed to have special military intelligence, warning that "in the early 1980s . . . the Soviets will be capable of wiping out our land-based ICBMs in a first strike." Sumner exhorted South Dakotans to "help [defeat] a man who has a long history of advocating the dismantling of our defenses and knuckling under to Soviet aggression."[138]

Yet McGovern's focus on military issues turned out to be a mistake. As important as it was, defense was not the only thing on voters' minds. In the late 1970s, South Dakotans had also become increasingly concerned about cultural issues and saw that McGovern's positions on everything from the ERA, gun rights, civil rights, prayer in school, and abortion diverged from their own. Furthermore they would come to make an important connection: a man who did not defend his country would also not defend the country's traditional family life. As such he personified the singular threat to American families that the "radical" Left had become.

South Dakotans deservedly could boast of a rich tradition of informed voting. Even so in 1980 they would get extra help reaching their conclusions. Beginning in 1978 conservative activists responded to a 1976 Supreme Court ruling allowing outside groups to donate unlimited funds to candidates so long as the candidate stayed uninvolved. Terry Dolan, Paul Weyrich, Richard Viguerie, and others formed the National Conservative Political Action Committee (NCPAC). Hardly going door-to-door, NCPAC activists used direct mail, conservative radio, and huge amounts of television advertising—one hundred thousand dollars' worth in South Dakota —to spread conservative views on defense, taxes, regulation, homosexuality, feminism, busing, and prayer in schools.[139] For the 1980 election they targeted ten liberal senators who were up for reelection—with George McGovern near the top of the list. As Terry Dolan told the *New York Times*, "McGovern is a liberal Senator from a conservative state and his record really is outrageous. Not every member of the U.S. Senate pals around with Castro. We felt we could make McGovern vulnerable."[140]

While McGovern logically worried that conservatives would try to make him look "soft on patriotism," NCPAC broadened voters' awareness of issues beyond defense.[141] A particularly "informative" mailing used the guise of looking like a poll. Each "question" was followed by an inflammatory statement of McGovern's "record" on the relevant issue. For example, voters were asked to check "approve" or "disapprove" "on capital punishment." Below it in bold font were the words: "McGovern states: 'I am against the death penalty.'" Of the twenty-four "questions" on the poll, only two asked about any topic related to the military or foreign affairs. The other twenty-two addressed concerns about taxation, regulation, gun control, sexuality, or women's rights. Some introduced topics that voters in South Dakota may have known nothing about, like the acquittal of black activist Angela Davis—"McGovern says . . . this is a 'Cause for Rejoicing.'"[142]

NCPAC also urged South Dakota voters to conclude that McGovern did not really represent common sense, "South Dakota thinking" any more. McGovern was vulnerable to these attacks. McGovern had lived in Washington, DC, for over two decades; it was the only home his youngest children had ever known. On the campaign trail in 1968, his daughter Susan had to dress in different clothes than she wore at home in DC so she would fit in.[143] A television spot paid for by "People for an Alternative to McGovern" ended each segment with a chorus of "McGovern doesn't represent South Dakota." Its final scene highlighted McGovern's "globetrotting junkets to Cuba and Africa." Associating McGovern with African Americans, the narrator also said, "Globe trotter is a great name for basketball players but it's a terrible name for a United States senator."[144] It did not help when

McGovern tried to go pheasant hunting but did not qualify for a state hunting license because he did not have a South Dakota driver's license.[145]

The most effective and powerful attacks on McGovern were those that accused him of "supporting abortion on demand." Some conflated his views on Vietnam with those on abortion. One pamphlet reminded voters that McGovern and others had "piously wrung their hands" in protest of the killing of babies in Vietnam, but supported killing babies through abortion at home.[146] Picketers forced McGovern to cancel a speech at a Catholic school in Sioux Falls. An antiabortion group put pamphlets on cars in the parking lot outside a church that juxtaposed images of McGovern and an aborted fetus. Letters to the editors of local papers and to McGovern himself poured in.[147] George Zacher of Leola, for example, asked McGovern to "take me off your mailing list. I have been a supporter of you every [sic] since you ran for office the first time." The abortion issue changed his mind. McGovern's campaign manager added a note to the letter: "this is the kind of letter that 'hurts.' "[148] Two elderly women stopped McGovern in a grocery store parking lot to give him the same news face-to-face. That likely hurt even more.

From the beginning, McGovern struggled to find a way to counteract these attacks. He tried warning voters against the lies circulated by the PACs. He urged them not to become "single issue" voters, creating more memos, taking more surveys, writing more letters that explained his positions. But he refused to change his views. Just as in the 1968 election, when South Dakota voters had first expressed concern over his liberal positions, he decided, "I want to be reelected . . . but I do not want re-election so badly that I will ever sacrifice my convictions to achieve it."[149] In 1980 he also stuck to his beliefs and his campaign's game plan: he worked to increase voter participation on Indian reservations by offering free lunch near polling sites.[150] He shored up support among better-educated white voters in Minnehaha County by hosting a Peter, Paul, and Mary reunion concert in Sioux Falls. He even asked feminist leader Gloria Steinem to write a fundraising letter.

None of these strategies helped. Some probably hurt. Every appeal to a liberal voter in Sioux Falls likely reinforced the impression held by more conservative rural voters that McGovern represented a radical leftist movement tearing at the fabric of traditional American life. Worse than his failed strategy, though, was McGovern's failure of imagination. He could never imagine that South Dakota voters would believe the "disinformation" they heard from PACs on the right. How could a man with five children, he asked, be reasonably portrayed as "anti-family"? How could a man who had been a minister be reasonably considered unchristian?[151] To McGovern, the rise of right-wing cultural issues seemed unbelievably—even irresponsibly—irrelevant, given the pressing questions of poverty and peace that he still considered far more vital to democracy. He told the *New York Times*, "I'm always answering negative questions: 'Is it true you're a pal of Fidel Castro's, that you sold the Panama Canal to the Communists, that you want to 'kill the unborn?' It's all these off-the-wall right-wing ideas."[152]

As it turned out, by 1980 most voters in South Dakota did not think that the ideas associated with the New Right were "off the wall." In fact some had not thought so for quite some time. Most importantly, they also did not think that the ideas of the New Right were disconnected from issues of war and peace. In the early years of the Vietnam War, South Dakotans had supported—or perhaps tolerated—a war hero who hated war. He and they hailed from a region where anti-militarism had once been the norm. But increasingly after 1968, South Dakotans changed their minds. They had no tolerance for McGovern's celebrity, his willingness to march with protesters, his outspoken support for every liberal cause from civil rights to reproductive rights, and his desire to travel the world. Most of all they did not want the peace he called for if it meant the decline of American superiority. On Election Day in November 1980, McGovern earned only 39 percent of the vote. Years later he recalled that he had watched the returns with a longtime friend and adviser, Joe Floyd, the owner of KELO in Sioux Falls, and his wife. "You might find [it] hard to believe . . . but this television executive—they couldn't believe it, and they literally wept. His wife left the room and sobbed and Joe had tears running down his face."[153] The McGoverns and the Floyds shed tears not just for that night's loss but for all that had been lost over years, even decades, on the Northern Plains. And even for the fact that, in their grief, they were, as McGovern remembered of that night, "pretty much alone."[154]

* * *

The people of North and South Dakota continued to care about the issues associated with new conservatism, redefining what it meant to have "common sense" and to be a "real" South Dakotan well into the twenty-first century. Like McGovern, other politicians learned what mattered most to voters the hard way: North Dakota governor George "Bud" Sinner, a devout Catholic who had introduced Billy Graham at his crusade in Fargo and shepherded the state through the 1980s Farm Crisis, vetoed a state law restricting access to abortion because he felt it was not the government's role to do so. His obituary noted that this single controversial decision largely determined his legacy; some voters argued he should not be honored even in death.[155] Larry Pressler lost his reelection bid in 1996 due to his extensive world travels—and carefully planted rumors of a secret male companion.[156] Tom Daschle, the Senate majority leader, narrowly lost to Jon Thune who accused him of being a "Washington insider" and embracing national liberal causes.[157]

The most revealing recent contest in the Dakotas, however, may be one that few Americans outside of the region noticed. In the 2016 Republican primary for a state senate seat in the Thirty-Third Legislative District, northwest of Rapid City, state representative Jackie Sly thought she had found the issue that could upend her opponent—ultraconservative Phil Jensen. She had found documents that proved that Jensen had been a registered conscientious objector at the end of the Vietnam War. A PAC that supported Sly sent postcard-sized flyers to mailboxes around the district that asked, "Would you vote for a politician who refused to wear our country's uniform?"[158] In his blog, "Way to Go," Sly supporter and fundraiser Stan Adelstein suggested that Jensen's "draft dodging" differentiated him from the vast majority of South Dakotans: "We welcome soldiers home. We take aging soldiers on honor flights. We gather to celebrate those who live and to mourn those who have passed."[159]

As sure a bet as this seemed for Sly, she was wrong. Decades after the war ended, after the New Right had ascended to power in the state, after the world of George McGovern had been both lost and forgotten, no one really doubted that a man as conservative as Jensen supported the military. He was a man, after all, and in the post-Vietnam period Americans had successfully melded the image of the warrior with both masculinity and whiteness.[160] As one commentator said, "Do pols really want to open this can of worms? Aren't campaigns smutty enough without scrutinizing every decision your opponent ever made?"[161] What mattered far more, as it turned out, than the Vietnam "can of worms" was Sly's own "weak" record on pressing cultural issues. By 2016 Jensen, a founder of the South Dakota Conservatives or "Wingnuts"—their term—was considered among the most aggressively conservative lawmakers in the state. He supported the death penalty for abortion providers, assailed lawmakers who had "hesitated" before voting for the right of students and teachers to carry guns to school, and demanded that the state's borders be closed to refugees. From that footing he reminded voters that Jackie Sly had led a movement to enact a small tax increase so that public school teachers, the lowest-paid in the nation, could get a raise. She had also supported Governor Daugaard after he had vetoed the state's transgender "bathroom bill."[162] In fall 2016 Jackie Sly learned the hard way what better-known politicians—George McGovern among them—had learned before her. Beginning in 1980 support for the military was an essential component for political success on the Northern Plains; in those same years, however, it was also revealed to be an insufficient definition of what the Rural New Right would become. Dakotans all support the military: it's how people are "in this part of the country." Bathrooms are the new divide.

CHAPTER 7

WOUNDED KNEE, 1973,
AND THE WAR AT HOME

WHEN THE GOVERNMENT DEPLOYED military force against the members of the American Indian Movement (AIM) who were occupying the hamlet of Wounded Knee, South Dakota, in the spring of 1973, it felt all too familiar. Russell Means remembered, "All of a sudden we saw these two fighter jets coming and they circled around. . . . We thought it was over. That's napalm." It was not napalm, but Jim Robideau told of men who reacted the same way. "They were shooting machine gun fire at us, tracers coming at us at night time just like a war zone. We had some Vietnam vets with us and they said, 'Man, this is just like Vietnam.' "[1] The last American soldiers and POWs had just left Southeast Asia but veterans inside Wounded Knee felt the war had followed them home. They were not alone in their perception. Their opponents, agents of the FBI and ATF, had a far "better" war in mind, however. When AIM leaders surrendered, three agents in military gear had their picture taken raising the American flag, imitating the capture of Mount Suribachi on Iwo Jima in World War II.[2] The trouble was, of course, that the "conquered" were neither Japanese nor Viet Cong; they were members of their tribal nations—American citizens all along.[3]

The Occupation of Wounded Knee lasted seventy-one days, drawing intense national and international attention. For Native people it was, as Phil Deloria and other Native scholars have written, "where Indian people and their challenges and possibilities achieved a political visibility they had not held for a century."[4] Moreover it stood as the most significant Native political action until the protests against the Dakota Access Pipeline at Standing Rock in 2016. For Euro-Americans in the Dakotas, by contrast, the Occupation of Wounded Knee represented the most significant cultural crisis of a turbulent era. It contributed significantly to white Dakotans' demands that "law and order" be reinstated and their support for candidates who promised to do so. As a result, while the New Right created a "new Republican majority" with a "southern strategy," that strategy depended on votes from the Central and Northern Plains. The Occupation and the support provided it by the liberal National Council of Churches (NCC) likewise fueled the ongoing movement away from mainline Protestantism into evangelical congregations, perceived as more concerned with personal salvation than social activism.[5] As one local man asked his left-leaning Methodist minister, "Pastor, we know what you think of the Vietnamese. We know what you think of the Indians. But what do you think of us?"[6]

Finally Dakotans' demand that the government end the Occupation violently if necessary evoked the role of the military in settler colonialism. But it also foretold how white Americans, in the wake of the civil rights movement and the loss in Vietnam, embraced new forms of state-sponsored violence to reestablish power in their communities. In South Dakota they would do so by electing their own self-proclaimed "Indian-fighting" governor, Bill Janklow, and later by opening new prisons, militarizing the police, and liberalizing gun laws.[7] From this perspective, the Occupation of Wounded Knee exemplified what Kathleen Belew calls Americans' desire to "bring the [Vietnam] war home" in the form of the violent white power movement and its better behaved associate, the New Right. The Occupation of Wounded Knee, in short, showed that the Cold War had "come home" not just in the form of bases and missiles, but "in ways bloody and unexpected."[8]

* * *

The Occupation of Wounded Knee began on February 27, 1973, when more than two hundred Oglala Lakota and other members of AIM seized and occupied the hamlet of Wounded Knee, South Dakota.[9] They stole provisions including guns and ammunition from a local store, captured—and

FIGURE 13. A tank rolls by a monument to Crazy Horse on the Pine Ridge
Reservation, during the Occupation of Wounded Knee in 1973. Getty Images.

later released—four white hostages, including store owners Clive and Agnes
Gildersleeve, blocked local roads, and in time declared the Independent
Oglala Nation.[10] They sought redress for the many forms of violence—from
forced removal, broken treaties, and stolen, allotted, and flooded land to
sexual assault, kidnapping, and genocide—that Native people had experienced since settler invasion and colonization had begun. But they had
another goal in mind. Because of the violence of forced assimilation in the
twentieth century, Russell Means, Dennis Banks, and other leaders of AIM
believed their entire way of life had been stolen, too. Means remembered,
"We were about to be obliterated culturally. Our spiritual way of life—our
entire way of life was about to be stamped out and this was a rebirth of our
dignity and self-pride."[11] AIM leaders named medicine man Leonard Crow
Dog to be their spiritual leader and built a sweat lodge for purification.
Among their proudest moments inside the village was the birth of Mary
Crow Dog's son, Pedro Bissonette, the first "free" Indian child born in
South Dakota in over one hundred years.[12] And yet the Native men and
women inside Wounded Knee also knew the risks they were taking. As
Carter Camp recalled later, "We wanted to give our lives in such a way that
would bring attention to what was happening in Indian Country and we
were pretty sure that we were gonna have to give our lives."[13]

The Occupation of Wounded Knee was hardly the only action taken by
the American Indian Movement, although it is the best known. AIM had

been founded in Minneapolis in 1968 to bring attention to police brutality; it would become one of the most central organizations of the Red Power movement.[14] But AIM did not represent all Native people in the region and, in fact, divisions within the Oglala Lakota were partially responsible for both the Occupation and its tragic aftermath. On the Pine Ridge Reservation, AIM sought to oust the Oglala tribal chairman, Dick Wilson, who they believed had been illegally elected and who used his considerable power to help mixed blood people, like himself, at the expense of full bloods or "traditionals."[15] When Wilson narrowly avoided impeachment, AIM accused him of buying votes and using his private paramilitary "GOONS (Guardians of the Oglala Nation)" to keep traditional Lakota from voting. Eventually Wilson banned AIM from Pine Ridge altogether.[16]

The conflict with Wilson was the immediate cause of the Occupation, but AIM leaders had additional reasons to take the advice of the Oglala chief Fools Crow and elders Gladys Bissonette and Ellen Moves Camp to "make your stand" at Wounded Knee.[17] First, AIM chose Wounded Knee because of its significance in Lakota history. On that site on December 29, 1890, members of the army's Seventh Cavalry hunted down and murdered over two hundred Indian men, women, and children—the vast majority of whom were unarmed. They buried all the murdered Lakota in a mass grave. During the Occupation, AIM leader Carter Camp felt the power of the place. "I walked over to a gully and I picked up some sage and I went and washed myself and I prayed to those ancestors that were there in that gully and I said, 'We're back. We have returned, my relations. We-bla-huh.'"[18] The massacre, described in detail in Dee Brown's best-selling 1970 book, *Bury My Heart at Wounded Knee*, also gave the location powerful symbolic meaning to observers around the world.[19]

The Occupation responded to recent violent attacks too, attacks that were meant to reinforce the racial hierarchy of the Northern Plains. They took place most often in border towns just outside reservations, where bars and liquor stores lined the streets. As Madonna Thunder Hawk recalled, "There were towns you didn't drive through, you didn't go through. Especially women."[20] On February 13, 1972, just south of the Pine Ridge Reservation in Gordon, Nebraska, four white men chased fifty-nine-year-old Raymond Yellow Thunder, stripped him to the waist, paraded him in front of people at the American Legion Hall, beat him, forced him into the trunk of a car, and left him to die.[21] Two were never charged; two were convicted of manslaughter and sentenced to only six

years in prison. Atrocities and miscarriages of justice like these were nothing new. For AIM that was exactly the point.[22] Dennis Banks summed up
Natives' feelings: "Hey, listen, White man! I have had all the bullshit from
your race as I can take!"[23]

Soon some AIM activists committed to combating the violence with
some of their own. Less than a year after Raymond Yellow Thunder's murder, in January 1973, a white man known to friends as "Mad Dog"—
notorious for having murdered an Indian before—stabbed Wesley Bad
Heart Bull in the heart outside a bar in Buffalo Gap, South Dakota. He also
was only charged with manslaughter.[24] On February 6, an AIM-organized
caravan moved into Custer, the site of the county courthouse. They initially
intended only to demand that "Mad Dog" face more serious charges, as
they had after Yellow Thunder's murder. This time, however, the local community prepared for the caravan to arrive. Heavily armed police shot tear
gas at protesters, including Wesley's mother, Sarah Bad Heart Bull, and beat
them with riot sticks and revolvers. In response AIM leaders threw bottles
and burned cars and an unoccupied building, the old Custer County courthouse. Local whites shouted "Injuns coming!" They organized armed
patrols, instituted curfews, and warned their wives and daughters not to
leave home unattended.[25]

The Occupation of Wounded Knee began just weeks later and this time,
the racial politics of the Northern Plains captured worldwide attention. As
it moved beyond its first week, images of Lakota men on horseback bran-
dishing rifles and federal marshals in battle fatigues appeared in newspapers
large and small. With AIM leaders announcing it "was a good day to die,"
hundreds of FBI and federal marshals surrounding the camp, and National
Guard units on standby, fears of a second massacre arose. In response,
South Dakota senators McGovern and Abourezk, federal mediators, and
several representatives of the NCC gathered on Pine Ridge to prevent
bloodshed. Hundreds of journalists and members of tribal nations in the
United States and Canada arrived to join the occupiers. Young whites from
California and Colorado hiked local trails to gain access to the village; the
anti-war activist Bill Zimmerman, who lived in Boston at the time, organized an airlift of two thousand pounds of supplies when food, medicine,
and other materials grew short.[26] Millions around the world watched as
Marlon Brando refused to accept his Academy Award due to the ongoing
crisis, joined later by Black Panther Angela Davis, country music star
Johnny Cash, and anti-war activist Jane Fonda.

Aware that the "whole world was watching," fearing the worst, and distracted by the growing Watergate scandal, President Nixon instructed the FBI to continue to try to "wait out" protesters rather than provoke bloodshed. An NCC-negotiated settlement in March fell apart when AIM leaders would not give up their weapons until their demand for a meeting in Washington, DC, had been met. When, on March 26, federal marshal Lloyd Grimm was gravely injured, a new Department of Justice official, Kent Frizzell, changed tactics drastically, preventing the press, most church members, and any new supporters from accessing the site. As Frizzell boasted later, "shortly after I arrived, the lifestyle was somewhat changed for the occupants. The electricity was cut, the water line was cut."[27] Food and medicine quickly ran low and fear that government informants had infiltrated the village provoked internal division. Until then the FBI had not been authorized to use military weapons against the occupiers; on Frizzell's orders, they began firing on the village day and night. On April 25, a Cherokee newcomer, Frank Clearwater, was killed by a bullet shot through the window of the church. On April 26, Buddy Lamont, an Oglala who had been inside Wounded Knee from the first day, was killed while collecting food from an air drop. For elders like Fools Crow, these violent deaths spelled the beginning of the end.

On May 5 AIM leaders agreed to give up their weapons and for the leaders to surrender. It seemed that the federal government had prevailed. Many occupiers simply walked out of the village under the cover of night. Arlene Means remembered, "The spirits had a lot to do with it. The one that brought us out was the owl. And every time he'd hoot in one direction . . . we would go that way, and [we] did it right under the marshals' noses."[28] Some activists who remained refused to give up their weapons. Later, the government's initial attempts to prosecute leaders of the Occupation would also fail when famed New York lawyer William Kunstler and the Wounded Knee Legal Defense/Offense Committee (WKLD/OC) proved that Banks could not get a fair trial in South Dakota. When the trial finally began in St. Paul, Judge Nichols threw out all charges against Banks due to prosecutorial misconduct, including tampering with witnesses and illegal electronic surveillance. Despite these embarrassments—or perhaps because of them—the state and federal governments were not done finding ways to "neutralize" AIM.[29] They would be back to win the war next time.

*   *   *

White Dakotans brought many decades of shared history and culture—not least a new "kinship" with the military—to the crisis at Wounded Knee. Whether their local histories said so or not, white men and women who "pioneered" on the Northern Plains did so within the larger structures of settler colonialism—the movement of whites onto indigenous land with the support of the military and the central government. Indeed the attacks on unarmed Native civilians were the original "American way of war."[30] The Second Amendment, Northwest Ordinance, Homestead Act, Dawes Act, and countless disregarded treaties likewise functioned to help whites subjugate and eliminate Native people while they converted stolen land into the gridded landscape of capitalist agriculture.[31] As historian Mark Lempke has written, even the "Law-abiding prairie republican" society that followed "often doubled as white privilege."[32]

Furthermore, stereotypes about Indians had a way of enduring for generations and influencing public policy. Far into the postwar period, many local whites generally agreed that Natives were lazy, stupid, undependable, and likely addicted to alcohol. They may have even agreed with a northwestern Minnesota radio journalist who in 1966 said that the Ojibwe people's "satisfaction level is so low that it corresponds to that of the most primitive of the earth's animals."[33] Thus, whites largely supported residential segregation, programs that forced Indian children to attend boarding school or promoted adoption by white families, and projects that destroyed Indian land "for the public good," such as the six dams created between 1946 and 1966 by the Pick-Sloan Missouri River Diversion plan.[34] Although significant, even the 1960 election of Ben Reifel to Congress from South Dakota's First District did not indicate a fundamental change in white attitudes. Reifel was a mixed-race Lakota, born on the Rosebud Reservation, who attended Harvard University; his support for full cultural assimilation of Native people and his contention that he had never experienced discrimination was a critical part of his appeal.[35] More revealing was Clint Roberts' election to Congress from South Dakota's Second District six years after the Occupation of Wounded Knee. Roberts, a local white rancher, had once auditioned to be the "Marlboro Man." He believed all reservations should be eliminated and won the election handily.[36]

In the years after World War II, most white Dakotans recognized that the state had an "Indian problem," although they would not acknowledge their own complicity in it. Tom Brokaw recounts, for example, that when he first saw broadcasts of the civil rights movement and its "young Negro leader, Dr. Martin Luther King Jr.," he felt completely disconnected, as if the racial problems of the South were a world away from his home, made real only by the occasional remarks of a southern neighbor.[37] He did admit, however, that his Indian "friends" lived utterly separate lives and when he played basketball on the reservation he felt uncomfortable and "encircled."[38] Studies conducted in 1973 and 1974 for the WKLD/OC likewise showed that many Dakotans still believed Indians were inferior to whites and had only themselves to blame for their problems. One survey demonstrated that nearly half the people in Custer County believed the Lakota were poor because they "lacked ambition."[39] In phone interviews of residents of Rapid City, whites openly admitted that if they were seated on the jury for the Dennis Banks trial, they would not be objective. Some even admitted that they preferred the vigilante justice of the "Old West." Subject #210 said, "We'll hang the bastard."[40] In short, while most white Dakotans felt disconnected from "the shame of the South," their racial practices and cultural affiliations were more like those of white southerners than they realized. Until the early twenty-first century, businesses across the state sold Confederate flags; until 2015 the Veterans Affairs office in Hot Springs displayed three in the rotunda of the building.[41] While whites may never have understood the flags solely as emblems of white power, Native people likely got the message loud and clear.

*   *   *

If Dakotans, like many other northerners, did not perceive similarities between their racial prejudices and those of white southerners, by 1970 some Republican politicians did. Furthermore, they hoped to make the two groups political allies. In 1964 George Wallace even surprised himself when he took his campaign for the Democratic nomination for President out of Dixie and into northern communities. He received so many votes in the Wisconsin primary—34 percent—that he purportedly said, "if I ever had to leave Alabama, I would like to live in South Milwaukee."[42] He also contended that both parts of the country practiced residential segregation while only southerners admitted it. He famously said to an aide after one enthusiastic rally, "Great God! That's it! They're all Southern! The whole United States is Southern."[43] While fewer than 5 percent of South Dakota voters

choose Wallace in the 1968 election, he found his largest group of supporters in the West River counties that bordered reservations.[44]

In the late 1960s the young Republican strategist Kevin Phillips built
on Wallace's observation that all white Americans shared racist views. He
predicted that over time conservatives could create "a new Republican
majority" from the ashes of a Democratic Party allied with "black and
brown" voters.[45] Because he believed the party should seek to attract white
Democrats who supported segregation and segregationist candidates, Phillips called it the "Southern Strategy." But the trick, he and other like-
minded young Republicans knew, would be to appeal to racial animus
without sounding racist. They advised candidates, including Richard
Nixon, to choose words and phrases that stood in for race and would trans-
late into race when white voters heard them. In a 1981 interview, Lee
Atwater recalled: "You start out in 1954 by saying 'Nigger, nigger, nigger.'
By 1968 you can't say 'nigger'—that hurts you, backfires, so you say stuff
like, uh, forced busing, states' rights, and all that stuff . . . now you're
talking about cutting taxes, and these things you're talking about are totally
economic things and a byproduct of them is, blacks get hurt worse than
whites . . . 'we want to cut this,' is . . . a hell of a lot more abstract than
'nigger, nigger.'"[46] Democrats soon called those rhetorical abstractions
"dog whistles." Whatever the name, they signaled the same outcome: a
Republican Party aiming to create a multiregional coalition of white people.
With an almost unbelievable degree of cynicism, Phillips even suggested
that Republicans stop trying to derail the Voting Rights Act: "The more
Negroes who register as Democrats in the South, the sooner the Negro-
phobe whites will quit the Democrats and become Republicans."[47]

Over time the "southern strategy" became so successful that few historians interrogated its correlative substrategy: maintaining the solid Republican allegiances of the rural states in the interior west—particularly the
Central and Northern Plains. It was no small thing to try to merge these
regions politically or culturally; before 1980, the states of the Northern
Plains had only voted in concert with those in the Deep South in three
presidential elections of the twentieth century: 1932, 1936, and 1964. Phillips nevertheless understood that keeping these states in the Republican
column was vital to creating a "New Republican majority." Apparently,
however, he did not think it would be difficult, devoting only forty of the
book's nearly six hundred pages to the topic and lumping six "Farm Belt"
states together.[48] He reasoned that the "essential social conservatism of the

region" together with its ethnic makeup and history of resentment toward Washington would be more than enough to keep voters on the Northern Plains from drifting to the Democrats. He considered the region, as James Boyd wrote for the *New York Times*, "the great electoral bastion of Republicanism that is against aid to blacks, against aid to big cities, and against the liberal lifestyle it sees typified by purple glasses, beards, long hair, bralessness, pornography, coddling to criminals, and moral permissiveness run riot."[49]

Phillips was spot on in predicting that voters on the Northern Plains would join southerners in the new conservative movement, although he should not have taken their allegiance for granted. Phillips acknowledged that in earlier decades, these "bastions" of Republicanism were filled with business-oriented Republicans as well as Populists, Progressives, socialists, and members of the Nonpartisan League; he also saw that the agrarian wing of the party had supported a variety of distinctly unconservative programs and policies, from state ownership of utilities to federal support for agriculture. But he barely mentioned that many in the Dakotas had also been ardent anti-militarists.[50] As a result, he must have been hard pressed to explain how, within a few years of his book's publication, a Democratic resurgence in both states in the late 1960s and early 1970s brought a raft of new governors and state legislators, as well as continued support for antiwar senators George McGovern and Quentin Burdick, demonstrating an ongoing attraction to progressive ideas of all kinds.

Even so, as we have seen, the conditions for the dominance of new conservatism had gradually emerged throughout the postwar years. The most important was the one Phillips overlooked entirely: the presence of the military, its personnel, and the kinship it created with Dakotans. That new reality in turn equipped local people to embrace anti-communism, evangelical Protestantism, and national defense. Likewise, living next door to secretive representatives of the nuclear state had helped Dakotans hone a fine distinction between supporting the military but not the federal government. The highly structured and surveilled culture of the military also reinforced the region's traditional views of race, gender, and sexuality.[51] Then, in the 1970s, the people of the Northern Plains confronted their own civil rights crisis with a backlash reminiscent of the Jim Crow South, made all the more violent by the region's easy access to military hardware and perspectives. Together these demographic, economic, religious, and cultural shifts enabled the people of the Northern Plains not just to "hear" the dog whistles of the new GOP but in time to blow them. Beginning in earnest in the late 1970s, the people of the Northern Plains linked arms with white southerners, working to constitute the New Right's Republican majority and voting in large and increasing majorities for every Republican candidate for president from Richard Nixon to Donald Trump.

This new coalition might have surprised some observers, but to the Oglala Lakota it made perfect sense. After all, as the Native woman LaDonna Harris told Tom Brokaw in the 1990s, "South Dakota . . . is the Mississippi of the Indian nation."[52]

*   *   *

As the Occupation of Wounded Knee continued, it became more evident that although still in its political infancy, the goals and language of the "southern strategy" had taken hold on the Northern Plains. Over the course of the late winter, Dakotan men and women put their concerns— and demands—in letters to elected officials, pastors, newspaper editors, and visiting officials. They were angry and wanted the government to bring the occupation to an end. But their letters rarely included explicit racial epithets. Instead nearly all who opposed the Occupation employed the very same codes that Lee Atwater had said the Republican Party could substitute for blunt racist attacks. They did not use the term "nigger," of course, but neither did they use the terms "redskins" or "savages."[53] Rather, they wrote about the breakdown of "law and order" in a society that "coddled" criminals, outlaws, radicals, renegades, and "hoodlums." They described themselves as aggrieved and overburdened "taxpayers" whose own rights were being taken away.[54] As Raymond French of Box Elder, South Dakota, asked Governor Kneip, "why are Indians . . . getting food stamps free. . . . Don't you think it's about time to stop playing around with taxpayers' money?"[55] They even wrote about the ways in which white people, not Indians, were being discriminated against. In a telegram he sent to Governor Kneip, Reverend Robert Wright asked: "How long must we tolerate the violent act of AIM or other groups who feel they have a right to burn loot and take hostages and walk away from the damage unchallenged. . . . [s]omething must be done to protect the rights of those whom they attack."[56]

While white Dakotans used coded language to express their resistance to racial equality, they did not mince words when demanding an end to the Occupation by any means necessary. Kenneth Munce put it bluntly in a letter to the Democratic governor, Richard Kneip: "law and order must be restored at any cost."[57] Furthermore, many letter writers, especially men, urged officials to behave in more masculine ways. In a letter to Senator McGovern, for example, H. Saunders of Hot Springs asked, "Why? Why? Has this been allowed to continue?? This type of action should be stopped once and for all. It seems to me that a government that allows such actions shows a weakness and not the strength that it has always been so proud of."[58] Rex Witte of Glad Valley demanded to know, "When is someone with authority in this state going to find enough guts to do something about these AIM Indians?"[59] Genevieve Layman went so far as to taunt the governor, asking, "Are you a servant of the people or a puppet of the Federal Government?"[60]

Dakotans also made it clear that they did not consider the Occupiers to be real Americans. The members of AIM, they said repeatedly, were not local people from Pine Ridge, even though some inarguably were. A few South Dakotans did not even think AIM itself could be responsible. On March 14, more than twenty days into the occupation, the *Rapid City Journal* reprinted an editorial from the *Arizona Republic* that argued, "Wounded Knee is simply too well-organized, too well-financed, too slick to have been the impromptu work of AIM."[61] Mrs. Harvey Hullinger was sure she had seen a photographer from Russia "taking pictures at some of these invasions." Or, she claimed, it was possible that the events at Wounded Knee had been incited by the same people responsible for the riots in the Los Angeles neighborhood of Watts.[62] Earl Allen, on the other hand, implicitly blamed an even more long-standing regional foe: Jews like New York attorney William Kunstler. Allen described these hidden foes as "sinister international powers . . . a foreign enemy press and media . . . [and] liberal activist attorneys" who aimed to promote "anarchy and defiance."[63]

Standing opposed to AIM, whites believed they were the "real Americans" of the Northern Plains. Decades before Sarah Palin boasted that small-town people were the country's "real Americans" and "pro-Americans," South Dakotans—who themselves had once been called dangerous radicals—were claiming these honorifics for themselves.[64] After South Dakota governor Richard Kneip had threatened to get tough with AIM, Earl Allen wrote: "heartfelt 'thanks' . . . for your red-blooded Americanism, manifest publicly at a time when the outlook is mighty bleak to the average conscientious American citizen."[65] Dan Gallimpore had an idea: "How about an America for the people who love it?"[66] No New Right Republican on the national stage, not Kevin Phillips, Lee Atwater, Pat Buchanan, Richard Nixon, Ronald Reagan, or George W. Bush could have said it better.

*   *   *

During a service one Sunday morning at the First Methodist church in Vivian, South Dakota, Vera Hullinger's pastor read a letter from the region's bishop, James Armstrong. Armstrong appealed to Methodists to donate to a special offering dedicated to buying food, clothing, and medicine for members of AIM inside Wounded Knee. Mrs. Hullinger did not hide her outrage. If there had been only one place where white South Dakotans were sure their anger about Wounded Knee would be understood, it was their local church. Why should her hard-earned money go to "criminals and renegades"? Was the church going to pay local ranchers back for the cattle that had been killed by the protesters? As a parting shot, she announced that she would not be returning to the Methodist church in Vivian. "Why go to Church anymore; to hear a letter read that makes me sick at my stomach and gives my husband a heart attack . . . I do not expect any answers. Only Excuses."[67] Mrs. Hullinger's criticisms were more in line with the teachings of the evangelical churches filling pews across the region. Focused on Bible readings, personal salvation, and conservative morality, leaders of these churches were not in league with violent protesters of color or, excepting African American evangelicals, any people of color at all.[68]

Vera was far from alone in her anger, sense of betrayal, and view that mainline Protestant officials were out of touch with the needs of local Dakotans. Many Dakotans argued that church leaders could not be "neutral" or "conciliatory" if they were inside Wounded Knee, providing food and medicine donated by parishioners. David Peterson, a trustee at the McCabe Methodist Church in Bismarck, demanded that any McCabe funds sent to AIM be returned immediately. "This is absolutely the most ridiculous thing that the United Methodist Church has done since I have been a member of it."[69] Harvey Hullinger excoriated Bishop Armstrong for appeasing AIM by "refusing to cut off food and supplies."[70] Not even all local pastors agreed with their leaders' approach. The Board of Directors at Trinity Lutheran Church in Rapid City voted to suspend any further donations from going to the Minneapolis-based American Lutheran Church. Pastor Burnell Lund explained: "you'd better take another look at your ethics in by-passing a host of clergy who neither invited nor wanted the NCC or you on the scene . . . you fraternise with AIM, promote their philosophy, aid their cause, and espouse their methods without ever befriending the local clergy."[71]

Dakotans perceived, quite correctly, that the NCC institutionally and mainline Protestant leaders individually had supported liberal causes ranging from peace activism and feminism to racial justice—about which whites in the region were ambivalent, at best. In fact Armstrong, named the executive director of the NCC and the "most influential church leader in America in 1982," personified this new kind of churchman-activist. His first churches were in Florida in the 1950s where he worked on behalf of local African Americans facing de jure racism. It was not easy. His son, Jim, remembered when "the letters and phone calls started" and when he "began getting into fights with kids on the street. . . . There were always threats."[72] In Indianapolis in the early 1960s, Armstrong created a church-affiliated day care center, staffed women's health clinics, and taught a course on the "urban church."

Like some missileers, Armstrong found being reassigned to the Dakotas "almost devastating."[73] He could not imagine how he could continue his social justice work in such an isolated, predominantly white region. Soon he realized, however, that "the irrational, intolerant, uninformed racism and vigilante mind-set, common in the rural South during those days, is present at our doorstep."[74] Unlike many Dakotans, though, once he realized the depth of the region's racial problems, he was more than ready to enter the fray. Soon Armstrong was joined by his Methodist colleague John P. Adams, a full-time NCC crisis mediator. Adams was behind the scenes in Selma, Jackson State, and Kent State, before he negotiated on behalf of AIM activists at Wounded Knee. He regarded his assignment as nothing less than "biblical . . . to seek justice and to care for the poor and oppressed."[75] As he would soon find out, South Dakotans' idea of what the Bible commanded was something else entirely.

The NCC redoubled its commitment to social justice activism, even though it knew that activist pastors like Armstrong and Adams were not what most parishioners in rural areas wanted.[76] In 1972, just a year before the Occupation, an NCC official "cited churchgoers' frustration with pastors and denominational leaders who embraced social issues and neglected parishioners' spiritual needs."[77] Moreover mainline churches seemed "lonelier" each year.[78] In 1970 most NCC-affiliated churches had already begun to see a decline in membership—it would increase to 15 percent in the next decade. At the same time evangelical churches grew at a breakneck pace. Pentecostal churches, for example, grew 300 percent in both North and South Dakota between 1970 and 1980.[79] Theologically, many evangelicals believed that personal salvation and guidance from the "inerrant" Bible was far more important than social uplift. Leaders of these churches promised, in Jerry Falwell's words, "not to be politicians, but to be soul winners."[80] And the context of the global Cold War, with nuclear holocaust never far away, also motivated the faithful to look inside themselves, not at society as a whole. As the evangelical Christian journalist Michael Gerson explained, "if Armageddon is coming soon, as most evangelicals believe, getting right with God is the only rational choice to make."[81]

But evangelical Protestant leaders' silence on civil rights—their choice to "sit out" rather than "sit in"—was itself a political action. They soon abandoned both their pretense of race neutrality and their disavowal of politics. Instead, evangelical leaders guided their flock into the public square in defense of white culture. In 1979, Jerry Falwell organized the "Moral Majority" to activate Christian conservatives, both evangelicals and Catholics, to join him in a Christian conservative coalition. Only four years later, the Supreme Court ruled in the *Bob Jones University* case that Christian schools would lose their nonprofit status if there was evidence of racial discrimination in admissions.[82] An early leader of the New Right, Richard Viguerie argued that the IRS controversy over race in Christian schools " 'kicked the sleeping dog. It galvanized the religious right. It was the spark that ignited the religious rights' involvement in real politics.' "[83] In the South, Christian schools had been established to circumvent school desegregation and provide a refuge for whites. So too were the churches that supported and sometimes housed the schools. Across the country, many evangelical Americans adopted the southern view that no "unelected bureaucrat" should have the right to take away the protected status of Christian organizations. With the spread of the Moral Majority in the 1980s, few elected Republicans would ever try.[84]

* * *

In the context of the Occupation of Wounded Knee—which itself occurred during the militarization of the region—the most significant difference between liberal leaders of mainline denominations and their increasingly racially resentful parishioners was their definition of violence and who had the right to use it. This was no mere esoteric or theological question, nor was its application limited to the conflict at Wounded Knee. Whether "militant" people of color would be granted full citizenship or disarmed, incarcerated, and killed by armed representatives of the state—who themselves had access to military equipment to use in response to "disturbances"—was a defining issue in late twentieth-century politics across the nation. Due to the ongoing activism of all nations on the plains, North and South Dakota served as the epicenter of this debate in the rural "Jim Crow North."[85]

As we have seen, in the 1960s and 1970s, liberal church leaders increasingly stood on the side of social justice. Furthermore, they came to see that commitment as justifying the limited use of violence. White northern churchmen such as Yale chaplain William Sloane Coffin had participated in nonviolent demonstrations organized by Southern Christian Leadership Conference (SCLC). Yet through those experiences, he and his peers came to sympathize with the view, held by Malcolm X and members of the Black Panther Party, that committed nonviolence had only begotten more violence—police dogs, water hoses, beatings, church bombings, arsons, torture, murders, and assassinations of people of color.[86] For some younger activists, the time had come "to arm for self-defense."[87] In the city jails of Minneapolis, these ideas also inspired organizers of the Red Power movement.

By learning from Black Power activists and African American leaders in the black church, liberal white leaders of mainline Protestant churches began to rethink what constituted violence or abuse of power. When used by the oppressed, they argued, violence did not indicate power or, necessarily, criminality. As John Adams wrote three years after Wounded Knee, "Violence can be a voice, a scream for help, and a hopeful piercing cry ending with a deep sigh of despair."[88] When used by powerful people or by the state, however, violence was the ultimate source of repression, and it could take multiple forms. "Remember," Adams told readers: "those who are privileged and powerful do not have to engage in public protest . . . they can make phone calls, or they can write letters. . . . They can even engage in violence, but it will be so subtle and discreet that it will hardly be

noticed. In contrast, the violence of the desperate is exposed and conspicuous."[89] In a private letter to a liberal-leaning constituent, Senator McGovern, a close ally of both Armstrong and Adams, suggested that prejudice
and poverty themselves were a kind of violence: "We cannot condone the
'daily violence' faced by almost every Indian citizen—the violence of poor
housing, inadequate medical care, lack of job opportunities, discrimination,
education, and almost every area of human activity where the Indian has
not shared equitably in the advantages available to most Americans."[90] A
sympathetic local newspaper editor put the familiar "law-and-order" trope
in a fresh light too, saying, "Let us have law and order, say those who
disapprove of the Indian protests. What could be more lawful than solemn
treaties entered into by our government? What could be more orderly than
thoughtful, practical interpretation and implementation of those treaties?"[91]

Dennis Banks and other AIM leaders saw violence in much the same
way as leaders of the Black Power movement and their liberal white allies: as
the root of white power. Clyde Warrior threatened: "If this country [only]
understands violence, then that is the way to do it."[92] Many of the activists
understood that racism, violence, and militarism were closely linked. Banks
had come by this view the hard way. At seventeen, he had enlisted in the
United States Air Force, serving enthusiastically as an aerial photographer
with a top-secret clearance at a large air force base outside Tokyo.[93] When
the military wanted to expand the base's runways, they seized "a large
chunk of useful farmland." Soon a massive protest drew Japanese university
students, monks, and local farmers to the fence that separated Japanese
land from the American airway. Dennis Banks, M-16 in hand, faced the
protesters with orders to "shoot to kill" any protester who breached it. He
knew he couldn't do it. The protesters simply wanted their land, no different from his people at home. "It was the hour of awakening. I had been
guarding the ramparts of the American Empire, but now I felt like those
Crow and Arikara Indians who, after scouting for Custer and fighting on
behalf of the whites, were pitted against their own brothers, the Cheyenne
and Lakota. . . . The American Air Force, which I had thought was a friend,
turned out to be an enemy."[94] Years later, Banks still thought of himself as
a warrior—but for his people, not for American empire. This time, with
other Native veterans, he would take on the FBI, the ATF, and even the
American military itself in the spirit of his own ancestors and elders. "The
message that went out was that a band of Indians could take on this government. Tecumseh had his day and Geronimo, Sitting Bull, Crazy Horse. And

we had ours."⁹⁵ Banks and others inside Wounded Knee did not shy away from threatening violence, using violence, or even claiming they had gone to war.⁹⁶ After the siege ended and many of the buildings were in disrepair, Vernon Bellecourt told the *New York Times*, "We were in an all-out war. There was little time for housekeeping."⁹⁷

White South Dakotans did not see the use of violence as a call for help or a method of protest for the oppressed. They did not think that people of color had the right to choose whatever form of protest they thought was most effective. They did not think that Natives had anything positive in common with the Japanese or Vietnamese. Instead they thought any people who declared war against America were traitors. Most importantly, they believed that if anyone in South Dakota had the right to take up arms in self-defense, it was the "responsible" local property owners and taxpayers. Again and again they objected to the "violent methods" AIM adopted and called the leaders criminals and hoodlums, while taunting officials for being too "weak" to take more aggressive action. One woman asked Bishop Armstrong, "Why are you so afraid of someone getting killed?" He responded, "Ma'am the church is not in the killing business."⁹⁸

Revealing their belief that only whites had the right to defend themselves, some South Dakotans organized vigilante groups and patrols, like the one formed in Custer after AIM protested the murder of Wesley Bad Heart Bull. There the sheriff had deputized local men and instituted a twenty-four-hour watch. Years later, he recalled that "there wasn't a male in town over sixteen years old that didn't walk around with some kind of weapon."⁹⁹ During a subsequent protest in Rapid City, Mayor Don Bartlett warned AIM that "if you want Rapid City to be as famous as Selma, I could take care of that in 15 minutes."¹⁰⁰ During the Occupation, local whites tried to block access along local roads to anyone arriving to support AIM. Some local ranchers began shooting into the occupied area at night, trying to incite a firefight that would end the stalemate.¹⁰¹ Many officials recognized the real threat of vigilantism. George McGovern, for example, encouraged the government to take more meaningful steps toward peace, before "'angry, private citizens' took matters into their own hands."¹⁰²

White vigilantes were not alone in their efforts to force AIM out of Wounded Knee and reclaim the right to use violence for whites. As ever in a settler colonial society, they had the help of the government. What surprised both critics and sympathizers was only that it had taken the FBI so long to infiltrate Wounded Knee and subdue AIM. From the beginning, the government had given the FBI a "blank check," agent Joseph Trimbach remembered, to buy as many rifles and as much ammunition as they could.[103] Even so, it was not until the first peace agreement collapsed in late March and Agent Grimm was nearly killed that Nixon authorized the use of a thoroughly militarized operation against AIM—one which would portend the militarized police operations against people of color, including those at Standing Rock, in the twenty-first century. By historian Jill Gill's accounting: "The US government responded with . . . army units from the 82nd Airborne, two F4 Phantom jets, several national Guard helicopters, 17 armored personnel carriers, machine guns, flares, about 150 FBI agents, over 200 US marshals, at least 100 police from the BIA, several Justice Department officials, CIA investigators, and Secret Service agents."[104] For AIM members just back from Vietnam, this "assemblage looked . . . like the Vietnam War had come home."[105]

Taking guns from the leaders of AIM had always been a primary goal of the government operation, just as it had been at the 1890 massacre. The first treaty had failed when activists would not disarm in exchange for the promise of future meetings in Washington, DC. Kent Frizzell explained, "The White House will not negotiate while guns are pointed at Federal officials at Wounded Knee! That is our Position! And I for one am prepared to stand by the agreement until hell freezes over. . . . The fun and games so far as I am concerned are over."[106] When the Occupation ended and AIM members only handed over "15 old guns," officials were furious yet again. "These guns are a lot of crap," Deputy Assistant Attorney General Richard Hellstern complained. "The arms dispossession part of the agreement has been violated."[107]

But the state-approved "fun-and-games" were not over. As described earlier, the government's prosecution of AIM leadership in St. Paul was an embarrassing failure, revealing the FBI's misconduct throughout the crisis. Nevertheless the FBI brought more than five hundred charges against other AIM members, costing the group tremendous amounts of money and time. Far more tragically, the state and federal government "looked the other way" while Dick Wilson and his GOONS made sure AIM members would pay for their actions—with their lives. Wilson warned, "The Oglala don't like what happened, and if the FBI don't get 'em, the Oglala will. We have our way of punishing people."[108] Between 1973 and 1976, the period Lakota called the "reign of terror," sixty members of AIM were killed on the reservation, giving Pine Ridge the highest murder rate in the country. The FBI investigated few of these crimes but responded fully and forcefully when two of their own agents, Jack Coler and Ronald Williams, were killed in a shootout on the reservation in 1975. After a nationwide manhunt, Leonard Peltier was arrested, convicted of the murders, and sentenced to two life terms. To this day, supporters regard Peltier as a political prisoner, rather than a convicted murderer.[109] Irregularities so marred the trial that in 2010 Amnesty International listed it as an "unfair trial."[110] Although he is in failing health and has served more than forty years in prison, Peltier has been denied parole and presidential pardon as recently as 2017.[111]

*   *   *

The people of the plains were far from the only white Americans, particularly men, determined to fight to "get their country back" after the civil rights movement and the defeat in Vietnam. Likewise, they were not the only ones in movie theaters who cheered the characters Rocky, Dirty Harry, Rambo, and "Top Gun" when they employed violence against people of color to protect America and its values.[112] But South Dakotans were alone in the late 1970s and 1980s in electing a governor who literally acted the part: self-proclaimed "Indian fighter" Bill Janklow. In his election for attorney general in 1974, Janklow vowed to crack down personally on AIM; he earned over two-thirds of the votes cast.[113] Janklow embraced violence in other spheres of public life, too. As a teen, Janklow chose a stint in the Marines over a stint in jail. As an elected official, he employed the lessons of military life to create new forms of incarceration and reform and reinstated the state's death penalty. Like many veterans, Janklow was also a gun lover and owned a collection that has long been rumored to have contained a bazooka.[114] During the late twentieth century, South Dakota gun laws became among the most relaxed in the country. They have remained so ever since.[115]

Janklow dropped out of high school and college but nonetheless graduated from University of South Dakota School of Law, taking a job as a legal aid attorney on the Rosebud Reservation. He first came to public attention when he switched sides and prosecuted members of AIM, including Sarah Bad Heart Bull, who had participated in the "riot" at the Custer Courthouse. The trial itself became a showcase for the struggle for authority between white South Dakotans and AIM after Natives in the courtroom refused to stand for Judge Joseph Bottum and Bottum responded by banning all but twenty Natives for the rest of the trial. When these twenty still did not act in accordance with courtroom etiquette, the state sent in a fully armed SWAT team that beat and arrested the unarmed Lakota. Sarah Bad Heart Bull and others were convicted and sentenced to prison terms.[116] Even before the Occupation at Wounded Knee had begun, Janklow was a local hero to some South Dakotans.

The subsequent Occupation of Wounded Knee outraged Janklow. He had represented many Lakota men and women, including some allied with Chairman Dick Wilson. To Janklow, AIM was a "renegade" group that put both moderate Native people and whites at risk. Thus when he ran for attorney general promising to restore "law and order," he meant it. Employed by Janklow, "law-and-order" was no euphemism, no carefully coded term, no cynical "southern strategy." Janklow promised South Dakotans that he would end AIM's role in the state by any means necessary, asserting: "The only way to deal with the Indian problem in South Dakota is to put a gun to the AIM leaders' heads and pull the trigger."[117] He also vowed to convict AIM leaders and either "put them in jail or under it."[118] According to Peter Matthiessen, Janklow worried about a race war and was determined to prevent it. As it turns out, he was not alone. Mary-Lee Chai recalled that her neighbors in Vermillion, hundreds of miles from Pine Ridge, also feared that "Indians wanted to kill white people for revenge."[119]

Not surprisingly, AIM vigorously opposed Janklow. In what would become one of their most controversial actions, AIM leaders held a news conference with twenty-two-year-old Jancita Eagle Deer. She alleged that when she was fifteen and served as Janklow's babysitter, Janklow had raped her. According to historian Peter Matthiessen, she had reported the assault when it happened—long before AIM had been organized—to the school principal. He had taken her to a doctor, who saw evidence of the attack.[120] A short time after the press conference, Jancita's body was found in a ditch.[121] No charges were ever brought against Janklow, although he was disbarred from the tribal court system. Janklow always strongly denied the charges.

As attorney general, Janklow moved to show that, if South Dakota were left alone to solve its "Indian problem," it would take strong action without delay. The first opportunity to do so came in May 1975 during an AIM-inspired occupation of the Yankton Sioux Meat processing plant in the reservation town of Wagner, where local Indians had long complained of underpay and underemployment. This occupation was actually the second action at the plant. The first, in March 1975, was like a miniature replay of the Occupation at Wounded Knee, with AIM leaders organizing local people to take over the plant and using the press to publicize their demands. Again the FBI waited out the occupiers and worked toward a peaceful resolution that included the arrest of the leaders and the disarming of other participants, with a local Methodist clergyman serving as an observer. But local whites grew fearful and impatient. According to Josh Garrett-Davis, "A vigilante force of fifty white farmers and ranchers with guns stowed in their pickup trucks stood ready to silence an Indian uprising if called upon."[122]

During the second occupation of the Wagner plant, vigilantes would be led by the attorney general himself, even though as a member of the state's Justice Department, he had no authority over most law enforcement.[123] With the support of local leaders, the BIA, and the state highway patrol, Janklow cut telephone wires to the plant, quarantined the area so other militants could not bring in arms and supplies, and imposed martial law on the tiny town. When an officer disobeyed orders and dispensed tear gas into the plant, forcing the occupiers out and ultimately into the hands of authorities, Janklow first said it was "one of these things that will happen." Later he "claimed credit for directing the tear-gas attack."[124] The press sang his praises across the region. The Sioux Falls *Argus Leader* commented, "The ending to this latest episode was as quick and clean as anyone could ask, or expect; Janklow deserves the credit."[125] Later Janklow prosecuted the occupiers to the fullest extent of the law. The trouble was that this action had not really been an AIM action after all, but the impulsive actions of seven young men, probably intoxicated at the time, who were not even sure why they had taken the plant. No matter: Janklow and the state had finally shown that it was "time to stop being soft on Indians just because they were a minority group."[126]

Because of term limits, Janklow served as governor for two separate eight-year periods, from 1978 to 1987 and from 1995 to 2003. During the Farm Crisis he acquired a national reputation for his populist style and innovative policies. But, along with diversifying the economy, Janklow added a touch of everyday racial extremism to his tenure in the statehouse. While he claimed to fear a "race war," he applauded efforts to track down any members of AIM.[127] He pushed relentlessly to expand uranium mining in the Black Hills, even though the 7.3-million-acre site was sacred ground for the Lakota and the Indian Claims Commission determined it had been seized from them illegally.[128] In 1995 when Lakota journalist Tim Giago suggested the state rename Columbus Day as Native American Day, Janklow replied, "We talk about reconciliation more than necessary."[129] In the fall of 2000, when Bill Clinton neared the end of his second term, Janklow "personally lobbied" the outgoing president not to pardon Leonard Peltier, later boasting about his role in keeping Peltier locked away.[130]

Janklow also employed his fondness for violent rhetoric and military-style governance by implementing new forms of incarceration. His famously tough-on-crime attitude emerged from his experience as an often-arrested teenager. Known to say that the discipline of the marines had saved his life, he sought similar ways to "rehabilitate" young offenders in the state. He modeled a new "youth training facility" in Plankinton after a military-style boot camp, with very little privacy or free time, strict rules, uniforms, constant drills, and compulsory exercise. On July 21, 1999, fourteen-year-old Gina Score, who had been sent to the facility after a "petty theft," was forced to run on an especially hot and humid day. She struggled from the beginning; camp leaders ignored her symptoms of heat exhaustion. "'Quit faking!'" several girls recalled a supervisor shouting, "'You're embarrassing us.'" According to an investigation done by *Mother Jones*, everyone knew the boot camp credo: "Quitting Is Not an Option." As a result, "When four girls encircled Gina to give her shade, counselors ordered them to back away."[131] She was left lying on the ground for three hours after she had collapsed, urinated on herself, and started to drool. EMTs recorded her temperature at 108 degrees; it was the worst case of heatstroke they had ever seen. A year after her death her parents still could not understand why the state would treat children so harshly. Gina's mother told a reporter from the *Rapid City Journal*, "After listening to what other parents say . . . [what] their kids have gone through there, I looked at my lawyer and at David and said, 'You know what? I'm glad she died. At least I know she didn't have to go through that mental stress afterwards.'"[132]

Janklow's prioritization of incarceration extended to transforming a state college in Springfield into a prison, over the strident objections of the community. At the same time, legislators made sweeping changes to sentencing laws and increased the budgets for local police departments. Mark Meierhenry, who served as Janklow's attorney general from 1979 to

1986, explained that in the 1980s, many legislators, like the governor, were veterans. They had fought in World War II or Korea, "had seen violence," and wanted retribution for victims' families. In 1980 only 609 people were in South Dakota prisons; ten years later 1,341 people were. In 2011 the number was 3,530.[133] The 2019 per capita incarceration rate was the highest in the country.[134] At the same time the number of police officers rose dramatically. In Mitchell, population 14,000, sometimes only an officer or two handled the night shift; over time that number increased by as much as 300 percent, even though the population stayed nearly the same. Mitchell's officers started to carry sophisticated equipment, including stun guns, sometimes obtained through military surplus.[135] In Custer, the hastily assembled force of citizen "deputies" who battled AIM members at the Custer County Courthouse were soon designated as a permanent "Sheriff's Reserve." They trained other local officials in search-and-rescue techniques —as well as the use of tear gas.[136]

Not surprisingly this increased incarceration rate has impacted— perhaps even targeted—Native people in the Dakotas more than whites. In fact, historian Nick Estes contends that "the rise in incarceration rates directly correlates with increased Native political activity in the 1970s."[137] While crimes committed on reservation lands are tried in tribal courts, those off reservation are tried in state or federal courts. Reflecting larger national trends, Native people have long been overrepresented in local jails, state prisons, and federal penitentiaries. But the numbers of incarcerated people, Natives in particular has risen drastically—500 percent—since 1977, in what Estes calls "a direct correlation with resistance and protest" and a new form of "the historical process of elimination."[138] In 2018 in South Dakota, Native people constituted 8.5 percent of the population, but 60 percent of federal prosecutors' caseload; in North Dakota, they made up less than 5 percent of the population and 25 percent of the caseload.[139] Studies demonstrate that Native people also received on average longer sentences for the same offenses as whites and are targeted—and killed— more often by police.[140] Finally the high rates of incarceration have contributed to high rates of Native suicide in the state. Some Native men openly call Sioux Falls, home to the largest state prison, "Suicide Falls."[141]

While Janklow was less active in promoting gun law reform than prison reform, his terms in office coincided with the liberalization of concealed carry laws in the state. In fact in 1985 South Dakota was one of the first six states to revise its concealed carry laws from those enacted in the 1930s in accordance with the federal Uniform Firearms Act. The earlier laws placed the burden on individuals to show that they *should* have the right to carry a concealed handgun; the later ones placed the burden on the state to show that they *should not*.[142] This change may seem minor but it was an important sign of the increasing influence and right-wing turn of the NRA. In 1977 conservative activist Harlon Carter captured control of the organization and radically changed its focus from marksmanship and safety to advocacy for a broad interpretation of the Second Amendment.[143] South Dakota was just the kind of state to embrace this change, as the state boasted a large number of hunters comfortable with guns and gun safety and a robust hunting-related tourist industry. But according to Roxanne Dunbar-Ortiz, the high percentage of military and military-affiliated residents in South Dakota would have also been a crucial factor influencing South Dakotans' views of gun rights. Veterans, like Governor Janklow, were far more likely than nonveterans to own guns and even be collectors. Likewise they were less likely to trust the federal government to protect individual rights.[144]

The Occupation of Wounded Knee undoubtedly deepened the urge white people of the Northern Plains felt to own guns and guarantee that the government could never take them away. They likely agreed with former Wyoming senator Alan Simpson when he boasted, "Without guns there would be no West"—but they did not mean in the hands of angry Natives.[145] In the anonymous space of an online forum for gun owners, a few South Dakotans admitted that their guns were needed for protection from Indians and the maintenance of white power. In response to a question asking whether non-Indians can bring weapons onto reservations, "460 sharpshooters" explained that "as a white man, I do not think I would be welcomed there for obvious reasons, i definately [sic] wouldn't go there unarmed."[146] Davek1977 could not have agreed more. Though he acknowledged that the "days of raiding parties and scalpings are over," he nevertheless portrayed Native people as dangerous and "reservations as hotbeds of criminal activity." "Many South Dakota residents realistically believe that they will be 'on their own' if the need for protection arises and [they] carry accordingly." In fact, Davek1977 could not remember a time when it had been illegal for South Dakotans to carry a concealed weapon almost anywhere they went.[147] If he had been born in 1977 as his online name suggests, he would have been just about right. Since he had been a young boy, there never had been any significant new restrictions on guns in South Dakota. In fact, since the rise of the American Indian Movement, the election of

Bill Janklow, and the consolidation of the New Right, there had not been, as he further alleged, a "more gun-friendly state" in the nation.[148]

* * *

To many Native people, the 2016 protests against the Dakota Access Pipeline at Cannon Ball, North Dakota, just outside the Standing Rock reservation, followed logically and took inspiration from the Occupation of Wounded Knee. Both actions brought diverse Native people together to protect treaty lands and promote traditional cultural practices and ways of knowing. But in many ways the Standing Rock actions also revised those taken by AIM in 1973, substituting nonviolence for threats of war, including female and two-spirit leaders alongside male "warriors," and allying themselves openly with international politics of decolonization. It even seemed that the protests had succeeded, when—at long last—in late fall 2016, President Obama ordered a stop to the construction of the pipeline under the sacred waterways of the Missouri River.[149]

But from a different perspective, the protest—or more precisely the state response to the protest—demonstrated the extent to which, as historian Nick Estes put it, "anti-Indianism has been reinforced under neoliberalism."[150] Nearly fifty years since his assassination, what Martin Luther King Jr. named as the three evils of modern society—capitalism, militarism, and racism—seemed more empowered, more entrenched, and more interconnected than ever. Even before the election of Donald Trump meant a victory for the pipeline, the signs that white conservatives and their corporate and military allies had consolidated power on the Northern Plains were everywhere. When protesters arrived on Black Friday to a mall near Bismarck, white shoppers identified them for the police—"they smell like smoke!"—and volunteered to help control and handcuff them. Police called those they arrested, "Prairie Niggers."[151] Months earlier, when North Dakota governor Jack Dalrymple declared a state of emergency, he paved the way for all forms of law enforcement and all manner of militarized response—from police dogs, tear gas, armored vehicles, chemical sprays, water cannons, rubber bullets, and assault weapons—to be deployed against his own residents. Perhaps most revealingly, the state engaged not

just state and federal forces, but TigerSwan, the private security organization of Energy Transfer Partners Corporation. One agent was overheard
recommending that they employ the same "brilliant" counterinsurgency
tactics that the Israelis use against Palestinians.[152]

As horrifying as these attacks on nonviolent demonstrators in the name
of corporate power were, to Standing Rock chairman David Archambault,
they were not surprising. "Perhaps only in North Dakota, where oil tycoons
wine and dine elected officials . . . would state and county governments act
as the armed enforcement for corporate interests."[153] It is doubtful that
North Dakota alone deserves the distinction. But the actions of the officers
and citizens of the "Peace Garden State" shined a bright light on its cruel
calculus everywhere.

CHAPTER 8

"THE COMPANIES YOU KEEP"

WHEN DEBRA MARQUART WAS growing up on a farm outside Napoleon, North Dakota, in the 1960s and 1970s, the grain elevator was the most important building in town. In her memoir *The Horizontal World*, she wrote that "the grain elevator props up the whole sky; it holds down the earth." Inside "the grain that sleeps fat and finished . . . comes from the sunshine and soil. It brings together heaven and earth."[1] In every country town along the railroad line, grain elevators collected the end product of the community's individual and collective labors. So much effort, risk, pain, danger, and loss—and so much wealth—were contained in local grain elevators that in 1922 the Nonpartisan League (NPL) had organized a state-owned mill and elevator. By sending grain to the state-owned and union-run elevator in Grand Forks, rather than those owned by large agricultural commodity corporations in the Twin Cities, farm families' profits were not siphoned off by "middlemen."[2] When the cooperatively owned grain elevator in Napoleon burned to the ground one day in the early 1970s—the "roaring" and "crackling" grains inside "going from yellow to orange to red"—it was "a catastrophe." The gathering townspeople felt "cut off from the world."[3]

A bell-bottom-wearing teen, Debra Marquart never wanted to be a farm wife, a teacher, or a nun, the options she felt were available to girls in Napoleon. After graduating from high school in 1974, she—like Hamlin Garland ninety years earlier—put the farm "in her rearview mirror" and planned never to return. But in time the land drew her back. When she returned decades later she was struck that the local grain elevator—rebuilt a year after the fire—was no longer the region's only defining construct and its contents no longer the region's only defining product. Furthermore, skepticism of large corporations—including those that profited from war—was no longer a defining element of the region's political culture. In a multisection poem from 2015, she demonstrated that the state now valued various "small, buried things" that were controlled and extracted by powerful, faraway organizations, and which put the public in harm's way.[4] First there were the two air force bases: "How many does one state need?" she asked. Next came the Minuteman missiles in their concrete underground "silos."[5] They had made North Dakota "ground zero" in any coming war, a potential "national zone of sacrifice" where anyone who lived above the ground would be "obliterated." Even so, she observed, "some people" liked the bases and servicepeople, missiles and missileers: they boosted the local economy and they made the state "strategic." A few people even felt "safer."[6]

But that was not all Marquart saw. Two miles under the soil of western North Dakota, far deeper than the missiles, was shale. With new hydraulic extraction (fracking) technology shale could produce oil—perhaps as much as four hundred billion barrels. By the early twenty-first century huge multinational energy corporations had constructed a different kind of edifice in western North Dakota: eleven thousand oil wells, pumping more than a million gallons per day. While it produced revenue for the state and kept unemployment low even during the Great Recession—North Dakota's "economic miracle"—fracking put expediency and private profit over public welfare. Extracting and processing shale required millions of gallons of water from underground aquifers, which was then filled with chemicals and "reinjected/in the land."[7] It also produced constant noise, flying dirt, land tremors, and radioactive waste. No one would know for years if the land or water had been permanently contaminated, if the region had become a "national zone of energy sacrifice."[8] Marquart described local politicians as "co-opted (or cowards or bought-out or honest and thwarted)." Rather than thinking about the long-term consequences of fracking, they simply "opened you up and said, *take everything.*" Imagining fracking's inevitable end-game, she wrote,

> north dakota who will ever be able to live with you
> once this is all over I'm speaking to you now
> as one wildcat girl to another be careful north dakota.[9]

By conjoining three seemingly unrelated structures—bases, missiles, and oil rigs—Marquart's poem mirrors the consolidation of military and private sectors in twenty-first-century America. Many North Dakotans, and other Americans, have justified fracking by saying that oil and gas produced this way would be "conflict-free"—requiring no wars on foreign soil to obtain it. Writing in the *Grand Forks Herald*, for example, Todd Fuchs contended that, "Using lessons from our state, oil producers have grown American production and lowered net energy imports from a high of 60 percent in 2005 to less than 17 percent, setting a 58-year record low."[10] But even with America's emerging "energy independence," no lasting peace in the Middle East appears near and the production of "conflict-free oil" has brought military-base-style conflicts to previously isolated American communities: increased crimes against women, sex trafficking, collapsing infrastructure. The crowded "man camps" in Williston reminded journalist Jeremy Miller of military bases because they were built in much the same way.[11] Likewise, many of the same multinational energy corporations—ExxonMobil, Halliburton, and ConocoPhillips, for example—that profited immensely from government subcontracting during our wars in Iraq and Afghanistan have profited immensely from similar work in the Bakken Formation. For shareholders in these corporations, the idea that "peace might break out" sounds like an off-color joke or, worse, a bad dream. In response to a question about the end of the war in Afghanistan, for example, a contractor from General Dynamics replied, "God Forbid!"[12]

As fracking supports the military, the military supports fracking. When North Dakotans became concerned about the small tremors caused by fracking and their proximity to ICBMs, military, oil, and gas officials pronounced confidently—if not entirely persuasively—that the numerous small earthquakes caused by drilling posed no danger. They said so despite the fact that, as in the Cold War, in the 2010s Dakotans were far more at risk of a devastating nuclear accident—a broken arrow—than a nuclear strike.[13] Marquart's poem relates the suspiciously well-coordinated responses of the authorities:

> the commander of the air base says,
>> *We can certainly co-exist with the oil industry*
> the petroleum council vice president says,
>> *we're communicating about how we share our territory*
> the air force commander reports,
>> *the drilling frenzy has presented no ill-effects to the ICBMS.*[14]

Who is the "we" these officials are referring to, Marquart seems to ask. Are they connected in any way with "we the people" of North Dakota? Or, are they merely the representatives of what Chris Hedges has called the military-industrial complex's "creeping coup d'état?"[15]

Finally, looming above these visible connections between bases, missiles, and oil wells is a more abstract, seemingly unanswerable concern—perhaps better posed as a question: What needs might local communities, counties, and states have prioritized; what other sources of funding for farming, the environment, healthcare, suicide prevention, addiction care, education, or infrastructure might they have received; and how much might their tax burden have been decreased if so much of the federal budget had not gone to the military over the past seventy years? Since the 1960s a handful of activists have been inserting dollar signs into the equation, arguing for "Farms not Arms": *New Yorker* writer Ian Frazier, for example, suggested that each missile silo represented the value to the county of "five years' worth of cattle, grain, and wheat."[16] Reverend L. J. Murtagh of Watertown, South Dakota, asked, "Do we want two billion dollars for a dumb weapon that will increase the arms race or more funds for programs to build the nation? The grain silo is a sign of life; the missile silo a sign of death."[17]

Marquart also wonders about the trade-off. Perhaps if Dakotans, like all Americans, had not welcomed the military and applauded its ever-growing budget, they might have imagined instead a world like the one their Populist predecessors did—with fewer weapons, far fewer wars, and more funding for human needs and the public good. In that world, North Dakotans might never have welcomed bases, bombs, and oil rigs. They might never have sought out "all these new friends" and "the companies you keep."[18] They may not have needed to risk land and lives and legacy in the first place—simply to pay their bills.

What had happened while Debra Marquart was away? How had it come about that two of the very organizations that generations of Dakotans had warned against—the military and wealthy corporations—had come to play such important, influential, and fully integrated roles in a region that was still largely rural? What had happened was a major transformation of Dakota politics, and that of the nation. Gradually, over the half century that followed World War II, Dakotans came to embrace all three of the major pillars of New Right–style conservatism. First and most fundamentally, beginning in the 1940s, most Dakotans turned away from their history of Populist anti-militarism and committed themselves to fighting communism both at home and abroad. They welcomed military bases and, albeit more cautiously, nuclear weapons to their communities and land. By 1980 they had largely banished outspoken anti-militarist politicians like George McGovern who questioned the use of American armed forces around the world. Partly as a consequence of having become "kin" with the military, they also learned to distinguish between a large and interventionist military—which they now supported—and a large and interventionist federal government—which they never had. Meanwhile, in response to 1960s and 1970s liberal activism, most Dakotans doubled down on traditional conservative social and cultural values. In sympathy with the values of national conservative organizations that had created the "new Republican majority," Dakotans found new words, political leaders, religious institutions, and legal mechanisms through which to protect white power and patriarchy. Over time Dakotans' allegiance to the Republican Party, made obvious in presidential contests but far more influential in elections for governor and state legislators, would prove just how essential the region was to the triumph of the New Right and even perhaps to the brand of conservatism to follow.

But full partnership with the New Right required one more commitment from people of the Northern Plains—at the worst possible time. It required a commitment to conservative economic principles of free markets, smaller government, lower taxes, and deregulation just as the agricultural sector began its worst economic decline since the Great Depression. Beginning in the late 1970s, as many as three hundred thousand farmers, most of them in the Midwest, lost their land when crop prices plummeted, interest rates skyrocketed, and they could not pay back loans. This downturn had an impact on states' revenues, local businesses' viability, and rural towns' survival.[19] The Farm Crisis was not limited to a year or two but continued to affect families throughout the 1980s and beyond. Farmers across the region, including many who had supported Reagan, expected the kind of emergency help and ongoing support from the federal government they had received for years; many were surprised when, due to the president's vow to help Americans learn "not to turn to the government to solve their problems," it did not arrive.[20] Soon new forms of radical agrarianism—what scholar/activist Harry Boyte called "New Populism"—arose in every Midwestern state, even motivating people who had scoffed at the student protesters of the recent past.[21] It had been a half century since Governor "Wild Bill" Langer told his Dust Bowl constituents threatened with foreclosure to "treat the banker like a chicken thief. Shoot him on sight." In the new hard times, a handful took his advice literally.[22] Far more used nonviolent action and political pressure to prioritize the NPL's "people first" agenda once again.[23]

The Farm Crisis lasted long enough to change the agricultural landscape permanently but farmers' impassioned commitment to "New Populism" did not. Even during the crisis itself, agrarian activism met opposition born of the ascendant force of new conservatism, sometimes expressed inside the New Populist organizations themselves. Meanwhile increasingly desperate state officials sought new ways to diversify state economies to limit the devastation of future agricultural downturns. Between 1980 and 1995 leaders in the Dakotas, including some Democrats, embraced fiscal conservatism, welcomed corporations, and cut public expenditures. In the wake of farm consolidations and the merger of large agribusinesses, the same trends crept into agriculture. While voters in both states passed legislation aimed to protect states against corporate farming, the increased size of "family" farms created a new reality of "family corporations" and LLCs, with large numbers of out-of-state owners and nonresident operators.[24] Looking back at the decade in which small operators, the backbone of radical agrarianism, simply disappeared on the Northern Plains, historian William Pratt reluctantly concluded, "The 1980s may have witnessed the last significant progressive rural insurgency in American history."[25]

In 1999, after two decades of depopulation, farm consolidation, and the rise of factory farming, the Federal Reserve Bank's Center for the Study of Rural America organized a conference on rural economic development in the bank's Kansas City office. They dubbed it, "Beyond Agriculture." Journalist William Greider wrote that the center's director was an open proponent of factory farming as a positive good for rural communities that found maintaining the family farm model a "burden": "Corporate consolidation allows rural communities to put aside farm issues so they can pursue brighter prospects for development."[26] While they would never have called family farming a "burden" and they largely stood by bans on corporate farming in the states, conservative leaders in the Dakotas certainly agreed about pursuing those "brighter prospects for development." In fact by the time of the conference they had already found what Marquart called their "new companies to keep," many of which were tied directly or indirectly to the military. As for her beloved grain elevators, in some towns they were operated by computer from a different state. In others they were designated historical sites. In the Bakken they were torn down.[27] They no longer propped up the sky and held down the earth in quite the way they once had.

FIGURE 14. Abandoned prairie church, 2016, North Dakota. Dozens of original settler churches have closed on the Northern Plains due to aging congregations and rural depopulation. Photo by Nancy Gephardt. Photo via Good Free Photos.

*　*　*

In January 1986, Bruce Litchfield of Elk Point, South Dakota, shot his wife and two children as they slept in their beds, and then turned the gun on himself. Litchfield was a Little League coach, a regular in the pews of the local Lutheran church, and a devoted member of the Lion's Club. But he wasn't a farmer. He was the county director of the Farmers Home Administration (FHA), the federal "lender of last resort for family farms."[28] There had been hard times in his county since the late 1970s but for 1983 and 1984, the government had banned FHA foreclosures. While this made his job much less painful, when the ban expired, at least twenty of his clients were behind—some way behind—on their loan payments. Litchfield was already known in town as "a stickler for rules"; he would soon be known for forcing farmers off land that might have been in their families for a century or more. " 'The job has got pressure on my mind, pain on my left side,' " he wrote in a suicide note.[29] The Litchfield family's deaths would not have been included in the state's official count of farm suicides: men, most often, who simply could not endure another day of back-breaking work, deprivation, debt, and shame.[30] But they should have been. The Farm Crisis was a disaster for whole families, entire communities, and the Midwest as a region. Litchfield's murder-suicide revealed the tragically broad reach of the Farm Crisis.

Downturns in the agricultural economy, the loss of farms, and the consolidation of land were not new phenomena in the 1980s. In fact the number of farms and farmers had never stopped decreasing on the Northern Plains since the Great Depression.[31] As anthropologist Caroline Tauxe noted, "Family farming in the United States has always been a commercial system highly integrated with, and dependent upon, the capitalist economy and the world market."[32] Farmers' profits have always relied on macroeconomic forces and structures—not to mention weather systems—far beyond their control. After strong crop prices and unusually wet weather in the late 1910s and early 1920s, for example, drought and depression combined to drive thousands of farmers from the land in the 1930s; more fled in the 1950s and 1960s. The problems of the 1980s began similarly: with strong crop prices, good weather, low interest rates, rising land values, and expanding export markets in the 1970s. President Nixon's secretary of agriculture, Earl Butz, echoed the secretary of agriculture under President Eisenhower, Ezra Benson, when he pushed farmers to plant "fencerow to fencerow" and to "get bigger or get out."[33] Young farmers heeded the call in large numbers; they took out loans, bought more land and equipment, and planted as much as they could. Despite their parents' and grandparents' warnings, few imagined that the good times could come to a sudden, devastating end.

But they did. The Farm Crisis began with three decisions in 1979, made by men far from the Northern Plains. First, in an attempt to curb inflation, new Federal Reserve chairman Paul Volcker initiated a series of increases to the central bank's prime interest rates, making it more expensive for farmers to pay back their loans; lower rates of inflation meant they received lower prices for their crops. Both combined to decrease the value of their land. That same year, the USSR's Leonid Ilyich Brezhnev gave the order for troops to invade Afghanistan; President Carter responded with an embargo on sales of grain to the USSR. The embargo eliminated a major market for these lower-priced crops, thus reducing demand, making prices fall lower still, and debts even harder to repay. Throughout the crisis, farmers saw land, equipment, and even livestock repossessed by banks and other lenders, including government lenders such as the "lender of last resort." In many small towns banks themselves closed up shop.[34]

On the Northern Plains, these larger geopolitical developments created the foundations for the economic and social disaster that stretched across the 1980s and into the 1990s. In 1984, 24 percent of North Dakota farm operators either made no money at all or had a "negative net farm income."[35] The same year 38 percent of North Dakota farmers had "debt [to asset] ratios in the ranges generally associated with considerable financial stress [over 40 percent]."[36] Fourteen percent had debt-to-asset ratios of over 70 percent. In many families married women sought off-farm jobs to supplement farm income, sending young children to stay with their grandmother or a sitter. After spending a year living among farmers in Mercer County, North Dakota, Caroline Tauxe observed that in the 1980s, "A farmstead was a lonely place during the day. No longer the bustling scene familiar to American nostalgia—a barnyard full of small animals and a kitchen busy with aproned women preparing ample midday meals—instead, the visitor finds an empty house with a deserted air, and only a car and a hen or two pecking around the old machinery scattered around the outbuildings."[37] This change in women's roles—from relatively coequal farm producers to part-time low-wage workers—decreased their overall value as the "complementary" partners they had been imagined to be in the past. That made some rural women even more resentful of the apparently fanciful ideas of second-wave feminism. At the same time, it opened up new opportunities for some women to involve themselves at high levels in farm activism.[38]

The crisis cut South Dakota even more deeply. Farm bankruptcies climbed each year until they peaked in 1986 at nearly 700. According to research done by Jessica Giard for the Mitchell *Daily Republic*, "between 1978 and 1988 South Dakota had 500 fewer farms on average each year. In 1978, 40,000 farms were operating in the state. In 1988, there were 35,000."[39] Less income and fewer farmers meant fewer customers for local businesses and, consequently, fewer opportunities for off-farm employment, just when farm women and teens were looking for jobs. Soon economists began to talk of the state having a "dual economy"—growing populations and employment levels in expanding urban areas and declines in the countryside.[40] In 1983 retail sales in the ten largest communities in South Dakota expanded over 13 percent, despite the hard times. In the rest of the state's communities, they rose only 5.9 percent.[41] Downtown Main Streets began to see shuttered buildings and an increased incidence of property crime, a trend that would only accelerate in the 1990s, with malls and big box stores like Walmart locating far from town centers.[42] Finally, the Farm Crisis contributed to significant out-migration of young people and the aging of the population in general. In the Woonsocket School District, a consolidated system serving communities in Sanborn County, the average high school graduating class fell by nearly 50 percent from around 20 students in the 1980s and 1990s to 11 or fewer in the 2010s.[43] The county itself lost 28 percent of its population: in 2000 just over 2,500 people lived there.[44] Farmsteads in Sanborn County were becoming lonely places, it seemed, at all times of day.

∗   ∗   ∗

Ronald Reagan won more votes in the 1980 presidential election in South Dakota than any Republican presidential candidate since Dwight Eisenhower in 1952. In North Dakota he did even better. Not only did Reagan win more votes than Ike, he won more votes than two recent Democratic candidates—Al Gore (2000) and Hillary Clinton (2016)—combined. Reagan checked every box that had come to define the new conservatism: commitments to defense, traditional cultural and religious values, "law and order," lower taxes, and decreased size of government. But some Reagan voters in 1980 may not have taken his vow to limit government spending seriously. As Richard Reeves wrote in 1984, "Perhaps American voters in 1980 thought they were just hiring Ronald Reagan to trim the excesses of the liberal and generous welfare state. . . . But that was not the way the new President and his men saw it . . . the Republicans seized the moment as a mandate for the agenda of Reaganism."[45] In retrospect it might be more accurate to say that conservative voters in rural America did not take his threats to lower government spending *personally*. Most still supported funding for programs that benefited them—Social Security and Medicare, for example. Racial codes in mind, however, they wanted Reagan to cut programs for the "undeserving poor," not for "hard-working" Americans. No Americans, they believed, worked harder than farmers.

Reagan's agricultural policy was deeply influenced by Don Paarlberg of the Heritage Foundation and David Stockman, Reagan's manager of the Office of Management and Budget.[46] Paarlberg and Stockman believed that agricultural subsidies were outrageously expensive—twenty billion dollars annually—and thus not just bad for the government, but bad for farmers too, creating dependence antithetical to American free enterprise. Stockman had grown up on a Michigan farm but he derided the federal government for sending his boyhood county so much money that officials built a tennis court: "It's all right, I suppose . . . but these people would never have taxed themselves to build that. Not these tight-fisted taxpayers!" [47] Similarly, the more the government spent on price supports, the more farmers were happy to accept them. Conservative strategists saw price supports as both wrong and wrong-headed: they encouraged farmers to grow more, leading to surpluses and lower prices. Wouldn't the farmer do better, they wondered, "turned loose" to plant what he wanted, where he wanted, and when he wanted, letting the free market determine his profits? In a speech to farmers in October of 1982, Reagan promised to find new international markets for their goods. But he reminded them, "I believe this government's proper role, indeed its only role, is to act as a friend, partner, and promoter of American farmers and their products." He compared farmers to "any small businessman . . . [who] sometimes has no option but to shut down his operation."[48] Furthermore, as Stockman put it, there was no reason why "taxpayers ought to be required to refinance the bad debt incurred by [greedy or marginal] farmers."[49]

Distressed farmers did not appreciate being blamed for macroeconomic developments far outside their control or being deemed "marginal." Instead of just getting mad, though, they got organized, putting their shared history of Populist, Progressive, and NPL politics to use by starting as many as 150 organizations throughout the United States.[50] Activist farmers worked on several fronts at once. They worked to elect a crop of "New Populist" representatives and elevate others to positions of leadership. Some—Iowa's Tom Harkin, Missouri's Dick Gephardt, South Dakota's Tom Daschle, North Dakota's Kent Conrad, and Illinois' Paul Simon—would affect Democratic politics for decades. Making sure their urban colleagues understood how dire the crisis was, they demanded government programs that would "save the family farm."[51]

But these New Populists, both elected officials and allies back home, did not want just a retread of old agricultural policies—the ones their predecessors had argued against fifty years earlier. They saw that, ever since the New Deal, federal agricultural support had gone disproportionately to the largest producers: in 1980, 60 percent of federal funds for agriculture went to 17 percent of operators. Thus, when they proposed the Harkin-Gephardt Bill in 1987, among other measures, they sought to elevate small- and moderate-sized producers' needs and to give them a voice in policy making, putting farmers on national commodities boards as advisers and allowing farmers to vote on referenda regarding proposed agricultural programs including production controls and conservation programs like wetlands protections supports.[52] In short, the New Populists did not believe that farmers were "like any other small businessmen." The risks they faced were exceptional; their importance in American society was irrefutable. They absolutely should not be "set loose" to see how they fared in the free market.[53]

While new Populist representatives worked in Congress, farm organizations sponsored direct actions in local communities and at local state houses, studying farm protest organizations' strategies from the past to ascertain which ones worked best. They sought to avoid, for example, actions like the National Farmers Organization's disastrous "hog kills" of 1968 that repelled members and their allies alike.[54] They also made use of the media to publicize their plight to the nation. Soon farmers were seen riding tractors into Washington, DC, and state capitals; silently standing with white crosses—each symbolizing a bankrupted farm or a farmer who had committed suicide—during legislative hearings; gathering at farmsteads to stop auctions by using the Depression-era convention of the "penny auction." But the new organizations also developed new strategies and found new resources. For example, they elevated local farm women to leadership roles.[55] They created coalitions with like-minded groups, including feminists, unionists, Latin American activists, environmentalists, faith leaders, and civil rights activists.[56] The Reverend Jesse Jackson was among the most prominent supporters of farm organizations. Announcing his bid for the presidency in 1988 from Iowa, Jackson declared that the problems of farmers were also the problems of "Detroit and Chicago."[57]

In this spirit of tradition, innovation, and cooperation, South Dakotans organized a local direct action campaign so successful that it eventually put the state's problems in the national spotlight. Leland Swenson of the South

Dakota Farmers Union announced his plan for a mass rally of farmers at the state capitol in Pierre for February 12, 1985. He hoped a few hundred would make it to the center of the state. "We began the plan," he recalled, "and it just grew." Local communities supported the effort by closing schools and businesses. Despite a cold winter day, six thousand arrived in Pierre. "The streets were packed with South Dakotans. Not just farmers and ranchers," remembered Swenson, "it was people from every rural community across the state."[58]

Impressed by the numbers who traveled to Pierre, Governor Janklow and 105 legislators proposed that their entire delegation travel to Washington on two chartered planes to pressure Congress to pass a meaningful farm bill. Even though the travelers were public officials, this sudden, extra-budgetary trip required funds from private donations. A Watertown radio station, KWAT, sponsored a "Give a Buck" campaign and received twenty thousand separate donations, for a total over $30,000. Once in Washington, Governor Janklow and state senator Jim Burg of Wessington Springs appeared on ABC's popular news show *Nightline*. Just as when he took charge of the "occupation" of the Turkey Processing Plant in Wagner, Janklow did not miss the opportunity to make an impression—this time in support of farmers. In his state of the state address, he argued that federal deficits ran up the price of American exports and ruined the farm economy: "The federal government, frankly, doesn't know how to balance a budget. They neither have the courage, nor the will, nor the guts, nor the talent, nor the political fortitude that it takes to get the job done."[59] He toned it down somewhat for Ted Koppel: "If this were 200 years ago, the Potomac would be full of tea."[60] Neither Janklow nor Koppel could have anticipated at the time, of course, that an actual national Tea Party would come from conservative voters in rural America, not the New Populist farm organizers of their day.

The crisis also inspired elected officials on the Northern Plains to take New Populist–style legal actions back home to protect farmers. Although Janklow was a Republican, he had a "complicated relationship" with the uncompromising movement conservatives in the Reagan camp.[61] While not a traditional economic Populist either, he was nevertheless creative enough to use populist-style actions when they would benefit the state—and his reputation. In May 1985, for example, Janklow called out state troopers to enforce a ban on shipments of Canadian hogs into South Dakota, citing a federal provision against the sale of livestock treated with antibiotics. Most hog farmers understood that something more elemental was at stake: Jank-low was protecting them at a very difficult time. "Just to have more people trying to help the producer . . . that's what makes me smile," said Leon Reiner of Tripp. "Maybe it takes our governor to do something like this?" Janklow also convinced Swift and Hormel, the state's largest packinghouses, to stop accepting the Canadian hogs. "How's that for victory?" he asked.[62] A year later—long after Canada had stopped using antibiotics—Janklow sought to extend the ban. "If Congress had done something," the local news editor in Spearfish explained, "[Janklow] wouldn't have had to go to such extremes."[63] Of course, going to extremes and getting publicity was one of Janklow's most effective political strategies.[64] He banned hogs again in 1998.

Janklow's purchase of seven hundred miles of tracks from the Milwau-kee Railroad in early 1981 was a similarly innovative public-private venture to help farmers. Many farmers still relied exclusively on the railroad tracks across the state to bring crops to market, but as the corporations that con-trolled the railroads neared bankruptcy with Carter-era deregulation of rates, the tracks fell into disrepair and Janklow sensed an opportunity. Few things might have made the original Populists from the late nineteenth century happier than a "railroad baron" facing the poor house—except perhaps a governor willing to buy his railroad for the state.

So important was this acquisition that Janklow called the legislature into an emergency 1981 session to approve both the purchase and a tempo-rary one penny sales tax increase to pay for it. They did so in a single day. Although conservatives accused him of entering into a "socialist venture," Janklow may have never actually intended for the state to run the railroad in perpetuity like North Dakota's state bank and mill. The state used Burl-ington Northern (BN) to operate the line; in 1986 they wrote provisions for a future purchase of the line into a new contract with BN. The sale ultimately took place in 2005, at a rumored price of $40 million—well above what it had cost the state over the twenty-five years it had owned it.[65] In 2000, Janklow sold the state-owned cement factory, first opened in 1924, to a private firm from Mexico.[66]

The powerful trio of Governor George "Bud" Sinner, Commissioner of Agriculture Sarah Vogel, and Tax Commissioner Heidi Heitkamp, all devoted members of the Democratic-NPL (D-NPL) party in North Dakota, also sought ways government could help farmers through the crisis. Sin-ner's view that government existed in part to improve people's lives in times of difficulty was inspired by years of Jesuit training in the Catholic social justice tradition, including care for the poor. These lessons also convinced him—despite his father's ardent anti-communism and his own service in Korea—that the war in Vietnam was wrong.[67] In the years when he was forced repeatedly to cut the state budget, he prioritized human services, "particularly helping the poor, the sick, and handicapped."[68] He was also unafraid to ask legislators and voters to pay higher taxes to help balance the budget without cutting these services. In North Dakota taxes were considered moderate compared with other states but the Farm Crisis' impact on revenues was severe. In 1985, legislators agreed to a modest increase in the state income tax which, at least temporarily, allowed newly elected Sinner to fund education and other programs at previous levels. When a Republican activist collected enough signatures to bring the tax increase to the voters via a referendum, it also passed—but by fewer than three thousand votes. This was an ominous sign of voters' reactions to similar initiatives in the near future.

As commissioner of agriculture, Sarah Vogel brought her inspiration from years on the road with her father, uncle, and grandfather, all of whom were active in the NPL and D-NPL.[69] She heard stories "about the role of government in bettering the lives of people; about the virtue of the family farm system; how the farmer could always be trusted; and about how the law and the legal system could be an instrument of justice for regular people." She also believed in the League's "people first principles . . . [as] the time-tested basis for political morality and serve as a model for public service."[70] Before Sinner's election in 1988, Vogel had made a name for herself as the lead attorney in *Coleman v. Block* (1983), a class action lawsuit that claimed the Farmers Home Administration (FmHA) did not provide all the information about alternative financing to farmers threatened with foreclosure. The decision in her favor, rendered by US District Court Judge Bruce Van Sickle in Bismarck, brought a two-year halt to threatened foreclosures of sixteen thousand farms across the country and increased rights for borrowers in both public and private lending systems.[71] As commissioner she also worked to create new processing cooperatives for producers to cut out the middleman, including one for durum wheat to be processed into pasta flour and another for the newly emerging bison industry.

While Heidi Heitkamp's family did not discuss politics as often, there was one important exception: her maternal grandmother was a faithful Roosevelt Democrat. She remembered clearly how FDR had designed

government programs to help the needy, not the wealthy. Like her predecessor Kent Conrad, as tax commissioner Heidi Heitkamp applied the time-
honored NPL skepticism of large corporations.[72] She was determined, for
example, to force companies that sold mail-order products in North
Dakota to pay North Dakota state sales taxes. In her first case, she won a
settlement from the Spiegel Corporation, an early interstate retailer that
also maintained warehouses in North Dakota.[73] She also ensured that a
family from Casper, Wyoming, that owned nineteen oil and gas companies
could not treat them as a single company for tax purposes and receive a $4
million tax refund.[74] After becoming attorney general in 1992, Heitkamp
led the effort of all attorneys general in the United States to collect a settlement from large tobacco corporations, resulting in the 1998 national
Tobacco Master Settlement.

All told, the 1980s were difficult times in the Dakotas and across the
Midwest, but high times for some Populist-inspired organizations and leaders. Mary Summers has argued, "The family farm movements proved that
it was possible—even in the 1980s—to organize a serious challenge to the
status quo."[75] But these New Populists could not find consistent and lasting
success. By the early 1980s, the South Dakota Democratic Party was in such
disarray, its chair Loila Hunking wryly recalled that "they decided that even
a woman could do a better job than what had been done."[76] Over time,
both in the state houses and in national elections, Democratic New Populists would begin to fade. Tom Daschle would be defeated by Jon Thune in
2004; Tim Johnson's seat would be won by Mike Rounds in 2014. In North
Dakota the trio of Sinner, Vogel, and Heitkamp would constitute the last
Democratic administration in Bismarck. By the turn of the century, signs
of a new conservative cultural and political realignment were everywhere.
Even the producer cooperatives that Sarah Vogel had worked so hard to
establish had been sold and reorganized into for-profit corporations.[77] In
fact, by the early twenty-first century farmers were such committed conservatives that, one regional political observer remarked, "it is hard to think
of all those farmers protesting in Pierre [during the Farm Crisis]. I wonder
if they would ever do that today."[78] Despite a few important victories,
including successful bans on corporate farming, by 2016 Democrats across
the region struggled to find candidates to run for statewide office.[79] That
same year Republicans swelled their ranks to 85 percent of the state legislature. Unlike in previous generations, there was no "progressive wing" of
the party.

*   *   *

Signs that new conservatism would ultimately triumph over New Populism and that big agriculture would triumph over the small family farm were visible even in the early days of the Farm Crisis. They were visible, first, in the rejection of reformist approaches to farm legislation and the persistence of Reaganomics in Washington, DC. In 1985 Reagan finally compromised his goal of getting the government out of the farm business. He was not happy about it. "I want to note here," he said at the signing ceremony, "that the Farm Bill of 1985 is not exactly what we wanted, but in government you can't let the perfect be the enemy of the good."[80] But the bill was not exactly what New Populists wanted, either. The Farm Bill of 1985 included some aspects of their agenda, including conservation provisions, but largely upheld the agricultural policy status quo with price supports primarily going to large landholders.[81] And it was the best they would ever do. In 1985, 1986, and 1987, New Populists learned that Reagan's supporters in Congress were done negotiating about agriculture and soon centrist Democrats would agree. None of the Populist attempts to reform family farming by introducing production controls and restoring a level of parity through grassroots farmer referenda succeeded—including the Harkin-Gephardt "Save the Family Farm Act" of 1987—or even made it out of Democratic-led committee. Less than a decade later, the Republican Congress led by Newt Gingrich revived the idea of "turning the farmer loose" and, with Bill Clinton's support, it prevailed. The 1996 Freedom to Farm Act decreased the amount of government subsidization of agriculture to zero over seven years. When low prices returned and export markets did not, farmers called it the "Freedom to Fail Act."[82]

A slew of other Reagan-Bush era policy changes—some ostensibly unrelated to agriculture—would affect farmers even more than the farm bills. For example, Reagan's concurrent increase in the military budget for the "Second Cold War" and his rhetoric about controlling deficits made some farm organizers, including the leadership of the Farmers Union, reluctant to ask for more government spending for fear they looked unpatriotic.[83] Likewise, interest rates rose because of increased deficits caused by spending and tax cuts for the wealthy. In this sense the left's calls for "farms not arms" signaled an important reality: the United States economy could not afford to invest broadly in military and social programs; the New Right preferred arms over farms.[84] In the mid-1990s, a rash of base closings and consolidations—including on the Northern Plains—further weakened farmers' ability to call for spending in their sector. After nearly thirty years of economic dependence on and kinship with the military, nothing else— not even the well-being of farmers—could be as important as keeping the military as close as possible.

Enormous changes to agriculture and rural society also came with the Reagan administration's aggressive liberalization of regulations on mergers and acquisitions, leading to rapid consolidation in agribusiness. Between 1995 and 1998, for example, Monsanto and Cargill acquired sixty-eight small seed companies. By 2000, four firms controlled 82 percent of beef packing and 75 percent of hogs and sheep.[85] Many of these firms were also partial owners of their competitors. Meanwhile, companies worked to vertically integrate their operations, acquiring everything from feedlots to processing and transportation services. Such near-monopolies prohibited farmers from participating fully in the free exchange of goods. Some even feared that soon they would be "indentured on their own land . . . the new serfs."[86] To make matters worse, these changes to agriculture occurred simultaneously with the first effects of the North American Free Trade Agreement (NAFTA), signed first by George H. W. Bush and finalized by Bill Clinton. NAFTA incentivized many businesses, including farm imple- ment manufacturers and food processors like stockyards, to leave rural America or—if they stayed—to slash wages, decertify unions, and encour- age immigrant laborers to move to the Midwest. No amount of emergency aid to farmers could return prosperity to rural communities that lost both farms and manufacturing facilities. A region of huge farms, multilevel agri- businesses, empty storefronts, dilapidated houses, and widespread metham- phetamine use could not have been further from the vision of democratic rural society that the New Populists had imagined.[87]

And yet it was not just when they negotiated legislation that New Popu- lists found their success limited by the emerging conservative political and cultural majority. Cory Haala has observed that congressional delegates from the Northern Plains were more ambivalent on cultural issues than previous Democratic leaders. Tom Daschle, for example, was far more cul- turally conservative than George McGovern or James Abourezk.[88] Many members of farm organizations—and certainly those farmers reluctant to join—considered themselves to be conservatives, had voted for Reagan, and endorsed his policies. And while farm protests drew large numbers and national attention, it was still a small proportion of farmers who attended.[89] If, for example, six thousand farmers came to Pierre—and each one came from a separate farming operation—that meant only one in seven of the state's forty thousand farm operators was represented. Furthermore, nearly 64 percent of farmers in the Midwest voted for Reagan's reelection in 1984—the very year Ronald Reagan refused to sign any emergency farm bills.[90]

Even more telling was the ideological self-representation of Midwestern farmers: 52 percent called themselves conservatives, while 46 percent were Republicans. Likewise while 43 percent called themselves Democrats, a paltry 13 percent said they were liberal.[91] Many farmers demonstrated their "powerful attraction" to Reagan and all his policies, blaming Carter rather than Reagan for the Farm Crisis and insisting that government programs in agriculture were not working. Furthermore, they recognized Reagan's familiar, albeit right-leaning, rhetoric of nostalgia, as he assailed "giantism" and called for a return to "the scale of the local fraternal lodge, the church organization, the book club, the farm bureau."[92] And, as we have seen, the vast majority of those on the Northern Plains supported Reagan's muscular approach to defense. In fact the only farmers who voted against Reagan by large percentages were those who described themselves as having "declining fortunes." By 2000 these voters had almost certainly moved off the farm or even away from the region altogether.

New Populist organizers surely observed the ambivalence of local farmers toward activism and understood it in part as a reaction to the upheavals and protests of the 1960s and 1970s. Denise O'Brien, like several other important farm activists, had gotten her start in the anti-war movement and had come to rural Iowa as part of a largely liberal back-to-the-land movement. Like Susan McGovern on the campaign trail, Denise discovered that she needed to look the part of a clean-cut farm woman "to have any credibility."[93] But, in their effort to gain public sympathy and publicity, farm organizers may have also reinforced the association of farming with conservatism and, however inadvertently, whiteness.[94] The motto of many organizations, for example, "Parity not Charity," implicitly distinguished struggling farmers from other Americans who depended on "handouts" or "welfare." Conservative radio host Paul Harvey got the same point across—and more—when he gave a speech called "On the Eighth Day, God Made a Farmer" to the Future Farmers of America in 1978, republishing it as a widely distributed newspaper column in 1986. Harvey listed the signal virtues of a hard-working country man: A farmer is "somebody with arms strong enough to wrestle a calf and yet gentle enough to deliver his own grandchild; somebody to call hogs, tame cantankerous machinery, come home hungry, have to await lunch until his wife's done feeding visiting ladies, then tell the ladies to be sure and come back real soon, and mean it."[95]

Six large-budget rural-themed Hollywood films released in 1984 and 1986—*The Dollmaker, The River, Country, Places in the Heart, Hoosiers,* and *Witness*—also reinforced American nostalgia for, in South Dakota Democratic governor Harvey Wollman's words, "the good old days" in rural America.[96] All portrayed their white protagonists, usually a married man and woman, as underdogs struggling to hang on to their families, religious faith, and moral values.[97] They fought valiantly against outside forces—floods, collapsing prices and sky-rocketing interest rates, unfeeling bureaucrats, urban immorality, poverty, and crime. Two of the films were not set during the Farm Crisis or Great Depression, but nevertheless evoked tremendous nostalgia for rural America. In them the racial divide between the purity of the countryside and the corruption of city life is as unapologetic as it is plain. In both *Hoosiers* and *Witness*, innocent and morally grounded white men and boys must vanquish their brutish opponents who happen to be the only African American characters in the films.

A third sign of the conservative turn in rural America was the degree to which farm organizations sought private funds from foundations, corporations, and individual philanthropists. While they demanded public action and democratic civic participation, they undermined themselves by allying with big, wealthy organizations that the original Populists had resisted. The best known of these private initiatives was the "Farm Aid" concert that Willie Nelson and John Mellencamp began. With a host of other stars—nearly all white—they performed in front of eighty thousand fans at the University of Illinois in 1985 and raised nine million dollars for local programs such as food banks and suicide prevention hotlines.[98] Regional football fans also know the "America Needs Farmers (ANF)" campaign started by legendary coach Hayden Fry that linked the Iowa Hawkeyes football program with the conservative-leaning Iowa Farm Bureau. Ranked number 1 ahead of a nationally televised game at number 9 Ohio State in November 1985, the Hawkeyes donned ANF stickers on their helmets to draw attention to the Farm Crisis.[99] Even local people organized small benefits to provide money for neighbors struggling to buy groceries or pay a doctor's bill. When President Reagan joked at the Gridiron Dinner in Washington in March of 1985 that "we should keep the grain and export the farmers," Bev Mader of the Lake County (South Dakota) Farm Alliance made bumper stickers that read, "Save the Farm. Export Reagan" and sold over six thousand for a dollar each.

But as Denise O'Brien recalled, once the Farm Crisis moved off the front page, private foundations moved to their next projects and private funds dried up, even while farmers were still hurting.[100] Other organizations offering ongoing support—including the Iowa Farm Bureau—had far more conservative political ambitions than ordinary men and women would realize, supporting, for example, the continued erosion of price supports. Large private donations likewise often came with strings attached and, of course, could not guarantee a long-term public solution to large economic problems. And as for small private donations that went directly to help local farmers, these were the very forms of charity—not parity—that farmers claimed they did not want.[101] Solutions to public problems were not best found through the generosity of private funding sources, but absent government intervention and reform, reliance on charity would have to suffice.

Finally the Farm Crisis years saw the spread not just of nostalgia-tinged conservatism in the region, but of white power groups like the KKK, Aryan Nation, and the Posse Comitatus. While they remained largely on the margins—in part because, as Summers put it, the left "out-organized" the right—they nevertheless revealed a previously unseen level of "white rage" and resentment focused on Jewish Americans, immigrants, African Americans, LGBT Americans, and government officials in the postwar period.[102] In fact, many of the best-known right-wing radicals of the 1990s experienced the devastations of the downturn in the Midwestern farm economy. Randy and Vicki Weaver, for example, had grown up in Iowa before moving to Ruby Ridge, Idaho. Likewise Timothy McVeigh and Terry Nichols, both military veterans, plotted to bomb the Murrah Federal Building in Oklahoma City at the indebted Nichols farm in central Michigan. Less notorious were the members of the Midwestern-based Posse Comitatus, a group that believed the Israeli Mossad controlled the federal government and aimed to kill Christians. Gordon Kahl, a Vietnam veteran from Medina, North Dakota, refused to pay taxes or repay his farm debts.[103] When surrounded by federal authorities, he killed two state troopers and injured four more. He then went on the run, hiding in one safe house after another, before a hand grenade detonated thousands of rounds of ammunition and blew him to pieces.[104]

* * *

In their work in North and South Dakota, local elected officials also encountered obstacles when they tried to increase taxes, leading them all eventually to try, in the Federal Reserve's words, "something new" to generate revenue and employment. The largest obstacle came in the form of taxpayers' resistance to tax increases, even in times of severe budget restriction. South Dakota governor Bill Janklow learned from his Democratic predecessor, Dick Kneip, who twice failed to pass a personal and corporate income tax. Janklow ran instead on the slogan "Putting Taxpayers First." But keeping his pledge not to raise taxes—other than the temporary one penny increase for the purchase of the railroad—meant undermining some of Janklow's constituents' real needs. In the 1980s South Dakota ranked second-to-last in state contributions to education. It also meant making substantial changes to the structure of public services as Janklow merged some state agencies, sold the state-owned creamery, and converted a college into a prison. He even used prison labor—with its disproportionate number of Native people—to install internet in public schools and keep costs low.

In North Dakota, Governor Bud Sinner counted his inability to convince voters to increase the sales tax, income tax, and gas tax in November 1989 among his most significant failures as a leader. He had traveled across the state, giving "five or six presentations a day," warning that, if voters did not pass the tax increase, they would face cuts to services, huge increases to their property taxes to pay for primary and secondary education, falling home values, and large hikes in state college and university tuition. He reflected later, "Few [politicians] would stand up and fight and say the tough stuff that you have to say to get new taxes. . . . This weird obsession [of the Republicans] with cutting taxes obliterates every other kind of rationality in public policy."[105] But Sinner could also see that keeping taxes relatively low, as they already were in North Dakota, did not appeal only to Republican voters. In the special election of 1989, the tax increases were defeated by substantial margins cutting across party lines. His budget chief turned off the holiday lights on the capitol building in Bismarck in protest.[106]

When governors and legislators across the political spectrum needed to find new sources of revenue—and when neither new taxes nor deficit spending was an option—they began to look for what Debra Marquart would call "new friends," some of whom the original Populist and NPL leaders would not have invited in for a cup of coffee. In these maneuvers, as in the race to get bases and missiles, South Dakota took an early lead. First, term-limited Janklow and his Republican successor, George Mickelson, oversaw the establishment of a state lottery, including a video lottery that could be located in any public or private space. South Dakota's original constitution—written by a Populist-dominated territorial legislature and influenced by the conservative Protestant prohibitions against drinking and gambling—forbade any "games of chance." As late as 1970, voters had rejected amendments allowing for church bingo and other games that profited religious or charity organizations.[107] Subsequent attempts also failed. Finally at the high point of the Farm Crisis, voters approved a state lottery. The controversy was far from over, however. Between 1986 and 1994 video lottery—as a supplement to scratch-off games—was approved, then revoked, then approved again through yet another referendum. Some religious conservatives continued to believe that gambling was sinful and allied with liberals who saw lotteries as a form of regressive taxation.[108] Yet nearly from the beginning, revenues from the various forms of lottery in South Dakota were the second-largest source of funds for the state budget; they even allowed Janklow, upon his return to the governor's office in 1994, to lower property tax rates and rid the state of its inheritance tax.

Janklow's attempts to diversify the state's economic infrastructure beyond agriculture had even more wide-reaching consequences, helping to establish the powerful credit card industry nationwide. In 1979, Janklow worked with the state legislature to remove the required ceiling from the state's interest rates, a provision to protect borrowers that dated from the Populist era. He did so because the prime rates had gone so high that credit had nearly dried up: lenders could not afford to provide capital to borrowers at rates lower than they paid to obtain it. At the same time, the credit card division of Citibank was limited by New York laws in the amount of interest on credit card debt that they could charge. As Citibank was losing millions every day and was desperate to find a solution, Janklow recalled, South Dakota "was slowly bleeding to death, they [Citibank] were gushing to death."[109] A Citibank official from Aberdeen spoke with leading bankers in Sioux Falls and they devised a plan: move the entire operation to Sioux Falls. Citibank guaranteed the state four hundred jobs to start. It took less

than three weeks for Janklow to close the deal and less than a single day for
the state legislature to approve it. By 2000, 16 percent of all workers in
South Dakota were part of the financial services sector and the Sioux Falls
metropolitan area experienced growth unmatched in the region's modern
era.[110] Meanwhile, the federally required Bank Franchise tax provided tens
of millions of dollars a year to state coffers. Meanwhile South Dakota still
had no personal or corporate income tax. All of this contributed to a culture of easy credit and rising personal indebtedness—within an unregulated
and poorly supervised financial sector—that led in turn to the Great Recession of 2008.

In making "new friends" and "keeping company"—for the long term—
with the big banks, Janklow openly broke with the values of early twentieth-
century Populism and Progressivism. After all, Populists had seen banks
and other lenders as among the worst of the middlemen, people with no
productive work of their own, who took ordinary people's money and then,
as Hamlin Garland put it, "sat around gassing with the boys." Janklow,
however, was tired of seeing bigness with suspicion; he felt it led South
Dakotans to have "an inferiority complex."[111] In fact Janklow was surprised
by how much he liked the "biggest" banker of all—Citibank CEO Walter
Wriston. Janklow, in his own words, wasn't "afraid of all these ogres from
the big corporations or big America or big world. I met some of the classiest
people I ever met . . . Every deal they ever made with me, they kept."[112]
Again and again in the elections that followed, Janklow reminded voters
that he was responsible for the "South Dakota Advantage." Many voters
saw it that way too. One said in the run-up to his 1994 campaign, "He kind
of got Citibank in here. He's . . . nationally known."[113]

But what did the state want to be known for? While the warning signs
came earlier, by 2008, most Americans perceived that the credit card industry
and other branches of finance were unsustainable. Some found them morally
reprehensible. Enabled by Reagan-era rollbacks of banking regulations, companies found new ways to charge ever higher interest rates—often without
disclosing them—and developed fee and penalty structures that profited them
even more. By 2004 many card companies even offered low-or-no interest
opening rates—similar to subprime mortgages—knowing that most consumers would only pay their minimum and never fully understand how deeply
in debt they were falling.[114] These were national trends that Janklow later
claimed he never foresaw.[115] But he could have foreseen the consequences of
unlimited interest rates within the state itself. After all, the unlimited usury

rate was available not just to the big banks but to local lenders too—payday lenders, car salesman, and even lenders who preyed specifically on men and women in the military. In 2016, nearly forty years after Janklow had welcomed Citibank with open arms, South Dakota voters approved a 36 percent ceiling on rates for payday lenders who preyed on the poorest in their communities. While still very high, this new rate was a significant decrease from the average rate charged before: 574 percent.[116]

Janklow may or may not have understood the ways in which the credit card industry and the finance sector had long been enmeshed in the military-industrial complex. Military families are among the credit issuers' "best"—that is, most indebted—customers. Service members tend to carry more debt than civilians because it can be difficult for military spouses to find employment quickly after a move to cover unreimbursed costs associated with deployments.[117] In 2006 and 2015, the Department of Defense issued regulations limiting the interest that could be charged to active-duty servicepeople—36 percent on credit cards, payday loans, or any other commercial loan. Beyond personal finance, however, wars are "big business" for banks. As Populist anti-militarists pointed out in 1915, banks have long profited from war by lending to belligerent nations, betting they will prevail and repay their debts with interest. At times banks have even lent to both sides to "hedge" these bets. More recently the Department of Defense has encouraged strategists and officers to see "money as a weapons system." In the new permanent war, investing in infrastructures of wartime countries and sometimes just giving cash to war-torn people has been seen both as good policy and a good business move.[118]

When the Citibank prospect was developing, South Dakota legislators revoked a little-used "emergency" exception to the rule that all major legislation had to be allowed to go through the initiative and referendum process. In other words, not a single voter in South Dakota got to decide about Citibank. The state had drifted far from the "people first" Populism and anti-militarism of the past. But, even if they got no say, South Dakotans did get to pay. Some new friends can be really expensive.

*   *   *

It took far more than three weeks for North Dakotans to transform their economy, but like the Citibank deal, the creation of an enormous corporate energy presence in the state had its roots in the boom and bust period of the 1970s and 1980s. In those years, private companies pushed legislators and farmers in the western part of the state to allow the industrial development of lignite coal—first for the generation of electricity and then, with new technology, for the conversion of coal into natural gas, called "gasification." North Dakota has the second largest lignite reserves in the country; coal had been mined in small quantities across western North Dakota throughout the century, usually by cooperatives.[119] Beginning in the 1960s, however, new private interests were planning much larger operations and, for the first time, proposing that they rely mostly on strip mining. Strip mining takes off the first layers of topsoil from farm and ranch land—between 150 and 500 acres per year depending on the size of the plant or its function—often leaving gaping holes and unproductive, toxic acres behind.

In 1975, Mike Jacobs, student author of the controversial 1967 essay "The Prostitution of Patriotism," was an activist with the Farmers Union. In that role he published a book, *One Time Harvest*, to warn against the potential consequences of the development of coal. He revealed the complex connections between energy corporations, railroads, and the finance industry, which shared members of their boards of directors and other interests, including investments. He also showed that while many powerful out-of-state investors sought an aggressive approach to development of local land, many farmers would see little material gain and incalculable loss. Most farmers in the countryside, as it happened, did not even own their mineral rights. Their fathers and grandfathers had sold them years before, when making it through the 1930s required doing anything to survive.[120]

In the late 1960s and early 1970s, when energy prices were high, state business leaders and industrial executives worked hard to convince local townspeople to give development a "red-carpet welcome."[121] Boosters met with sixty chambers of commerce, produced radio and television ads, paid local stations to play "Be Proud You Know a Coal Mining Man!" over and over, and held dozens of "town hall" meetings. Industry officials also tried hard to fit into the communities, a public relations man even bringing his small son with him to meetings to look more like a "family man." Like South Dakotans during the Citibank deal—and many residents of the Northern Plains when they heard the bases and missiles were coming to the region—local people in western North Dakota largely supported the expansion of private mining interests because they hoped to put that part of the state "on the map." They hoped, for example, that the boom would bring national franchises—fast food, even a Super Kmart or a Walmart. Some also hoped to profit from it, through real estate, housing construction, or increased wages. As the editor of the *McLean County Independent* wrote in 1973, "Something big and wonderful is about to happen [here]. . . . With environmental standards satisfied, the complex should be nothing but good for the people of this county."[122]

But some farmers along with many D-NPL leaders were not so sure that "big coal"—or big anything—would be so wonderful. In the private sphere, it rarely had been before. Tax Commissioner Byron Dorgan worried in 1979 that, "North Dakotans have been exploited for decades by out-of-state interests who want to buy what we produce at fire sale prices."[123] Anthropologist Caroline Tauxe suggested that the opposition might have been stronger if local people had not grown accustomed to smaller, cooperatively owned mines in town, where they had sometimes found off-season employment. They could not foresee the impact of larger scale industrialization on their water supplies, the health of their cattle, or the landscape itself. But given the economic realities facing North Dakota, many leaders and farmers insisted, like Dorgan, that the state at least get its fair share. The legislature worked, for example, to levy a severance tax that would go to local communities as well as a long-term trust for the General Fund. Governor Arthur Link, who had grown up on a ranch, likewise insisted that coal companies "reclaim" the land by saving the top soil and replanting it over the course of several seasons until it was able to be returned to grass or hay. In a speech in 1973, Link warned, "Let us not permit the opportunity of quick economic gain to overshadow our concern for the long-range benefit and prosperity of succeeding generations. We do not want to halt progress . . . we simply want to insure the most efficient and environmentally sound method of utilizing our precious coal and water resources for the benefit of the [most] people."[124]

Even if the D-NPL leadership succeeded in negotiating a modest severance tax and number of regulations, they could not forestall the bust that came when coal prices collapsed and production was curtailed. Just as quickly housing prices plunged, businesses on Main Street that had already lost business to the big box stores shuttered, and the construction of new schools and roads stalled. In 1986 the unemployment rate in coal-rich Mercer County was nearly twice as high as the state's average; in 1987 the child abuse and neglect rate was the highest of all.[125] Towns that had gone deeply in debt to improve services suddenly had a vastly reduced share of coal tax revenues with which to repay them. Of most concern was Great Plains Energy Corporation's abandonment of the coal gasification plant in which the state had invested heavily. When they heard of the impending default, townspeople held a special church service to pray for God's assistance with their troubles. Soon the state auctioned the plant to a cooperative venture but only after lowering the severance tax. Given that the coal bust came at the same time as the Farm Crisis, many people in western North Dakota could not see anything positive, only "helplessness and despair, a growing realization of their collective dependence on unpredictable forces."[126] As a newspaper columnist in Beulah wrote in 1987, "If there is a lesson to be learned from what's happening in Mercer County, it is that being honest and working hard will not bring success. . . . Everyone seems dispensable these days and profit pictures dictate what will be done."[127] If that was true, more than the coal boom was over.

Since 2010 the experiences of towns in the Bakken oil shale region have echoed those in lignite coals counties, only at far, far higher decibels. The rise in global prices for energy due to American wars in the Middle East, the development of new extraction technology, the entrance of enormously powerful global energy corporations, the influx of male workers, and the attempts at modest taxation and regulation had all occurred in North Dakota before. So had an earlier fall in prices created a raft of deserted homes and shops, a rise in unemployment and drug use, and a state budget crisis. But the Bakken boom was also like nothing anyone in the Dakotas had seen before. As C. S. Hagen has written for the *High Plains Reader*, "North Dakota is not fly-over country anymore."[128] For ordinary people, the reasons for the newfound fame, aside from the low unemployment rate, can be more worrisome than reassuring as national attention mounts. Towns that boasted 4-H clubs and church picnics are now towns where strippers can make $1,000 a night; where so many men have arrived to work that an evangelical pastor allowed as many as two hundred to stay "overnight" on the floor of his church; where a Walmart had so few workers that it simply dumped merchandise in the parking lot; where some people lucky enough to have mineral rights became millionaires while everyone else just tried to endure the interminable noise, dirt, vibrations, broken roads, and increased crime; and, most importantly, where sex crimes against Native women, as well as murders and "disappearances," literally cannot be counted—in part because no one has kept track.[129] It is the place where one Republican candidate after another has received large campaign contributions from energy corporations and mineral rights owners like Harold Hamm and lawsuits brought by Democratic activists have mysteriously been "slow walked" or thrown out of court altogether.[130] It is the place where there is no peace and no garden. It is the place where a grain elevator has been torn down and replaced with a chemical delivery site.[131]

As people in South Dakota discovered during the credit card crisis, it is one thing to be famous and another to be notorious. It is a third to find yourself fully integrated into the very system of corporate capitalism and militarism against which you had long staked your legacy. But, as Mike Jacobs wrote in 2014 on the occasion of North Dakota's 125th anniversary of statehood, this is the "new North Dakota."[132] It is the new South Dakota, Rural New Right, and it threatens to be the "new America" as well. As stark as the transformation has been on the Northern Plains, it is the same one all Americans have experienced, whether they can see it or not. Our democratic society agreed to expose its land and communities to nuclear annihilation in the belief that America was exceptionally good and others were exceptionally evil and went on to build a global military empire through massive budgets that citizens can neither fully access nor easily rescind. Everything that followed—all the walls we have built—has been easy.

APPENDIX

METHODOLOGY: TOTAL POPULATION OF MILITARY PERSONNEL AND DEPENDENTS STATIONED IN THE DAKOTAS, 1955–1995

GRAND FORKS AFB, ELLSWORTH AFB, and Minot AFB (henceforth referred to as GF, EW, and MT, respectively) had, in 1970, combined military and civilian populations of 10,474, 5,805, and 12,077. No census data is present before 1970, which presents a significant difficulty, since during the 1970s, the US military was in the process of becoming an all-volunteer force. The overall estimate of three hundred thousand is thus based on extending the following estimate model for the 1970s, to the four-decade period of the Cold War, with assumptions that the 1960s and 1980s had similar population numbers, but that the periods from 1955 to 1960 and from 1990 to 1995 were lower. It also does not account for air force personnel deployed to Vietnam and then replaced temporarily, some of whom returned to the base but some of whom were killed in action. By definition, it also does not include the numbers of military personnel and their families who have been assigned to bases on the Northern Plains between 1995 and 2019.

MT AFB will be used as an example to demonstrate the model. Rough breakdown of the USAF officer-to-enlisted ratio is 1-to-5,[1] with 84.9 percent of the officers and 47.5 percent of the enlisted being married and the average military family having two children.[2] As such, MT AFB has 9,822 enlisted (+ families) and 2,857 officers (+ families) (this rather imprecise calculation accounts for most of the uncertainty). Due to longer contracts of the officers (especially so before the transition to the all-volunteer model), the theoretical turnover rate for the officers every four years is 25 percent, in comparison with the 75 percent of the enlisted (little to no hard figures are available regarding this). At this time, due to switching to the all-volunteer model, reductions in force (RIF) affected all three AFBs. For example, the complement of GF AFB was reduced from 10,474 to 9,390 by 1980. RIFs are handled much the same way as the turnover rates. Total RIF is divided by ten (an annual model), with 75 percent of the result being subtracted from the enlisted (+ families) figure and the 25 percent from the officers (+ families) figure. After plugging MT AFB into the model, the resulting data indicated that 33,020 personnel and family members rotated through MT AFB over the ten-year span between 1970 and 1980. Taking into account that, at the time, roughly a full third of the USAF was stationed overseas (Norway, Germany, etc.), under the staggered long/short CONUS/overseas tour system,[3] the full figure for MT AFB is 40,001.

After plugging the values of all AFBs into the model individually, the final range for all three bases for the period from 1970 to 1979 is 85,741–87,941. The difference is accounted for by the discrepancy between the predicted values (as arrived to by the multiplication of the married personnel by three on account of the average size of the military families of the period) and the observed values (as in the figures present on the US Census data for the three AFBs). The final range is arrived at by subtracting the discrepancy from the final high-end estimate to get a clearer picture regarding the figure of personnel and families rotated through the AFBs in question.

NOTES

Preface

1. Tom Brusegaard, conversation with the author, October 5, 2017, Grand Forks, North Dakota; Tim Pavek, interview, "National Park Service, Minuteman Missile Historic Site," https://www.nps.gov/people/timpavek.htm?utm_source = person&utm_medium = website& utm_campaign = experience_more.

2. Delphine Red Shirt, conversation with the author, September 2001, New London, Connecticut.

3. Among other works, see Delphine Red Shirt, *Bead on an Anthill: A Lakota Childhood* (Lincoln: University of Nebraska Press, 1997).

4. Sonia Narang, "Elderly Women on Okinawa United Against Plans to Move U.S. Military Base," https://www.upi.com/Top_News/Voices/2017/02/20/Elderly-women-on-Okinawa -unite-against-plans-to-move-US-military-base/7221487604758/.

5. On Americans' inability to "see" empire, see Daniel Immerwahl, *How to Hide an Empire: A History of the Greater United States* (New York: Farrar, Straus, and Giroux, 2019), 3–20. On the concept of "shareholder whiteness," see Manu Karuka, *Empire's Tracks: Indigenous Nations, Chinese Workers, and the Transcontinental Railroad* (Oakland: University of California Press, 2019), 149–67.

6. Quoted in Gretchen Heefner, *The Missile Next Door: The Minuteman in the American Heartland* (Cambridge, MA: Harvard University Press, 2012), 144.

Introduction

1. "Grand Forks Herald Publisher to Retire," *Bismarck Tribune*, June 19, 2013, https:// bismarcktribune.com/news/state-and-regional/grand-forks-herald-publisher-to-retire-next -year/article_032f45ec-d960–11e2-ad61–001a4bcf887a.html.

2. Mike Jacobs, "The Prostitution of Patriotism," *Dakota Student*, September 15, 1967.

3. No author to Mike Jacobs, no date, George Starcher Papers, Elwyn Robinson Department of Special Collections, Orin G. Libby Library, University of North Dakota, Grand Forks, North Dakota, OGLMC 238, Box 7, Folder 26.

4. Mike Jacobs, "Starcher Remains a Presidential Model," *Grand Forks Herald*, May 31, 2018, https://www.grandforksherald.com/opinion/columns/4453866-mike-jacobs-starcher -remains-presidential-model.

5. Mike Jacobs, *A Birthday Inquiry: North Dakota at 125; A Collection of Essays*, ed. Steve Wagner (Fargo, ND: Forum Communications, 2014). Kindle only.

6. https://www.washingtonpost.com/posteverything/wp/2017/01/25/south-dakota-lawmakers-are-showing-us-that-populism-is-a-lie/?utm_term = .dcde9972afdd. North Dakota voters preferred Trump by 35 points.

7. The New Right had roots in the anti–New Deal coalition, the postwar conservative movement among intellectuals like William F. Buckley, anti-communism, and the conservative Catholic and evangelical Protestant traditions. Rick Perlstein, *Before the Storm: Barry Goldwater and the Unmaking of the American Consensus* (New York: Nation Books, 2009).

8. Phillip Barlow and Mark Silk, eds., *Religion and Public Life in the Midwest: America's Common Denominator?* (Lanham, MD: AltaMira, 2004), 33–37. Several denominations largely seen as culturally conservative today worked for left-leaning social and economic causes too. In the Dakotas many Catholic leaders supported Populist reforms and, later, the antinuclear and family farm movements. North Dakota bishops Vincent Wehrle and Aloysius Muench, for example, worked with "Wild Bill" Langer and the Nonpartisan League. And yet their support had limits. While Wehrle and Muench supported initiatives to control the power of big business, their fear of socialism reined them in. Charles M. Barber, "A Diamond in the Rough: William Langer Reexamined," *North Dakota History* 65 (Fall 1998): 2–18. See also Bishop H. B. Hacker, *The Catholic Church in Western North Dakota, 1738–1960* (Mandan, ND: Diocese of Bismarck, 1960), 55. Furthermore some "mainline" Protestant denominations that we think of today as liberal had what one leader called an "old school" approach to doctrine. Kenneth L. Smith, "Presbyterianism, Progressivism, and Cultural Influence: William M. Blackburn, Coe E. Crawford, and the Making of Civic Dakota," in Jon K. Lauck, John E. Miller, and Paula M. Nelson, eds., *The Plains Political Tradition: Essays on South Dakota Political Culture*, vol. 3 (Pierre: South Dakota State Historical Society Press, 2018), 104. Nearly all Christian groups worked to maintain the "social order" in areas of religious practice, race, and gender. Many did not support women's suffrage. With far more devastating consequences, Catholic, Episcopalian, Presbyterian leaders founded and administered boarding schools for Native children, where conversion to Christianity was involuntary and abuse and neglect accompanied the "civilizing" mission. Brenda J. Childs, *Boarding School Seasons: American Indian Families, 1900–1940* (Lincoln: University of Nebraska Press, 1998); Linda M. Clemmons, " 'Business Is Business Even If We Are Christians': The Politics of Grant's Peace Policy in Dakota Territory," in Lauck, Miller, and Nelson, *The Plains Political Tradition: Essays on South Dakota Political Culture*, 3:32–57.

9. Even many white moderates in the region demonstrate what Eddie Glaude Jr. calls the "soft bigotry" of those who support civil rights but not full equality. "Don't Let the Loud Bigots Distract You," *Time*, September 6, 2018, http://time.com/5388356/our-racist-soul/. For Native people, full equality would require redress of treaty violations, something no Republican or Democratic candidate for national office from the region has fully endorsed. The ongoing conflict over the "Fighting Sioux" mascot at the University of North Dakota reflects many Dakotans' desire to maintain control over the symbols and myths of settler colonialism. See Catherine McNicol Stock, " 'Reading the Ralph': Privatization in the 'New' North Dakota," in Jon K. Lauck and Catherine McNicol Stock, eds., *The Conservative Heartland: A Political History of the Postwar American Midwest* (Lawrence: University of Kansas Press, 2020), 323–345.

10. Samuel Day, *Nuclear Heartland: A Guide to the 1,000 Missile Silos of the United States* (Madison, WI: Progressive Foundation, 1988), 10. The best discussion of how the missiles came to be located on the plains is Gretchen Heefner, *The Missile Next Door: The Minuteman in the American Heartland* (Cambridge, MA: Harvard University Press, 2012).

11. According to Vance, "To these Americans, the military isn't just an organ of the national security state; it is a safety net, health care provider, employer, educator and landlord." J. D. Vance, "How Trump Won the Troops," *New York Times*, November 25, 2016, https://www.nytimes.com/2016/11/25/opinion/how-trump-won-the-troops.html?_r = 0.

12. See, for example, Mikkel Pates, "Flags on Farms," *Ag Week*, July 2, 2018, http://www.agweek.com/business/agriculture/4467500-give-us-old-glory-flags-farms.

13. A study of 2015 recruits found that the states of North and South Dakota both ranked in the top ten for number of "high quality recruits": high school graduates and others well prepared for service. Aline Quester and Robert Shuford, "Population Representation in Military Services (2015)" Washington, DC: CNA Reports, 2017, 27. According to the National Priorities Project, 44 percent of all military recruits come from rural areas largely in the South and Great Plains states. Montana has three counties in the top twenty for recruitment; Nebraska has two, South Dakota one. See National Priorities Project, "Military Recruitment 2008: Significant Gap in Army's Quality and Quantity Goals," http://www.nationalpriorities.org/militaryrecruiting2008, accessed July 1, 2018. This data is summarized in Bill Ganzel, "Rural America Supplies More Recruits," Living History Farm, 2009, https://livinghistoryfarm.org/farminginthe70s/life_07.html. See also National Priorities Project, "Military Recruitment 2010," https://www.nationalpriorities.org/analysis/2011/military-recruitment-2010/.

14. Historian Ahrar Ahmad has written "most people [in South Dakota] know someone in the military." Ahmad, "War and Peace in South Dakota," in Jon K. Lauck, John E. Miller, and Donald C. Simmons Jr. eds., *The Plains Political Tradition: Essays on South Dakota Political Culture*, vol. 1 (Pierre: South Dakota State Historical Society Press, 2011), 203; Ahmad draws his data from "US Casualties: State-by-State Troop Deaths," *PBS News Hour*, https://web.archive.org/web/20130424084902/http://www.pbs.org/newshour/indepth_coverage/middle_east/iraq/honorroll/map_flash.html.

15. David Finkel, *The Good Soldiers* (New York: Farrar, Straus and Giroux, 2007), 209. Soon enough, Adam found, the experience of war began to "sour" (ibid.).

16. The question of how radical or conservative Dakota politics were before World War II has inspired lively debate. While Jon K. Lauck, Tom Isern, and others have called South Dakota a land of "agrarian conservatism" from its inception, others point to definitional leftist movements in both states. On the tradition of political conservatism, see Thomas D. Isern, "Confessions of an Agrarian Conservative," *South Dakota History* 36 (Summer 2006): 218–23. On the history of the left, see William C. Pratt, "Another South Dakota; or, The Road Not Taken: The Left and the Shaping of South Dakota Political Culture," in Lauck, Miller, and Simmons Jr., *The Plains Political Tradition*, 1:105–32; Steven A. Stofferahn, "The Persistence of Agrarian Activism: The National Farmers' Organization in South Dakota," in Jon K. Lauck, John E. Miller, and Donald C. Simmons Jr., eds., *The Plains Political Tradition: Essays on South Dakota Political Culture*, vol. 2 (Pierre: South Dakota State Historical Society Press, 2014), 209–41. Genuine economic and political radicalism endured the longest in North Dakota. See Michael Lansing, *Insurgent Democracy: The Nonpartisan League in North American Politics* (Chicago: University of Chicago Press, 2015).

17. Sarah M. Vogel, "Advocate for Agriculture," in Susan E. Wefald, *Important Voices: North Dakota's Women Elected State Officials Share Their Stories, 1893–2013* (Fargo, ND: Institute for Regional Studies Press, 2014), 87.

18. Throughout this work, the word Populist is capitalized any time it refers to the broad ideas of economic and political reform first articulated by the Farmers Alliance and People's Party. Thus it is used to describe organizations and leaders who came decades later, even if they may not have adhered to every aspect of the original Populist agenda or movement culture. Most importantly, it includes Populist anti-militarism, which found expression as late as 1970, because Populists saw the struggle against war as part of their struggle against the power of large corporations. On the other hand, when right-leaning politicians who work on behalf of corporate interests and the military industrial complex, use populist-style rhetoric to appeal to broad swaths of Americans, the term appears with a lower case "p."

19. The literature on Populism is vast and sometimes contentious. Two of the most influential works are Lawrence Goodwyn's revisionist classic, *The Populist Moment: A Short History of the Agrarian Revolt in America* (New York: Oxford University Press, 1978); and Charles Postel's more recent, *The Populist Vision* (New York: Oxford University Press, 2009). Scholars are also interested in the ways in which populist rhetoric and ideals have appealed to the right. See Dan Carter, *The Politics of Rage: George Wallace, the Origins of the New Conservatism, and the Transformation of American Politics* (Baton Rouge: Louisiana State University Press, 2000); and Michael Kazin, *The Populist Persuasion: An American History* (Ithaca, NY: Cornell University Press, 2009).

20. Brooke L. Blower, "Nation of Outposts: Forts, Factories, Bases, and the Making of American Power," *Diplomatic History* 41 (2017): 455.

21. One new book reminds readers of the connection between Populism and anti-imperialism. Nathan Jessen, *Populism and Imperialism: Politics, Culture, and Foreign Policy in the American West, 1890–1900* (Lawrence: University Press of Kansas, 2017).

22. Michael Kazin, *War Against War: The American Fight for Peace, 1914–1918* (New York: Simon and Schuster, 2017).

23. David Wyman, *The Abandonment of the Jews: America and the Holocaust, 1941–1945* (New York: New Press, 2007); Bradley W. Hart, *Hitler's American Friends: The Third Reich's Supporters in the United States* (New York: Thomas Dunne, 2018).

24. The America First Committee is more frequently referred to as "isolationist" than anti-militarist. But, as Brooke L. Blower has shown, the term "isolationist" was in fact used as a term of disparagement by prewar interventionists and postwar military expansionists. For this reason, I do not use it in this book except in quotations, and, while Blower prefers the term "neutralists" in the interwar period, I refer to all those who sought to remain at peace throughout the late nineteenth and early twentieth centuries in the Dakotas as Populist anti-militarists. "From Isolationism to Neutrality: A New Framework for Understanding American Political Culture, 1919–1941," *Diplomatic History* 38 (2014): 345–76.

25. Quoted in David T. Nelson and Richard G. Cole, "Behind German Lines in 1915: The Letters Home of David T. Nelson," *Journal of Military History* 65 (October 2001): 1058–59.

26. Quoted in Robert Griffith, "Old Progressives and the Cold War," *Journal of American History* 66 (September 1979): 342.

27. Marilyn B. Young, "'I Was Thinking, as I Often Do These Days, of War': The United States in the Twenty-First Century," *Diplomatic History* 36 (January 2012): 1. See also Michael

S. Sherry, *In the Shadow of War: The United States Since the 1930s* (New Haven, CT: Yale University Press, 1995); and Michael S. Sherry, "War as a Way of Life," *Modern American History* 1, no.1 (2018): 1–4. I agree with Sherry that at its most concrete, militarization is "'the contradictory and tense social process in which civil society organized itself for the production of violence'" and, further, that the impact of militarization on society extends to "the memories, models, and metaphors that [have] shaped broad areas of national life." *In the Shadow of War*, xi; Sherry is quoting John R. Gillis (who is employing Michael Geyer's definition), from Gillis, *Militarization of the Western World* (New Brunswick, NJ: Rutgers University Press, 1989), 1. Third, I agree that war, rather than an anomaly in American history, is "what the nation does." "War as a Way of Life," 3.

28. Rosa Brooks, *How Everything Became War and the Military Became Everything: Tales from the Pentagon* (New York: Simon and Schuster, 2017).

29. By 2011 some historians thought the literature on American conservatism had begun to rely on overused tropes and chronologies. See Matthew D. Lassiter, "Political History Beyond the Red-Blue Divide," *Journal of American History* 98 (December 2011): 760–64. Not surprisingly, the 2016 presidential election sharpened the field's focus on whiteness and the rural experience, and brought important works of sociology, journalism, and memoir to the public. See Kathleen Cramer, *The Politics of Resentment: Rural Consciousness in Wisconsin and the Rise of Scott Walker* (Chicago: University of Chicago Press, 2016); Arlie Russell Hochschild, *Strangers in Their Own Land: Anger and Mourning on the American Right* (New York: New Press, 2016); J. D. Vance, *Hillbilly Elegy: A Memoir of a Family and Culture in Crisis* (New York: Harper, 2016); Jonathan Metzl, *Dying of Whiteness: How the Politics of Racial Resentment Is Killing America's Heartland* (New York: Basic Books, 2019); Sarah Smarsh, *Heartland: A Memoir of Working Hard and Being Broke in the Richest Country on Earth* (New York: Scribners, 2019). Two excellent books that examine the impact of militarization and the experience of war on politics and culture are Heefner, *The Missile Next Door*; and Kathleen Belew, *Bring the War Home: The White Power Movement and Paramilitary America* (Cambridge, MA: Harvard University Press, 2018).

30. Since 2013 historians have reexamined the field of Midwestern history. Jon K. Lauck, *The Lost Region: Toward a Revival of Midwestern History* (Iowa City: University of Iowa Press, 2013).

31. Kim Phillips-Fein, "Conservatism: A State of the Field," *Journal of American History* 98 (December 2011): 723–43. On the Sunbelt and the urban North, see among many others, Lisa McGirr, *Suburban Warriors: The Origins of the New American Right* (Princeton, NJ: Princeton University Press, 2002); Jason Sokol: *There Goes My Everything: White Southerners in the Age of Civil Rights* (New York: Knopf, 2006); Jason Sokol, *All Eyes Are upon Us: Race and Politics from Boston to Brooklyn* (New York: Basic Books, 2014); Matthew Lassiter, *The Silent Majority: Suburban Politics in the Sunbelt South* (Princeton, NJ: Princeton University Press 2007); Thomas Sugrue, *The Origins of the Urban Crisis: Race and Inequality in Postwar Detroit* (Princeton, NJ: Princeton University Press, 2005).

32. Quoted in Bruce J. Schulman, ed., *The Seventies: The Great Shift in American Culture, Society, and Politics* (New York: Da Capo Press, 2002), xiv; see also Kevin Phillips, *The Emerging Republican Majority* (New Rochelle, NY: Arlington, 1969). Phillips included a short chapter on the "farm states" (42 pages of 557) in which he recognizes the importance of immigrant heritage, New Deal farm programs, and a history of anti-militarism to regional politics. But

he seems unable to explain a small pocket of support for segregationist candidate George Wallace in southwestern South Dakota—counties that border large reservations (451).

33. Nicole Hemmer, *Messengers of the Right: Conservative Media and the Transformation of American Politics* (Philadelphia: University of Pennsylvania Press, 2016).

34. Burgess Everett, "North Dakota's Last Democrat?," *Politico*, June 22, 2017, https://www.politico.com/story/2017/06/22/heidi-heitkamp-north-dakota-239805.

35. In *How to Hide an Empire: A History of the Greater United States* (New York: Farrar, Straus and Giroux, 2019), Daniel Immerwahr argues that the American West was the site of empire building during the "Indian Wars"; I contend that the region was a continuous site of this "hidden" process throughout its history. As Brooke Blower has written, "the United States has always been a nation of outposts" but in the Cold War years, American exceptionalism required the nation and its citizens to deny this history, embrace the notion of the "accidental" empire, and imagine that occupation (either at home or abroad) served the purpose of keeping local people "safe." Blower, "Nation of Outposts," 445, 456–59.

36. Maria Höhn and Seungsook Moon, eds., *Over There: Living with the U.S. Military Empire from World War Two to the Present* (Durham, NC: Duke University Press, 2010), 7. Other works that focus on bases within the emerging "new military history" include Mark Gillem, *America Town: Building the Outposts of Empire* (Minneapolis: University of Minnesota Press, 2007); David Kieran and Edwin A. Martini, eds., *At War: The Military and American Culture in the Twentieth Century and Beyond* (New Brunswick, NJ: Rutgers University Press, 2018); David Vine, *Base Nation: How U.S. Military Bases Abroad Harm America and the World* (New York: Henry Holt, 2017); Blower, "Nation of Outposts," 455.

37. David Vine, "Where in the World Is the U.S. Military?," *Politico Magazine*, July/August, 2015, https://www.politico.com/magazine/story/2015/06/us-military-bases-around-the-world-119321; Immerwahr, *How to Hide an Empire*, 355–71.

38. In *On the Move for Love: Migrant Entertainers and the U.S. Military in South Korea* (Philadelphia: University of Pennsylvania Press, 2013), Sealing Cheng reveals the complexity of Filipinas' motivations for working at American air force bases in South Korea.

39. Vine, *Base Nation*, 183, 186. See also Cynthia Enloe, *Bananas, Beaches, and Bases: Making Feminist Sense of International Relations* (Berkeley: University of California Press, 2000).

40. Dennis Banks with Richard Erdoes, *Ojibwa Warrior: Dennis Banks and the Rise of the American Indian Movement* (Norman: University of Oklahoma Press, 2004), 44. Native soldiers in Vietnam would at times struggle with the idea of attacking "people who looked too much like ourselves." Valerie Barber, interview, Twin Cities PBS and Vision Maker Media, *The People's Protectors*, produced by Leya Hale, 2018, https://www.visionmakermedia.org/films/peoples-protectors.

41. Vine, *Base Nation*, 329.

42. White men have also remarked on the "peer pressure to 'try a prostitute' " that exists on bases as a semirequired form of male bonding. Ibid., 166, 182. The military actively contrasts local sex workers with the USO entertainers and others women usually recruited from the United States. Rather than to provide sex, these "girls" were meant to "keep up [soldiers'] morale." Kara Dixon Vuic, *The Girls Next Door: Bringing the Home Front to the Front Lines* (Cambridge, MA: Harvard University Press, 2019), 3.

43. Banks, *Ojibwa Warrior*, 44–45.

44. Ibid., 50–55. See also Dustin Wright, "From Tokyo to Wounded Knee: Two Afterlives of the Sunagawa Struggle," *The Sixties: A Journal of History, Politics, and Culture* 10 (Winter 2017): 133–49.

45. Catherine A. Lutz, *Homefront: A Military City and the American Twentieth Century* (Boston: Beacon Press, 2001).

46. The Northern Plains were home to several forts, including Fort Buford and Fort Sully, which were maintained by the Army of the West during the late nineteenth century. Robert Utley, *The Indian Frontier, 1860–1890* (Albuquerque: University of New Mexico Press, 1984.)

47. Lutz, *Homefront*, 3; John Harrington, "America's Largest Bases," September 6, 2018, https://247wallst.com/special-report/2018/09/06/americas-largest-military-bases/8/. For a searchable map see https://militarybases.com/.

48. Vine, *Base Nation*, 14.

49. Lutz, *Homefront*, 58–59, 134–36. Some people both inside and outside the military joked that Fayetteville was a place to "get a dozen beers and a disease" (7).

50. While some African American leaders and historians have seen the military as a source of increased equality of opportunity, others have argued that the military has institutionalized or even amplified the racism present in society at large. Gerald F. Goodwin, "Black and White in Vietnam," *New York Times*, July 18, 2017; Jeremy P. Maxwell, *Brotherhood in Combat: How African Americans Found Equality in Korea and Vietnam* (Norman: University of Oklahoma Press, 2018); Beth Bailey, *America's Army: Making the All-Volunteer Force* (Cambridge, MA: Harvard University Press, 2009), 78, 257–58. More recently historians have identified the ways in which the military was tasked with enforcing structures of racism and inequality beginning in the colonial period, including "removal" of Native people from their lands. Maj. Gen. Grenville Dodge "urged the army to 'follow the Indians day and night, attacking them at every opportunity until they are worked out, disbanded or forced to surrender,'" writes Manu Karuka. "Nakedly indiscriminate, constant violence would be the means for establishing U.S. sovereignty and stabilizing U.S. property claims." *Empire's Tracks: Indigenous Nations, Chinese Workers, and the Transcontinental Railroad* (Oakland: University of California Press, 2019), 69. See also Roxanne Dunbar-Ortiz, *Loaded: A Disarming History of the Second Amendment* (San Francisco, CA: City Lights Publishing, 2018).

51. Racial tensions rose on many bases in the 1960s and 1970s. At the Minot AFB, a group of African American servicemen published three issues of a newsletter called *My Knot*. http://cdm15932.contentdm.oclc.org/cdm/ref/collection/p15932coll8/id/24694.

52. Belew, *Bring the War Home*.

53. Lutz, *Homefront*, 207, 240.

54. Centralized government support of private industry in wartime began during World War I and came to full expression in the 1940s and 1950s. James Sparrow, *Warfare State: World War II and the Age of Big Government* (New York: Oxford University Press, 2011). Even though these innovations in public and private cooperation made the production of incredible amounts of war material possible, business historian Mark Wilson suggests that a concerted effort to diminish the role of the public sphere in the 1950s and 1960s helped to lay the groundwork for the triumph of private enterprise as part of the ideology of new conservatism in the 1980s and 1990s. *Destruction Creation: American Business and the Winning of World War II* (Philadelphia: University of Pennsylvania Press, 2016).

55. Valerie Kuletz, quoted in Heefner, *The Missile Next Door*, 12.

56. Robin Riley, "Hidden Soldiers: Working for the 'National Defense,'" in Höhn and Moon, *Over There*, 203–30.

57. Kristen Iverson, *Full Body Burden: Growing Up in the Nuclear Shadow of Rocky Flats* (New York: Broadway Books, 2012), 189, 132, 148.

58. Brooks, *How Everything Became War*.

59. Lutz, *Homefront*, 3.

60. Heefner, *The Missile Next Door*, 7.

61. Kathleen Belew writes that war cannot be "neatly contained in the time and space legitimated by the state . . . [war] comes home in ways bloody and unexpected." Belew, *Bring the War Home*, 16.

62. A growing number of veterans are speaking out against the war on terror and the empty patriotic gestures that have prolonged it. See Andrew J. Bacevich, *American Empire: The Realities and Consequences of U.S. Diplomacy* (Cambridge, MA: Harvard University Press, 2002); Andrew J. Bacevich, "American Imperium: Untangling Truth and Fiction in an Age of Perpetual War," *Harpers*, May 2016, https://harpers.org/archive/2016/05/american-imperium/; Phil Klay, "Left Behind," *Atlantic*, May 2018, https://www.theatlantic.com/magazine/archive/2018/05/left-behind/556844/; Phil Klay, "The Warrior at the Mall," *New York Times*, April 14, 2018, https://www.nytimes.com/2018/04/14/opinion/sunday/the-warrior-at-the-mall.html.

63. https://watson.brown.edu/costsofwar/.

64. Mary Dudziak, *War Time: An Idea, Its History, Its Consequences* (New York: Oxford University Press, 2012), 6.

65. Jessica T. Mathews, "America's Indefensible Defense Budget," *New York Review of Books*, July 18, 2019, 1.

66. Heefner, *The Missile Next Door*, 152. Anti-military activist and rancher, Marvin Kammerer, understood, as did the South Dakota Peace and Justice Center, that "the best kept secret of the gutting of American agriculture is the degree to which military spending is responsible" (quoted from Heefner, *The Missile Next Door*, 154). Heefner also quoted journalist Ian Frazier's calculation that "in each county that housed a Minuteman, a single silo cost five years' worth of cattle, grain, and wheat" (155).

67. Quoted in Vine, *Base Nation*, 212.

68. In *What's the Matter with Kansas?: How Conservatives Won the Heart of America* (New York: Henry Holt, 2004), Thomas Frank argues that cultural conservatism largely convinced rural voters to vote for New Right Republicans, even though many of their fiscal policies could hurt them financially. He does not consider the impact of the presence of several military facilities and Minuteman missiles. In this book I do not assume that something is "the matter" with rural people, however much I disagree with their views on many issues today.

69. Robert F. Kennedy, "Remarks at the University of Kansas," March 18, 1968, https://www.jfklibrary.org/Research/Research-Aids/Ready-Reference/RFK-Speeches/Remarks-of-Robert-F-Kennedy-at-the-University-of-Kansas-March-18–1968.aspx.

70. Steven Lee, "Pistol-Packing Grand Forks Mayor Says He Refuses to Be a Victim," *Grand Forks Herald*, December 19, 2012, https://www.grandforksherald.com/news/government-and-politics/2185561-pistol-packing-grand-forks-mayor-says-he-refuses-be-victim.

71. Lassiter, "Political History Beyond the Red-Blue Divide," 764.

72. Martin Luther King Jr., "The Three Evils of Society," August 31, 1967, https://www .scribd.com/doc/134362247/Martin-Luther-King-Jr-The-Th ree-Evils-of-Society-1967. King argues that racism, militarism, and capitalism as mutually interdependent and destructive forces.

73. Kazin, *War Against War*.

74. Martin Luther King Jr., "Beyond Vietnam," http://kingencyclopedia.stanford.edu/ encyclopedia/documentsentry/doc_beyond_vietnam/.

75. Lutz, *Homefront*, 253.

Chapter 1

1. Hamlin Garland, *Son of the Middle Border* (New York: Macmillan, 1917), 374. "Under the Lion's Paw" is part of Garland's first publication, *Main-Travelled Roads*, originally published in 1891. See also Robert F. Gish, "Hamlin Garland's Dakota: History and Story," *South Dakota History* (1979): 193–209.

2. Hamlin Garland, "Under the Lion's Paw," in *Main Travelled Roads*, with introductions by William Dean Howells and Joseph B. McCullough (Lincoln: University of Nebraska Press, 1995), 139, 141.

3. Ibid., 144.

4. Garland first advocated for the single tax movement. See Caroline Fraser, *Prairie Fires: The American Dreams of Laura Ingalls Wilder* (New York: Holt, 2017), 164–67. For a more complete discussion of Garland's radical politics in the 1880s and 1890s, see Donald Pizer, ed., *The Radical Hamlin Garland: Writings from the 1890s* (Urbana: University of Illinois Press, 2010), introduction; Jonathan Berliner, "The Landscapes of Hamlin Garland and the American Populists," *American Literary Realism* 47 (2015): 219–34.

5. Garland, "Under the Lion's Paw," 135, 136, 141.

6. Robert L. Morlan, *Political Prairie Fire: The Nonpartisan League, 1915–1922* (Minneapolis: University of Minnesota Press, 1955).

7. Lawrence Goodwyn, *The Populist Moment: A Short History of the Agrarian Revolt in America* (New York: Oxford University Press, 1978).

8. William Pratt, "Farmers, Communists, and the FBI in the Upper Midwest," *Agricultural History* 63 (Summer 1989): 61–80; Lowell K. Dyson, *Red Harvest: Communism and American Farmers* (Lincoln: University of Nebraska Press, 1982.)

9. There is now a rich literature on racial formation in the US between 1870 and 1930. For immigrant groups from Europe, learning the "cultural logic" of racism was essential to defining themselves as "white." See Matthew Jacobson, *Whiteness of a Different Color: European Immigrants and the Alchemy of Race* (Cambridge, MA: Harvard University Press, 1999); Noel Ignatiev, *How the Irish Became White* (New York: Routledge Classics, 2008); David Roediger, *The Wages of Whiteness: Race and the Making of the American Working Class*, rev. ed. (New York: Verso, 2007); Ian Haney-Lopez, *White by Law: The Legal Construction of Race* (New York: New York University Press, 2006). On the common logic of the plains, see Karen V. Hansen, *Encounter on the Great Plains: Scandinavian Settlers and the Dispossession of Dakota Indians, 1890–1930* (New York: Oxford University Press, 2013), 15.

10. Garland, "Under the Lion's Paw," 138.

11. Mel Piehl, "Perspectives on Religion in Twentieth-Century American History," in Bruce J. Schulman, ed., *Making the American Century: Essays on the Political Culture of Twentieth Century America* (New York: Oxford University Press, 2014), 141–54. Mel Piehl reminds us not to equate the fundamentalist views of Populists like William Jennings Bryan with the "new evangelism" of the 1970s and 1980s. See also Michael Kazin, *A Godly Hero: The Life of William Jennings Bryan* (New York: Anchor Books, 2006). For the denominational representation and importance of religiosity in the Midwest, see Phillip Barlow and Mark Silk, eds., *Religion and Public Life in the Midwest: America's Common Denominator?* (Lanham, MD: AltaMira, 2004). On the experiences of non-Christians see Rachel Calof, *Rachel Calof's Story: A Jewish Homesteader on the Northern Plains* (Bloomington: Indiana University Press, 1995); Samuel G. Freedman, "North Dakota Mosque a Symbol of Muslims' Deep Ties in America," *New York Times*, May 28, 2016, A13; Eric Steven Zimmer, Art Mamorstein, and Matthew Remmich, "Fewer Rabbis Than U.S. Senators: Jewish Political Activism in South Dakota," in Jon K. Lauck, John E. Miller, and Paula M. Nelson, eds., *The Plains Political Tradition: Essays on South Dakota Political Culture*, vol. 3 (Pierre: South Dakota Historical Society Press, 2018), 112–39.

12. Sara Egge, *Woman Suffrage and Citizenship in the Midwest, 1870–1920* (Iowa City: University of Iowa Press, 2018), 14–20, 86–89.

13. Elliot West, "Reconstructing Race," *Western Historical Quarterly* 34, no. 1 (2003): 6–26. The unstated tenets of settler colonialism were understood by new immigrants, the vast majority of whom were white; adopting them was part of their assimilation process, even if it did not always protect them from interethnic discrimination and xenophobia. Hansen, *Encounter on the Great Plains*, 15–16. Sara Egge, quoting Andrew Cayton, puts it bluntly: "Most Midwesterners believed passionately that the United States 'was by rights a white nation, a Protestant nation,' a nation in which true Americans were native-born men with Anglo-Saxon ancestors.'" *Woman Suffrage and Citizenship in the Midwest*, 8.

14. Richard White, *The Republic for Which It Stands: The United States During Reconstruction and the Gilded Age, 1865–1896* (New York: Oxford University Press, 2017). White contends that "Americans had long regarded Indians as a collection of deficiencies. Their religions were deficient, their economies were deficient, their cultures were deficient, and their families were deficient. American efforts to 'civilize' Indians focused on . . . making them Protestant, organizing them into patrilineal families, and giving them homes" (151). Native scholar Nick Estes has written that "elimination"—through segregation or incarceration—is the "unfinished business of settler colonialism." Nick Estes, *Our History Is the Future: Standing Rock Versus the Dakota Access Pipeline, and the Long Tradition of Indigenous Resistance* (London: Verso, 2019), 185.

15. Jason Pierce, *Making the White Man's West: Whiteness and the Creation of the American West* (Boulder: University of Colorado Press, 2016), 14.

16. At the turn of the century, nearly half of the population of North Dakota had been born outside the US; more than a quarter of the population of South Dakota had. See Elwyn B. Robinson, *History of North Dakota* (Lincoln: University of Nebraska Press, 1966); William C. Sherman and Playford V. Thorson, eds., *Plains Folk: North Dakota's Ethnic History* (Fargo: North Dakota Institute for Regional Studies, 1988); Herbert T. Hoover, *A New South Dakota History* (Sioux Falls, SD: Center for Western Studies, 2005).

17. David Laskin, *The Children's Blizzard* (New York: HarperCollins, 2004).

18. Kristin L. Hoganson, *The Heartland: An American History* (New York: Penguin, 2019).

19. R. Alton Lee, *Principle over Party: The Farmers' Alliance and Populism in South Dakota, 1880–1900* (Pierre: South Dakota Historical Society Press, 2011), 71.

20. Ibid., 187.

21. Robinson, *History of North Dakota*, 226.

22. Jon K. Lauck, *Prairie Republic: The Political Culture of Dakota Territory, 1879–1889* (Norman: University of Oklahoma Press, 2010), 107.

23. David B. Danbom, *Born in the Country: A History of Rural America* (Baltimore: Johns Hopkins University Press, 1995), 153. Danbom comments, "For farmers, the stick had two short ends" (ibid).

24. Steven Hahn, *The Roots of Southern Populism: Yeoman Farmers and the Transformation of the Georgia Upcountry, 1850–1890* (New York: Oxford University Press, 1983).

25. Norman K. Risjord, *Dakota: The Story of the Northern Plains* (Lincoln: University of Nebraska Press, 2012), 180.

26. Goodwyn, *Populist Moment*, 230–32 and *passim*.

27. Quoted in Kazin, *A Godly Hero*, 61.

28. Howard R. Lamar, "Perspectives on Statehood: South Dakota's First Quarter Century, 1889–1914," *South Dakota History* 19 (Spring 1989): 13–14.

29. Lee, *Principle over Party*, 36–41. See also Brad Tennant, "People's Democracy: The Origins of the Initiated Measure in South Dakota," in Jon K. Lauck, John E. Miller, and Donald C. Simmons Jr., eds., *The Plains Political Tradition: Essays on South Dakota Political Culture*, vol. 2 (Pierre: South Dakota State Historical Society, 2014), 8–29.

30. Lee, *Principle over Party* , 169–72.

31. Elizabeth Sanders, *Roots of Reform: Farmers, Workers, and the American State, 1877–1917* (Chicago: University of Chicago Press, 1999).

32. Gilbert Courtland Fite, *Peter Norbeck: Prairie Statesman* (Pierre: South Dakota State Historical Society Press, 2005), xi.

33. Herbert T. Hoover and Steven C. Emery, "South Dakota Governance Since 1945," in Richard Lowitt, ed., *Politics in the Postwar American West* (Norman: University of Oklahoma Press, 1995), 222.

34. Fite, *Peter Norbeck: Prairie Statesman*, 27, 57. A million dollars in 1920 would be worth over fifteen million in 2019.

35. Michael J. Lansing, *Insurgent Democracy: The Nonpartisan League in North American Politics* (Chicago: University of Chicago Press, 2015), 108–10. According to Lansing, Norbeck said the leaders of the NPL " 'live and grow on trouble' " (110).

36. Jeffrey Ostler, *Prairie Populism: The Fate of Radical Agrarianism in Kansas, Nebraska, and Iowa* (Lawrence: University Press of Kansas, 1993), 128–29.

37. Lee, *Principle over Party*, 22–23.

38. Paula M. Nelson, "Home and Family First: Women and Political Culture," in Jon K. Lauck, John E. Miller, and Donald C. Simmons Jr., eds., *The Plains Political Tradition: Essays in South Dakota Political Culture*, vol. 1 (Pierre: South Dakota Historical Society Press, 2011), 137–38; Egge, *Woman Suffrage and Citizenship in the Midwest*; Lori Ann Lahlum, "Women, Work, and Community in Rural Norwegian America, 1840–1920," in Betty A. Berglund and Lori Ann Lahlum, *Norwegian American Women: Migrations, Communities, and Identities* (St. Paul: Minnesota Historical Society Press, 2011), 79–118.

39. William C. Pratt, "Another South Dakota; or, The Road Not Taken," in Lauck, Miller, and Simmons Jr., *The Plains Political Tradition*, 1:113.

40. US House of Representatives: History, Art and Archives, "Gladys Pyle," http://history .house.gov/People/Detail?id = 20002.

41. Quoted in Risjord, *Dakota*, 191, 193.

42. By the 1970s Romness would be well inside the Grand Forks Air Base's "missile field."

43. Document Four, "Minutes from the Romness Farmers Alliance (1892)" http://ndstu dies.gov/gr8/content/unit-iii-waves-development-1861–1920/lesson-4-alliances-and -conflicts/topic-5-bosses-and-reformers/section-3-farmers%E2%80%99-alliance.

44. Curt Eriksmoen, "Populist Fought for Initiative, Referendum," *Bismarck Tribune*, December 25, 2011, http://bismarcktribune.com/news/columnists/curt-eriksmoen/populist -fought-for-initiative-referendum/article_52b08f14–2da8–11e1-a39b-001871e3ce6c.html.

45. Charles N. Glaab, "John Burke and the Progressive Revolt," in Thomas Howard, ed., *The North Dakota Political Tradition* (Ames: Iowa State University Press, 1981), 40–65.

46. Quoted in Risjord, *Dakota*, 195.

47. Robert Vogel, *Unequal Contest: Bill Langer and His Political Enemies* (Mandan, ND: Crain Grosinger, 2004), 10–11; Glenn Smith, "Bill Langer and the Art of Personal Politics," in Howard, *The North Dakota Political Tradition*, 123–50.

48. Quoted in Lansing, *Insurgent Democracy*, 172–73. See also Kim E. Nielsen, " 'We All Leaguers by Our House': Women, Suffrage, and Red-Baiting in the National Nonpartisan League," *Journal of Women's History* 6 (Spring 1994): 31–50.

49. Frazier knew almost nothing about protocol, so he hired Tony Thompson, an African American who had worked as a driver in the previous administration, as a personal messenger. His daughter, Era Bell Thompson, published *American Daughter: The Life of a Negro* (Chicago: University of Chicago Press, 1946).

50. Lansing, *Insurgent Democracy*, xi–xii.

51. Ann Marie Low, *Dust Bowl Diary* (Lincoln: University of Nebraska Press, 1984), 33.

52. Richard Lowitt and Maurine Beasely, eds., *One-Third of a Nation: Lorena Hickok Reports on the Great Depression* (Urbana: University of Illinois Press, 1981), 82.

53. Quoted in Theodore Salutos and John D. Hicks, *Agricultural Discontent in the Middle West: 1900–1939* (Madison: University of Wisconsin Press, 1951), 443. See also John E. Miller, "Restrained, Respectable Radicals: The South Dakota Farm Holiday," *Agricultural History* 59 (July 1985): 429–47.

54. Pratt, "Another South Dakota," 116–19.

55. Quoted in Charles Conrad and Joyce Conrad, *Fifty Years: North Dakota Farmers Union* (n.p, 1976), 38.

56. As much as white farmers have long claimed to hate farm programs, they have also been privileged by them. The Roosevelt administration could not pass New Deal legislation without the votes of white southern Democrats; as a result many of the programs, including the AAA, included mechanisms whereby blacks were excluded from receiving benefits. Nathan A. Rosenberg and Bryce Wilson Stucki, "The Butz Stops Here: Why the Food Movement Needs to Rethink Agricultural History," *Journal of Food Law and Policy* 13 (2017): 19–20. Ira Katznelson calls this the "southern cage." *Fear Itself: The New Deal and the Origins of Our Time* (New York: Liveright, 2013), 14–16, 133–226.

57. James C. Scott, *Weapons of the Weak: Everyday Forms of Peasant Resistance* (New Haven, CT: Yale University Press, 1987).

58. US Senate, Committee on Agriculture and Forestry, *Agricultural Emergency Act to Increase Farm Purchasing Power*, 73rd Congress, 1st Sess., 1932, Hearings of H.R. 3835, 109–12.

59. Ibid. See also US Senate, Committee on Agriculture and Forestry, *To Abolish the Federal Farm Board and Secure for the Farmer the Cost of Production*, 72nd Congress, 1st Sess., 1932, Hearings of S. 3133.

60. Quoted in Elizabeth Evenson Williams, *Emil Loriks: Builder of a New Economic Order* (Sioux Falls, SD: Center for Western Studies, 1987), 157.

61. Catherine McNicol Stock, *Main Street in Crisis: The Great Depression and the Old Middle Class on the Northern Plains* (Chapel Hill: University of North Carolina Press, 1992), 145–47.

62. Ibid., 146. David Danbom explores the ways local boards on the Northern Plains could also deny certain people benefits. See David B. Danbom, "National Ideas and Local Power in Fargo, North Dakota, During the Great Depression," in Schulman, *Making the American Century*, 37–50.

63. David B. Danbom, "A Part of the Nation and Apart from the Nation: North Dakota Politics Since 1945," in Lowitt, *Politics in the Postwar American West*, 174–84.

64. Kristin L. Hoganson, "Meat in the Middle: Converging Borderlands in the US Midwest, 1865–1900," *Journal of American History* 98 (January 2012): 1025–51.

65. Robert E. Wright, *Little Business on the Prairie: Entrepreneurship, Prosperity, and Challenge in South Dakota* (Sioux Falls, SD: Center for Western Studies, 2015).

66. https://www.cargill.com/about/cargill-timeline.

67. Michael Kazin, *The Populist Persuasion: An American History* (New York: Basic Books, 1995), 40.

68. Quoted in *Sioux Falls Argus Leader*, April 13, 1925, 2.

69. Kimberly Phillips-Fein, *Invisible Hands: The Businessmen's Crusade Against the New Deal* (New York: Norton, 2010).

70. Robinson, *History of North Dakota*, 223.

71. Ibid.

72. Quoted in ibid., 224.

73. Ibid., 340–41.

74. Lansing, *Insurgent Democracy*, 136.

75. Vogel, *Unequal Contest.*

76. United States Senate, "William Langer Expulsion Case," https://www.senate.gov/artandhistory/history/common/expulsion_cases/123WilliamLanger_expulsion.htm.

77. Stock, *Main Street in Crisis*, 125–26.

78. R. Alton Lee, *A New Deal for South Dakota: Drought, Depression, and Relief, 1920–1941* (Pierre: South Dakota Historical Society Press, 2016), 34.

79. Lois Phillips Hudson, *Reapers of the Dust: A Prairie Chronicle* (St. Paul: Minnesota Historical Society Press, 1984), 8.

80. This was not an entirely specious concern. See Thomas Biolsi, "New Deal Visions v. Local Culture: The Agony of the South Dakota State Planning Board, 1934–1939," in Lauck, Miller, and Simmons Jr., *The Plains Political Tradition* 2:4.

81. Quoted in ibid., 88.

82. Quoted in ibid., 91–92.

83. John E. Miller, "McCarthyism Before McCarthy: The 1938 Election in South Dakota," *Heritage of the Great Plains* 15 (1982): 1–21.

84. Quoted in ibid., 11. See also Scott N. Heidepriem, *A Fair Chance for a Free People: Biography of Karl E. Mundt, United States Senator* (Madison, SD: Leader, 1988).

85. George McGovern, interview by Jon K. Lauck and John E. Miller, November 25, 2003, Mitchell, South Dakota, 16. By permission of interviewers.

86. South Dakota banned the showing of the Pare Lorentz classic documentary *The Plow That Broke the Plains* (1936). On the controversy over the film, see John E. Miller, "Two Visions of the Great Plains: *The Plow That Broke the Plains* and South Dakotans' Reactions to It," *Upper Midwest History* 2 (1982): 1–12.

87. Hansen, *Encounter on the Great Plains*, 15–16.

88. No history of agrarian radicalism that praises its democratic ideals or otherwise distinguishes it from the conservatism of its day is complete if it does not also fully reckon with its distinctly undemocratic ideals and practices. Most recent historians acknowledge this contradiction, albeit rather weakly. Charles Postel, for example, writes that "populism's relationship to democracy [was] complex" particularly in an era when race relations "turned especially menacing." *The Populist Vision* (New York: Oxford University Press, 2009), 18. Michael Kazin explains that the Populists "shared the era's core belief in white supremacy." *Populist Persuasion*, 42. None explores the possibility that the desire to protect not just class status but race privilege may have lain at the core of agrarian radicalism.

89. Pierce, *Making the White Man's West*.

90. Ibid., ix.

91. Nell Irvin Painter, *The History of White People* (New York: Norton, 2010), 325–26.

92. In the1950s historians like Richard Hofstadter decried the antisemitism within Populist politics, even arguing that William Jennings Bryan's "Cross of Gold" speech employed the crucifixion metaphor as a rhetorical vehicle for coded antisemitism. Since the 1970s revisionist historians who see Populism as radically democratic rather than protofascist have argued that antisemitic language was limited to a few Populist leaders, largely from its "shadow movements," and thus was not a defining component of the party's original political worldview. Jeff Ostler is closer to the truth when he argues that "some Populists could have been susceptible to the anti-Semitism that pervaded American culture and how they might have given the theory of an English conspiracy an anti-Semitic turn." Ostler, "The Rhetoric of Conspiracy and the Formation of Kansas Populism," *Agricultural History* 69, no. 1 (1995): 26. See also Charles Postel, "Populism and Race: Separate and Unequal," https://digital.lib.niu.edu/illinois/gildedage/populism.

93. Quoted in David H. Bennett, *The Party of Fear: From Nativist Movements to the New Right in American History* (Chapel Hill: University of North Carolina Press, 1988), 178.

94. Quoted in ibid., 181.

95. Zimmer, Mamorstein, and Remmich, "Fewer Rabbis Than U.S. Senators."

96. Leonard Dinnerstein, "Jews and the New Deal," *American Jewish History* 72 (1983): 461.

97. President Starcher kept handwritten notes on Camelback Inn stationary. They are included among his papers in the Orin G. Libby Manuscript Collection #238, Elwyn Robinson Department of Special Collections, Chester Fritz Library, University of North Dakota,

Grand Forks, North Dakota. On undergraduate activism, author conversation and email exchange with Sara Garland, October 4, 2017.

98. Jon K. Lauck, "'You Can't Mix Wheat and Potatoes in the Same Bin': Anti-Catholicism in Early Dakota," *South Dakota History* 38 (Spring 2008): 1–46.

99. Kazin, *Populist Persuasion*, 39–40.

100. Painter, *History of White People*, 317–23.

101. James Madison, *A Lynching in the Heartland: Race and Memory in America* (New York: Palgrave Macmillan, 2001); Nancy MacLean, *Behind the Mask of Chivalry: The Making of the Second Ku Klux Klan* (New York: Oxford University Press, 1995); Linda Gordon, *The Second Coming of the KKK: The Ku Klux Klan of the 1920s and the American Political Tradition* (New York: Norton, 2017). Nell Irvin Painter says the motto for some klans was "Catholics, Kikes,and Koloreds." Painter, *History of White People*, 324.

102. William Harwood, "The Ku Klux Klan in Grand Forks, North Dakota," *South Dakota History* 1 (Fall 1971): 301–35. F. Hadley Ambrose was also known to be a prominent member of the IVA and tremendously opposed to the NPL. Michael Lansing, email to author, June 1, 2019.

103. Lauck, "'You Can't Mix Wheat and Potatoes in the Same Bin,'" 42. See also Charles Ranbow, "The Ku Klux Klan in the 1920s: A Concentration on the Black Hills," *South Dakota History* 4 (Winter 1973): 74.

104. Lauck, "'You Can't Mix Wheat and Potatoes in the Same Bin.'"

105. George McGovern, interview by Jon K. Lauck and John E. Miller, 3–4. See also Tom Lawrence, "JFK at 100," May 22, 2017, https://www.aberdeennews.com/news/opinion/lawrence-john-f-kennedy-at/articleb1e32dcc-891e-5117–89df-50efde4849a8.html.

106. Sherman and Thorson, *Plains Folk*, 190–92, 234–35.

107. Kenneth Smith, "Presbyterianism, Progressivism, and Cultural Influence: William M. Blackburn, Coe I. Crawford, and the Making of Civic Dakota," in Lauck, Miller, and Nelson, *The Plains Political Tradition* 3:104.

108. Egge, *Woman Suffrage and Citizenship in the Midwest*, 38–41. On the "timid" campaigns in North Dakota and the "daily, dirty politics of a prohibition state largely controlled by railroads and milling interests," see Barbara Handy-Marchello, "Quiet Voices in the Prairie Wind: The Politics of Woman Suffrage in North Dakota, 1868–1920," in Lori Ann Lahlum and Molly P. Rozum, eds., *Equality at the Ballot Box: Votes for Women on the Northern Great Plains* (Pierre: South Dakota Historical Society Press, 2019), 71.

109. http://files.usgwarchives.net/sd/women/suffrage.txt.

110. Paula M. Nelson, "Defending Separate Spheres: Anti-Suffrage Women in South Dakota Suffrage Campaigns," in Lahlum and Rozum, *Equality at the Ballot Box*, 128–68.

111. Sara Egge, "Leadership, Immigrants, and the Fight for Woman Suffrage on the Northern Great Plains" (paper presented at the Organization of American Historians, Annual Meeting, Providence, RI, April 2, 2015). See also Egge, "Ethnicity and Woman Suffrage on the South Dakota Plains," in Lahlum and Rozum, *Equality at the Ballot Box*, 218–39.

112. Egge, "Leadership, Immigrants, and the Fight for Woman Suffrage," 1.

113. Ibid., 4.

114. Nelson, "Defending Separate Spheres."

115. Toni Morrison, *Playing in the Dark: Whiteness and the Literary Imagination* (Cambridge, MA: Harvard University Press, 1992). I adhere to Nell Irvin Painter's contention that

"race is an idea, not a fact, and its questions demand answers from the conceptual rather than the factual realm." *History of White People*, ix–x.

116. Quoted in Kate Brown, "Gridded Lives: Why Kazakhstan and Montana Are Nearly the Same Place," *American Historical Review* 106 (February 2001): 31.

117. Quoted in Biolosi, "New Deal Visions," 93.

118. Manu Karuka, *Empire's Tracks: Indigenous Nations, Chinese Workers, and the Transcontinental Railroad* (Oakland: University of California Press, 2019).

119. Louis S. Warren, *God's Red Son: The Ghost Dance Religion and the Making of Modern America* (New York: Basic Books, 2017).

120. Jerome A. Greene, *American Carnage: Wounded Knee, 1890* (Norman: University of Oklahoma Press, 2014); David Treuer, *The Heartbeat of Wounded Knee: Native America from 1890 to the Present* (New York: Riverhead Books, 2019); Estes, *Our History Is the Future.*

121. Historian Eric Zimmer, a volunteer with the Rapid City Native Lands project, has been retracing the history of segregation in Rapid City. Chynna Lockett, "Presentation Links Rapid City Housing to Segregation," *South Dakota Public Radio*, http://listen.sdpb.org/post/presentation-links-rapid-city-housing-segregation.

122. Nathan Sanderson, "The Roots of West River Republicanism," in Lauck, Miller, and Simmons Jr., *The Plains Political Tradition*, 2:67–68. The Garrison Dam project of the postwar period would force many Natives off their lands again. See Estes, *Our History Is the Future*, 133–68.

123. Chuck Lewis, "Frontier Fears: The Clash of Dakotas and Whites in the Newspapers of Mankato, Minnesota, 1863–1865," *Minnesota's Heritage* 5 (January 2012): 36–37.

124. White, *The Republic for Which It Stands*, 605. See also Ben Johnson, "Red Populism? T. A. Bland, Agrarian Radicalism, and the Debate over the Dawes Act," in Catherine McNicol Stock and Robert D. Johnston, eds., *The Countryside in the Age of the Modern State: Political Histories of Rural America* (Ithaca, NY: Cornell University Press, 2001), 15–37.

125. For a fascinating discussion of the "failed moment" when woman suffrage activists might have collaborated with those who supported the vote for Native men, see Molly P. Rozum, "Citizenship, Civilization, and Property: The 1890 South Dakota Vote on Woman Suffrage and Indian Suffrage," in Lahlum and Rozum, *Equality at the Ballot Box*, 240–61.

126. Greene, *American Carnage*, 373–80.

127. Charles Barber, "Reason on the Rez in the Age of Joe McCarthy: Senate Judiciary Chair William Langer's (R-ND) Hearings on Juvenile Delinquency, Ft. Yates, New Town, Rolla and Bismarck, ND, October 11–14, 1954," (paper presented at the Northern Great Plains History Conference, Mankato, MN, September 21, 2018).

128. West, "Reconstructing Race," http://www.studythepast.com/his378/recon structingrace_elliottwest.pdf, 7.

129. Richard R. Chenoweth, "Francis Case: A Political Biography," *South Dakota Historical Collections* 39 (1978): 323.

130. Quoted in Michael Patrick Hearn, "Little Myths on the Prairie," in Nancy Tystad Koupal, ed., *Pioneer Girl Perspectives: Exploring Laura Ingalls Wilder* (Pierre: South Dakota Historical Society Press, 2017), 132.

131. Ibid.

132. Stock, *Main Street in Crisis*, 199–200; Cynthia Culver Prescott, *Pioneer Mother Monuments: Constructing Memory* (Norman: University of Oklahoma Press, 2019), 20–21, 112–14.

133. http://www.netstate.com/states/mottoes/sd_motto.htm.

Chapter 2

1. Quoted in Michael Kazin, *War Against War: The American Fight for Peace, 1914–1918* (New York: Simon and Schuster, 2017), 266. See also Jeanette Keith, *Rich Man's War, Poor Man's Fight: Race, Class, and Power in the Rural South During the First World War* (Chapel Hill: University of North Carolina Press, 2004).

2. On Alvin York's actual experience in combat, beyond what is represented in the film *Sergeant York* (Hawke, 1941), see https://kentuckypress.wordpress.com/2014/06/11/the-con troversy-of-sergeant-york-uncovering-the-wwi-iconic-heros-battleground/.

3. I use the terms Populist anti-militarist, anti-militarist, and, when needed for clarity, anti-interventionist rather than the more familiar term isolationist when writing about the movement against intervention in Europe in the 1930s and early 1940s. As Brooke Blower explains, "isolationist" was used by prowar forces before, during, and after World War II as a bludgeon and a rallying cry. See Brooke L. Blower, "From Isolationism to Neutrality: A New Framework for Understanding American Political Culture, 1919–1941," *Diplomatic History* 38, no. 2 (2014): 345–76. The term Populist anti-militarist also clarifies that the views of those "isolationists" from the upper Midwest were distinct because they were based in the radical agrarian views on the economy and centralized power first articulated nationwide by the Populist Party. This is largely the same view advanced by Wayne S. Cole in his work *Senator Gerald P. Nye and American Foreign Relations* (Minneapolis: University of Minnesota Press, 1962).

4. Jack Warner supported FDR in 1932, later refusing a diplomatic position and telling Roosevelt he could do more for American foreign relations by making films. Harry was even closer to the president. Warner Brothers produced more prowar films, and produced them sooner, than any other studio. See Nancy Snow, "Confessions of a Hollywood Propagandist: Harry Warner, FDR, and Celluloid Persuasion," https://learcenter.org/pdf/WWSnow.pdf.

5. On how the film navigated the "narrow ridge between capitalizing on Appalachian local color and exploiting it," see Richard Gray and Owen Robinson, *A Companion to the Literature and Culture of the American South* (New York: Wiley, 2007), 37.

6. Ibid. See also Adrianna Abreu, "Art vs. Propaganda: How to Prepare the Public for an Indeterminate Course of Action," http://digital.lib.lehigh.edu/trial/reel_new/films/list/0_43_9.

7. Lynne Olson, *Those Angry Days: Roosevelt, Lindbergh, and America's Fight over World War II, 1939–1941* (New York: Random House, 2014), 369.

8. When Nye learned of the attack on Pearl Harbor, he said, "Just what the British had planned for us. . . . We have been maneuvered into this by the President." Quoted in David W. Mills, *Cold War in a Cold Land: Fighting Communism on the Northern Plains* (Norman: University of Oklahoma Press, 2015), 10.

9. Quoted in Abreu, "Art vs. Propaganda." See also Olson, *Those Angry Days*, 360.

10. Quoted in Clayton R. Koppes and Gregory D. Black, *Hollywood Goes to War: How Politics, Profits, and Propaganda Shaped World War II Movies* (Berkeley: University of California Press, 1990), 40.

11. Ronald Schaffer, *America in the Great War: The Rise of the War Welfare State* (New York: Oxford University Press, 2011), 213.

12. Kazin, *War Against War*, 207. Hutterites wore traditional clothing, grew long beards, owned land communally, and spoke mostly German, making them particular targets of the Wilson administration's vicious "loyalty" campaign.

13. Ibid., 207. See also Duane C. S. Stoltzfus, "Standing in Chains at Alcatraz: When Hutterites Were Called to War," https://themennonite.org/feature/standing-chains-alcatraz/.

14. Just before the Hofers were drafted, their Rockland colony had refused to buy war bonds. Local people stole their cattle, sold it, and purchased the bonds "for them." Stoltzfus, "Standing in Chains at Alcatraz."

15. Quoted in Kazin, *War Against War*, 279.

16. Historians of Populism from Hicks and Hofstadter to Goodwyn, Sanders, and Ostler have evinced little curiosity about anything beyond the People's Party's important proposals to reform the American economy and political process. Even Charles Postel, whose innovative work takes on Populist religious and intellectual life, seems to care little about Populist views of America's role in the world, saying that "most Populists paid little heed to foreign affairs." Charles Postel, *The Populist Vision* (New York: Oxford University Press, 2009), 240. A recent exception is Nathan Jessen's *Populism and Imperialism: Politics, Culture, and Foreign Policy in the American West, 1890–1900* (Lawrence: University Press of Kansas, 2018). Jessen also disputes previous claims that Populists acted as collaborators in the imperialist project overseas, however much they benefited from settler colonialism and dispossession at home.

17. Postel, *Populist Vision*, 99–100, 122–23, 239–41. On the global and outward-looking nature of the Midwestern experience, see Kristin L. Hoganson, *The Heartland: An American History* (New York: Penguin, 2019).

18. Postel, *Populist* Vision, 240.

19. David Lee Amstutz, "A Populist Approach to Foreign Policy: Governor William A. Poynter, the South African War, and the Indian Famine, 1899–1901," *Great Plains Quarterly* 34 (Winter 2014): 12.

20. For the full platform of the American Anti-Imperialist League, see https://source books.fordham.edu/mod/1899antiimp.asp.

21. Kazin, *Godly Hero*, 85, 240–41. See also Merle Curti, *Bryan and World Peace* (Northampton, MA: Department of History at Smith College, 1931).

22. Kazin, *Godly Hero*, 87–90.

23. Quoted in Kazin, *Godly Hero*, 89.

24. William Jennings Bryan, "The Paralyzing Influence of Imperialism," from the *Official Proceedings of the Democratic National Convention Held in Kansas City, Mo., July 4, 5, and 6, 1900*, Chicago, 1900, 205–27, accessed March 30, 2012, https://www.mtholyoke.edu/acad/intrel/bryan.htm.

25. Ibid.

26. Kenneth Elton Hendrickson Jr., "The Public Career of William F. Pettigrew of South Dakota, 1848–1926," (PhD diss., University of Oklahoma, 1962), 231.

27. Kristin L. Hoganson, *Fighting for American Manhood: How Gender Politics Provoked the Spanish-American and Philippine-American Wars* (New Haven, CT: Yale University Press, 1998); G. Edward White, *The Eastern Establishment and the Western Experience: The West of Frederic Remington, Theodore Roosevelt, and Owen Wister* (Austin: University of Texas Press, 1986).

28. Hoganson, *Fighting for American Manhood*, 22–23.

29. Quoted in Rachel Maddow, *Drift: The Unmooring of American Military Power* (New York: Crown Publishers, 2012), 45.

30. Hendrickson, "Public Career," 214.

31. Pettigrew to William Augustus Croffut, October 28, 1899, quoted in Hendrickson, "Public Career," 245.

32. Quoted in Hendrickson, "Public Career," 218.

33. Ibid., 223.

34. Quoted in ibid., 226.

35. Terrence J. Lindell, "Populists in Power: The Problems of the Andrew E. Lee Administration in South Dakota," *South Dakota History* 22 (Winter 1992): 343–65.

36. R. Alton Lee, *Principle over Party: The Farmers' Alliance and Populism in South Dakota, 1880–1900* (Pierre: South Dakota Historical Society Press, 2011), 163–64.

37. Ibid., 164.

38. Ibid.

39. Ibid., 164–65.

40. Quoted in Lindell, "Populists in Power," 361.

41. Robert Lee Mattson, "Politics Is Up! Grigsby's Cowboys and Roosevelt's Rough Riders, 1898," *South Dakota History* 9 (Fall 1979): 303–15.

42. Lee, *Principle over Party*, 222n37.

43. *Rapid City Journal*, April 8, 1898, quoted in Daniel Simundon, "The Yellow Press on the Prairie: South Dakota Daily Newspaper Editorials Prior to the Spanish American War," *South Dakota History* 2 (1972): 226.

44. Herman F. Krueger, "A South Dakotan's Experience in the Spanish American War," *South Dakota Historical Collections* 39 (1978): 229.

45. Ibid.

46. Steven J. Bucklin, ed., "'We Were All Mustered in Uncle Sam's Army': The Journal of Thomas H. Briggs in the Philippines, 1898–1899," *South Dakota History* 34 (Fall 2004): 256, 257, 274.

47. Krueger, "A South Dakotan's Experience in the Spanish American War," 269. It would be reasonable to wonder if some South Dakotans actually had learned such brutality back in "Indian Country." Katharine Bjork argues that their officers, including General John Pershing, carried the "lessons" of waging war against Natives in the American West with them to the Philippines and later to Mexico. Katharine Bjork, *Prairie Imperialism: The Indian Origins of American Empire* (Philadelphia: University of Pennsylvania Press, 2019).

48. Krueger, "A South Dakotan's Experience in the Spanish American War," 275.

49. Michael Kazin, "If the U.S. Had Not Entered World War I, Would There Have Been a World War II?," https://newrepublic.com/article/118435/world-war-i-debate-should-US-have-entered.

50. Kazin, *War Against War*, xii.

51. Quoted in Kazin, *Godly Hero*, 240.

52. Blower, "From Isolationism to Neutrality."

53. Joel Andrew Watne, "Public Opinion Toward Non-Conformists and Aliens During 1917, as Shown by the *Fargo Forum*," *North Dakota History* 34 (1967): 5–29, http://history.nd.gov/publications/public-opinion.pdf.

54. "Time for Good Sense and Moderation," *Fargo Forum*, February 28, 1917, 4, quoted in Watne, "Public Opinion," 10.

55. Quoted in Watne, "Public Opinion," 19.

56. Ibid., 21.

57. Michael J. Lansing, *Insurgent Democracy: The Nonpartisan League in North American Politics* (Chicago: University of Chicago Press, 2015), 101.

58. Quoted in ibid., 100.

59. Quoted in ibid., 99–100.

60. Quoted in H. C. Peterson and Gilbert C. Fite, *Opponents of War, 1917–1918* (Madison: University of Wisconsin Press, 1957), 155.

61. Quoted in Lansing, *Insurgent Democracy*, 100.

62. Keith, *Rich Man's War, Poor Man's Fight*. Keith argues that as many as half a million rural men in the South may have avoided or refused conscription.

63. Lansing, *Insurgent Democracy*, 130. See also 121–24.

64. Quoted in Peterson and Fite, *Opponents of War*, 154. Pettigrew was in ill health and in 1919 the case was dropped. While he was under indictment, a mob painted his house yellow.

65. Lansing, *Insurgent Democracy*, 121.

66. Rex C. Myers, "An Immigrant Heritage: South Dakota's Foreign-Born in the Era of Assimilation," *South Dakota History* 19 (Summer 1989): 147. See also Frederick Luebke, *Bonds of Loyalty: German Americans and World War One* (DeKalb: Northern Illinois University Press, 1974).

67. Quoted in Lansing, *Insurgent Democracy*, 125.

68. Peterson and Fite, *Opponents of War*, 195.

69. Quoted in Charles M. Barber, "The Impact of World War One on German-Americans in North Dakota and the Midwest" (paper presented at the Heritage Center, Bismarck, ND, April 9, 2017).

70. Quoted in Barber, "Impact of World War One," 11.

71. Lansing, *Insurgent Democracy*, 95; Barber, "Impact of World War One," 8.

72. David T. Nelson and Richard G. Cole, "Behind German Lines in 1915: The Letters Home of David T. Nelson," *Journal of Military History* 65 (October 2001): 1058, 1059.

73. Steven Trout, *On the Battlefield of Memory: The First World War and American Remembrance, 1919–1941* (Tuscaloosa: University of Alabama Press, 2010), 167.

74. David M. Lubin, *Grand Illusions: American Art and the First World War* (New York: Oxford University Press, 2016), 173.

75. Ibid. For more examples of Dunn's combat art see https://unwritten-record.blogs.ar chives.gov/2015/02/02/wwi-combat-artists-harvey-dunn/.

76. Lubin, *Grand Illusions*, 252–53. See also John Steuart Curry's *Return of Private Davis from the Argonne* (1940), https://www.mfah.org/art/detail/111400?returnUrl = %2Fart %2Fsearch%3Fdepartment%3DAmerican%2520Painting%2520%2526%2520Sculpture.

77. http://history.nd.gov/hp/WWImemorials.html.

78. Ibid.

79. "International Peace Garden: Preface and History," April 14, 1932, unpublished manuscript, courtesy of Lorna B. Meidinger, State Historical Society of North Dakota.

80. "Statement of Significance: CCC Lodge, International Peace Garden, Rolette County, ND," US Department of the Interior, National Park Service, National Register of Historic Places Continuation Sheet, Section 8, 2. Courtesy of Lorna B. Meidinger, State Historical Society of North Dakota.

81. Bradley W. Hart, *Hitler's American Friends: The Third Reich's Supporters in the United States* (New York: St. Martin's, 2018); Blower, "Isolationism to Neutrality," 345.

82. Cole, *Senator Gerald P. Nye and American Foreign Relations*; Wayne S. Cole, *America First: The Battle Against Interventionism, 1940–1941* (Madison: University of Wisconsin Press, 1953). While treading far too lightly, Cole does not dispute the antisemitism of some antimilitarists, even arguing that antisemitism "was in tune with" rural culture (Cole, *Senator Gerald P. Nye and American Foreign Relations*, 192).

83. David Horowitz, *Beyond Left and Right: Insurgency and the Establishment* (Urbana: University of Illinois Press, 1996), 180; Sylvie Murray and Robert D. Johnston, *Writing World War II: A Student's Guide* (New York: Hill and Wang, 2011), part 1.

84. Kazin, *War Against War*, 281.

85. Quoted in Michael S. Sherry, *In the Shadow of War: The United States Since the 1930s* (New Haven, CT: Yale University Press, 1995), 26.

86. Quoted in Larry Woiwode, *The Aristocrat of the West: The Story of Harold Schafer* (Fargo, ND: Institute for Regional Studies, 2001), 67.

87. Resolution of the South Dakota American Legion, April 16, 1939, http://plains humanities.unl.edu/homefront/homefront.rec.0011; Extension of Remarks of Hon. Chan Gurney, Friday, January 10, 1941, http://plainshumanities.unl.edu/homefront/home front.rec.0005.

88. http://plainshumanities.unl.edu/homefront/homefront.rec.0014.

89. Extension of Remarks of Hon. Chan Gurney.

90. On August 1, 1940, Nye and Senator Bennett Clark (D-MO) advanced Senate Resolution 152 which set up a congressional committee to investigate "war propaganda" coming out of Hollywood. Olson, *Those Angry Days*, 359–74.

91. Lindbergh's father, a Minnesota politician, opposed entry into World War I. Charles Lindbergh likewise was committed to maintaining American neutrality, even after the invasion of Poland and the bombing of Britain. Having left the US after his son's kidnapping in 1935, Lindbergh put his commitment to neutrality into action by advising Hitler's Luftwaffe and gladly accepting a medal from Hermann Göring just weeks before Kristallnacht. His refusal to return the medal began a series of accusations of disloyalty that ended with him giving up his position in the US Air Force. After the war, he returned to the military and flew bombers in the Pacific theater. See Susan Dunn, "The Debate Behind U.S. Intervention in World War II," *Atlantic*, July 8, 2013, https://www.theatlantic.com/national/archive/2013/07/the-debate-behind-US-intervention-in-world-war-ii/277572/. On Lindbergh's racism and interest in eugenics, see Olson, *Those Angry Days*, 72–75, 459–60.

92. Quoted in Hart, *Hitler's American Friends*, 181.

93. Ibid., 180.

94. Ibid., 182. See also Cole, *Senator Gerald P. Nye and American Foreign Relations*, 188–90.

95. Sherry, *In the Shadow of War*, 29.

96. Ibid., 21.

97. Schaffer, *America in the Great War*, 214–16; Sherry, *In the Shadow of War*, 21–29; James T. Sparrow, *Warfare State: World War II Americans and the Age of Big Government* (New York: Oxford University Press, 2011), 19–47.

98. Alden Whitman, "Burton K. Wheeler, Isolationist Senator, Dead at 92," *New York Times*, January 8, 1975, https://www.nytimes.com/1975/01/08/archives/burton-k-wheeler-iso lationist-senator-dead-at-92.html.

99. Ronald Rodosh, "Lindy the Peacenik," http://www.nytimes.com/books/98/09/27/spe cials/lindbergh-battle.html.

100. Quoted in Elwyn P. Robinson, *History of North Dakota* (Lincoln: University of Nebraska Press, 1966), 423–24.

101. Robert P. Wilkins, "The Non-Ethnic Roots of North Dakota Isolationism," *Nebraska History* 44 (September 1963): 221.

102. Kazin, *War Against War*, 287.

103. Blower, "From Isolationism to Neutrality," 352.

Chapter 3

1. David S. Mills, *Cold War in a Cold Land: Fighting Communism on the Northern Plains* (Norman: University of Oklahoma Press, 2015), 93, 97. See also David S. Mills, "Politics, Piety, and Patriotism: Early Cold War Politics in South Dakota," in Jon K. Lauck, John E. Miller, and Donald C. Simmons Jr., eds., *The Plains Political Tradition: Essays on South Dakota Political Culture*, vol. 2 (Pierre: South Dakota Historical Society Press, 2014), 126–50.

2. Mills, *Cold War in a Cold Land*, 100.

3. Quoted in Mills, *Cold War in a Cold Land*, 35.

4. Senator Francis Case, for example, worried that a bill promoting universal military training would "commit the country to a permanent form of military direction—if not domination." Quoted in Richard R. Chenoweth, "Francis Case: A Political Biography," *South Dakota Historical Collections* 39 (1978): 362.

5. As a single example of this ongoing revisionism, in 2011 the *Bismarck Tribune* described the Farmers Alliance as a group that "sought to unite farmers in an effort to establish a free market." Curt Eriksmoen, "Populist Fought for Initiative, Referendum," *Bismarck Tribune*, December 25, 2011, http://bismarcktribune.com/news/columnists/curt-eriksmoen/ populist-fought-for-initiative-referendum/article_52b08f14–2da8–11e1-a39b-001871 e3ce6c.html.

6. Mary Dudziak, *Wartime: An Idea, Its History, Its Consequences* (New York: Oxford University Press, 2012), 6.

7. Mills, *Cold War in a Cold Land*, 10.

8. Ibid. See also Richard R. Chenoweth, "Francis Case: A Political Biography" (PhD diss., University of Nebraska, Lincoln, 1977), 73–89.

9. Mills, *Cold War in a Cold Land*, 12.

10. Walter Lippmann, "America's Greatest Mistake," *Life*, July 21, 1941, 74.

11. *Fargo Forum*, May 14, 1950.

12. Brooke L. Blower, "From Isolationism to Neutrality: A New Framework for Understanding American Political Culture, 1919–1941," *Diplomatic History* 38, no. 2 (2014): 347. Blower also suggests that Cold Warriors could use the isolationist movement to explain that the US was but a "reluctant" empire, thus in a sense having it both ways (347).

13. Another complicating factor was that a staunchly anti-Nye candidate, Lynn Stambaugh, national president of the American Legion, ran as an independent. Curt Eriksmoen, "North Dakotan Was on Hitler's Enemies List," *Bismarck Tribune*, May 16, 2010.

14. Elwyn B. Robinson, *The History of North Dakota* (Lincoln: University of Nebraska Press, 1966), 437–39. See also Dan Rylance, "Fred G. Aandahl and the ROC Movement," in

Thomas W. Howard, ed., *The North Dakota Political Tradition* (Ames: Iowa State University Press, 1981), 151–82.

15. David Danbom, "A Part of the Nation and Apart from the Nation: North Dakota Politics Since 1945," in Richard Lowitt, ed., *Politics in the Postwar American West* (Norman: University of Oklahoma Press, 1995), 178.

16. Quoted in Richard R. Chenoweth, "Francis Case: A Political Biography" (PhD diss., University of Nebraska, Lincoln, 1977), 61. See also Richard R. Chenoweth, "The Black Hills—United Nations Capital," *South Dakota History* 5, no. 2 (1975): 150–64. Charlene Mires, *Capital of the World: The Race to Host the United Nations* (New York: New York University Press, 2013), 9–12.

17. Quoted in "In the US Tradition," *Time Magazine*, December 10, 1945, 30.

18. Ibid.

19. Quoted in Mills, *Cold War in a Cold Land*, 3.

20. Robert P. Wilkins, "The Nonpartisan League and Upper Midwest Isolationism," *Agricultural History* 39 (April 1965): 106. Many fewer South Dakotans supported the plan, reflecting perhaps the large numbers of Germans and German Russians in North Dakota. Sioux Falls *Argus Leader*, January 10, 1951.

21. *Bismarck Tribune*, January 15, 1951, 4.

22. *Bismarck Tribune*, February 1, 1951, 4. See also *Fargo Forum*, August 30, 1950.

23. *Grand Forks Herald*, March 9, 1951, 9.

24. *Dakota Farmer*, July 16, 1938, 293.

25. Ibid., May 7, 1938, 205.

26. Ibid.

27. *Bismarck Tribune*, February 21, 1951, 4.

28. Charles Barber, "Against the Grain: William Langer, the NPL, and the Left Wing Anti-Communist Tradition in North Dakota, 1918–1959" (paper presented at the Annual Meeting of the Northern Great Plains History Association, Grand Forks, ND, October 4–7, 2017).

29. Ibid., 2. Langer had broken with the NPL in 1919 over A. C. Townley's socialism.

30. *Fargo Forum*, May 21, 1950, 4.

31. *Bismarck Tribune*, March 29, 1951, 4.

32. *Fargo Forum*, August 20, 1950, 9; *Bismarck Tribune*, March 13, 1951, 4.

33. *Bismarck Tribune*, January 30, 1951, 1.

34. John E. Miller, "McCarthyism Before McCarthy: The Election of 1938 in South Dakota," *Heritage of the Great Plains* 15 (Summer 1982): 1–21.

35. Communist organizations were concentrated in subregions of the plains, including Brown and Roberts Counties in South Dakota and the southwestern sections of North Dakota, with activity peaking in the 1930s and early 1940s. William C. Pratt, "Farmers, Communists, and the FBI in the Upper Midwest," *Agricultural History* 63 (Summer 1989): 61–80.

36. William C. Pratt, "Rural Radicalism on the Northern Plains, 1912–1950," *Montana: The Magazine of Western History* 42 (Winter 1992): 51.

37. Quoted in Miller, "McCarthyism Before McCarthy," 7.

38. Quoted in ibid., 9. See also, "The Farmer Is the Man," in Studs Terkel, *Hard Times: An Oral History of the Great Depression* (New York: Avon Books, 1971), 261–66.

39. John E. Miller, "Historical Musings: Defining Moments in Twentieth-Century South Dakota Political History," *South Dakota History* 42, no. 2 (2012): 183.

40. Matthew Pehl, "The Frustrations of Organized Labor in South Dakota and the Making of a Conservative Coalition in the Midcentury United States," in Lauck, Miller, and Simmons Jr., *The Plains Political Tradition*, 2:103. Pehl argues that the 1940s were "key to the revivification of American conservatives and no issue proved more unifying for conservatives of many stripes than a rollback of organized labor's newly achieved rights" (104).

41. Quoted in Pehl, "Frustrations of Organized Labor in South Dakota," 115–16.

42. Ibid., 111.

43. See Jonathan F. Wagner, " 'The Greatest Thing I Ever Did Was Join a Union': A History of the Dakota Teamsters in the Great Depression," *Great Plains Quarterly* 8 (Winter 1988): 16–28.

44. Quoted in Pehl, "Frustrations of Organized Labor in South Dakota," 113.

45. Quoted in Chenoweth, "Francis Case," *South Dakota History*, 366.

46. Danbom, "A Part of the Nation and Apart from the Nation," 179.

47. Mark R. Wilson points out that creating the postwar consensus around the importance of free markets and private enterprise was a particularly difficult task given the public-private partnership that had made possible the production of enough war material to win World War II. *Destructive Creation: American Business and the Winning of World War II* (Philadelphia: University of Pennsylvania Press, 2016).

48. Rylance, "Fred G. Aandahl and the ROC Movement," 172.

49. Quoted in ibid., 182.

50. R. Alton Lee, " 'New Dealers, Fair Dealers, Misdealers, and Hiss Dealers': Karl Mundt and the Internal Security Act of 1950," *South Dakota History* 10 (Fall 1980): 277–90.

51. Ibid., 289.

52. Quoted in Michael S. Sherry, *In the Shadow of War: The United States Since the 1930s* (New Haven, CT: Yale University Press, 1995), 175.

53. Richard Halworth Rovere, *Senator Joe McCarthy* (Berkeley: University of California Press, 1995), 208.

54. Quoted in Mills, *Cold War in a Cold Land*, 35.

55. Robert Griffin, "Old Progressives and the Cold War," *Journal of American History* 66 (September 1979): 334–47.

56. Quoted in Mills, *Cold War in a Cold Land*, 49. See also Scott N. Heidepriem, *A Fair Chance for a Free People: A Biography of Karl E. Mundt, United States Senator* (Madison, SD: Leader, 1988), 180–82.

57. "The Congress: The Censure of Joe McCarthy," *Time*, October 4, 1954; "The Congress: Elbow Grease," *Time*, November 29, 1954.

58. Many pro-McCarthy letters also came in to the region's other political leaders, including some from members of the John Birch society. Mills, *Cold War in a Cold Land*, 53–55.

59. Quoted in Jon K. Lauck, "George S. McGovern and the Farmer: South Dakota Politics, 1953–1962," *South Dakota History* 32 (Winter 2002): 339.

60. Ibid., 341.

61. Ibid., 339–49.

62. R. Alton Lee, "McCarthyism at the University of South Dakota," *South Dakota History* 19 (Spring 1989): 434–35.

63. Ibid., 436.

64. Ibid., 438.

65. Quoted in ibid., 430.

66. Ibid., 431–32.

67. Quoted in ibid., 433–34.

68. William C. Pratt, "Another South Dakota; or, The Road Not Taken: The Left and the Shaping of South Dakota Political Culture," in Jon K. Lauck, John E. Miller, and Donald C. Simmons Jr., eds., *The Plains Political Tradition: Essays in South Dakota Political Culture*, vol. 1 (Pierre: South Dakota State Historical Society Press, 2011), 105–32.

69. Elizabeth Evenson Williams, *Emil Loriks: Builder of a New Economic Order* (Sioux Falls, SD: Center for Western Studies, 1987).

70. Ibid., 146–47.

71. William C. Pratt, "The Farmers Union, McCarthyism, and the Demise of the Agrarian Left," *The Historian* 58 (Winter 1996): n.p.

72. Quoted in Mills, *Cold War in a Cold Land*, 41–42.

73. Pratt, "The Farmers Union, McCarthyism, and the Demise of the Agrarian Left," n.p.

74. William C. Pratt, "Glenn Talbott, the Farmers Union, and American Liberalism After World War II," *North Dakota History* 55, no.1 (1988): 3.

75. Ibid.

76. Quoted in Pratt, "Glenn Talbott," 6.

77. Quoted in ibid., 13.

78. Pratt, "Another South Dakota; or, The Road Not Taken," 123.

79. Pratt, "Glenn Talbott," 13. See also Bruce E. Field, *Harvest of Dissent: The National Farmers Union and the Early Cold War* (Lawrence: University Press of Kansas, 1998).

80. Alec Campbell, "The Sociopolitical Origins of the American Legion," *Theory and Society* 39 (January 2010): 1–24.

81. Tom Brokaw, *A Long Way from Home: Growing Up in the Heartland in the Forties and Fifties* (New York: Random House, 2003), 131.

82. Jim Fuglie, "Remembering a Great Man," June 16, 2019, https://theprairieblog.com/2019/06/16/remembering-a-great-man-on-fathers-day/.

83. Matthew Farish, "The Ordinary Cold War: The Ground Observer Corps and Midcentury Militarization in the United States," *Journal of American History* 103 (December 2016): 629–55.

84. Mills, *Cold War in a Cold Land*, 143.

85. Ibid., 139.

86. Mark A. Lempke, "Senator George McGovern and the Role of Religion in South Dakota Political Culture," in Lauck, Miller, and Simmons Jr., *The Plains Political Tradition*, 2:153.

87. Stephen J. Whitfield, *The Culture of the Cold War* (Baltimore: Johns Hopkins University Press, 1991).

88. Ibid., 86–87. See also Jonathan P. Herzog, *The Spiritual Industrial Complex: America's Religious Battle Against Communism in the Early Cold War* (New York: Oxford University Press, 2011). Some officials in the federal government believed that part of spreading the idea of America was, in the 1950s, spreading the idea of religious belief and practice. John Foster Dulles, for example, hoped Americans would "extend their conception of morality and spirituality to the rest of the world." Quoted in Sherry, *In the Shadow of War*, 159.

89. Darren Dochuk, "'They Locked God Outside the Iron Curtain': The Politics of Anticommunism and the Ascendancy of Plain-Folk Evangelicalism in the Postwar West," in Jeff Roche, ed., *The Political Culture of the New West* (Lawrence: University Press of Kansas, 2008), 97–134, esp. 102–5. Dochuk also points out that the "wildcat drillers" of the Southwest were evangelicals and, as such, fought against the representatives of corporate America and mainline Protestantism, like John D. Rockefeller, at the same time. Darren Dochuk, *Anointed with Oil: How Christianity and Crude Made Modern America* (New York: Basic Books, 2019).

90. Dochuk, "'They Locked God Outside the Iron Curtain.'" Some members of the 1960s counterculture also found their way to evangelism, though evidence of this trend on the Northern Plains is minimal. See Larry Eskridge, *God's Forever Family: The Jesus People Movement in America* (New York: Oxford University Press, 2018).

91. Mills, "Politics, Piety, and Patriotism," 138.

92. Quoted in ibid.

93. Ibid.

94. "Images of the Black Hills Passion Play," http://www.sdpb.org/blogs/images-of-the -past/the-black-hills-passion-play-1939–2008/.

95. Mills, *Cold War in a Cold Land*, 77.

96. Nicole Hemmer, *Messengers of the Right: Conservative Media and the Transformation of American Politics* (Philadelphia: University of Pennsylvania Press, 2016).

97. Kevin M. Kruse, "Billy Graham: 'America's Pastor'?," *Washington Post*, February 22, 2018.

98. Melani McAlister, "Billy Graham's Legacy," *Process: A Blog for American History*, March 21, 2018, https://www.processhistory.org/mcalister-billy-grahams-legacy/. McAlister asserts that, while Graham seemed open to issues around social justice, he was more interested in changing "hearts than laws."

99. Roxanne B. Salonen, "Faith Conversions: 30 Years After Billy Graham Visited Fargo, Crusade Attendees Share Memories," *Dickinson Press*, June 10, 2017, 1.

100. Kirk Johnson, "Mormons on a Mission," *New York Times*, August 22, 2010.

101. Ibid.

Chapter 4

1. Tom Brokaw, *A Long Way from Home: Growing Up in the American Heartland in the Forties and Fifties* (New York: Random House, 2003), 24.

2. Ibid., 147–51.

3. James T. Sparrow, *Warfare State: World War II Americans and the Age of Big Government* (New York: Oxford University Press, 2011), 7–13.

4. Brokaw, *Long Way from Home*, 225.

5. Ibid.

6. Ibid., 61, 22.

7. David Mills explains that "the war was an important turning point in the history of the West, marking a transition from resistance to opportunism." *Cold War in a Cold Land: Fighting Communism on the Northern Plains* (Norman: University of Oklahoma Press, 2012), 181. In this book I try to examine in more detail why this shift occurred and what its long-term political and cultural consequences were.

8. Brokaw, *Long Way from Home*, 75; see also David B. Danbom, "A Part of the Nation and Apart from the Nation: North Dakota Politics Since 1945," in Richard Lowitt, ed., *Politics in the Postwar American West* (Norman: University of Oklahoma Press, 1995), 178.

9. Brokaw, *Long Way from Home*, 65.

10. Ibid., 190.

11. Ibid., 78.

12. Ibid., 75. Southern workers were recruited for many large federal construction projects in the West during and after the war. See Kate Brown, *Plutopia: Nuclear Families, Atomic Cities, and the Great Soviet and American Plutonium Disasters* (New York: Oxford University Press, 2013), 20.

13. Brokaw, *Long Way from Home*, 152.

14. I borrow the word ordinary from Matthew Farish, "The Ordinary Cold War: The Ground Observer Corps and Midcentury Militarization in the United States, "*Journal of American History* 103 (December 2016): 629–55.

15. https://www.usgovernmentspending.com/defense_spending. See also Michael S. Sherry, *In the Shadow of War: The United States Since the 1930s* (New York: Oxford University Press, 1995), 5–6.

16. Charles H. Anderson and Walter Isard, "The Geography of Arms Manufacture," in David Pepper and Alan Jenkins, eds., *The Geography of Peace and War* (New York: Basil Blackwell, 1985), 90; Catherine Lutz, "Making War at Home in the United States: Militarization and the Current Crisis," *American Anthropologist* 104 (September 2002): 726–35.

17. Lutz, "Making War at Home in the United States," 730.

18. The people of the Northern Plains are hardly alone in their practice of deriding the federal government while also benefiting from its financial support. Princeton sociologist Robert Wuthnow describes similar attitudes in the rural Midwestern community where he grew up. *Remaking the Heartland: Middle America Since the 1950s* (Princeton, NJ: Princeton University Press, 2011), 259.

19. Even "Wild Bill" Langer, who maintained many Populist anti-militarist views, saw the upside of making "lemonade from lemons." He worked to get an ammunition plant built near the Turtle Lake reservation to provide employment for Native people. Charlie Barber, email message to author, September 24, 2018.

20. Sparrow, *Warfare State*, 6.

21. Jeffrey Engel and Catherine Carte Engel, "Introduction: On Writing the Local Within Diplomatic History," in Jeffrey Engel, ed., *The Local Consequences of the Global Cold War* (Washington, DC: Woodrow Wilson Center Press, 2007), 3.

22. Ibid., 21.

23. Lutz, "Making War at Home in the United States," 372.

24. Maria Höhn and Seungsook Moon, eds., *Over There: Living with the U.S. Military Empire from World War Two to the Present* (Durham, NC: Duke University Press, 2010), 6–7.

25. Valerie Kuletz, *The Tainted Desert: Environmental and Social Destruction in the American West* (New York: Routledge, 1998), 38; Gerald B. Nash, "The West and the Military-Industrial Complex," *Montana: The Magazine of Western History* 40 (Winter 1990): 72.

26. Gerald B. Nash, *The Federal Landscape: An Economic History of the Twentieth-Century West* (Tucson: University of Arizona Press, 1991), 96, 98–99.

27. Ibid., 95. See also Roger Bolton, *Defense Purchases and Regional Growth* (Washington, DC: Brookings Institution, 1966).

28. Ann Markusen, Peter Hall, Scott Campbell, and Sabina Deitrick, *The Rise of the Gunbelt: The Military Remapping of Industrial America* (New York: Oxford University Press, 1991).

29. In 1997, after Senator Kent Conrad procured a large new defense contract, Ian Swanson of the *Grand Forks Herald* explained: "Keeping the Air Force base open in Grand Forks and Minot . . . is an issue all of North Dakota's politicians will back. It's a pork issue, too, but unlike the trade issues it isn't pork at the expense of a greater good (non-proliferations issues aside)." "Conrad Comes Home After $794 Million Pork Delivery," *Grand Forks Herald*, November 25, 1997.

30. Mills, *Cold War in a Cold Land*, 182.

31. The story of the coming of the base to Minot is relatively short, if also a bit confounding: the town of less than 20,000 had never asked to have the base located solely in its community. Instead leaders had proposed a joint "Bismarck-Minot" region. So, while the residents in Minot were rather surprised when their town was chosen, they too looked forward to its many economic benefits. Its population increased by over 50 percent, growing to 33,000 in 1957. Samuel H. Day, ed., *Nuclear Heartland: A Guide to the 1,000 Missile Silos of the United States* (Madison, WI: Progressive Foundation, 1988), 17. See also Richard J. Nolan, "The Air Force Comes to North Dakota: A Study in the Site Selection of Grand Forks and Minot Air Force Bases" (master's thesis, University of North Dakota, 1990).

32. Redford H. Dibble, "Location of Base Result of Hard Work by Many Persons," *Rapid City Daily Journal*, October 10, 1942. See also Mills, *Cold War in a Cold Land*, 264n19.

33. Mills, *Cold War in a Cold Land*, 179.

34. A pilot stationed at the Grand Forks AFB reflected later on the dangers of living near a practice range. "I don't know if I would like to live near there! But they haven't killed anyone yet." Dennis Almer, interview, State Historical Society of North Dakota (SHSND), Missile Site Oral Histories (MSOH), 32314–00001. While no ICBMs were placed on Native land, part of the gunnery range used during World War II was on the Pine Ridge reservation. That land has never been fully cleaned up or returned to tribal control. Seth Tupper, "Area of Former Badlands Bombing Range Could Remain Off-Limits," *Rapid City Journal*, February 10, 2019, https://rapidcityjournal.com/news/local/area-of-former-badlands-bombing-range -could-remain-off-limits/article_71ebe406–508a-52c3–8fc4-b6f836379630.html.

35. Interview with Gretchen Heefner quoted in Heefner and Catherine McNicol Stock, "Missiles and Militarization: How the Cold War Shaped South Dakota Political Culture," in Jon K. Lauck, John E. Miller, and Donald C. Simmons Jr., eds., *The Plains Political Tradition: Essays on South Dakota Political History*, vol. 1 (Pierre: South Dakota State Historical Society Press, 2011), 226.

36. Gretchen Heefner, *The Missile Next Door: The Minuteman in the American Heartland* (Cambridge, MA: Harvard University Press, 2012), 115–16. Columnist Paul Harvey wrote, "You and I sowed a hundred million dollars on the prairies of Montana. Now, before the crop has matured, Uncle Sam wants to plow it under." Quoted in Mills, *Cold War in a Cold Land*, 196. On the base closing in Glasgow, see ibid., 197–98.

37. Quoted in Richard J. Nolan, "Grand Forks Air Force Base: The Beginning," unpublished manuscript in author's possession, 1988, 8. Much of this material also appears in Nolan, "The Air Force Comes to North Dakota," but sometimes in slightly altered form. For clarity, I provide cites to both sources.

38. Richard Nolan, "Grand Forks Air Force Base," 8; Nolan, "The Air Force Comes to North Dakota," 48.

39. Nolan, "Grand Forks Air Force Base" 8; Nolan, "The Air Force Comes to North Dakota," 40.

40. Quoted in Nolan, "Grand Forks Air Force Base," 11; Nolan, "The Air Force Comes to North Dakota," 49.

41. Nolan, "Grand Forks Air Force Base," 8; Nolan, "The Air Force Comes to North Dakota," 46–47.

42. Quoted in James McKenzie, *Nuclear Weapons of Grand Forks: An Interpretive Catalog, Peace Issues* (Grand Forks: University of North Dakota Center for Peace Studies, 1986), 2.

43. Quoted in Day, *Nuclear Heartland,* 16.

44. Nolan, "Grand Forks Air Force Base," 11; Nolan, "The Air Force Comes to North Dakota," 47.

45. Quoted in Nolan, "Grand Forks Air Force Base," 12; Nolan, "The Air Force Comes to North Dakota," 49.

46. Nolan, "Grand Forks Air Force Base," 12–13; Nolan, "The Air Force Comes to North Dakota," 53.

47. City leaders from Newington, New Hampshire, and Plattsburgh, New York, asked the military to reconsider its decision to build bases in their communities. They worried that a Soviet attack meant "bringing death and destruction to a heavily populated area." The Plattsburgh site also required the acquisition and demolition of Champlain College, which in 1953 held its last graduation ceremony before moving to a new location in Vermont. Quoted in Mills, *Cold War in a Cold Land,* 187–89.

48. Nolan, "Grand Forks Air Force Base," 20; Nolan, "The Air Force Comes to North Dakota," 84.

49. Nolan, "The Air Force Comes to North Dakota," 87, 94–99.

50. Tom Brusegaard, conversation with the author, October 5, 2017, Grand Forks, North Dakota.

51. For the methodology used to estimate this figure, see Appendix.

52. The Northern Plains were not the only place where the ratio of military to civilian population swelled in 1940s and 1950s. In Arizona, the 144,000 military people stationed there in 1940, "equaled the entire workforce in the state." Nash, "The West and the Military-Industrial Complex," 73. Nash writes further that the political alliances that developed to keep federal funds flowing influenced politics throughout the region (73).

53. Wade Bertrand, interview, State Historical Society of North Dakota (SHSND), Missile Site Oral Histories (MSOH), 32314–00004.

54. https://www.census.gov/population/www/cen2000/censusatlas/pdf/12_Military -Service.pdf. See p. 201.

55. https://dakotafreepress.com/2017/09/10/population-notes-veterans-8–32-of-sd -population-higher-proportion-in-black-hills/.

56. https://www.census.gov/population/www/cen2000/censusatlas/pdf/12_Military -Service.pdf. See pp. 200, 204. See also "Economic Impact Study: Grand Forks Air Force Base Realignment," (for presentation by the Grand Forks Region Base Realignment Impact Committee [BRIC], November 17, 2006), 7, http://gfcounty.nd.gov/sites/default/files/pdf/ Economic%20Impact%20Study%20-%20Final%20November%202006.pdf.

57. Nash, "The West and the Military-Industrial Complex," 74.

58. Ahrar Ahmad, "War and Peace in South Dakota," in Lauck, Miller, and Simmons Jr., *The Plains Political Tradition,* 1:203–4. Ahmad also details the total federal expenditures in the state, mostly from military spending and agricultural programs: 1.9 billion in 2011 (210n52).

59. Michael Brown, interview, State Historical Society of North Dakota (SHSND), Missile Site Oral Histories (MSOH), 32314–00006. Brown comments on how many military people he knew who "stayed or came back" to Grand Forks and are active in the community, one as a city commissioner, another as the president of the local rod-and-gun club.

60. Mike Brule, "BRAC Closing Would Be 'Man Made' Disaster After '97 Grand Forks Flood," *Grand Forks Herald*, April 30, 2005. See also Kimberly Porter, "1997 Grand Forks Flood: When History Became Personal," *North Dakota History* 82 (Summer 2017): 18–34.

61. Porter, "1997 Grand Forks Flood"; "Remembering the Flood of 1997," *Grand Forks Herald*, April 22, 2012, https://www.grandforksherald.com/news/2174209-rememberingflood-97-red-river-crests-15-years-ago-today. Air force personnel helped residents of Rapid City in 1972 when their community also suffered a devastating flood. Accommodations for housing victims of the flood were segregated by race. See Nick Estes, *Our History Is the Future: Standing Rock Versus the Dakota Access Pipeline, and the Long Tradition of Indigenous Resistance* (London: Verso, 2019), 186–88.

62. Michael S. Sherry, *The Rise of American Air Power: The Creation of Armageddon* (New Haven, CT: Yale University Press, 1987), 216.

63. African Americans joined the air force gradually during the 1950s and 1960s. By the late twentieth century all branches of the military had high populations of people of color. By 2000, there were four thousand African Americans in North Dakota; 58 percent of them lived in either Grand Forks or Ward counties, the two counties with bases. The base populations themselves that year were around 10 percent black. http://factfinder.census.gov/servlet/Basic FactsTable/Dec_2000PL-U_GCTPL_ST7&_geo_id=04000U538. Accessed January 16, 2018. This version of Fact Finder is no longer available. Its data is currently compiled at https://factfinder.census.gov/faces/tableservices/jsf/pages/productview.xhtml?src=bkmk and https://www2.census.gov/census_2000/datasets/demographic_profile/North_Dakota/2kh38.pdf.

64. Quoted in David Vine, *Base Nation: How U.S. Military Bases Abroad Harm America and the World* (New York: Henry Holt, 2017), 182.

65. For a complete demographic breakdown of military service after 9/11, see Tim Kane, "Who Bears the Burden? Demographic Characteristics of the U.S. Military Recruits Before and After 9/11," November 7, 2005, Washington, D.C.: Heritage Foundation, https://www.heritage.org/defense/report/who-bears-the-burden-demographic-characteristics-us-military-recruits-and-after-911.

66. Jeanette Keith, *Rich Man's War, Poor Man's Fight: Race, Class, and Power in the Rural South During the First World War* (Chapel Hill: University of North Carolina Press, 2004), 6. Keith also reminds the reader of the South's history of Populist antimilitarism in World War One.

67. Thomas Borstelmann, "The Cold War and the American South," in Engel, *Local Consequences of the Cold War*, 82–83. See also Kari Frederickson, *Cold War Dixie: Militarization and Modernization in the American South* (Athens: University of Georgia Press, 2013).

68. James N. Gregory, *The Southern Diaspora: How the Great Migrations of Black and White Southerners Transformed America* (Chapel Hill: University of North Carolina Press, 2005). Gregory writes that southerners who left their region "changed America" (xii). This migration involved the movement of both whites and African Americans, though they often moved to different locations. The military eventually provided "one clear pathway" out of the region for both groups. By 1970, 41 percent of black and 20 percent of white veterans who had been born in the South lived outside their region (37).

69. Sean Braswell, "Why the U.S. Military Is So Southern," http://www.ozy.com/acumen/why-the-us-military-is-so-southern/72100. For the broader transformation of the Armed Forces and the mass marketing of military service, see Beth Bailey, *America's Army: Making the All-Volunteer Force* (Cambridge, MA: Harvard University Press, 2009).

70. Braswell, "Why the U.S. Military Is So Southern."

71. James N. Gregory, *American Exodus: The Dust Bowl Migration and Okie Culture in California* (New York: Oxford University Press, 1989); Annual state-by-state military population breakdowns can be found in Department of Defense, *Population Representation in the Military Services*, https://www.cna.org/research/pop-rep.

72. Gregory encourages his readers to think of the southern migration as both "a circulation" and as "fluid," with families outside the region maintaining their regional ties and cultural practices. *Southern Diaspora*, xii, 7–8. Former secretary of the navy, Jim Webb, explains that in the South "military virtues have been passed down at the dinner table." Quoted in Braswell, "Why the U.S. Military Is So Southern." Statistics also show that 80 percent of volunteers have a parent or sibling who served.

73. In 2000, approximately 17,500 people born in the South were living permanently in North Dakota. This number increased with the recent migration of energy workers from Texas and other states with oil and gas production. For graphs of where Southerners have migrated, see "Mapping the Southern Diaspora," http://depts.washington.edu/moving1/map_diaspora.shtml. In the air force even those who were not born in the South did live there for a time, as one of the only training facilities for new recruits was at Lackland Air Force Base in San Antonio, Texas.

74. www.churchofchrist-sd.com/histphoto.html. The Destiny Foursquare Church near Ellsworth began in much the same way, in the basement of a home and with largely military membership. According to a representative of the church, many of these military personnel "have been involved 110% and have become trusted leaders who rotate out but stay in touch with the congregation." Weston Stephens, telephone conversation with Foursquare Church administrator as relayed to the author, July 2018.

75. Steve Lee "New Churches Spring Up," *Grand Forks Herald*, April 17, 2009, https://www.grandforksherald.com/news/2096614-new-churches-spring. The numbers of new evangelical churches can be hard to measure with precision as they do not necessarily belong to a denominational organization but can pop up as unaffiliated congregations. See http://www.usreligioncensus.org/maps2000.php. The religious census of the US began including "independent" churches as a category in 2010.

76. Quoted in Day, *Nuclear Heartland*, 17.

77. Frances Fitzgerald, *The Evangelicals: The Struggle to Shape America* (New York: Simon and Shuster, 2017). See also Gregory, *Southern Diaspora*, 222–35.

78. Army Wife 101, "How Many Wal-Marts Are Near Your Military Base?," http://armywife101.com/2012/07/how-many-walmarts-are-near-your-military-base-walmart-petition-for-military-discount.html.

79. Sam Walton, *Made in America: My Story* (New York: Doubleday, 1992), 139–60.

80. Army Wife 101, "How Many Wal-Marts?"

81. Anna Jauhola, "During 80s, Downtown Transitioned," *Mitchell Daily Republic*, March 21, 2014, https://www.mitchellrepublic.com/news/2473044-during-80s-downtown-transitioned-cafes-retailers-niche-stores-coffee-shops.

82. Bethany Moreton, "It Came from Bentonville: The Agrarian Roots of Wal-mart," in Nelson Lichtenstein, ed., *Wal-mart: The Face of Twenty-First Century Capitalism* (New York: New Press, 2006), 61.

83. Bethany Moreton, *To Serve God and Wal-Mart: The Making of Christian Free Enterprise* (Cambridge, MA: Harvard University Press, 2010). Kevin M. Kruse makes much the same argument, albeit more broadly, in *One Nation Under God: How Corporate America Invented Christian America* (New York: Basic Books, 2015).

84. Moreton also points out that Walton overcame Populist resistance to chain stores and monopolies by portraying himself as no "foreigner" but a "small town boy made good." "It Came from Bentonville," 70, 74.

85. David L. Leal and Jeremy M. Teigen, "Recent Veterans Are More Republican Than Older Ones," *Washington Post*, November 11, 2015, https://www.washingtonpost.com/news/monkey-cage/wp/2015/11/11/recent-veterans-are-more-republican-than-older-ones-why/?noredirect=on&utm_term=.5419b6e927c1.

86. Adam Clymer, "Sharp Divergence Found in Views of Military and Civilians," *New York Times*, September 9, 1999, http://www.nytimes.com/1999/09/09/us/sharp-divergence-found-in-views-of-military-and-civilians.html. See also a Gallup poll that demonstrates the more conservative views among veterans: http://news.gallup.com/poll/118684/military-veterans-ages-tend-republican.aspx. This trend began after the Vietnam War and accelerated after 9/11. Until 2016, the connection between military service and conservatism extended to Congress. See Tim Hsia, "The Role of the Military and Veterans in Politics," *New York Times*, February 1, 2013, https://atwar.blogs.nytimes.com/2013/02/01/the-role-of-the-military-and-veterans-in-politics/.

87. Thomas E. Ricks, "The Widening Gap Between Military and Society," *The Atlantic*, July 1997, https://www.theatlantic.com/magazine/archive/1997/07/the-widening-gap-between-military-and-society/306158/.

88. Steve Kornacki, *The Red and the Blue: The 1990s and the Birth of American Tribalism* (New York: Harper Collins, 2018).

89. Clymer, "Sharp Divergence."

90. Ricks, "Widening Gap Between Military and Society."

91. Soybeans are a hardier and more drought-resistant crop, writes Mike Jacobs, giving farmers more economic security. "Subtle Soybean Becomes Conspicuous," *Grand Forks Herald*, August 28, 2018, https://www.grandforksherald.com/opinion/columns/4490941-mike-jacobs-subtle-soybean-becomes-conspicuous.

92. Ahmad, "War and Peace," 204.

93. J. D. Vance, "How Trump Won the Troops," *New York Times*, November 25, 2016, https://www.nytimes.com/2016/11/25/opinion/how-trump-won-the-troo ps.html?_r=0. See also Clymer, "Sharp Divergence."

94. For two examples, see Jack Dalrymple's attacks on Kent Conrad in the 1992 Senate special election and Conrad's increasingly defensive responses. *Bismarck Tribune*, November 18, 1992. Four years later Kevin Cramer would take a similar approach in his contest against Earl Pomeroy. *Bismarck Tribune*, August 23, 1996.

95. See the public Instagram account for Senator Heidi Heitkamp, October 30, 2018, for three images of the senator meeting with military members and visiting the Minot AFB; see also James Arkin, "How to Win in North Dakota," *Politico*, November 1, 2018, https://

www.politico.com/magazine/story/2018/11/01/north-dakota-2018-senate-election-heitkamp
-cramer-222094.

96. So many communities tried to enforce segregationist policies on service personnel assigned to nearby bases that the Kennedy administration asked a panel to investigate. In communities at home, as in the rear areas of combat, African American air force members were far more likely to face racial discrimination than they did in combat itself. See Jeremy Maxwell, *Brotherhood in Combat: How African Americans Found Equality in Korea and Vietnam* (Norman: University of Oklahoma Press, 2018), 15, 17, 138.

97. Some Dakotans consider Rapid City to be an outlier in terms of race relations. But several legal cases and regional commissions found widespread discrimination against Natives in communities across the Northern Plains in the 1970s and 1980s. See Susan Peterson, "Discrimination and Jurisdiction: Seven Civil Rights Cases in South Dakota, 1976–1982," *Journal of the West* 25 (1986): 44–48; Montana-North Dakota-South Dakota Joint Advisory Committee to the United States Commission on Civil Rights, *Indian Civil Rights Issues in Montana, North Dakota, and South Dakota*, August, 1974; United States Commission on Civil Rights, *American Indian Issues in the State of South Dakota*, hearing held in Rapid City, SD, July 27–28, 1978.

98. South Dakota Advisory Committee to the United States Commission on Civil Rights, *Report on Rapid City*, March 1963, https://www2.law.umaryland.edu/marshall/usccr/documents/cr12r18.PDF, 20–37.

99. The Cold War military had long-standing practices of encouraging or at least tolerating de facto segregation in its base communities. Nightclubs on "Hooker Hill" in Itaewon, South Korea, were racially segregated. Maria Höhn and Seungsook Moon, eds., *Over There*, 16–19, 22. Residential neighborhoods in Hanford, Washington, where plutonium for atomic bombs was processed, were also segregated so that white workers, especially those from the South, would feel comfortable there. Kate Brown, *Plutopia: Nuclear Families, Atomic Cities, and the Great Soviet and American Plutonium Disasters* (repr., New York: Oxford University Press, 2014), 26–31.

100. South Dakota Advisory Committee to the United States Commission on Civil Rights, *Report on Rapid City*, 9, 38–39.

101. Brokaw, *Long Way from Home*, 188.

102. South Dakota Advisory Committee to the United States Commission on Civil Rights, *Report on Rapid City*, 32.

103. Since the early twentieth century Natives in Rapid City, as in other communities, had been relegated to a series of "Indian towns" which had been relocated repeatedly when city leaders discovered the sites had value for whites. See Paul Chaat Smith and Robert Allen Warrior, *Like a Hurricane: The Indian Movement from Alcatraz to Wounded Knee* (New York: New Press, 1996), 170. See also Estes, *Our History Is the Future*, 186–88.

104. Aaron Belkin, *Bring Me Men: Military Masculinity and the Benign Façade of American Empire, 1898–2001* (New York: Columbia University Press, 2012); Alan Berube, *Coming Out Under Fire: The History of Gay Men and Women in World War II* (Chapel Hill: University of North Carolina Press, 1990); Mary Louise Roberts, *What Soldiers Do: Sex and the American GI in World War II France* (Chicago: University of Chicago Press, 2013); Cynthia Enloe, *Maneuvers: The International Politics of Militarizing Women's Lives* (Berkeley: University of California Press, 2000); Margot Canaday, *The Straight State: Sexuality and Citizenship in Twentieth Century America* (Princeton, NJ: Princeton University Press, 2009).

105. Vine, *Base Nation*; Höhn and Moon, *Over There*.

106. Dennis Banks with Richard Erdoes, *Ojibwa Warrior: Dennis Banks and the Rise of the American Indian Movement* (Norman: University of Oklahoma Press, 2004), 44–45.

107. Vine, *Base Nation*, 182; quoted on 166.

108. Robert Draper, "The Military's Rough Justice on Sexual Assault," *New York Times*, November 26, 2014, https://www.nytimes.com/2014/11/30/magazine/the-militarys-rough -justice-on-sexual-assault.html.

109. Ibid.

110. Sara Egge, *Woman Suffrage and Citizenship in the Midwest, 1870–1920* (Iowa City: University of Iowa Press, 2018), 38–61.

111. Debra Marquart, *The Horizontal World: Growing Up in the Middle of Nowhere* (New York: Counterpoint, 2006), 97–99, 119.

112. Several historians have recently suggested that rural America offered more opportunities for gay men and women than "urban-centric" academics often imagine. While they lived without a vibrant community, queer men and women were often accepted by their communities as "eccentric." See Colin R. Johnson, *Just Queer Folks: Gender and Sexuality in Rural America* (Philadelphia: Temple University Press, 2013); Mary L. Gray and Brian J. Gilley, eds., *Queering the Countryside: New Frontier in Queer Studies* (New York: New York University Press, 2016). The dearth of queer scholarship on the Dakotas does not reflect a dearth of queer life. The Democratic mayor of Fargo in the 1980s, Jon Lingren, was publically supportive of gay rights, held the states' first gay pride parade in 1982, and was an advocate for the first gay bar in the state. Cory Haala, email to author, June 25, 2019.

113. Leon G. Lewis to Oscar Lunseth, 11/12/1959, Oscar Lunseth Papers (hereafter OL), Orin G. Libby Manuscript Collection 372, Elwyn B. Robinson Department of Special Collections, Chester Fritz Library, University of North Dakota, Box 7, File 1.

114. "Minutes of the Base-Community Council of the Grand Forks Air Force Base, March 24, 1960," OL Papers, Box 7, File 1, 1–2.

115. Like Minot, Rapid City had a long-established sex trade in the gambling towns of the Black Hills. In 1980 the base commander shut down a popular and well-known brothel in Deadwood, Pam's Purple Door, because he felt that too many airmen were making the thirty-minute drive. Thadd M. Turner, *Wild Bill Hickok and Deadwood City: End of the Trail* (Irvine, CA: Universal Publishing, 2001), 44. It may be that Deadwood's attractions were replicated closer to home, since Box Elder, South Dakota, has been called "a strip club with a large mobile home park." "Comment" from cuiser20, February 6, 2010, http://www.city-data .com/forum/rapid-city/837307-moving-ellsworth-afb-2-weeks-3.html.

116. Minot Junior Chamber of Commerce, *Why Minot?* (Minot, ND: R-L-M Printing, 1961), 19. See also coverage in the *Bismarck Tribune* in 1960 and 1961, including "Vogel Charges Minot Wide Open, Blames Apathy," *Bismarck Tribune*, December 14, 1960.

117. *Why Minot?*, 15–16.

118. *Why Minot?*, 31.

119. "Vogel Charges Minot Wide Open, Blames Apathy."

120. *Why Minot?*, 21–22.

121. https://law.justia.com/cases/north-dakota/supreme-court/1963/123-n-w-2d-1 10-2.html.

122. Brad Schlossman, "In Emerado, Contractors, Retirees Express Concern," *Grand Forks Herald*, May 13, 2005.

123. Niraj Chokshi, "What Each State's Veteran Population Looks Like in 10 Maps," *Washington Post*, November 11, 2014, https://www.washingtonpost.com/blogs/govbeat/wp/2014/11/11/what-each-states-veteran-population-looks-like-in-10-maps/?noredirect=on&utm_term=.c86f4dcbaa5c.

124. To combat suicide, see new programs in "resiliency" at the Minot base: http://www.minot.af.mil/Base-Units/Resiliency/.

125. https://www.census.gov/population/www/cen2000/censusatlas/pdf/12_Military-Service.pdf; Jennifer Mittelstadt, *The Rise of the Military Welfare State* (Cambridge, MA: Harvard University Press, 2015); Administrator of Head Start of Grand Forks, conversation with author, October 5, 2017.

126. Dan Lamothe, "Air Force Launches Investigation into Drug Use Among Troops Protecting Nuclear Weapons," *Washington Post*, March 18, 2016.

127. Diana Jean Schemo, "Rate of Rape at Academy Is Put at 12 Percent in Survey," *New York Times*, August 29, 2003, http://www.nytimes.com/2003/08/29/us/rate-of-rape-at-academy-is-put-at-12-in-survey.html. On a scandal involving a prominent female pilot stationed at Minot, see Marilyn Gardner, "Kelly Flinn's Tale: The Military Applies the Scarlet Letter," *Christian Science Monitor*, May 22, 1997, 13.

128. Karen Houppert, "Base Crimes: The Military Has a Domestic Violence Problem," *Mother Jones*, July 2005.

129. Lucinda Marshall, "Why Male Military Veterans Are Committing Sexual Assault at Alarming Rates," Alternet, May 25, 2007, https://www.alternet.org/2007/05/why_male_military_veterans_are_committing_sexual_assault_at_alarming_rates/. See also Daniel Engber, "Is There a Lot of Crime on Military Bases?," *Slate*, November 5, 2009, https://slate.com/news-and-politics/2009/11/are-shootings-at-military-bases-common-or-was-fort-hood-unusual.html.

130. Bill Donovan, "S.D. Case May Allow Claims Against U.S.," *Navajo Times*, May 7, 2009, http://www.navajotimes.com/news/2009/0409/050709court.php.

131. "Minot AFB More Than a Good Neighbor," *Minot Daily News*, February 8, 2018.

132. "2005 BRAC Regional Hearing," Rapid City, SD, Tuesday, June 21, 2005, transcript. This document and many others can be found at a website dedicated to the successful effort to save Ellsworth. See http://www.ellsworthauthority.org/2005-brac—the-battle-to-save-ellsworth-.html. In 2019 the air force announced an expansion of Ellsworth's responsibilities.

133. "2005 BRAC Regional Hearing, Rapid City, South Dakota," transcript, 11.

Chapter 5

1. Shirley Norgard, interview, State Historical Society of North Dakota (hereafter SHSND), Missile Site Oral Histories (hereafter MSOH), 32314–00020.These interviews are only available on videotape. When audio is unclear, author transcription may contain slight errors.

2. Ibid.

3. Ibid. Mrs. Norgard's interviewer, former missileer Mark Sundlov, attempts to explain midway through the interview why SAC personnel may not have made good neighbors. He says, of his time in Minot, "I couldn't even tell you if the sites had neighbors." Shirley thanks him for explaining and adds, "Other people felt like I did."

4. Catherine Lutz, "Making War at Home in the United States: Militarization and the Current Crisis," *American Anthropologist* 104 (September 2002): 726–35.

5. The term "national sacrifice zone" is found in Samuel H. Day Jr., ed., *Nuclear Heartland: A Guide to the 1,000 Missile Silos of the United States* (Madison, WI.: Progressive Foundation, 1988), 10.

6. "Command and Control: The Long-Hidden Story of the Day Our Luck Almost Ran Out," PBS, *American Experience*, transcript, 3, http://www.pbs.org/wgbh/americanexperience/films/command-and-control/.

7. North Dakota missileer Hans Heinrich remembered that the Titan was so slow they sometimes called it the "at last" missile. Hans Heinrich, interview, SHSND, MSOH, 32314–0009.

8. The SHSND created a four-part video about the development of the Minuteman missile. See "America's Ace in the Hole," http://history.nd.gov/historicsites/minutemanmissile/oscarzeroexhibits.html. For technical history, see John C. Lonnquest and David F. Winkler, *To Defend and Deter: The Legacy of the Cold War Missile Program* (Rock Island, IL: Defense Publishing Services, 1996). The Soviets were not as far ahead in missile technology in the 1950s as Americans thought, but they rapidly caught up in the 1960s and 1970s. See David W. Mills, *Cold War in a Cold Land: Fighting Communism on the Northern Plains* (Norman: University of Oklahoma Press, 2012), 200. John Lewis Gaddis suggests that nuclear weapons "exchanged destructiveness for duration" and thus kept the Cold War going longer than it otherwise would have. *We Now Know: Rethinking Cold War History* (New York: Oxford University Press, 1997), 240, 291–92.

9. Ian Frazier, *The Great Plains* (New York: Picador, 2001), 200.

10. Sharon Cohen, "In Farm Belt Silos U.S. Sowed Are Being Reaped," *Washington Post*, August 20, 2000, https://www.washingtonpost.com/archive/politics/2000/08/20/in-farm-belt-silos-us-sowed-are-being-reaped-missile-silos/1fd8d39f-2a87–4c4d-8d3e-e3f130451528/?utm_term = .a759bbad0e4e.

11. Gretchen Heefner, *The Missile Next Door: The Minuteman in the American Heartland* (Cambridge, MA: Harvard University Press, 2012), 74–75.

12. Lutz, "Making War at Home in the United States," 727–28.

13. For an explanation of the mix of "boosterism" and reportage provided in midcentury newspapers in the region, see Rebecca Berens Matzke, "Cold War Missiles Meet the Press: Local Newspaper Coverage of the Atlas F Missile Project, Lincoln Air Force Base, 1959–1961," *Great Plains Quarterly* 35 (Summer 2015): 249–67.

14. Quoted in Gretchen Heefner and Catherine McNicol Stock, "Missiles and Militarization: How the Cold War Shaped South Dakota Political Culture," in Jon K. Lauck, John E. Miller, and Donald C. Simmons Jr., *The Plains Political Tradition: Essays on South Dakota Political History*, vol. 1 (Pierre: South Dakota State Historical Society Press, 2011), 227–28.

15. *Rapid City Daily Journal*, January 17, 1961, p. 1. The other days the series ran were January 10 and 18, 1961.

16. "Minuteman Promises Economic Lift," *Rapid City Journal*, January 5, 1961, quoted in Heefner and Stock, "Missiles and Militarization," 228.

17. Ibid. For a more complete discussion, see Gretchen Heefner, "Missiles and Memory: Dismantling South Dakota's Cold War," *Western Historical Quarterly* 38 (Summer 2007): 185–87.

18. *Grand Forks Herald*, September 12, 1962, 22.

19. For images of the massive construction project, see National Park Service (hereafter NPS) Minuteman Missile Historic Site (hereafter MIMI), "The Missile Plains, Frontline of America's Cold War: Historical Resource Study, Minuteman Missile National Historic Site, South Dakota," https://www.nps.gov/mimi/getinvolved/upload/MIMI%20HRS%202006.pdf, 75–80.

20. Nathan A. Johnson, "The Economic Impact of North Dakota's Minuteman Missile Silos," (unpublished paper presented at the Northern Great Plains History Conference, Fargo, ND, October 2003), 5–6. Conversation with the author, October 2004.

21. Ted Hustead, interview, NPS-MIMI, https://www.nps.gov/mimi/learn/historycul ture/upload/MIMI-OH_TedHustead_2003.pdf, transcript, 8.

22. Quoted in Heefner and Stock, "Missiles and Militarization," 228.

23. Quoted in Johnson, "The Economic Impact of North Dakota's Minuteman Missile Silos," 2–3.

24. Ibid., 3.

25. Quoted in ibid. During the potentially catastrophic accident at Damascus, Arkansas, Vice President Walter Mondale asked Vice Colonel Ryan of the 308th strategic bomber wing if the damaged silo contained a nuclear weapon. Ryan told him, "I can't confirm or deny." "Command and Control," PBS, *American Experience*.

26. Milton Young to Mrs. Peter Peterson, 9/13/61, in Milton Young Papers (hereafter MY), Orin G. Libby Manuscript Collection 0020, Elwyn Robinson Department of Special Collections, Chester Fritz Library, University of North Dakota, Box 315, File 11.

27. Gretchen Heefner demonstrates that the "map-makers" in the nuclear security state made decisions long before interventions by congress members had even begun. *The Missile Next Door*, 49–76.

28. Mills, *Cold War in a Cold Land*, 203–5.

29. Ted Hustead, interview, NPS-MIMI, 9.

30. Shirley Norgard, interview, SHSND, MSOH, 32314–00020. Heefner demonstrates that the landowners group had relatively more impact on decisions during the deactivation stage in the 1990s. "Missiles and Memory," 190–94.

31. Gene S. Williams, interview, January 7, 2003, NPS-MIMI, https://www.nps.gov/ mimi/learn/historyculture/upload/MIMI-OH_GeneSWilliams2003.pdf, transcript, 4.

32. Ibid.

33. Shirley Norgard, interview, SHSND, MSOH, 32314–00020.

34. Quoted in Day, *Nuclear Heartland*, 9.

35. John Laforge, interview, NPS-MIMI, https://www.nps.gov/mimi/learn/historycul ture/upload/MIMI-OH_JohnLaForge_2003.pdf, transcript, 5.

36. Tom Brusegaard, conversation with author, October 4, 2018. By permission.

37. Heefner, "Missiles and Memory," 202. See also Michael Brown, interview, SHSND, MSOH.

38. *Rapid City Journal*, November 27, 1983, 4.

39. Wendy McNiel, interview, NPS-MIMI, https://www.nps.gov/mimi/learn/historycul ture/upload/MIMI-OH_WendyMcNiel_2003.pdf, transcript, 13–14.

40. John LaForge, interview, NPS-MIMI, https://www.nps.gov/mimi/learn/historycul ture/upload/MIMI-OH_JohnLaForge_2003.pdf, transcript, 4.

41. Quoted in Day, *Nuclear Heartland*, 8.

42. "Minuteman III," Fact Sheet, http://www.jonahhouse.org/archive/WMD%20Here%20Plowshares/WMD%20Here%20Fact%20Sheet.htm.

43. Shirley Norgard, interview, SHSND, MSOH, 32314–00020.

44. Ibid.

45. Steve Bucklin to Tim Pavek, interview, NPS-MIMI, https://www.nps.gov/mimi/learn/historyculture/upload/MIMI-OH_TimPavek_1999.pdf, transcript, 27.

46. Mrs. Robert Lefevre to Milton Young, 3/28/1962, MY Papers, Box 169: File 1; Dennis Carter to Milton Young, 11/21/1962, MY Papers, Box 169, File 2.

47. Quoted in Karl Mundt to Milton Young, 4/1/1969; Milton Young to Karl Mundt, 4/2/1969, MY Papers, Box 342, File 13.

48. "Command and Control," PBS, *American Experience*, transcript, 25.

49. Hans Heinrich, interview, SHSND, MSOH, 32324–0009.

50. Eric Schlosser, *Command and Control: Nuclear Weapons, The Damascus Accident, and the Illusion of Safety* (New York: Penguin, 2013), 430–32.

51. http://www.atomicarchive.com/Almanac/Brokenarrows_static.shtml.

52. Seth Tupper, "South Dakota's Secret Nuclear Missile Accident Revealed," *Rapid City Journal*, November 3, 2017, http://rapidcityjournal.com/news/local/south-dakota-s-secret-nuclear-missile-accident-revealed/article_92b6722d-9cd5-5551-8831-f61964da70b2.html.

53. Ibid. There was also faulty wiring but the air force report blamed the accident on "airman error."

54. Quoted in ibid.

55. Ibid.

56. Louis Brothag, interview, SHSND, MSOH, 32314–00005.

57. David Blackhurst, interview, NPS-MIMI, https://www.nps.gov/mimi/learn/historyculture/upload/MIMI-OH_DavidBlackhurst_1999.pdf, transcript, 6.

58. Shirley Norgard, interview, SHSND, MSOH, 32314–00020.

59. Ibid. Colorado rancher Charlie McKay, whose outfit bordered the Rocky Flats nuclear weapons facility, remembered a similarly strange set of maneuvers taking place nearby: "I'm over here fooling with the calves and feeding. . . . And these Rambo idiots will get out and lie down on the ground and crawl up to the fence and pull out their binoculars and start watching me." Quoted in Len Ackland, *Making a Real Killing: Rocky Flats and the Nuclear West* (Albuquerque: University of New Mexico Press, 2002), 1.

60. Shirley was right that some helicopter pilots flew as low as they could. Louis Brothag described an airman who tried to "buzz" the launch facility regularly. Louis Brothag, interview, SHSND, MSOH, 32314–00005. In northern Canada, Innu people have accused the government of "sonorous aggression" after four thousand test flights per year began to take off from large air force bases nearby; the constant noise made people and animals ill. See Winona LaDuke, *All Our Relations: Native Struggles for Land and Life* (Cambridge, MA: South End Press, 1999), 53–58.

61. Heefner, "Missiles and Memory," 188.

62. Some missileers mentioned that the local people were "stand-offish" toward them too. See Curtis Anderson, interview, SHSND, MSOH; Wade Bertrand, interview, SHSND, MSOH.

63. Mark Sundlov, a crew commander in Minot from 1999 to 2003, provides an overview of the many procedures the missileers followed every day. "The Atomic Age: North Dakota

and the Cold War," http://history.nd.gov/mediaroom/markSundlovPodcast.mp3. See also his explanations for crews' unfriendly behavior in his interview with Shirley Norgard; Shirley Norgard, interview, SHSND, MSOH, 32314–00020. For a 2014 report on missileer culture, see Josh Harkinson, "Hanging Out with the Disgruntled Airmen Who Baby-Sit America's Aging Nuclear Weapons," https://www.motherjones.com/politics/2014/11/air-force-missile -wing-minuteman-iii-nuclear-weapons-burnout-1/.

64. Michael Brown, SHSND, MSOH, 32314–00006.

65. Ibid.

66. Tim Pavek, interview, NPS-MIMI, https://www.nps.gov/mimi/learn/historyculture/ upload/MIMI-OH_TimPavek_1999.pdf, transcript, 4.

67. David Blackhurst, interview, NPS-MIMI, https://www.nps.gov/mimi/learn/history culture/upload/MIMI-OH_DavidBlackhurst_1999.pdf, transcript, 4.

68. Wade Bertrand, interview, SHSND, MSOH, 32314–00004.

69. Mark Sundlov remembered his wife's face as they drove out Highway 83 on their way to the Minot Air Force Base. Nearly in tears, she said, "I hope there are more trees to see soon. Or something!" Louis Brothag, interview, SHSND, MSOH, 32314–00005.

70. Curtis Anderson, interview, SHSND, MSOH, 32314–00002.

71. Aaron Bass and Chad Smith, interview, SHSND, MSOH, 32314–00003.

72. Hannah Rappleye, "The Missileers: Air Force Has Trained 247 Women for Nuclear Launch," https://www.nbcnews.com/news/military/missileers-air-force-has-trained-247 -women-nuclear-launch-n822486.

73. Hans Heinrich called the air force a "classed system." Hans Heinrich, interview, SHSND, MSOH, 32314–0009.

74. Michael S. Sherry, *The Rise of American Air Power: The Creation of Armageddon* (New Haven, CT: Yale University Press, 1987), 213.

75. Tim Pavek, interview, NPS-MIMI, https://www.nps.gov/mimi/learn/historyculture/ upload/MIMI-OH_TimPavek_1999.pdf, transcript, 24.

76. As Michael Brown put it, "We had to be a credible deterrent. We were part of what kept world peace." Michael Brown, interview, SHSND, MSOH, 32314–00006.

77. Curtis Anderson, interview, SHSND, MSOH, 32314–00002.

78. Wade Bertrand, interview, SHSND, MSOH, 32314–00004.

79. Tim Pavek, interview, NPS-MIMI, https://www.nps.gov/mimi/learn/historyculture/ upload/MIMI-OH_TimPavek_1999.pdf, transcript, 27.

80. Dennis Almer, interview, SHSND, MSOH, 32314–00001.

81. Tim Pavek, interview, NPS-MIMI, https://www.nps.gov/mimi/learn/historyculture/ upload/MIMI-OH_TimPavek_1999.pdf, transcript, 12.

82. Tinhatranch Productions, "Oscar Zero: Conversations with a Minuteman Nuclear Missile Combat Crew," https://www.youtube.com/watch?v = WLNTJ6LUuUk; Michael Brown, interview, SHSND, MSOH, 32314–00006.

83. Tupper, "South Dakota's Secret Missile Accident Revealed."

84. The smallest launch control centers were less than 336 square feet, and the crew shared space with a large number of file cabinets. Eric Leonard, email, Minuteman Missile Historic Site, July 7, 2019. The air force was well aware that the small quarters combined with the constant stress of attack, like the heavy bomber crew experienced in World War II, could create mental "emotional instability" in the crews, and categorized physical attraction or

intimacy to be among these "mental health" problems. See Sherry, *The Rise of American Air Power*, 205–6.

85. Randy Shilts, *Conduct Unbecoming: Gays and Lesbians in the U.S. Military* (New York: St. Martin's, 1993), 3.

86. Alan Berube, *Coming Out Under Fire: The History of Gay Men and Women in World War II* (Chapel Hill: University of North Carolina Press, 2010), 67–97. Berube describes how gay and straight servicemen in World War II could transgress gender lines because once they were soldiers, their masculinity was "established." Furthermore, they could "reap the benefits of the . . . wartime relaxation of rigid gender roles (68)." After the war, however, these roles were far less relaxed.

87. For examples of the surveillance of sexuality in the military in the Cold War, see Margot Canaday, *The Straight State: Sexuality and Citizenship in Twentieth-Century America* (Princeton, NJ: Princeton University Press, 2009). Several observers have argued that the crackdown on gays in the military actually worked to create a stronger gay community and more advocacy for change. Likewise, gays and lesbians in the service created opportunities for community-building with civilians in their base communities. Berube, *Coming Out Under Fire*, 271–76; Ross Benes, "How Exclusion from the Military Strengthened Gay Identity in America," *Rolling Stone*, October 3, 2016, https://www.rollingstone.com/culture/news/how-exclusion-from-the-military-strengthened-gay-identity-in-america-w441663.

88. Michael Brown, interview, SHSND, MSOH, 32314–00006. Of course, these masculinist performances had long histories in the military. For example, the practice of naming weapons, especially airplanes, for women was widespread in WWII. See Robert B. Westbrook, "'I Want a Girl, Just Like the Girl That Married Harry James': American Women and the Problem of Political Obligation in World War II," *American Quarterly* 42 (December 1990): 587–614.

89. Michael Brown, interview, SHSND, MSOH, 32314–00006.

90. Dennis Almer, interview, SHSND, MSOH, 32314–00001. Almer was not happy that his wife discussed this on camera.

91. Ibid. Dennis Almer described his first day: "There we were with our .38 calibers strapped on. Looking pretty tough and mean."

92. David Blackhurst, interview, NPS-MIMI, https://www.nps.gov/mimi/learn/history culture/upload/MIMI-OH_DavidBlackhurst_1999.pdf, transcript, 32.

93. Ibid.

94. SHSND podcasts, "The Atomic Age in North Dakota: Interview with Mark Sundlov, Former Missileer," http://podbay.fm/show/264349109/e/1194289200.

95. Aaron Bass and Chad Smith, interview, SHSND, MSOH, 32314–00003.

96. Dennis Almer, interview, SHSND, MSOH, 32314–00001.

97. Many missileers recalled the tight quarters in the Launch Control Facility. Eric Leonard, NPS-MIMI, conversation with the author, July 3, 2019.

98. Aaron Bass and Chad Smith, interview, SHSND, MSOH, 32314–00003.

99. Dennis Almer, interview, SHSND, MSOH, 32314–00001. In an interview with former missileer David Blackhust, historian Steven Bucklin asked what he thought of gays in the military. Blackhurst laughed and said, "That's a hard one to answer. It really is." David Blackhurst, interview, NPS-MIMI, https://www.nps.gov/mimi/learn/historyculture/upload/MIMI-OH_DavidBlackhurst_1999.pdf, transcript, 15–16.

100. Senator William Proxmire thought missile work would be appropriate for women because they were "unlikely to be in the line of fire." "Female Missileers," https://www.nps .gov/articles/femalemissileers.htm.

101. The air force commissioned studies in 1980 and 1985. The 1980 study is summarized in the 1985 report: Strategic Air Command, "A Study of Females on Minuteman/Peace keeper Crews," January 31, 1985, ii, https://apps.dtic.mil/dtic/tr/fulltext/u2/a584971.pdf. Military wives held a special place in all branches of the armed forces; thus their negative opinion of female missileers was taken quite seriously. A handbook for military wives from the Cold War era asserted, "When a married man entered the service, the government gained not just one—but two—the man and his wife." Quoted in Lynne R. Dubrofsky and Constance T. Batterson, "The Military Wife and Feminism," *Signs* 2 (Spring 1977): 675. In an interview years later, Dennis Almer's wife remembered clearly what the wives' objections had been. It was "tough enough" having a husband away from home on alert so much, she explained. If women were integrated into the crews, "your husband would be talking with the other woman for twenty-four hours a day and sharing everything and if there was anything wrong at home, you never know [what might happen]." She added later, "The wives basically killed it." Dennis Almer, interview, SHSND, MSOH, 32314–00001. David Blackhurst's jocular attitude toward female missileers demonstrated why wives might be concerned: "I'm not sure how my wife thought [about women coming into the missileers], but I thought it was OK. [Laughter from interviewer]." David Blackhurst, interview, NPS-MIMI, https://www.nps.gov/mimi/learn/his toryculture/upload/MIMI-OH_DavidBlackhurst_1999.pdf, transcript, 15.

102. No data was provided on risks during pregnancy. SAC, "A Study of Females on Minuteman/Peacekeeper Crews," 3–12, 3–14.

103. Brooke L. Blower, "V-J Day, 1945, Times Square," in Blower and Mark P. Bradley, eds., *The Familiar Made Strange: American Icons and Artifacts after the Transnational Turn* (Ithaca, NY: Cornell University Press, 2015), 70–87.

104. Dennis Almer, interview, SHSND, MSOH, 32314–00001.

105. Wade Bertrand, interview, SHSND, MSOH, 32314–00004.

106. Gene S. Williams, interview, January 7, 2003, NPS-MIMI, https://www.nps.gov/ mimi/learn/historyculture/upload/MIMI-OH_GeneSWilliams2003.pdf, transcript, 10.

107. Tim Pavek, interview, NPS-MIMI, https://www.nps.gov/mimi/learn/historyculture/ upload/MIMI-OH_TimPavek_1999.pdf, transcript, 10.

108. The Peace Studies program included, along with coursework and a proposed minor, a "student exchange program aimed at the Soviet Union and China." According to President Clifford, the rationale for the program was based in the "dangers of this nuclear age and the need for peace within and among human communities." Between 1988 and 1995 more than sixty-nine faculty members from different departments were affiliated with the program and as many as a hundred students, including those in ROTC. Janet Moen, "The History of the Center for Peace Studies at UND," unpublished manuscript, with permission of the author.

109. Charles Ray, "Bucking the Trends: Black Hills Crusader Marvin Kammerer," *High Country News*, September 27, 2004, https://www.hcn.org/issues/283/15021.

110. Heefner, *The Missile Next Door*, 153–57. See also North American Farm Alliance Education Program, "Farms Not Arms: Forging the Links Between Peace and Agriculture," (Ames, IA: n.p., June 1988).

111. Gene S. Williams, interview, NPS-MIMI, https://www.nps.gov/mimi/learn/history culture/upload/MIMI-OH_GeneSWilliams2003.pdf, transcript, 7.

112. Ibid., transcript, 3.

113. Ibid., transcript, 21.

114. Curtis Anderson, interview, SHSND, MSOH, 32314–00002,

115. *Grand Forks Herald*, September 12, 1962, 22.

116. One possible consequence of the construction projects was the election of George McGovern to the Senate in 1962. Unionized out-of-state construction workers organized aggressively to support the Democrat, who won a very tight contest. Don Barnett, email exchange with Jon K. Lauck, June 26, 2018. By permission.

117. Mr. and Mrs. Nels Peterson to Milton Young, 2/16/67, MY Papers, Box 342, File 14.

118. George Johanssen to Milton Young, 2/15/67, MY Papers, Box 342, File 14.

119. Melvin Jensrud to Milton Young, 5/23/1970, MY Papers, Box 342, File 14.

120. Gene S. Williams, interview, NPS-MIMI, https://www.nps.gov/mimi/learn/history culture/upload/MIMI-OH_GeneSWilliams2003.pdf, transcript, 14–15.

121. David Mills, *Cold War in a Cold Land*, 216–35.

122. Matthew Gault, "America's Abandoned $6 Billion Missile Pyramid," https://me dium.com/war-is-boring/americas-abandoned-6-billion-missile-pyramid-398d2dfe40c9.

123. Quoted in Mills, *Cold War in a Cold Land*, 216.

124. "The Missile Flop," *Grand Forks Herald*, 8/16/68, n.p., MY Papers, Box 342, File 14.

125. "Is This Protection?," *Devils Lake Journal*, 8/15/68, n.p., MY Papers, Box 342, File 14.

126. Lawrence Woehl to Milton Young, 8/16/1968, MY Papers, Box 342, File 14.

127. Gene S. Williams, interview, NPS-MIMI, https://www.nps.gov/mimi/learn/history culture/upload/MIMI-OH_GeneSWilliams2003.pdf, transcript, 9.

128. Ibid., 1–2, 6, 22.

129. Ibid., 16, 19.

130. Ibid., 2.

Chapter 6

Note to chapter title: The term "lost world" derives from Josh Garrett-Davis, "The Lost World of George McGovern," *New York Times*, October 21, 2012, https://www.nytimes.com/2012/10/22/opinion/the-lost-world-of-george-mcgovern.html.

1. James M. Moon, interview, Public Broadcasting Service and Prairie Public Broadcasting (PBS/PPB), *Prairie Memories: The Vietnam War Years*, https://www.youtube.com/watch?v=C_r7xkhqI8I.

2. In its introduction, the film purported to show how the war "changed the lives" of both "those who fought" and "those who protested."

3. "Vietnam: Why Does This Matter?" https://www.ndstudies.gov/gr8/content/unit-iv -modern-north-dakota-1921-present/lesson-4-alliances-and-conflicts/topic-3-experience -war/section-4-vietnam-war. A "Summary of North Dakota History" on the State Historical Society of North Dakota's website does not refer to the war at all. See http://history.nd.gov/ ndhistory/summaryintro.html. At least one scholarly treatment of the region's history also gives the war extremely short shrift. See Norman K. Risjord, *Dakota: The Story of the Northern Plains* (Lincoln: University of Nebraska Press, 2013).

4. "William Janklow Dedicates the South Dakota World War II Memorial," https:// www.youtube.com/watch?v=j6rzELpPLVg.

5. Rounds said, "This is not about the war. This is not about politics. This is not about history. It is about you [the veterans]." "South Dakota Welcomes Home Vietnam/Era Veterans," https://www.youtube.com/watch?v = MtCZVAts1m4. In a video produced for the "History Day" contest in 2012, South Dakota students Aimee Allcock and Amanda Greenmyer also erased the history of protest in the region. In "Hawks and Doves: South Dakotans React to the Vietnam War," one "dove" apologizes, saying, "We didn't really know what we were talking about." Their video was selected for the national finals. See https://www.youtube.com/watch?v = F6p4LG28cOI.

6. Garrett-Davis, "The Lost World of George McGovern."

7. Jefferson Cowie, *Stayin' Alive: The 1970s and the Last Days of the Working Class* (New York: New Press, 2010), 1.

8. The strategies employed to evade or avoid the draft ranged from simply staying in college to feigning all manner of illnesses. See Lawrence M. Baskir and William A. Strauss, *Chance and Circumstance: The Draft, the War and the Vietnam Generation* (New York: Vintage Books, 1978).

9. Quoted in Jack Beatty, "Vietnam: Sorrow, Rage and Remembrance," *Washington Post*, June 3, 1984, https://www.washingtonpost.com/archive/entertainment/books/1984/06/03/vietnam-sorrow-rage-and-remembrance/ca669d48–0358–4a4b-8e3e-7a1ae00e3cf7/?utm_term = .7b9b00f2e20c.

10. Tim O'Brien, "Writing Vietnam," April 21, 1999, http://cds.library.brown.edu/projects/WritingVietnam/obrien.html, n.p.

11. Kyle Longley, "A Small Town's Sacrifice to Vietnam," *New York Times*, August 11, 2017, https://www.nytimes.com/2017/08/11/opinion/a-small-towns-sacrifice-to-vietnam.html.

12. "In Country: Tales of the Vietnam War from the Veterans Who Lived It," South Dakota Department of Veterans Affairs, John Sweet, accessed October 16, 2019, https://vetaffairs.sd.gov/memorials/Vietnam/incountry.aspx.

13. "In Country," Mark Young, accessed October 16, 2019, https://vetaffairs.sd.gov/memorials/Vietnam/incountry.aspx.

14. "In Country," Richard Decker, accessed October 16, 2019, https://vetaffairs.sd.gov/memorials/Vietnam/incountry.aspx.

15. "In Country," Anthony Rangel, accessed October 16, 2019, https://vetaffairs.sd.gov/memorials/Vietnam/incountry.aspx.

16. "In Country," Mark Young, accessed October 16, 2019, https://vetaffairs.sd.gov/memorials/Vietnam/incountry.aspx.

17. Ibid.

18. "In Country," Timothy Werlinger, accessed October 16, 2019, https://vetaffairs.sd.gov/memorials/Vietnam/incountry.aspx.

19. George Shurr, "Suspended Succession: How the Vietnam War Impacted a Family Farm in the Eastern Great Plains" (paper given at the Fiftieth Annual Dakota Conference, Center for Western Studies [CWS], Augustana College [AC], Sioux Falls, SD, April 20, 2018). George's brother was ordered to take photographs in a dangerous mountain zone and was killed.

20. Bill Anderson, interview, PBS/PPB, *Prairie Memories: The Vietnam War Years*, https://www.youtube.com/watch?v = ZVw6jz-7KyE.

21. Andrew Maragos, interview, PBS/PPB, *Prairie Memories: The Vietnam War Years*, https://www.youtube.com/watch?v = iYW7tJCaGmk.

22. Bill Rose, interview, PBS/PPB, *Prairie Memories: The Vietnam War Years*, https://www.youtube.com/watch?v = fgfVAsqUv1A.

23. "In Country," John Sweet, accessed October 16, 2019, https://vetaffairs.sd.gov/memorials/Vietnam/incountry.aspx; see also "In Country," Don Fechner, accessed October 16, 2019, https://vetaffairs.sd.gov/memorials/Vietnam/incountry.aspx.

24. "In Country," Berwyn Place, accessed October 16, 2019, https://vetaffairs.sd.gov/memorials/Vietnam/incountry.aspx.

25. "In Country," Robert Riggio, accessed October 16, 2019, https://vetaffairs.sd.gov/memorials/Vietnam/incountry.aspx.

26. Kristen Iverson, *Full Body Burden: Growing Up in the Nuclear Shadow of Rocky Flats* (New York: Random House, 2012), 12.

27. Darrell Dorgan, interview, PBS/PPB, *Prairie Memories: The Vietnam War Years*, https://www.youtube.com/watch?v = 7lnSdtPttxg.

28. Jon Hanna, interview, PBS/PPB, *Prairie Memories: The Vietnam War Years*, https://www.youtube.com/watch?v = UR8sYQUwDng.

29. John Rootham, interview, PBS/PPB, *Prairie Memories: The Vietnam War Years*, https://www.youtube.com/watch?v = DS3eHqhCXzg.

30. "In Country," Jerome Cleveland, accessed October 16, 2019, https://vetaffairs.sd.gov/memorials/Vietnam/incountry.aspx.

31. "In Country," Victor Robertson, accessed October 16, 2019, https://vetaffairs.sd.gov/memorials/Vietnam/incountry.aspx.

32. "In Country," Calvin F. Olsen, accessed October 16, 2019, https://vetaffairs.sd.gov/memorials/Vietnam/incountry.aspx

33. "In Country," Dennis Lau, accessed October 16, 2019, https://vetaffairs.sd.gov/memorials/Vietnam/incountry.aspx.

34. "In Country," Leo Powell, accessed October 16, 2019, https://vetaffairs.sd.gov/memorials/Vietnam/incountry.aspx.

35. http://www.nd.gov/veterans/news/north-dakota-vietnam-veterans-america.

36. Ahrar Ahmad, "War and Peace in South Dakota," in Jon K. Lauck, John E. Miller, and Donald C. Simmons Jr., eds., *The Plains Political Tradition: Essays in South Dakota Political Culture*, vol. 1 (Pierre: South Dakota Historical Society Press, 2011), 202.

37. "On Vietnam War: Public Split on McGovern's Stand," *Sioux Falls Argus Leader*, May 31, 1967.

38. Jon K. Lauck, "Binding Assumptions: Karl E. Mundt and the Vietnam War, 1963–1969," *Mid-America* 76 (Fall 1994): 292. This data contradicts surveys taken by college groups with smaller data sets. At Northern State College in 1966, for example, 69 percent of students surveyed called themselves "hawks." See Daryl Webb, " 'There Is No Place in Our Institutions for Radicals': The Vietnam War on South Dakota Campuses, 1965–1973," *South Dakota History* 45 (Spring 2015): 5.

39. Milton Young Papers (hereafter MY Papers), Orin G. Libby Manuscript Collection, Elwyn D. Robinson Department of Special Collections, Chester Fritz Library, University of North Dakota, 20–626–48.

40. MY, 20–626–113.

41. MY, 20–627–6.

42. MY, 20–276–7.

43. MY, 20–485–20.

44. MY, 20–276–6.

45. MY, 20–279–6.

46. MY, 20–276–6.

47. See, for example, MY, 20–276–7.

48. MY, 20–409–16.

49. MY, 20–276–6.

50. MY, 20–279–6.

51. MY, 20–409–16.

52. MY, 20–627–6.

53. The AP described the protest this way: "An Anti-War Sign That Included the Words, 'America the Insane' Was Hoisted in the Crowd by Two or Three Persons." This report was used in papers across the state. See, for example, Harl Andersen, "Slight Ripples Mar Nixon Visit," *Rapid City Journal*, June 4, 1969, 1.

54. John T. Schneider, "Pacifist Students Plan Anti-Viet Nam War Protest," *Spectrum*, March 23, 1966, 1.

55. Webb, "'No Place in Our Institutions for Radicals.'"

56. Ibid., 20.

57. Larry Peterson, email to author, June 18, 2018. Peterson requested and received his FBI file under the Freedom of Information Act.

58. Quoted in Webb, "'No Place in Our Institutions for Radicals,'" 18.

59. John Rigert, "Dakota State's 'Silent Majority' Is Upset over War," *Minneapolis Tribune*, May 17, 1970, 43.

60. The broadest interpretation of the "Movement's" critique of American society incorporated all forms of oppression—at least in theory. In practice it worked out quite differently. Sara Evans, *The Personal Is Political: The Roots of Women's Liberation in the Civil Rights Movement and the New Left* (New York: Knopf, 1979).

61. Jenifer Wolf, "Comment," June 2, 2017, in response to Kim Phillips-Fein, "The Two Women's Movements," *The Nation*, June 1, 2017, https://www.thenation.com/article/two-womens-movements/.

62. "Peace Rally Turns into Rap Session," *Spectrum*, April 1, 1971, 1.

63. Ibid.

64. Jon K. Lauck, "'It Disappeared as Quickly as It Came': The Democratic Surge and the Republican Comeback in South Dakota Politics, 1970–1980," *South Dakota History* 46 (Summer 2016): 139–40. For many more examples of this argument, see Cory Haala, "Replanting the Grassroots: The South Dakota Democratic Party from McGovern to Daschle, 1980–1986," in Jon K. Lauck, John E. Miller, and Paula M. Nelson, eds., *The Plains Political Tradition: Essays in South Dakota Political Culture*, vol. 3 (Pierre: South Dakota Historical Society Press, 2018), 202nn2,6.

65. "Peace Rally Turns into Rap Session."

66. Richard M. Chapman, "The Black Campus Movement at Concordia College, Moorhead, 1968–1978" (paper prepared for the Annual Meeting of the Northern Great Plains History Conference, Mankato, MN, September 21, 2018).

67. President Clifford and his successors would find this issue far more divisive than they imagined, especially after a conservative alumnus, Ralph Engelstad, donated over $100 million for a new hockey rink but threatened to destroy it if the mascot were ever changed. See Catherine McNicol Stock, "Reading the 'Ralph': Privatization in the New North Dakota," in Jon K. Lauck and Catherine McNicol Stock, eds., *The Conservative Heartland: A Political History of the Postwar American Midwest* (Lawrence: University of Kansas Press, 2020), 323–345.

68. Cara Beck, " 'Let Them Use the Back Seat of a Car': The Fight for Co-Ed Living on South Dakota Campuses" (paper presented at the 49th Dakota Conference, CWS, AC, April 2017), 17. On a similar fight at the University of Kansas, see Beth Bailey, *Sex in the Heartland* (Cambridge, MA: Harvard University Press, 1999), 205–11.

69. Beck, " 'Let Them Use the Back Seat of a Car'," 17.

70. Shurr, "Suspended Succession."

71. Ruth Ann Alexander, "South Dakota Women Stake a Claim: A Feminist Memoir, 1964–1989," *South Dakota History* 19 (Winter 1989): 544–48.

72. Quoted in Matthew Pehl, "Gender Politics on the Prairie: The South Dakota Commission on the Status of Women in the 1970s," in Lauck, Miller, and Nelson, *The Plains Political Tradition*, 3:163. Pehl argues that the triumph of conservative views on gender roles, beginning with the rescission of the ERA, was not "pre-ordained" in South Dakota. Perhaps not, but the ERA debate had striking parallels with earlier efforts to gain woman suffrage. As Pehl himself admits—or, in my view, understates—the highly valued notion of gender "complementarity" in rural settings was "not the quite the same as equality" (160, 162).

73. Garrett-Davis, *Ghost Dances (Proving Up on the Plains)* (New York: Little, Brown, 2012), 54. Josh recounts that there were also head shops in Fargo, Sioux Falls, and Rapid City.

74. Ibid., 56.

75. Ibid., 60. To be fair, Josh's father, Jay Davis, says this was an "isolated incident" and that drug paraphernalia was but a small part of the store's business. Jay Davis, email to author, July 3, 2019.

76. Ibid., 119–35. See also Garrett-Davis, "The Lost World of George McGovern."

77. Garrett-Davis, *Ghost Dances*, 102.

78. Debra Marquart, *The Horizontal World: Growing Up Wild in the Middle of Nowhere* (Philadelphia: Counterpoint, 2006), xii–xxiii.

79. Rick Perlstein, "I Thought I Understood the American Right; Trump Proved Me Wrong," *New York Times Magazine*, April 11, 2017.

80. Historians have recently called attention to the importance of *Bob Jones University v. United States* (1983) and the cases that preceded it, arguing that they may have galvanized some Christian leaders more than *Roe v. Wade* (1973). Randall Balmer, "The Real Origins of the Religious Right," *Politico*, May 27, 2014, https://www.politico.com/magazine/story/2014/05/religious-right-real-origins-107133.

81. In the 1980s and 1990s, several influential right-wing radio hosts emerged on the Northern Plains, including John Ruby of KFYR in Bismarck, Scott Hennan of KCNN 1590 in Grand Forks, and Ed Schulz, who would later become nationally known for his progressive views, on KFGO 790 in Fargo. Sarah Vogel, Darrell Dorgan, and Tom Brusegaard, email exchange with author, July 3, 2019.

82. Phyllis Schlafly's Pro-Life Pro-Family rally in 1977 drew ten thousand conservative women to Houston. One of them was a Bismarck mother of nine who traveled to the rally

with six other women in her yellow van. As she drove, "we felt we had the Lord knocking on the top of the van all the way down." Quoted in Phillips-Fein, "Two Women's Movements."

83. Ibid.

84. Lauck, "Binding Assumptions," 298–99n65.

85. Karl Mundt, "Another Opinion: Stop the Poor People's March," *New York Times*, May 12, 1968, https://timesmachine.nytimes.com/timesmachine/1968/05/12/issue.html?action = click&contentCollection = Archives&module = ArticleEndCTA&region = Archive Body&pgtype = article.

86. Quoted in Lauck, "Binding Assumptions," 298.

87. "Sexuality in the Beat Generation," https://qssfc.wordpress.com/2012autumn/sexuality-in-the-beat-generation/.

88. Quoted in Webb, "'No Place in Our Institutions for Radicals,'" 4.

89. Herbert Schell, *History of South Dakota*, 4th ed. (Pierre: South Dakota State Historical Society, 2004), 322.

90. Webb, "'No Place in Our Institutions for Radicals,'" 22. See also "Governor Wants No Nonsense Allowed in College System," *Pierre Daily Journal*, February 21, 1969.

91. Daniel Spillman, "Combative Conservatism at the 'Berkeley of the Midwest': The *American Spectator* and Baby Boomer Conservative Intellectuals, 1967–1980," in Lauck and Stock, *The Conservative Heartland*, 133–152.

92. Quoted in Webb, "'No Place in Our Institutions for Radicals,'" 7.

93. Ibid., 9.

94. Quoted in ibid., 10.

95. *Sioux Falls Argus Leader*, October 19, 1969.

96. Quoted in Webb, "'No Place in Our Institutions for Radicals,'" 2, 4, 9.

97. Ibid., 14.

98. Bonnie Meibers, "Zap Will Celebrate Fiftieth Anniversary of Zip to Zap," *Grand Forks Herald*, March 4, 2019, https://www.grandforksherald.com/news/4579950-zap-will-celebrate-50th-anniversary-zip-zap.

99. Quoted in Beck, "'Let Them Use the Back Seat of a Car,'" 10. See also Schell, *History of South Dakota*, 322.

100. Quoted in Beck, "'Let Them Use the Back Seat of a Car,'" 17.

101. "Schlafly to Debate ERA," *Rapid City Journal*, April 17, 1977.

102. Veronica Monique Lerma, "The Equal Rights Amendment and the Case of the Rescinding States: A Comparative Historical Analysis" (master's thesis, University of California-Merced, 2015), https://escholarship.org/uc/item/7bg4s908.

103. Pehl, "Gender Politics on the Prairie," 161.

104. Jon K. Lauck, "The Decline of South Dakota Democrats and the Fall of George McGovern, 1974–1980," in Lauck and Stock, *The Conservative Heartland*, 247–266.

105. Quoted in Faye D. Ginsburg, *Contested Lives: The Abortion Debate in an American Community* (Berkeley: University of California Press, 1998), 79.

106. Two dozen evangelical ministers in the Fargo area were given a private showing of the antiabortion documentary *Assignment Life*. They reported that the stronger their admonishment of abortion the more congregants at other denominations began to "church hop" over to them. Ginsberg, *Contested Lives*, 85–87, 271–72n5.

107. Robin Huebner, "Site of Former Abortion Clinic, Major Protests, to be Demolished," *Fargo Forum*, April 29, 2018, http://www.inforum.com/news/4438741-piece-fargo-history-site-former-abortion-clinic-major-protests-be-demolished.

108. Cory Haala, email to author, July 2, 2019.

109. Daniel T. Rodgers, *The Age of Fracture* (Cambridge, MA: Harvard University Press, 2012).

110. Robert Griffith, "Old Progressives and the Cold War," *Journal of American History* 66 (September 1979): 334–47.

111. Dan Rylance, *Quentin Burdick: The Gentle Warrior* (Fargo, ND: Institute for Regional Studies, 2007), 359.

112. Darrell Dorgan, interview, "The Legacy of Quentin Burdick," Prairie Public Broadcasting, https://www.youtube.com/watch?v=XNguPupHmj4.

113. Michael J. C. Taylor, "The Violence of War and the Mark of Leadership: The Significance of McGovern's Air Force Service During World War II," in Robert P. Watson, ed., *George McGovern: A Political Life, a Political Legacy* (Pierre: South Dakota State Historical Society Press, 2004), 19–37.

114. George McGovern, *Grassroots: The Autobiography of George McGovern* (New York: Random House, 1977), 30–31.

115. George McGovern, interview with Jon K. Lauck and John E. Miller, Mitchell, SD, November 25, 2003, 8. By permission of interviewers.

116. Quoted in Taylor, "The Violence of War," 31.

117. Mark A. Lempke, *My Brother's Keeper: George McGovern and Progressive Christianity* (Amherst: University of Massachusetts Press, 2017), 4–5.

118. Ibid., 5.

119. Ibid., 90. See also Daryl Webb, "Crusade: George McGovern's Opposition to the Vietnam War," *South Dakota History* 28 (Fall 1998): 161–90.

120. "Why as a Christian I Cannot Vote for McGovern," George McGovern (GM) Papers, Department of Rare Books and Special Collections, Seeley Mudd Library, Princeton University (PU), Box 941, Folder: 1980 Senate Re-election Campaign.

121. In 1967 he said, "To remain silent in the face of policies we do not believe in is not patriotism; it is . . . a form of treason." Robert Sam Anson, *McGovern: A Biography* (New York: Holt, Rinehart, and Winston, 1972), 165.

122. Quoted in Thomas J. Knock, "George McGovern, Vietnam and the Democratic Crackup," *New York Times*, December 5, 2017.

123. George McGovern, "On the Military Budget," *New York Times*, June 10, 1980.

124. Rylance, *Quentin Burdick*, 286–87. See also PPB, "Legacy of Quentin Burdick."

125. Rylance, *Quentin Burdick*, 288.

126. PPB, "Legacy of Quentin Burdick."

127. Anson, *McGovern*, 160–71. In later years McGovern was still flabbergasted by the flyers that read "Target McGovern" when King and Kennedy had only recently been assassinated. McGovern, interview with Lauck and Miller, 15.

128. John Mollison, luncheon remarks, Dakota Conference, CWS, AU, April 6, 2018. See also http://ww2fighters.blogspot.com/2012/10/final-flight-george-mcgovern-455th-bg.html.

129. Lauck, "The Decline of South Dakota Democrats," in Lauck and Stock, *The Conservative Heartland*, 247–266.

130. Lauck, "'It Disappeared as Quickly as It Came.'"

131. Abourezk, a Lebanese American, was an outspoken critic of US foreign policy in the Middle East and an advocate for civil rights, including Native rights.

132. Cambridge Survey Research, "An Analysis of Political Attitudes in the State of South Dakota," 1976, 18, GM-PU, Box 187, Folder "Surveys 1980."

133. In the 1968 campaign, a retired air force general warned Republicans that they might lose Ellsworth Air Force Base if they reelected McGovern. Thomas J. Knock, *The Rise of a Prairie Statesman: The Life and Times of George McGovern* (Princeton, NJ: Princeton University Press, 2016), 429–30.

134. "B-1 Bomber," GM-PU, Box 186, Folder "1980 Campaign Issues."

135. "Cuba," GM-PU, Box 186, Folder "1980 Campaign Issues."

136. Kathleen Belew, *Bring the War Home: The White Power Movement and Paramilitary America* (Cambridge, MA: Harvard University Press, 2018).

137. Abdnor supported the B-1 bomber program, the MX missile system, the deregulation of the energy industry, and the expansion of the military budget. "James Abdnor, Former South Dakota Senator Dies," https://www.nytimes.com/2012/05/17/us/james-abdnor-former -south-dakota-senator-dies-at-89.html?_r = 0. In a flyer he sent to voters, Abdnor listed each of his many local clubs and organizations, in contrast to McGovern, who likely belonged to none. "Jim Abdnor: A Senator for South Dakota," GM-PU, Box 186, Folder "Abnor Ads."

138. Target McGovern Committee, "Letter from Lt. General Gordon A. Sumner (RET)," no date, GM-PU, Box 941, Folder "1980 Re-election Campaign."

139. Haala, "Replanting the Grassroots," 184–85.

140. Leslie Bennetts, "National Anti-Liberal Crusade Zeroing in on McGovern in South Dakota," *New York Times*, Monday, June 3, 1980.

141. Anthony Lewis, "Backlash in South Dakota?," *New York Times*, October 13, 1980.

142. Mid-America Communications, "A Citizen's Survey of South Dakotan's [*sic*] Reaction to Senator McGovern's Record," n.d., GM-PU, Box 941, Folder "1980 Senate Reelection Campaign."

143. Knock, *The Rise of a Prairie Statesman*, 417.

144. People for an Alternative to McGovern, "Texts of PFAMM Television Spots to Be Aired March 17–24," n.d., GM-PU, Box 941, Folder "1980 Senate Re-election Campaign."

145. Alan L. Clem, "The 1980 Election in South Dakota: End of an Era," *Public Affairs* 80 (March 1981): 3.

146. Quoted in Lempke, *My Brother's Keeper*, 176.

147. In a letter to the editor, Mrs. Charles Englert from Vienna, SD, wrote: "Our Constitution was based on the Ten Commandments. It is always a crime that calls to heaven for vengeance to kill an innocent person." Sioux Falls *Argus Leader*, January 14, 1979, GM-PU, Box 187, Folder "Abortion Letters: Anti-McGovern Stand."

148. George Zacher to George McGovern, January 22, 1979, GM-PU, Box 187, Folder "Abortion Letters: Anti-McGovern Stand."

149. Quoted in Anson, *McGovern*, 165.

150. Clem, "The 1980 Election in South Dakota," 3.

151. Haala, "Replanting the Grassroots," 185. See also Lewis, "Backlash in South Dakota?"

152. Quoted in Anson, *McGovern*, 165.

153. McGovern, interview with Lauck and Miller, 11.

154. In the days after the election, McGovern admitted that he might have been out of touch with the values of his voters, saying "Maybe it's true." Clem, "The 1980 Election in South Dakota," 4.

155. Patrick Springer, "Former Governor George Sinner Dies at Age 89," *Fargo Forum*, March 9, 2018; Melissa Woinarowicz, "Sinner Should Not Be Honored for Vetoing Abortion Ban," *Fargo Forum*, March 22, 2018, https://www.inforum.com/opinion/columns/4421285 -woinarowicz-sinner-should-not-be-honored-vetoing-abortion-ban.

156. On Pressler see, Jon D. Schaff, "The Politics of Defeat: Senate Elections in South Dakota," in Lauck, Miller, and Simmons Jr., *The Plains Political Tradition*, 1:325.

157. Haala, "Replanting the Grassroots," 201. See also Jon K. Lauck, *Daschle vs. Thune: The Anatomy of a High-Plains Senate Race* (Norman: University of Oklahoma Press, 2007).

158. Seth Tupper, "Campaign Flyer: Sen. Jensen Dodged Draft During Vietnam War," *Rapid City Journal*, May 27, 2016, http://rapidcityjournal.com/news/election/campaign-flyer -sen-jensen-dodged-draft-during-vietnam-war/article_243a2e48–80c6–5886-a16f-e5c 0c83879be.html.

159. Stan Adelstein, "While Others Served—Jensen Wouldn't Wear Our Country's Uniform," May 24, 2016, https://way2gosd.com/2016/05/24/while-others-served-jensen-wouldnt -wear-our-countrys-uniform/.

160. James Gibson, *Warrior Dreams: Paramilitary Culture in Post-Vietnam America* (New York: Hill and Wang, 1994).

161. "Mike from Iowa," comment, *Dakota Free Press*, May 31, 2016, https://dakotafree press.com/2016/05/31/forty-years-later-draft-dodging-stirs-jensen-sly-primary-in-rapid-city/ #comments.

162. The bifurcation of the Republican Party dates back organizationally to 2007 when a handful of local men, some of whom were military veterans, met to discuss the "leftward drift" of the Republican Party in the state. They had been disappointed, for example, that some Republicans "had hesitated" before casting a vote in favor of allowing students and teachers to carry guns in schools. In 2014 more than thirty ultraconservative candidates ran for state office. In 2018 both Republican candidates for governor, Jackley and Noem, supported the "bathroom bill" and other planks in the ultraconservative movement's agenda. See http://rapidcityjournal.com/news/local/wingnuts-pledge-to-push-republican-party-further -right/article_6a0e13f4–8e3e-5f08–99e2–3af726f3803e.html; and http://rapidcityjournal.com/ news/local/top-stories/mayor-elect-hanks-defends-use-of-wing-nut-mailing/ article_6457337b-a364–5042-af50–43207a066be1.html. Some members of the "Wingnuts" also belong to a more conventional Tea Party style group called the South Dakota Citizens for Liberty. See http://www.sdcitizensforliberty.com/index.html.

Chapter 7

1. "We Shall Remain: Wounded Knee," PBS, *American Experience*, transcript, 5, 9. Native people have had a long tradition of service in the US armed forces. For an overview of Lakota and Dakota (Sioux) experiences in Vietnam, see John A. Little, "Between Cultures: Sioux Warriors and the Vietnam War," *Great Plains Quarterly* 33 (Fall 2015): 357–75.

2. To see the image, go to https://www.usmarshals.gov/history/wounded-knee/ index.html.

3. As Alexandra Fuller writes regarding the military response to the AIM Occupation, "In the United States, domestic war looks a lot like a foreign invasion. It doesn't hurt that the enemies . . . are almost always Black or Brown." *Quiet Until the Thaw* (New York: Penguin, 2017), 125.

4. Phil Deloria, K. Tsianina Lomawaima, Bryan McKinley Jones Brayboy, Mark N. Trahant, Loren Ghiglione, Douglas Medin, and Ned Blackhawk, "Unfolding Futures: Indigenous Ways of Knowing for the Twenty-First Century," *Daedalus* 147 (Spring 2018): 6–7. White historians tend to be more critical of the Occupation, saying for example, that "Indians stood on more solid ground when they challenged injustices through legal cases brought in the court system." Herbert Schell, *History of South Dakota*, 4th rev. ed. (Pierre: South Dakota Historical Society Press, 2004), 363. AIM contended that the judicial system was as much a part of the problem of injustice as a solution.

5. The National Council of Churches (NCC), an ecumenical organization of largely mainline Protestant denominations, was founded in 1950. See http://nationalcouncilof churches.us/.

6. Quoted in Gail Richardson, "S.D.'s Social Conscience Prepares to Move On," *Sioux Falls Argus Leader*, June 8, 1980, 1B.

7. Peter Matthiessen, *In the Spirit of Crazy Horse* (New York: Viking, 1980), 107–10. See also Nick Estes, *Our History Is the Future: Standing Rock Versus the Dakota Access Pipeline, and the Long Tradition of Indigenous Resistance* (London: Verso, 2019), 197.

8. Kathleen Belew, *Bring the War Home: The White Power Movement and Paramilitary America* (Cambridge, MA: Harvard University Press, 2018), 16.

9. For an overview of the Occupation and events that preceded it, see Paul Chaat Smith and Robert Allen Warrior, *Like a Hurricane: The Indian Movement from Alcatraz to Wounded Knee* (New York: New Press, 1996); Mary Crow Dog with Peter Erdoes, *Lakota Woman* (New York: Grove Press, 1990); Dennis Banks with Peter Erdoes, *Ojibwa Warrior: Dennis Banks and the Rise of the American Indian Movement* (Norman: University of Oklahoma Press, 2005); Nick Estes, *Our History Is the Future*. For the view of the FBI, see Stanley David Lyman, *Wounded Knee, 1973: A Personal Account* (Lincoln: University of Nebraska Press, 1993).

10. In their interviews for the PBS account of the Occupation, "We Shall Remain: Wounded Knee," the former hostages claimed they had not wanted to be called hostages and, furthermore, had not wanted to leave the village because then the FBI would begin killing the activists. But the FBI saw the matter very differently, calling AIM a terrorist organization. To see how controversial any discussion of the Occupation still is—even one at an academic conference—see Stew Magnuson, *Wounded Knee 1973: Still Bleeding* (Arlington, VA: Court Bridge Publishing, 2013).

11. "We Shall Remain: Wounded Knee," PBS, *American Experience*, 1.

12. Crow Dog, *Lakota Woman*, 161–64.

13. "We Shall Remain: Wounded Knee," PBS, *American Experience*, 2–3.

14. AIM, only one organization within the Red Power movement, was founded in Minneapolis, where many Natives had been forcibly relocated in the 1950s and 1960s or displaced due to the flooding of Native land by the Oahe Dam. The Lakota connected with Native people from other nations there as well as with activists in the African American community, including members of the Black Panther party. Members founded "survival schools," including the Little Red School House to preserve Native culture. The Occupation followed other well-publicized actions, including a protest march known as the Trail of Broken Treaties, the occupation of the Bureau of Indian Affairs (BIA) building in Washington, DC, and smaller local actions at the Naval Air Station in Minneapolis, Sheep Mountain in the Badlands, and Mount Rushmore. Estes, *Our History Is the Future*, 169–80.

15. David Treuer, *The Heartbeat of Wounded Knee: Native America Since 1890* (New York: Riverhead Books, 2019), 320.

16. Estes, *Our History Is the Future*, 38–39.

17. "We Shall Remain: Wounded Knee," PBS, *American Experience*, 8; Estes, *Our History Is the Future*, 192.

18. "We Shall Remain: Wounded Knee," PBS, *American Experience*, 11. For a new interpretation of the Ghost Dance and its role in the massacre, see Louis Warren, *God's Red Son: The Ghost Dance Religion and the Making of Modern America* (New York: Basic Books, 2017).

19. Dee Brown, *Bury My Heart at Wounded Knee: An Indian History of the West* (New York: Holt, Rinehart, and Winston, 1970). Another book of that era that gave voice to Native history and politics was Vine DeLoria Jr., *Custer Died for Your Sins: An Indian Manifesto* (Norman: University of Oklahoma Press, 1969).

20. "We Shall Remain: Wounded Knee," PBS, *American Experience*, 7.

21. Matthiessen, *In the Spirit of Crazy Horse*, 59–61.

22. The habit of assaulting Indians was hardly limited to the border towns of the Northern Plains. A civil rights case was brought against the city of Farmington, New Mexico, after it was revealed that several intoxicated Navajo men had died after being "rolled" by local teenagers, a common practice in the area. New Mexico Advisory Committee to the US Commission on Civil Rights, *The Farmington Report: A Conflict of Cultures* (July 1975).

23. "We Shall Remain: Wounded Knee," PBS, *American Experience*, 7.

24. Smith and Warrior, *Like a Hurricane*, 182–83. For a full description of the events in Custer and how they were later recalled see Justin C. Hammer, "Race and Perception: The 1973 American Indian Movement Protest in Custer, South Dakota" (master's thesis, University of South Dakota, 2011).

25. Smith and Warrior, *Like a Hurricane*, 183–86; Matthiessen, *In the Spirit of Crazy Horse*, 62–63; Hammer, "Race and Perception," 58–61.

26. Bill Zimmerman, *Airlift to Wounded Knee* (Chicago: Swallow Press, 1976), 9.

27. "We Shall Remain: Wounded Knee," PBS, *American Experience*, 18.

28. Ibid., 22.

29. Smith and Warrior, *Like a Hurricane*, 271–72.

30. John Grenier, *The First Way of War: American War-Making on the Frontier, 1607–1814* (Cambridge: Cambridge University Press, 2005).

31. Roxanne Dunbar-Ortiz, *Loaded: A Disarming History of the Second Amendment* (San Francisco: City Lights Publishers, 2018).

32. Mark A. Lempke, *My Brother's Keeper: George McGovern and Progressive Christianity* (Amherst: University of Massachusetts Press, 2017), 178.

33. Quoted in David Treuer, *Rez Life: An Indian's Journey Through Reservation Life* (New York: Grove Press, 2011), 139.

34. Michael Lawson, *Dammed Indians: The Pick Sloan Project and the Missouri River Sioux, 1944–1980* (Norman: University of Oklahoma Press, 1994).

35. Sean J. Flynn, "Bicultural Conservatism: Native American Congressman Ben Reifel and the GOP," in Jon K. Lauck, John E. Miller, and Donald M. Simmons Jr., eds., *The Plains Political Tradition: Essays on South Dakota Political Culture*, vol. 2 (Pierre: South Dakota Historical Society Press, 2014), 179–208. See also Sean J. Flynn, *Without Reservation: Benjamin Reifel and American Indian Acculturation* (Pierre: South Dakota Historical Society Press, 2018).

36. Jonathan Ellis, "More Than 30 Years Ago, Another S.D. Politician Called for Abolishing Reservations," *Argus Leader*, May 31, 2018, https://www.argusleader.com/story/news/2018/05/31/more-than-30-years-ago-south-dakota-rep-clint-roberts-called-abolishing-reservations/660963002/.

37. Tom Brokaw, *A Long Way from Home: Growing Up in the American Heartland in the Forties and Fifties* (New York: Random House, 2002), 188–91.

38. Brokaw, *A Long Way from Home*, 107.

39. Harris Survey, Wounded Knee Legal Defense/Offense Committee: An Inventory of Its Records (hereafter WKLD/OC), Box 91, Jury Selection surveys, Minnesota State Historical Society, St. Paul, MN.

40. "Comments on the Main Purpose of AIM" and "Comments on Fair Trial in Custer County," WKLD/OC, Box 6, Custer County Opinion Survey: Methods and Results with Comments. See also "Comments Made in Addition to Response to Survey," WKLD/OC, Box 92, Juror Selection Surveys; "Minnehaha County Survey, Jay Schulman, 1975," WKLD/OC, Box 91, Jury Selection Surveys. Mary Crow Dog did not need to see the survey data: she described Rapid City as "the most racist city in the country as far as Indian people are concerned." *Lakota Woman*, 48.

41. Most stores on the Northern Plains ended the practice of selling or displaying Confederate flags in the 2010s, although it had been common practice until then. See Jerry Shaw, "Where You Can Find Confederate Flag Flying in South Dakota," https://www.newsmax.com/fastfeatures/confederate-flag-south-dakota/2015/09/03/id/673513/; https://bismarcktribune.com/news/state-and-regional/flag-of-confederacy-flies-in-hebron/article_511855a7-c9bd-55fc-8f08-d704523368d5.html; Kevin Woster, "Confederate Flag Removed at Hot Springs VA Center," https://rapidcityjournal.com/news/confederate-flag-removed-at-hot-springs-va-center-as-officials/article_bddac104-c6cd-5698-907e-52925ae7d80b.html. But there are important exceptions. A local internet radio host, Reb Rider, incorporates a Confederate flag into his logo. See https://www.facebook.com/profile.php?id = 100010268624131. In 2017 and 2018 a rumor circulated that the extreme left-wing group "Antifa" had planned to riot at the Sturgis rally because there would be "too many American and Confederate flags there." See https://www.snopes.com/fact-check/antifa-protest-sturgis-2018/.

42. Matthew Prigge, "Dixie North: George Wallace and the 1964 Wisconsin Primary," https://shepherdexpress.com/news/what-made-milwaukee-famous/dixie-north-george-wallace-1964-wisconsin-presidential-primary/#/questions.

43. Quoted in Ian Haney-Lopez, *Dog Whistle Politics: How Coded Racial Appeals Have Reinvented Racism and Wrecked the Middle Class* (New York: Oxford University Press, 2014), 16.

44. See map of Wallace vote on the Northern Plains in Kevin Phillips, *The Emerging Republican Majority* (New York: Arlington House, 1969), 451. Of course, Wallace appealed to northern whites on issues other than race. He was also a critic of the federal bureaucracy, describing its officials as "pointy headed bureaucrats." This appealed to anti–New Deal voters. Joseph E. Lowndes, *From the New Deal to the New Right: Race and the Southern Origins of Modern Conservatism* (New Haven, CT: Yale University Press, 2008), 77–105. See also Dan T. Carter, *The Politics of Rage: George Wallace, the New Conservatism, and the Transformation of American Politics* (New York: Simon and Schuster, 1995).

45. Phillips, *Emerging Republican Majority*.

46. Rick Perlstein, "Exclusive: Lee Atwater's Infamous 1981 Interview on the Southern Strategy," *The Nation*, November 13, 2012, https://www.the nation.com/articles/exclusive-lee-atwaters-infamous-1981-interview-southern-strategy/.

47. Phillips, *Emerging Republican Majority*, quoted in James Boyd, "Nixon's Southern Strategy," *New York Times*, May 17, 1970, 215. On "dog whistles," their origins, and their consequences, see Haney-Lopez, *Dog Whistle Politics*; and Carol Anderson, *White Rage: The Unspoken Truth of Our Racial Divide* (New York: Bloomsbury, 2016). Historians who argue that class rather than race and the experience of suburbanization drove southerners to the Republican Party are Byron E. Shafer and Richard Johnston, *The End of Southern Exceptionalism: Class, Race, and Partisan Change in the Postwar South* (Cambridge, MA: Harvard University Press, 2009); and Matthew D. Lassiter, *The Silent Majority: Suburban Politics in the Sunbelt South* (Princeton, NJ: Princeton University Press, 2007). This thesis does not help explain why Dakotans, from largely rural communities and very few affluent suburbs became attracted to the ideas of the New Right.

48. Phillips, *Emerging Republican Majority*, 410–51.

49. Boyd, "Nixon's Southern Strategy."

50. On "isolationism," see Phillips, *Emerging Republican Majority*, 428–32.

51. In 1970, a Democrat, James J. Barnett, suggested a factor that most strategists had missed and which, in his mind, explained the growth of conservatism in the region: the presence of "national security military institutions." Quoted in Boyd, "Nixon's Southern Strategy."

52. Brokaw, *A Long Way from Home*, 194.

53. Of course there were exceptions: letters and editorials that were openly racist. The editor of the Chadron, Nebraska, newspaper stated that "the Natives were getting restless." Quoted in Kevin C. Abourezk, "From Red Fears to Red Power: The Story of Newspaper Coverage of Wounded Knee, 1890, and Wounded Knee, 1973" (master's thesis, College of Journalism and Mass Communications, University of Nebraska, 2012), 60. George McGovern received an equally blunt letter. "I have had men tell me we are heading toward the same situation that is going on over in Ireland. Only the Indians and Collard [*sic*] people will be killing the white people." Harold Waldt to George McGovern, March 22, 1973, George McGovern Papers (GM), Department of Special Collections, Seeley Mudd Library, Princeton University (PU), Princeton, New Jersey.

54. Richard Tate, for example, wrote, "Our country is a sad state of affairs when tax dollars are used to pay a radical revolutionary group to go around destroying property on any pretext they can think up." Richard Tate to Richard Kneip, n.d., Richard F. Kneip Papers, Box 28, Mabel Richardson Collection, University of South Dakota (USD), Vermillion, South Dakota.

55. Raymond French to Richard Kneip, May 2, 1974, Kneip Papers, Box 28, USD.

56. Reverend Robert D. Wright to Richard Kneip, February 28, 1973, Kneip Papers, Box 28, USD.

57. Kenneth Munce to Richard Kneip, n.d., Kneip Papers, Box 28, USD.

58. H. Sanders to George McGovern, March 23, 1973, McGovern Papers.

59. Rex Witte to Richard Kneip, May 9, 1974, Kneip Papers, Box 28, USD.

60. Genevieve Layman to Richard Kneip, n.d., Kneip Papers, Box 28, USD.

61. Quoted in Rolland Dewing, "South Dakota Newspaper Coverage of the 1973 Occupation of Wounded Knee," *South Dakota History* (1982): 54.

62. Vera Hullinger to James Armstrong, March 23, 1973, "Correspondence 1973–1974," Church and Society Records, General Commission on Archives and History, The United Methodist Church, Drew University, Madison, New Jersey (hereafter CSR-UMC-DU).

63. Earl Allen to Richard Kneip, May 10, 1974, Kneip Papers, Box 28, USD.

64. Lyndsey Layton, "Palin Apologizes for 'Real America' Comments," *Washington Post*, October 22, 2008.

65. Earl Allen to Richard Kneip, May 10, 1974, Kneip Papers, Box 28, USD.

66. Dan Gallimore to Richard Kneip, May 15, 1974, Kneip Papers, Box 28, 3, USD.

67. Vera Hullinger to James Armstrong.

68. Michael Gerson, "The Last Temptation," *The Atlantic*, April 2018, https://www.the atlantic.com/magazine/archive/2018/04/the-last-temptation/554066/.

69. David L. Peterson to Bishop James Armstrong, June 26, 1973, James Armstrong Papers, Correspondence 1973–1974, CSR-UMC-DU.

70. Harvey Hullinger to "whom it may concern," March 26, 1973, James Armstrong Papers, Correspondence 1973–1974, CSR-UMC-DU.

71. Burnell A. Lund to James Armstrong, April 5, 1973, James Armstrong Papers, Correspondence 1973–1974, CSR-UMC-DU. See also "Church Suspends ALC Support over AIM Funding," *Rapid City Journal*, April 7, 1973.

72. Richardson, "S.D.'s Social Conscience Prepares to Move On," 1B.

73. Ibid.

74. Quoted in Dewing, "South Dakota Newspaper Coverage," 56. Dewing also quotes the Right Reverend Walter Jones of Sioux Falls, bishop of the Episcopal diocese of South Dakota, "I am heartsick over the number of letters and telephone calls I have received full of hate and vindictiveness telling me how wrongly the Episcopal Church has acted" (56).

75. Majorie Hyer, "Peacekeeping Minister of Crisis Dies," *Washington Post*, December 13, 1983, https://www.washingtonpost.com/archive/local/1983/12/17/peace-keeping-mini ster-of-crisis-dies/f40d00cf-375a-47a8-a16b-4066f754c2bd/?utm_term=.478a42b94a8e.

76. Methodists in Sioux Falls signed a letter of protest when Armstrong publicly endorsed George McGovern for president. Mark A. Lempke, "Senator McGovern and the Role of Religion in South Dakota Political Culture," in Lauck, Miller, and Simmons Jr., *The Plains Political Tradition*, 2:168–69.

77. Paul Boyer, "The Evangelical Resurgence in 1970s American Protestantism," in Bruce J. Schulman and Julian E. Zelizer, eds., *Rightward Bound: Making America Conservative in the 1970s* (Cambridge, MA: Harvard University Press, 2008), 35.

78. Lempke, *My Brother's Keeper*, 178–80.

79. Paul Boyer, "The Evangelical Resurgence in 1970s American Protestantism," 33–35. While Pentecostals are a small subset of evangelicals, they are nationally organized enough to count—unlike many other evangelical churches that operate independently. Albeit small in real numbers, then, the relative growth of Pentecostal churches in the region beginning in 1970 is remarkable. By 2010 a higher percentage of religious believers in North Dakota affiliated themselves with Pentecostalism than with Presbyterianism or Congregationalism combined. In South Dakota they were neck and neck. See http://religionatlas.org/?page_id=18.

Jay M. Price has recently documented the spread of evangelical Protestantism into Kansas and north into Iowa and South Dakota, arguing that it blurs regional boundaries between the South and Midwest and Great Plains. "Where the Midwest Meets the Bible Belt: Using Religion to Explore the Midwest's Southwestern Edge," in Jon K. Lauck, ed., *The Interior Borderlands: Regional Identity in the Midwest and Great Plains* (Sioux Falls, SD: The Center for Western Studies, Augustana University, 2019): 229–42.

80. Quoted in Lempke, *My Brother's Keeper*, 35.

81. Gerson, "The Last Temptation."

82. Joseph Crespino, "Civil Rights and the Religious Right," in Schulman and Zelizer, *Rightward Bound*, 90–105.

83. Quoted in ibid., 91.

84. Through the 1980s and 1990s, Christian schools, radio stations, bookstores, and home-schooling organizations would also come in large numbers to the Dakotas. Weston Stephens, "Religious Institution Data, North and South Dakota, 1970–2000" (unpublished manuscript in author's possession, 2017). By permission. For the 14 schools in South Dakota that belong to the Association of Christian Schools International, see https://www.private schoolreview.com/south-dakota/association-of-christian-schools-international-(acsi) -members. For an overview of the decline of mainline congregations and the growing dominance of evangelical Protestantism among Protestants as a whole, see Pew Research Center, "America's Changing Religious Landscape," May 15, 2015, https://www.pewforum.org/2015/ 05/12/americas-changing-religious-landscape/.

85. Brian Purnell and Jeanne Theoharis with Komozi Woodard, eds., *The Strange Careers of Jim Crow North: Segregation and Struggle Outside the South* (New York: New York University Press, 2018).

86. In 1967 Huey Newton wrote, "There is a great similarity between the occupying army in Southeast Asia and the occupation of our communities by the racist police." Quoted in Joshua Bloom and Waldo E. Martin Jr., *Black Against Empire: The History and Politics of the Black Panther Party* (Berkeley: University of California Press, 2016), 2.

87. Ibid., 72, 199.

88. John P. Adams, *At the Heart of the Whirlwind* (New York: Harper and Row, 1976), 5.

89. Ibid., 6.

90. McGovern to Redmond, March 21, 1973, McGovern Papers, Princeton University.

91. "Forked Tongue?," *Lincoln Evening Journal*, March 27, 1973, 4, quoted in Abourezk, "From Red Fears to Red Power," 56.

92. Quoted in Heppler, "The American Indian Movement and South Dakota Politics," in Jon K. Lauck, John E. Miller, and Donald M. Simmons Jr., eds., *The Plains Political Tradition: Essays on South Dakota Political Culture*, vol. 1 (Pierre: South Dakota Historical Society Press, 2014): 272.

93. Banks, *Ojibwa Warrior*, 44.

94. Ibid., 55.

95. "We Shall Remain: Wounded Knee," PBS, *American Experience*, transcript, 1.

96. Ibid., 4.

97. Quoted in Abourezk, "From Red Fears to Red Power," 64.

98. Quoted in Dewing, "South Dakota Newspaper Coverage," 56.

99. Quoted in Hammer, "Race and Perception," 61.

100. Quoted in Estes, *Our History Is the Future*, 191.

101. "Reverend John Adams Discusses Role of the FBI at Wounded Knee," *Minnesota Public Radio*, http://archive.mprnews.org/stories/19740326/reverend-john-adams-discusses-role-fbi-wounded-knee.

102. Heppler, "The American Indian Movement and South Dakota Politics," 276.

103. "We Shall Remain: Wounded Knee," PBS, *American Experience*, 5.

104. Jill K. Gill, "Preventing a Second Massacre at Wounded Knee, 1973: United Methodists Meditate for Peace," *Methodist History* 43 (October 2004): 45.

105. Quoted in ibid.

106. "We Shall Remain: Wounded Knee," PBS, *American Experience*, 19.

107. Quoted in Andrew H. Malcolm, "Occupation of Wounded Knee Is Ended," *New York Times*, May 9, 1973, 1.

108. "We Shall Remain: Wounded Knee," PBS, *American Experience*, transcript, 23.

109. Peltier's trial is covered in Matthiessen, *In the Spirit of Crazy Horse*, 83–102. In 1980, Governor Bill Janklow sued to stop the sale of Matthiessen's book. After eight years of litigation, his case was thrown out by the South Dakota Supreme Court. See Elizabeth Mehren, "Suit Against 'Spirit of Crazy Horse' Ends," *L.A. Times*, November 16, 1990, https://www.latimes.com/archives/la-xpm-1990–11–16-vw-4902-story.html.

110. https://www.amnesty.org/en/documents/amr51/9791/2019/en/.

111. Estes, *Our History Is the Future*, 195.

112. James Gibson, *Warrior Dreams: Violence and Manhood in Post-Vietnam America* (New York: Hill and Wang, 1994); Susan Jeffords, *Hard Bodies: Hollywood Masculinity in the Reagan Era* (New Brunswick, NJ: Rutgers University Press, 1993).

113. Janklow won almost 71 percent of the vote in Pennington Country, home to Rapid City. Lorna A. Herseth, South Dakota Secretary of State, comp., "Official Election Returns for South Dakota: General Election," November 5, 1974, 6, https://sdsos.gov/elections-voting/assets/74SDGEN.pdf.

114. Josh Garrett-Davis, *Ghost Dances: Proving Up on the Great Plains* (Boston: Little, Brown, 2012), 41.

115. The most recent change to the state gun laws is the passage of "constitutional carry"—a law that permits carrying a concealed weapon without a permit. It was the first bill signed by the new governor, Kristi Noem. "South Dakota No Longer Requires Permit for Concealed Weapon," *Sioux City Journal*, July 3, 2019, https://siouxcityjournal.com/news/state-and-regional/south-dakota/south-dakota-no-longer-requires-permit-for-concealed-carry/article_ca11c81b-0d9f-5374-a118–8c2a08895124.html.

116. Matthiessen, *In the Spirit of Crazy Horse*, 106.

117. Quoted in ibid., 107.

118. Quoted in Heppler, "The American Indian Movement and South Dakota Politics," 278.

119. Mary-Lee Chai, *Hapa Girl: A Memoir* (Philadelphia: Temple University Press, 2007), 120–24.

120. Matthiessen, *In the Spirit of Crazy Horse*, 108–9.

121. Ibid., 119. See also Garrett-Davis, *Ghost Dances*, 42.

122. Joshua Garrett-Davis, "The Red Power Movement and the Yankton Sioux Industries Pork Processing Plant Takeover of 1975," *South Dakota History* 36 (Summer 2006): 197.

123. Ibid., 179.

124. Ibid., 180.

125. Ibid., 205.

126. Quoted in Matthiessen, *In the Spirit of Crazy Horse*, 194.

127. Ibid., 107, 132.

128. Wayne King, "Bradley Offers Bill to Return Land to the Sioux," *New York Times*, March 11, 1987, https://www.nytimes.com/1987/03/11/us/bradley-offers-bill-to-return-land -to-sioux.html.

129. Quoted in Garrett-Davis, *Ghost Dances*, 44.

130. Heppler, "The American Indian Movement and South Dakota Politics," 286n48.

131. Bruce Selcraig, "Camp Fear," *Mother Jones*, November/December 2000, https:// www.motherjones.com/politics/2000/11/camp-fear/.

132. Denise Ross, "Gina Score's Parents Still Hurting," *Rapid City Journal*, December 8, 2000.

133. "1980s Crime: From 8-Tracks to Stun Guns," *Mitchell Republic*, February 8, 2014, www.mitchellrepublic.com/lifestyle/2226378-1980s-crime-8-tracks-stun-guns.

134. Arielle Zionts, "South Dakota Incarceration Rate Highest in Country," *Rapid City Journal*, October 7, 2019, https://rapidcityjournal.com/news/local/crime-and-courts/south -dakota-jails-most-per-capita-study-says/article_34584f2b-8a2f-52ec-8bdc-6c98b24 84958.html.

135. "1980s Crime: From 8-Tracks to Stun Guns."

136. Mary Garrigan, "Custer's Sheriff's Reserve Came Out of 1973 Riot," *Rapid City Journal*, May 12, 2011.

137. Estes, *Our History Is the Future*, 197.

138. Ibid.

139. Nationally, Native people are incarcerated at a rate of 38 percent higher than national average. Native men are incarcerated at four times the rate of white men; Native women at six times the rate of white women. Jake Flanagin, "Reservation to Prison Pipeline," *Quartz*, April 27, 2015; Lakota People's Law Project, https://www.lakotalaw.org/.

140. Estes, *Our History Is the Future*, 190–91.

141. Steve Lapointe, conversation with author, October 2018.

142. Clayton C. Cramer and David B. Kopel, "'Shall Issue': The New Wave of Concealed Carry Permit Laws," *Tennessee Law Review* 62 (Spring 1995): 679–757, http://www.davekopel .com/2A/LawRev/ShallIssue.htm#c1. See also Seth Tupper, "Concealed-Carry Bills Would Reverse 155 Years of State-Territorial Policy," *Rapid City Journal*, January 20, 2019, https:// rapidcityjournal.com/news/local/concealed-carry-bills-would-reverse-years-of-state -territorial-policy/article_ceef18e9-7047-52d2-8977-b4ce2b6ddc82.html.

143. Steven Rosenfeld, "The NRA Once Supported Gun Control," *Salon*, January 14, 2013; Adam Winkler, *Gunfight: The Battle over the Right to Bear Arms in America* (New York: Norton, 2013).

144. Dunbar-Ortiz, *Loaded*, 165. In 2016 military service was the best predictor of gun ownership. Kathleen Belew has shown how service in the military during Vietnam also led to the creation of new radical White Power organizations and the rise of paramilitary violence. Belew, *Bring the War Home*.

145. Quoted in Dunbar-Ortiz, *Loaded*, 202. Simpson also boasted, "How steady you hold your rifle; that's gun control in Wyoming." In 2015 South Dakota had more than twenty-four guns per person; North Dakota had more than seventeen per person. See https://hunting mark.com/gun-ownership-stats/.

146. #24, September 20, 2015, https://www.thehighroad.org/index.php?threads/south -dakota.788366/.

147. "What Are South Dakota's Firearms Laws?," *Argus Leader*, February 22, 2018, https://www.argusleader.com/story/news/2018/02/22/what-south-dakotas-firearm-laws/ 359387002/. See also the NRA site which links to specific state legislation: https://www.nraila .org/gun-laws/state-gun-laws/south-dakota/.

148. #25, September 21, 2015, South Dakota, The High Road, https://www.thehighroad .org/index.php?threads/south-dakota.788366/.

149. Estes, *Our Past Is the Future*, 33–35.

150. Ibid., 196.

151. Ibid., 4–5.

152. Ibid., 251.

153. Quoted in ibid., 48.

Chapter 8

Note to chapter title: This term used here and throughout the chapter is from Debra Marquart's poem, "small buried things," from Marquart, *Small Buried Things: Poems* (Moorhead, MN: New Rivers Press, 2015), 52.

1. Debra Marquart, *The Horizontal World: Growing Up Wild in the Middle of Nowhere* (New York: Counterpoint, 2006), 97.

2. Michael J. Lansing, *Insurgent Democracy: The Nonpartisan League in North American Politics* (Chicago: University of Chicago Press, 2015), 149–51.

3. Marquart, *The Horizontal World*, 97–98.

4. Marquart, "small buried things," 41.

5. Ibid., 42.

6. Ibid., 41.

7. Ibid., 49.

8. Debra Marquart, interview, Iowa Public Radio, https://www.iowapublicradio.org/ post/debra-marquart-chin-whiskers-fracking-things-not-put-your-mouth#stream/0.

9. Marquart, "small buried things," 53.

10. Todd Fuchs, "Oil Boom on the Bakken Helped Strengthen National Security," *Grand Forks Herald*, May 10, 2018, http://www.inforum.com/opinion/letters/4443983-oil-boom -bakken-helped-strengthen-national-security.

11. Jeremy Miller, "The Shining: A Night in the Heart of Energy Independence," in Taylor Brorby and Stefanie Brook Trout, eds., *Fracture: Essays, Poems, and Stories on Fracking in America* (North Liberty, IA: Ice Cube Press, 2016), 250–51.

12. Quoted in David Vine, *Base Nation: How U.S. Military Bases Abroad Harm Americans and the World* (New York: Henry Holt, 2017), 231.

13. In 2017 a nuclear bomb was flown across the country in error before any officials in Minot realized it was missing. In 2018 officials in Minot had to ask local people to help them

find lost explosives and a machine gun. See "Air Force Base That Lost Explosives: We're Also Missing a Machine Gun," *Washington Post*, May 18, 2018, https://www.washingtonpost.com/news/checkpoint/wp/2018/05/18/air-force-base-that-lost-explosives-were-also-missing-a-machine-gun/?utm_term=.39112e44b193.

14. Marquart, "small buried things," 50–51.

15. Chris Hedges, "Live at Politics and Prose," August, 2018, https://player.fm/series/live-at-politics-and-prose-2355583/chris-hedges-live-at-politics-and-prose.

16. Gretchen Heefner, *The Missile Next Door: The Minuteman in the American Heartland* (Cambridge, MA: Harvard University Press, 2012), 155, 267n32.

17. Rev. L. J. Murtaugh, "Support Silos, Not Missiles," letter to the editor, *Argus Leader*, March 20, 1985, 8.

18. Marquart, "small buried things," 52.

19. Rates of child neglect and abuse, divorce, drug use, domestic violence, and suicide all climbed during the Farm Crisis. Pamela Riney-Kehrberg, "Children of the Crisis: Farm Youth in Troubled Times," *Middle West Review* 2 (Fall 2015): 11–25.

20. Richard Reeves, "The Ideological Election," *New York Times*, February 19, 1984, https://www.nytimes.com/1984/02/19/magazine/the-ideological-election.html.

21. Harry C. Boyte, Heather Booth, and Steve Max, *Citizen Action and the New American Populism* (Philadelphia: Temple University Press, 1986).

22. In rural Minnesota, a farmer and his son asked their banker to come to their farm where they ambushed and killed him. Catherine McNicol Stock, *Rural Radicals: Righteous Rage in the American Grain*, 2nd ed. (Ithaca, NY: Cornell University Press, 2017), 87–90.

23. On "people-first principles," see Sarah M. Vogel, "Advocate for Agriculture," in Susan E. Wefald, *Important Voices: North Dakota's Women Elected State Officials Share Their Stories, 1893–2013* (Fargo, ND: Institute for Regional Studies Press, 2014), 65.

24. In 2019, the North Dakota legislature passed a bill redefining a "family" member to include second cousins. "Second Cousins Added to North Dakota's Corporate Farming Law," *Fargo Forum*, April 18, 2019, https://www.inforum.com/news/government-and-politics/1007441-Second-cousins-added-to-North-Dakotas-corporate-farming-law.

25. William C. Pratt, "Using History to Make History? Progressive Farm Organizing During the Farm Revolt of the 1980s," *Annals of Iowa* 55, no. 1 (Winter 1996): 45.

26. William Greider, "The Last Farm Crisis," *The Nation*, November 2, 2000, https://www.thenation.com/article/last-farm-crisis/.

27. Robert Wuthnow, *The Left Behind: Decline and Rage in Rural America* (Princeton, NJ: Princeton University Press, 2018), 94; "Days are Numbered for Pair of Weathered Grain Elevators," *Bismarck Tribune*, May 6, 2007, https://bismarcktribune.com/news/state-and-regional/days-are-numbered-for-weathered-pair-of-grain-elevators/article_38301606–68d3–5467–9403–3cfac4ebad6b.html.

28. Scott Kraft, "Were Foreclosure Pressures to Blame? Family Farm Deaths Shock a Hamlet," *Los Angeles Times*, January 10, 1986, http://articles.latimes.com/1986–01–10/news/mn-839_1_farm-crisis.

29. Quoted in ibid. See also "Broken Heartland," *The Nation*, February 8, 1986, https://www.thefreelibrary.com/Broken+heartland.-a04129459.

30. Kathryn Marie Dudley, *Debt and Dispossession: Farm Loss in the American Heartland* (Chicago: University of Chicago Press, 2000).

31. Nathan A. Rosenberg and Bryce Wilson Stucki, "The Butz Stops Here: Why the Food Movement Needs to Rethink Agricultural History," *Journal of Food Law and Policy* 13 (2017): 19–20.

32. Caroline Tauxe, "Family Cohesion vs. Capitalist Hegemony: Cultural Accommodation on the North Dakota Farm," *Dialectical Anthropology* 17, no. 3 (1992): 297. See also Kristin L. Hoganson, *The Heartland: An American History* (New York: Penguin, 2019).

33. Rosenberg and Stucki argue that these infamous words were actually first uttered by President Eisenhower's secretary of agriculture, Ezra Benson. "The Butz Stops Here," 17–19.

34. Iowa Public Television, "The Farm Crisis: Causes of the Crisis," http://www.iptv.org/mtom/classroom/module/13999/farm-crisis.

35. F. Larry Leistritz, Arlen Leholm, and Harlan Hughes, "Coping with the Farm Crisis in North Dakota," http://agris.fao.org/agris-search/search.do?recordID = US8866478, 56.

36. Ibid.

37. Tauxe, "Family Cohesion vs. Capitalist Hegemony," 313.

38. Rebecca Stoll, "Desperate Farm Wives: Gender, Activism, and Traditionalism in the Farm Crisis," *Middle West Review* 2 (Fall 2015): 33–49.

39. Jessica Giard, "Farm Crisis Unites a State," *Daily Republic*, February 14, 2014, https://www.mitchellrepublic.com/news/2236577–1980s-series-farm-crisis-unites-state.

40. Herbert S. Schell, *History of South Dakota*, 4th rev. ed. (Pierre: South Dakota State Historical Society Press, 2004), 351–53.

41. Ibid., 353.

42. Anna Jauhola, "During '80s, Downtown Transitioned," *Mitchell Daily Republic*, March 21, 2014, https://www.mitchellrepublic.com/news/2473044-during-80s-downtown-transitioned-cafes-retailers-niche-stores-coffee-shops.

43. Chris Mueller, "Population Decline Hits Rural Areas Hard," *Daily Republic*, March 1, 2014, https://www.mitchellrepublic.com/news/2352700-population-decline-hits-rural-areas-hard.

44. Ibid.

45. Reeves, "The Ideological Election."

46. Jay Ward, "Agriculture During the Reagan Years" (PhD diss., University of Missouri, 2015), 14–15, 297; Don Paarlberg, "Agriculture," in Charles L. Heatherly, ed., *Mandate for Leadership: Policy Management in a Conservative Administration* (Washington, DC: Heritage Foundation, 1981), chapter 1.

47. Quoted in William Greider, "The Education of David Stockman," *The Atlantic*, December 1981, https://www.theatlantic.com/magazine/archive/1981/12/the-education-of-david-stockman/305760/.

48. Ronald Reagan, "Radio Address to the Nation on Agriculture and Grain Exports," October 15, 1982, https://www.reaganlibrary.gov/research/speeches/101582a. See also Jonathan Harsch, "Reagan Farm Policy Will Continue Bipartisan Effort to 'Turn Farmers Loose,'" *Christian Science Monitor*, November 14, 1980.

49. Jason Manning, "The Midwest Farm Crisis of the 1980s,"http://eightiesclub.tripod.com/id395.htm.

50. Pratt, "Using History to Make History?," 24–45.

51. Cory Haala, "Replanting the Grassroots: The South Dakota Democratic Party from McGovern to Daschle, 1980–1986," in Jon K. Lauck, John E. Miller, and Paula M. Nelson,

eds., *The Plains Political Tradition: Essays on South Dakota Political Culture*, vol. 3 (Pierre: South Dakota Historical Society Press, 2019), 182–209.

52. Jim Hightower, "Saving the Family Farm," *Washington Post*, October 1, 1985; James Risen, "Four Candidates Back Liberal Programs: Militant Farmers Wield Power in Iowa Caucuses," *Los Angeles Times*, November 24, 1987, http://articles.latimes.com/1987–11–24/news/mn-24284_1_iowa-farm-unity/2.

53. Quoted in Manning, "Midwest Farm Crisis of the 1980s."

54. Steven A. Stofferahn, "The Persistence of Agrarian Activism: The National Farmers Organization in South Dakota," in Jon K. Lauck, John E. Miller, and Donald C. Simmons Jr., eds., *The Plains Political Tradition: Essays on South Dakota Political Culture*, vol. 2 (Pierre: South Dakota Historical Society Press, 2014), 209–41.

55. Denise O'Brien, "Memories of the Crisis," *Middle West Review* 2 (Fall 2015): 51–68; Stoll, "Desperate Farm Wives."

56. Farm Crisis organizers would have been well aware of the stunning victory experienced by the United Family Farmers, which had brought a halt to the flooding of one hundred thousand acres of land by the Army Corps of Engineers at the Oahe dam. Rather than promote violence, they made coalitions with environmental groups, Native people, and local scholars to bring a new perspective to the plan. See Peter Carrells, *Uphill Against Water: The Great Dakota Water War* (Lincoln: University of Nebraska Press, 1999).

57. "Jesse Jackson Donned a Farmers Cap," April 1, 1985, https://www.upi.com/Archives/1985/04/01/Jesse-Jackson-donned-a-farmers-cap-Monday-climbed-aboard/2843481179600/.

58. Giard, "Farm Crisis Unites a State."

59. *Argus Leader*, January 9, 1985, 1.

60. *Argus Leader*, May 30, 1985, 4.

61. Eric Steven Zimmer, Art Marmorstein, and Matthew Remmich, "'Fewer Rabbis Than U.S. Senators': Jewish Political Activism in South Dakota," in Lauck, Miller, and Nelson, *Plains Political Tradition*, 3:112–39. Janklow's father was Jewish, and although Janklow was a practicing Lutheran, he had close ties to Stan Adelstein, an important conservative organizer from Rapid City.

62. "South Dakota Governor Calls Out Troopers to Stop Canadian Hogs," https://www.apnews.com/cd3d382cc1f05620bc26d52bfd081b09.

63. Quoted in the Spearfish *Daily Queen City Mail*, June 13, 1986, 1.

64. Emily Wanless, "Understanding South Dakota's Political Culture Through the 1994 Election of Governor William Janklow," in Lauck, Miller, and Nelson, *Plains Political Tradition*, 3:210–31.

65. "Governor Announces Sale of Core Rail Line," https://siouxcityjournal.com/news/state-and-regional/governor-announces-sale-of-core-rail-line/article_877f97c5-d489–5336-a4f1-c688b26c0814.html.

66. Bill Harlan, "Legislators to Consider $252 Million S.D. Cement Plant Offer," *Rapid City Journal*, December 23, 2000, https://rapidcityjournal.com/legislators-to-consider-million-s-d-cement-plant-offer/article_4eba44cc-5c32–574d-bb4b-2168f2d2b76f.html.

67. George A. Sinner and Bob Jansen, *Turning Points: A Memoir* (Fargo: North Dakota Institute for Regional Studies, 2011), 30.

68. Ibid., 136.

69. Sarah Vogel's grandfather, Frank Vogel, was a close associate of Bill Langer and, among other positions in the NPL, was the manager of the Bank of North Dakota.

70. Vogel, "Advocate for Agriculture," in Wefald, *Important Voices*, 65, 88.

71. Curt Stofferahn, "Farm Advocate Elected Ag Commissioner," *North American Farmer*, December 1988, 4. Vogel was inspired by her study of the legal actions taken by Governor Bill Langer and the North Dakota state legislature in 1933, including Langer's halt to all foreclosures. She wrote that "the legal developments of the 1930's are no longer simply of academic or historical interest" given the problems of the farm credit crisis in the 1980s. Sarah M. Vogel, "The Law of Hard Times: Debtor and Farmer Relief Actions of the 1933 North Dakota Legislative Session," *North Dakota Law Review* 60, no. 489 (1988): 512.

72. Before Conrad was tax commissioner, Byron Dorgan was; he attempted to tax the missile silos as a state utility. Cory Haala, email to author, July 10, 2019.

73. North Dakota ultimately lost a second, somewhat similar case against an office retailer, Quill Corporation, because, the state supreme court ruled, the company maintained no physical presence in the state. In 2018 the US Supreme Court took up a similar question brought by the state of South Dakota regarding taxing internet companies, finding that states could charge taxes on internet sales in *South Dakota v. Wayfair, Inc.*

74. "Court Affirms State's Way of Taxing Firms," *Bismarck Tribune*, May 24, 1991, 9A.

75. Mary Summers, "From the Heartland to Seattle: The Family Farm Movement of the 1980s and the Legacy of Agrarian State Building," in Catherine McNicol Stock and Robert D. Johnston, eds., *The Countryside in the Age of the Modern State: Political Histories of Rural America* (Ithaca, NY: Cornell University Press, 2001), 323.

76. Quoted in Haala, "Replanting the Grassroots," 186.

77. When asked years later what she thought of the fact that nearly all the producer cooperatives she had begun had been turned into corporations, Sarah Vogel replied that, "You could have knocked me over with a feather on that one. That was pretty shocking because the spirit of the co-op was to have a plant that was subject to farmer control and ownership, and to compete. That's been lost. And to a Canadian company? That's unbelievable. On the other hand, it wasn't a takeover. The farmers did the voting and gave up on their dream." Quoted in "Sarah Vogel Remains a Force Outside Politics," *Grand Forks Herald*, July 17, 2010.

78. Anonymous, email correspondence with author, August 10, 2018.

79. Cally Musland, "Jim Fuglie: What's a Democrat to Do in North Dakota?," February 9, 2016, http://kfgo.com/podcasts/news-views-with-joel-heitkamp/1703/jim-fuglie-whats-a -democrat-to-do-in-north-dakota/.

80. Quoted in Ward, "Agriculture During the Reagan Years," 298.

81. Ibid., 297–98.

82. Ibid., 290–302.

83. Summers, "From the Heartland to Seattle," 307.

84. Michael Stewart Foley, "'Everyone Was Pounding on Us': Front Porch Politics and the American Farm Crisis of the 1970s and 1980s," *Journal of Historical Sociology* 28 (March 2015): 110. See also Barry J. Barnett, "The U.S. Farm Financial Crisis of the 1980s," in Jane Adams, ed., *Fighting for the Farm, Rural America Transformed* (Philadelphia: University of Pennsylvania Press, 2003), 160–74.

85. Greider, "The Last Farm Crisis."

86. Ibid. See also https://historyrat.wordpress.com/2012/05/31/the-1985-farm-crisis -what-one-hand-giveth-the-other-taketh-away/.

87. Nick Reding, *Methland: The Death and Life of an American Small Town* (New York: Bloomsbury, 2009), 16–17, 47, 187–88. Reding explains that it was "no accident" that the meth epidemic developed at the height of the Farm Crisis. He quotes rural sociologist William Heffernan who claims that "most rural economic development specialists discount agriculture as a contributor to rural development [after 2000]" (189). He also describes the low-wage work that has taken the place of farming or manufacturing in many Midwestern communities. One man used meth and made it in his home. "The way he saw it, life in Greenville was a prison anyway. It was better to live well for a time and go back to jail than to pretend to make ends meet on [the] two hundred dollars a week and no health insurance that [his friend] Sean said a job at Wal-Mart would get him" (17). He also points to the closure of military bases in the 1990s as a contributing factor to the epidemic (59).

88. Haala, "Replanting the Grassroots," 187.

89. Lee Sigelman, "Economic Pressures and the Farm Vote: The Case of 1984," *Rural Sociology* 52, no. 2 (1987): 151–65. Sigelman quotes a journalist's conclusion that many farmers had just "reconciled to their doom" (161).

90. Ibid., 153.

91. Ibid., 153, 155.

92. Quoted in Boyte, Booth, and Max, *Citizen Action and the New American Populism*, 17.

93. O'Brien, "Memories of the Crisis," 62.

94. Summers, "From the Heartland to Seattle," 304–5.

95. Paul Harvey, "On the Eighth Day, God Made a Farmer," *Altus Times* (OK), May 19, 1986. For the 2013 Super Bowl ad which included Harvey's own narration and depicted only two nonwhite farmers, see https://www.youtube.com/watch?v=AMpZ0TGjbWE.

96. Quoted in Haala, "Replanting the Grassroots," 186.

97. Jon Lauck writes that the depiction of the Farm Crisis in *Country* (Pearce 1984) was so powerful that many South Dakotans who saw the film had to leave the cinema. See Jon K. Lauck, *American Agriculture and the Problem of Monopoly: The Political Economy of Grain Belt Farming, 1953–1980* (Lincoln: University of Nebraska Press, 2000), ix. Three of the lead actors from these films—Jane Fonda, Sissy Spacek, and Jessica Lange—testified to Congress about the Farm Crisis.

98. For the continued focus on the rural economy, but also a continued reliance on white performers (despite the use of the African American country star, Yola, on the first page), see https://www.farmaid.org/.

99. As of 2018 they still wore these stickers. Cory Haala, "'America Needs Farmers': Hawkeye Football and State Exceptionalism in 1980s Iowa" (paper delivered at the Midwestern History Association Annual Meeting, Grand Rapids, MI, June 6, 2018). Haala demonstrates that the Farm Bureau supported seemingly nonpolitical campaigns like ANF rather than the more radical Prairie Fire or Farm Aid programs. He argues that it set Iowa aside as an exceptional example of the crisis and of traditional values adding to the overall conservative nature of the media attention to and political outcomes of the crisis.

100. O'Brien, "Memories of the Crisis," 65. O'Brien was especially disappointed when the funding for her organization's women's project dried up.

101. An example of privately funded aid for farmers is the Ralph Engelstad Foundation's generous support for the Farm Rescue program, which uses volunteers to help farmers injured in accidents or who suffered weather disasters. See https://farmrescue.org/.

102. Summers, "From the Heartland to Seattle," 316.

103. Stock, *Rural Radicals: Righteous Rage in the American Grain*, 143–76. See also Kathleen Belew, *Bring the War Home: The White Power Movement and Paramilitary America* (Cambridge, MA: Harvard University Press, 2018). Belew argues that the experience of defeat in the Vietnam War inspired some white power radicals more than their experiences in the Farm Crisis.

104. Stock, *Rural Radicals: Righteous Rage in the American Grain*, 171–74. The tiny town of Leith, North Dakota, has been trying to fend off being taken over by a neo-Nazi group since 2012. See Samantha Schmidt, "The Mayor of Tiny North Dakota Town Shaken by Neo-Nazi Wants to Dissolve City Government," *Washington Post*, June 27, 2018, https://www.washingtonpost.com/news/morning-mix/wp/2018/06/27/the-mayor-of-tiny-north-dakota-town-shaken-by-neo-nazi-wants-to-dissolve-its-government/?utmterm=.474fcffec056.

105. Sinner and Jansen, *Turning Points*, 135.

106. Ibid., 137.

107. Terry Worster, "Crack Down Led to Proposed Amendment," *Rapid City Journal*, October 12, 1970, 8.

108. Linda Lea M. Viken, email conversation with author, September 16, 2018. See also Bob Mercer, "State Legislators Decide Video Lottery Must Stay," *Rapid City Journal*, February 16, 2018, https://rapidcityjournal.com/news/local/state-legislators-decide-video-lottery-must-stay/article_2381ce9f-2b90–5326–91fa-b659e93c879c.html.

109. Bill Janklow, interview, "Secret History of the Credit Card," PBS, *Frontline*, https://www.pbs.org/wgbh/pages/frontline/shows/credit/interviews/janklow.html. Early signs of deregulation of the financial sector were also important to the Citibank deal: in 1956, Congress relaxed some provisions of the Depression-era Glass Steagall Act, including one that had prohibited banks from crossing state lines to set up branches.

110. In 2004 Ralph J. Brown completed a study that showed the difference the arrival of Citibank and other firms had made to the Sioux Falls economy by comparing it with his "sister city," Sioux City, Iowa, eighty miles east on Interstate 29. See Brown, "A Tale of Two Cities: Sioux Falls and Sioux City," *South Dakota Business Review* 62 (December 2004): 1–8.

111. Governor Dennis Daugaard, quoted in Wanless, "Understanding South Dakota's Political Culture Through the 1994 Election of Governor William Janklow," 214.

112. Janklow, interview, "The Secret History of the Credit Card," PBS, *Frontline*, 3.

113. Quoted in Wanless, "Understanding South Dakota's Political Culture Through the 1994 Election of Governor William Janklow," 213.

114. Janklow, interview, "The Secret History of the Credit Card."

115. Ibid., 7. Janklow also blamed consumers for their "lack of sophistication" about handling their debt (6).

116. "South Dakota Voters Approve Interest Rate Cap on Payday Loans," November 8, 2016, http://www.ksfy.com/content/news/South-Dakota-voters-approve-interest-rate-cap-on-payday-loans-400489561.html.

117. "More Military Families Struggle with Debt," https://www.military.com/money/personal-finance/credit-debt-management/more-military-families-struggle-with-debt.html; "Department of Defense Issues Final Military Lending Act Rule," https://www.defense.gov/News/News-Releases/News-Release-View/Article/612795/department-of-defense-issues-final-military-lending-act-rule/.

118. Emily Gilbert, "Money as a 'Weapons System' and the Entrepreneurial Way of War," *Critical Military Studies* 1, no. 3 (2015): 202–19.

119. https://www.ndstudies.gov/energy/level2/module-3-coal/where-coal-found.

120. Mike Jacobs, *One Time Harvest: Reflections on Coal and Our Future* (Jamestown: North Dakota Farmers Union, 1975).

121. Caroline Tauxe, *Farms, Mines, and Main Streets: Uneven Development in a Dakota County* (Philadelphia: Temple University Press, 1993), 94.

122. Quoted in Tauxe, *Farms, Mines, and Main Streets*, 110.

123. *Beulah Beacon* (ND), March 8, 1979, quoted in Tauxe, *Farms, Mines, and Main Streets*, 106.

124. "Coal Land Reclamation," https://www.ndstudies.gov/gr8/content/unit-iv-modern -north-dakota-1921-present/lesson-1-changing-landscapes/topic-5-energy/section-2-coal.

125. Tauxe, *Farms, Mines, and Main Streets*, 213.

126. Ibid., 224.

127. *Beulah Beacon*, December 10, 1987, quoted in Tauxe, *Farms, Mines, and Main Streets*, 229.

128. C. S. Hagen, "Master of Puppets," *High Plains Reader*, August 1, 2018, https:// hpr1.com/index.php/fcature/news/master-of-puppets.

129. For two films about the Bakken boom, see *The Overnighters* (Moss, 2014) and *My Country No More* (Baghdadi and Hemmerling, 2018). See also Brorby and Brook Trout, *Fracture*. On the impact of fracking on women see John Eligon, "An Oil Town Where Men Are Many and Women Are Hounded," *New York Times*, January 15, 2013, www.nytimes.com/ 2013/01/16/us/16women.html; Susan Elizabeth Shepard, "Wildcatting: A Stripper's Guide to the Modern American Boomtown," *Buzzfeed*, July 25, 2013, https://www.buzzfeed.com/su sanelizabethshepard/wildcatting-a-strippers-guide-to-the-modern-american-boomtow; "Native Leaders Bring Attention to the Impact of Fossil Fuel Industry on Missing and Murdered Indigenous Women and Girls," *Indigenous Environmental Network*, May 3, 2017, http:// www.ienearth.org/native-leaders-bring-attention-to-impact-of-fossil-fuel-industry-on -missing-and-murdered-indigenous-women-and-girls/; Nick Estes, *Our History Is the Future: Standing Rock Versus the Dakota Access Pipeline, and the Long History of Indigenous Resistance* (London: Verso, 2019), 32–33; Lisa Kaczke, "We Don't Know How Many Native American Women Are Missing in South Dakota: That's About to Change," *Argus Leader*, June 26, 2019, https://www.argusleader.com/story/news/politics/2019/06/27/indigenous-women-missing -murdered-south-dakota-new-law-changes/1525751001/. On the struggle to maintain a balanced budget despite the fluctuations of the energy economy see "Burgum Vows to Curb Spending Despite Additional Oil Revenue," KFGO, July 19, 2018, https://kfgo.com/news/arti cles/2018/jul/19/burgum-vows-to-curb-spending-despite-additional-oil-revenue/; Ernest Scheyder, "In North Dakota's Oil Patch, a Humbling Comedown," *Reuters*, May 18, 2016, www.reuters.com/investigates/special-report/usa-northdakota-bust/.

130. Hagen, "Master of Puppets"; Jim Fuglie, "600 Illegal Water Permits? Unacceptable Behavior by a State Agency," https://theprairieblog.com/2017/04/17/state-agency-breaks-the -law-600-times-how-much-jail-time-do-you-get-for-that/.

131. Mark Trechock, "Down the Road," in Brorby and Brook Trout, *Fracture*, 360.

132. Mike Jacobs, *A Birthday Inquiry: North Dakota at 125; A Collection of Essays*, ed. Steve Wagner (Fargo, ND: Forum Communications, 2014). Kindle only.

Appendix

1. https://diversity.defense.gov/LinkClick.aspx?fileticket = gxMVqhkaHh8%3D&po rta lid = 51.

2. https://pdfs.semanticscholar.org/c567/b17bc58e83e93e68e28f1cfe270473593a48.pdf.

3. https://apps.dtic.mil/dtic/tr/fulltext/u2/661594.pdf.

INDEX

Figures are indicated by page numbers followed by fig.

ACKNOWLEDGMENTS

THIS BOOK HAS BEEN the project on my desk, the rattle of an idea in my mind, for nearly my entire career. For this reason I owe thanks to many scholars, political activists, journalists, military officials, archivists, and friends who have helped me complete it. I fear its conclusions may come as an unhappy surprise to some. If so, I am even more deeply in their debt. Among many others who answered my questions and emails, provided materials, and suggested revisions are Charlie Barber, Janet Moen, Larry Peterson, Tom Isern, Steve Bucklin, David Mills, David Danbom, Marshall Damgaard, Bob Mercer, Tom Brusegaard, Kristin Hoganson, Paula Nelson, Daryl Webb, John Miller, Harry Thompson, Jerry Wilson, Delphine Red Shirt, Ian Toller-Clark, Kim Stenehjem, Jay Davis, Lori Lahlum, Kim Porter, Molly Rozum, Mark Lempke, Mark Sundlov, Robert Branting, Sarah Walker, Eric Leonard, Chuck Lewis, Sarah Egge, Frances Lyons-Bristol, Diane Frigge, Richard Chapman, Jack Zaleski, Steve Lapointe, Catharine Franklin, Sarah Vogel, Sara Garland, Jim Fuglie, Bill Taylor, Curt Hanson, Linda Lea M. Viken, Lorna Meidinger. I am especially grateful to a luncheon table full of graduate students at the 2018 meeting of the Northern Great Plains History Association who nodded their heads and smiled enthusiastically when I described this project in a public setting for the first time.

Many members of the Connecticut College community have weighed in on early versions of this work, assisted with research, or simply extended a hand when I needed one—which was often. They include colleagues and former colleagues in the History Department, American Studies program, Center for the Critical Study of Race and Ethnicity, Peace and Conflict pathway, and, most importantly, the research and interlibrary loan offices of Shain Library. Along the way student research assistants have found essential materials. They include Mel Thibeault, Wesley Chrabasz, Weston Stephens, Bettina Weiss, Andrew Miller, Ethan Underhill, John Dunham, Charlotte Hecht, Avery Gobbo, Matt Wagman, Irakli Svanidze, Connor Reardon, Brendan Reardon, Brian Irving, Erin Knox, and Nathan Johnson. The research funds provided by Barbara Zaccheo Kohn made much of their work and mine possible. Gretchen Heefner, Cory Haala, and Jon Lauck's willingness to collaborate on shared interests made the book smarter and made writing it much more fun. Editorial suggestions from James Downs, Jeff Wells, Graham Finney, Regina Kunzel, Michael Lansing, Jeremy Maxwell, Cory Haala, Pamela Haag, the two anonymous readers for the Press, and my friend and mentor, Peter Agree, improved the book immeasurably.

Working with a historian who is trying to complete a many-years-long project is one thing; living with one is quite another. This book is for my husband, Peter. It comes with my deepest gratitude for the love we have shared, the parents and grandparents who have guided us, and the children we have raised. It is also accompanied by a timeless prayer: for a peaceful and just world in which our infant grandchildren and all the souls as yet unknown to us and to families and communities across the world may grow and thrive.